Civilian
Nuclear
Power

TWENTIETH CENTURY FUND

The Fund is a nonprofit, philanthropic foundation conducting research and public education on economic and social problems. It was founded in 1919 and endowed by Edward A. Filene. The Fund's income, administered as a public trust by a Board of Trustees, is devoted to its own research and educational activities. The Trustees choose subjects for research studies and vote the appropriation to cover the expenses of each project. The Trustees, however, assume no responsibility for the facts and opinions contained in research reports.

Civilian Nuclear Power

ECONOMIC ISSUES

AND POLICY FORMATION

BY PHILIP MULLENBACH

THE TWENTIETH CENTURY FUND

New York 1963

Printed in the United States of America

By Wm. F. Fell Company, Philadelphia, Pennsylvania

Library of Congress Catalog Card Number: 63-10431

FOREWORD

The prospect of power drawn from nuclear energy evoked, only a few years ago, large hopes. It was easy to see this source of power as substantially cheaper than that now available to the industrialized regions and also a boon to those less developed countries determined upon rapid growth. These hopes for the peaceful uses of nuclear energy have been disappointed—in part because of the favorable factor that new sources of oil and gas have been discovered and made available to Western Europe. Elsewhere the costs and complexity of nuclear technology have made it appear less than suitable for the immediate needs of the underdeveloped world.

In the present stage of planning for this new source of power for mankind, careful account needs to be taken of the basic factors and possibilities involved. This book seeks to be a contribution to this process of sober second thought. It is concerned with the economic issues which must influence United States policy making in regard to the development of civilian nuclear energy. It recognizes that the policy choices of the United States must be related to foreign as well as domestic considerations, and that in no part of this field are the relevant factors simple or the necessary choices obvious.

Philip Mullenbach, who began work on this volume toward the end of 1957, had been director of research for the nuclear energy project of the National Planning Association. He had been, before that, an economist with the Atomic Energy Commission. The reader will recognize in these pages the work of a man who is a careful craftsman and an observer who is not ready to accept unanalyzed assumptions. The Twentieth Century Fund is grateful to Mr. Mullenbach for having undertaken the work and for having given to it so much of himself.

AUGUST HECKSCHER, *Director*
The Twentieth Century Fund

41 East 70 Street, New York
October 1962

vii

PREFACE

This study is intended to provide an evaluation of policy formation that is based on economic analysis of the issues underlying power reactor development during the period 1953–1961. Its purpose is to help private and public policy makers find sound solutions to the controversial economic issues that arise as the area of private development and participation enlarges. Over the shoulders of policy makers I am also addressing fellow economists, particularly those intrigued by the "institutional" footings of public policy. I hope this study is in the challenging tradition of Edward A. Filene's expectations for the work of the Fund in "these new times."

I have tried, but with less satisfaction and feeling of success, to be faithful to the demands of precision in discussing technical matters and power reactor technology. Though the study is long, it is intended to be simplified enough that the nontechnical reader can readily see the range of issues and will not feel overwhelmed by the complexity of detail. This simplification has perhaps entailed a use of technical data which may seem highhanded to the technical reader.

In examining the controversial issues of policy one might take a safely historical approach, merely reporting opposing positions and arguments and hoping for a synthesis of conflicting views. Instead I have chosen to take an analytical view of the economic issues and to join in their appraisal, as a more stimulating and illuminating approach to both past and future public policy formation. That approach has helped to shape the structure of the study. In Chapter 2 I stress the intimate interaction of reactor technology and administrative economic policies. In Chapters 3, 4 and 5 I review the debated economic need for nuclear power in the United States against the background of our nuclear resources and programs for development. These findings provide a basis for critical appraisal of the economic policies influencing private and public reactor development. In Chapters 6, 7 and 8 I analyze the expressed foreign needs and programs, with special attention to the economic differences of the industrialized and the less developed countries. With this background it is then possible to assess the nation's foreign policies for nuclear power and to observe how a partial synthesis of divergent domestic and foreign policies has been occurring recently. In the concluding chapter I set down a few economic guidelines to which policy makers might well be sensitive when attacking the issues that are likely to challenge the Congress, the administration and industry during the next few years.

Writing on nuclear energy well in advance of publication is vulnerable to unpredictable events. The cutoff date of this volume is June 1962 when the manuscript went to the printer. It has not been possible to do more about developments since then than to note briefly in the text certain major ones that have occurred. Among these the most important have been the second reduction by the AEC in the prices of enriched uranium (effective July 1); the passage by the Congress of legislation authorizing the proposal of Washington state public power groups to finance and operate electric generating facilities using heat from the AEC's New Production Reactor at Hanford, Washington; and the recent announcement by India of its intention to purchase a large nuclear power reactor from the General Electric Company. Certain other developments, however—such as the forthcoming study of the civilian nuclear power program now being prepared by the AEC in response to the President's request last March—could not be covered.

The Fund has provided me maximum freedom and opportunity to undertake this study, including a trip to Western Europe in the summer of 1958 to attend the Second International Conference on the Peaceful Uses of Atomic Energy (Geneva) and to consult with the staffs of Euratom (Brussels), the European Nuclear Energy Agency (Paris) and the IAEA (Vienna). I am grateful to Ben Moore and to August Heckscher for their encouragement and support at every stage of the study. The original research took place in the Fund's Washington office in 1958–1959. Completion of the study in Chicago after mid-1959 called for the understanding cooperation of my colleagues on the staff of Growth Research, Inc., investment managers. I want to express my gratitude to each of them, particularly Harland H. Allen, who encouraged me throughout.

I am indebted to Kenneth A. Bohr and Robert A. Sadove (of the IBRD) for their paper on the problem of measuring potential foreign exchange savings, to John Hardt (Research Analysis Corporation) for reviewing the nuclear power program of the USSR, to Victor A. Salkind (consultant) for providing technical background on the relation of nuclear power to various methods of recovering fresh water from saline water, to Norman L. Gold (formerly of the UN Secretariat) for advice on potential capital savings in India and to Krishen D. Mathur (Aroostook State Teachers College) for help on the worldwide projections of nuclear power capacity.

I am grateful for the constructive criticism of a number of friends and associates who have read and commented on the manuscript, in whole or in part, including: Bennett Boskey, Harold P. Green and James Morrisson (all formerly on the legal staff of the U. S. Atomic Energy Commission); David Herron (of the Advanced Technology Laboratories), Philip Powers (Purdue University) and Chauncey Starr (President, Atomics International), who gave scientific and technical criticism; my fellow economists, Robert Blum (FPC), Ralph K. Davidson (Purdue University), Leo Fishman (West Virginia University), George Y. Jordy (AEC), Louis Lister (New School for Social Research), Sam H. Schurr and Perry D. Teitelbaum (Resources for the Future, Inc.), Richard A. Tybout (Ohio State University) and Thomson Whitin (University of California). Other reviewers were Robert Barlow (Atomic Industrial Forum), James Grahl (formerly of the American Public Power Association), John Kenton (McGraw-Hill), Richard Hewlett (AEC), Harold Bengelsdorf (AEC) and G. J. Petretic (AEC). Early discussions of energy problems with Paul W. McGann (formerly of the Bureau of Mines) and Harold D. Gresham were especially helpful.

I thank the following persons for helpful advice on specific items: Corbin Allardice (IBRD) on the SENN Project; Professor Manson Benedict (Massachusetts Institute of Technology) on the pricing of fissionable material by AEC; Professor Lyle B. Borst (New York University) on Chapter 2; Professor Harrison Brown (California Institute of Technology) on energy resources and prospects for India; Don Burrows (formerly AEC) on AEC pricing policies; S. K. Dhar (IAEA) on the position of less developed economies; Philip J. Farley (Department of State) on atoms-for-peace policies; P. H. Frankel (consultant) on petroleum in Western Europe; Max Kohnstamm on Euratom; Arnold Kramish (Rand Corporation) on atoms-for-peace programs and for review of John Hardt's background paper on the Soviet power reactor program; Leonard E. Link (ANL) on Chapter 2; Rudolph Regul (European Coal and Steel Community) on the energy problems of Western Europe; Robert Schaetzel (Department of State) and Clark Vogel (formerly of the AEC) on U. S. policies for Euratom and the IAEA. I am also grateful to Professor R. A. Moore (formerly of Macalester College) and Roderick P. Stewart (Growth Research, Inc.) for assistance in reviewing proofs. The Office of Classification, AEC, reviewed certain sections of the study.

In acknowledging my indebtedness to the individuals named above I do so without implying responsibility on their part for any findings or conclusions in the study.

I want to express my thanks to Gerhard Colm and to the National Planning Association for arranging for me to use the extensive source materials and other data gathered during the course of the NPA project on the Productive Uses of Nuclear Energy, of which I was research director (1954–1957). I am especially indebted to David Cushman Coyle for help in shortening the original manuscript. Also, Mrs. Frances Klafter of the Fund's Washington office has earned all the praise I can give for preparing a difficult manuscript for the printer. The fact that I was in Chicago and she in Washington placed upon her an especially heavy responsibility, which she fulfilled with skill and speed.

I hope that the generous help of these individuals and many others has been well used and that the study will fulfill the high purpose for which it was supported by the Fund.

PHILIP MULLENBACH

Wilmette, Illinois
September 30, 1962

CONTENTS

6 Foreign Need: The Strategic Economic Factors   187

World Energy Prospects, 189. Industrially Developed Economies, 202. Other Economies, 216

7 Foreign Programs and Resources   229

Major Economic Considerations, 230. National and Regional Programs, 237. Approaches to Nuclear Power by Less Developed Countries, 250. Projections of Free World Nuclear Power Capacity, Fuel Requirements and Plant Investment, 256. Self-Sufficiency Versus External Nuclear Assistance, 260

8 Nuclear Power and Foreign Policy   263

Atoms for Peace and for Power, 263. Programs and Instruments, 270. Problems of Policy, 281. Commercial Policy, 291. In Brief, 297

9 Partial Reconciliation   299

Grand Designs for Reconciliation, 301. Reconciliation of Plans and Goals, 306

10 Future Public Policy   317

Expanding Technical Knowledge, 318. Toward a Dynamic Price Policy, 326. Unifying Energy Policies, 334. Recognizing the Economic Imperatives, 341. Perspective, 345

Civilian
Nuclear
Power

CHAPTER 1

The Issues

Retrospect

The first phase of nuclear energy development following the war was marked by the passage, as the Atomic Energy Act of 1946, of the much-debated "civilian control" McMahon-Douglas bill. The central issue of the 1946 legislation was said to be "civilian versus military control" of the atom.[1] Yet, in fact, the civilian Atomic Energy Commission was compelled for years to concentrate attention on strengthening the nation's precarious position in military applications and to let inconsequential civilian applications follow the course already set by the Manhattan Engineer Project in the War Department. In this first phase, 1946–1949, nuclear power was developed only for naval propulsion and it was generally assumed that civilian use would ride on the coattails of naval development. The tougher economics of civilian power were thus avoided for a time. On the other hand, little support was voiced at this stage for the policy—followed later by the United Kingdom, France and the USSR—of giving civilian nuclear power a "military crutch," that is, of producing weapon-value plutonium in dual-purpose civilian power reactors.[2]

The first phase was shattered by the Russian atomic bomb test in 1949. This frightening event led at once to a program intended to keep the United States ahead of Soviet capabilities—a large expansion of the AEC's productive capacity and intensification of research on development of the hydrogen

1. James R. Newman and Byron S. Miller, *The Control of Atomic Energy*, McGraw-Hill, New York, 1948, p. 7.

2. Cf. Walker L. Cisler, "Economic Feasibility: The Dual Purpose Reactor," *Annals of the American Academy of Political and Social Science*, November 1953, pp. 45–49.

bomb. It also necessarily prolonged the neglect of the civilian nuclear power program. It is doubtful that any military agency would have been permitted to neglect development of civilian nuclear reactors as consistently as did the civilian AEC in the second phase—and largely without inviting criticism.

Meanwhile, private industry was growing restless with the continued government monopoly in atomic energy and was insisting on an opportunity to assess for itself the prospects for competitive nuclear power. The AEC therefore established in 1951 the "industry participation program," in which representatives of public utilities and equipment manufacturers were cleared for study of the classified technology and its commercial promise. At this time the notion gained currency, in and out of the AEC, that competitive nuclear power could be achieved "within a matter of a very few years," if the "cost-cutting" capabilities of private industry were brought to bear on the problem under a liberalized revision of the 1946 statute.

The third phase began in 1953, under a new administration, with congressional hearings on the prospective role of private industrial participation in reactor development.[3] The key premise of spokesmen from both the old and new administrations was that a "nationalized" industry should be normalized promptly. By the close of the hearings in 1954 the new policy was revealed. The objective of competitive nuclear power in the United States was to be sought by a novel and complex form of industry-government relations. On the optimistic assumption that the goal could be reached within a very few years— "certainly less than ten years"—electric utilities and equipment manufacturers were called upon to take the initiative, with strong government encouragement, in converting the AEC's budding technology into plants on the line.[4] The AEC's laboratory studies and experimental power reactors were to be continued, but with two important restraints—nothing was to be done that might lead, by accident or otherwise, to federal nuclear power, and nothing was to delay turning reactor development over to industry as rapidly as the AEC could do so. (The damage this new policy might do to the world leader-

---

3. *Atomic Power Development and Private Enterprise*, Hearings, Joint Committee on Atomic Energy, 83rd Cong., 1st Sess., 1953.

4. In 1950 former AEC Commissioner Lewis L. Strauss described as a fallacy the proposal to "turn the program over to private enterprise" and as premature the expectation that industry should compete in a nuclear power program. Within three years he was responsible, as Chairman of the Commission, for administering a program designed to accomplish, in some degree, both of the earlier "fallacies." In 1957 he expressed a firm belief that "within a decade we shall see established in the United States an industry that has completely taken over and has assumed its proper independent role in the field of the peaceful uses of atomic energy." See Lewis L. Strauss, "Some A-Bomb Fallacies Are Exposed," *Life*, July 24, 1950, pp. 80 ff.; and remarks of L. L. Strauss prepared for delivery to Atomic Industrial Forum–American Nuclear Society, New York, October 29, 1957.

ship of the United States was not generally recognized until several years later, when the sheer difficulty of achieving competitive nuclear power had become clear to all.)

It was in such an illusory economic setting that amendments to the original 1946 statute were hastily made, resulting in the Atomic Energy Act of 1954. Unfortunately, insufficient provision was made in the "interim" legislation for orderly transition from nationalization to effective private enterprise. The third phase was marked, indeed, by growing, not diminishing, federal assistance and subsidies to private and public electric utility groups. Dual purposes were involved—to avoid federal public power and to stimulate private development in support of U. S. nuclear foreign policy. The latter purpose was apparent in Euratom, the International Atomic Energy Agency and numerous bilateral power agreements with industrial nations.

"*Letting Loose*"

When the United States moved from the constraints of the 1946 act to the greater economic freedom of the 1954 act the nation was advancing a process that may best be described as one of "letting loose." Some critical observers called the step a "giveaway," while others described it as an act that "surrendered the government monopoly" or "freed the atom for private development." None of these is accurate. The 1946 act did not represent absolute government monopoly, nor did the 1954 act result in a return to free competitive enterprise.

The Manhattan Engineer District worked in cooperation with outside groups before passage of the 1946 act, as did the AEC thereafter. The operation of production plants, research laboratories, "company towns" and all the stages from extracting ore to stockpiling weapons were and still are being carried on, with only minor and irrelevant exceptions, by contract with private industrial and educational institutions. Despite government ownership of plants and fissionable materials—the major form of government monopoly —and utter dependence on congressional appropriations, there was a large degree of "private" participation but not "enterprise" before passage of the 1954 act.

Similarly, the 1954 act did not "turn over" atomic energy to full private development for profit, as had been customary with the results of government research. The 1954 statute amended the 1946 policy to permit, in a restricted and regulated manner, private enterprise to own and develop facilities useful in the wide field of nuclear energy. Still retained by the government, however, were ownership of fissionable materials, some measure of patent control, the responsibility for encouraging basic research and development and the right of determining the terms under which private owners might be licensed to build and operate reactors.

The 1954 Statute

Many current policy issues are imbedded in the legislative history of the 1954 statute.[5] The theory of strict control by a supersecret civilian agency was carried over to the 1954 statute and an "unhealthy isolation" of atomic energy from defense and foreign policy formation was thus maintained. The 1954 act also continued the administrative subordination of civilian nuclear power development—with ill effects on foreign policy, as explained later.

Figure 1-1   Public and Private Power, 1961

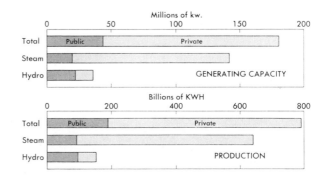

Source: Table 5-1. "Steam" includes internal combustion.

While the 1954 act did indeed "settle," for a time, a number of vexatious policy issues,[6] it also left a number of unresolved questions. It made clear that the peaceful atom would be "let loose" to some degree of controlled private-industry development for profit and that industry would be "let into" an increased range of reactor activities, but it left ambiguous the desired relations between government and industry. It made clear that, in the peaceful applications, the United States was to embark upon a more liberal policy of international cooperation, rather than continue the isolationist course of the

5. See in particular the classic analysis by John G. Palfrey, "Atomic Energy Law in the United States," *Law and Administration*, Series X, *Progress in Nuclear Energy*, Pergamon Press, New York, 1959, pp. 15–46.

6. James L. Morrisson, "Federal Support of Domestic Atomic Power Development—The Policy Issues," *Vanderbilt Law Review*, December 1958, pp. 195–222.

1946 statute. On the deep private-vs.-public-power controversy, it made possible working compromises or diversions which might avoid entanglement of
nuclear development in this bitter institutional struggle. Thus, the government
would not undertake the establishment of any "yardstick" plants, but it would
protect the historic, hard-won preferential right of public power to purchase electricity from experimental, government-owned facilities and from
materials production reactors. However, the novelty and complexities of
nuclear energy, as well as of the statute itself, have provided fertile ground for
dispute on policies and programs. The main domestic and foreign policy issues
are summarized below and treated in detail in the chapters which follow.

The Domestic Issues

Throughout the Eisenhower administration there were three dominant economic issues in the formulation of domestic policies for nuclear power development. The Kennedy administration inherited all three: the amount and
kind of public assistance that should be given to private industry; how best
to proceed with reactor development with least obstruction by the controversy
between private and public power; and the respective government and industry responsibilities for the construction of prototype or full-scale demonstration plants that could not, at the current stage, hope to be competitive and
make a profit.[7]

Financial Assistance

The 1954 act permits the AEC to grant money to groups outside the
government in order to encourage nuclear energy research and development
(Section 31). However, the AEC may not subsidize commercial—"licensed"—
facilities (Section 169).[8] Within the limits of this restriction the AEC has fully
employed almost all conceivable forms of direct and indirect aid to licensed
operators of noncommercial reactors. Among the forms of aid that have been
used, and are permitted under the act, are payments for research and development in advance of construction, the waiving of use charges on nuclear fuels
and other materials furnished by the AEC, fuel reprocessing and waste
storage and payments after construction for a specific period and purpose.

7. These issues and their significance in the formation of economic policies for nuclear power
development, briefly summarized here, are discussed in detail in Chapter 5.

8. The AEC has interpreted Sec. 31 as being an exception to Sec. 169; therefore, research and
development assistance, whether or not a subsidy, has been permitted. Any other assistance, such
as assistance toward construction, is thus prohibited.

Thus far the AEC has not provided construction funds for any investor-owned power reactors; in 1959 the Commission suggested, but did not receive, authority from Congress to do so. In 1962 the Commission recommended that the AEC be authorized to provide funds for the engineering design of private demonstration reactors.[9]

The alternative to AEC construction or construction subsidies has been progressively greater indirect financial assistance. Since the latter part of 1957, when the nuclear cost estimates jumped, equipment manufacturers, private utilities and publicly owned systems have agreed—for different reasons, to be sure—that the degree of government assistance for power reactor development has been too small. Equipment manufacturers have indicated that they are financially unable to expand the heavy research and development outlays that had proved necessary for the first few private projects. They have urged construction subsidies for private reactors. Private utilities have been prepared to build several prototypes (of under 75,000 kilowatts), but they have lacked the incentive and resources necessary for building any large number of full-scale units.[10] Public power systems (municipal and cooperative) have had no funds available for noncompetitive reactors. Managers of these systems have looked to the AEC for government plants and for full assurance that if demonstration reactors were built they would not jeopardize the financial position of the systems.

QUALITATIVE CRITERIA. The variety of public assistance to meet these demands has become great, hence danger obviously exists that subsidy will go undetected and unscrutinized by the critical public eye, particularly that of the Congress. Moreover, certain types of assistance—such as low "use" charges on government materials—may have become so "built-in" that they will be difficult to abandon as the commercial period approaches.[11] The form of assistance, too, should be such as to avoid exacerbation of the private-vs.-

9. *AEC Authorizing Legislation, Fiscal Year 1960*, Hearings, Subcommittee on Legislation, Joint Committee on Atomic Energy, 86th Cong., 1st Sess., 1959, p. 143.

AEC Authorizing Legislation, Fiscal Year 1963, Hearings, Subcommittee on Legislation, Joint Committee on Atomic Energy, 87th Cong., 2nd Sess., 1962, p. 159.

10. In addition to the original four full-scale nuclear power plants, underway in 1955 or earlier, private utilities have pursued plans (as of February 1962) for three other plants—in the Southern California Edison system, in the Pacific Gas and Electric system and in the New England Electric system.

11. In reporting out the 1954 act, the Joint Committee report contained an extensive minority view signed by Representatives Chet Holifield and Melvin Price. Among other points, they alluded to the "intermingled" private ownership of plant and federal ownership of fissionable material as a "built-in subsidy feature." (See *Amending the Atomic Energy Act of 1946, as Amended, and for Other Purposes*, House of Representatives, 83rd Cong., 2nd Sess., Report No. 2181, July 12, 1954.)

public-power controversy, mainly by assuring private and public power equal opportunity to secure assistance from the AEC without discrimination.

The appropriate standards for evaluating the scale of federal assistance are not easily established in economic terms. The material and technical resources now available for both military and civilian undertakings are vast, but assurance is necessary that civilian projects do not divert resources needed for military security. On the other hand, one should ask whether present resources are so fully engaged in nuclear technology that additional federal assistance would merely inflate costs of research, development and construction. Also, some attention needs to be given to the question of economies of scale, for, quite conceivably, the nature of nuclear power development is such that only the largest undertakings at the laboratory level can produce the results that are being sought. But the most fundamental question is what purposes justify the granting of aid at all. Owing to the limited domestic need for nuclear energy as a resource in the foreseeable future, the justifications have been multiple—to support foreign policy objectives, to accelerate development and hence reduce program costs, and to avoid government-owned plants.

The Private-vs.-Public-Power Controversy

The private-vs.-public-power controversy has become enmeshed in almost all aspects of domestic policy on nuclear power development.[11a] The bitter competition between the two sectors has encouraged the development of nuclear power by driving the private utilities to build demonstration plants which, in the absence of public power systems in the United States, would probably not have been built (or at least not so soon). Private power has been adamant in its opposition to federal construction of full-scale (as opposed to prototype) demonstration reactors.[12] Public power has generally insisted on application of the preference clause, though it did not do so in 1961, when approval of generating facilities for the New Production Reactor at AEC's Hanford, Washington, installation was debated and rejected. Public power has questioned large construction or operating subsidies to private utilities as alternatives to federal construction of demonstration reactors, although it has

11a. See the classic analysis by Herbert S. Marks, "Public Power and Atomic Power Development," *Law and Contemporary Problems*, winter 1956, Duke University School of Law, Durham, N. C., pp. 132–47. The relevance of the controversy is indicated by former AEC Chairman Lewis L. Strauss in his memoirs, *Men and Decisions*, Doubleday, New York, 1962, Chaps. 15 and 16.

12. Demonstration reactors may be either full-scale or prototype. By "full-scale" is meant a developmental reactor that approximates the size customarily required for commercial operation. By "prototype" is meant a pilot plant, without regard to size, that is designed with the subsequen construction of a full-scale plant in mind.

concurred in private development of nuclear energy as permitted by the 1954 statute. Public power insists, too, that federal construction of demonstration plants is necessary for rapid development of nuclear power, though it opposes federal distribution to ultimate consumers.

In this economic tempest the AEC, during the period 1953–1960, appeared to follow a policy more in harmony with that of the private utilities than of public power. It was, to be sure, not opposed to cooperative arrangements with local public power groups.[13] Yet, the AEC insisted that it was opposed to federal construction of demonstration plants, except when private enterprise was not prepared to proceed with a reactor concept that the AEC felt deserved demonstration.[14] Federal construction was viewed as increasing the difficulties involved and the time required in normalizing the industry. Hence, government reactor construction and development was delayed, to an indeterminate extent, by this by-product of the private-vs.-public-power controversy, and by the AEC's general acceptance of the private-power doctrine that federal demonstration plants would constitute a threat to the economic future of investor-owned utilities.

The ambiguity of private and government responsibilities for reactor development, plus the imprecise reasons for accelerating development, made the concrete question of construction by the federal government of full-scale plants the heart of the policy conflict during the Eisenhower administration. The precedent for government construction had been set, before the 1954 act, by AEC construction of the 60,000-kilowatt demonstration plant in a private utility system at Shippingport, Pennsylvania. No lack of legal authority prevented the AEC from doing so again elsewhere. Rather, the AEC under the Eisenhower administration chose to resist such construction as a matter of executive policy, for reasons stated above, and held out for fullest government assistance to secure private investment in plant, even at the cost of delay.

13. Indeed, Commissioner Harold S. Vance stated in 1957 that the AEC did not take a position in the private-vs.-public-power controversy, and intended to encourage participation by both private and public utilities. "If our assistance is in favor of one as against the other, it is in favor of public groups, such as cooperatives, not because we choose to take sides with them, but because their resources, financial and otherwise, are more limited than are the resources of private groups and, consequently, the measure of our assistance in some cases at least must be greater for them if it is to be effective." (Remarks at industrial preview of engineering test reactor, Idaho Falls, Idaho, October 2, 1957.)

14. "It is the Commission's policy," AEC Chairman Lewis L. Strauss said in 1957, "to give industry the first opportunity to undertake the construction of power reactors. However, if industry does not, within a reasonable period of time, undertake to build types of reactors which are considered to be promising, the Commission will take steps to build those reactors on its own initiative." (Remarks before the Atomic Industrial Forum–American Nuclear Society, New York, October 29, 1957.)

On the other hand, the proponents of the Gore-Holifield bill,[15] holding out for speed, questioned the wisdom of such wholesale "enticement" to private industry and abdication of AEC initiative. They urged construction of AEC demonstration plants to produce power for government installations—and so perhaps avoid the private-vs.-public-power issue of who might buy the resulting power. As is often the case in public affairs, events compelled unexpected and seemingly untidy compromises. Foreign developments, notably the Suez crisis in 1956, thrust forward Euratom as a potential meeting ground of U. S. interests and foreign needs. The private utilities, drawing on the pooled resources of their entire industry, proved able, when cajoled by the Joint Committee, to come forward with successive reactor proposals, though some proved abortive. Furthermore, the AEC slowly made arrangements with

Figure 1-2   Growth of Nuclear Power Capacity, 1957–1965[a]

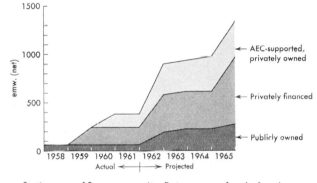

a. Stations over 10 emw. capacity. Data are as of end of each year.

Source: Section 202 Hearings, 1962, pp. 605 and 606.

public power systems for a few small nuclear stations to be owned by the AEC. The ultimate congressional battle over whether the AEC should build full-scale, government-owned power plants was avoided, or postponed. The real problem, then and later, was how to secure the demonstration of nuclear power in a number of full-scale plants, as the technology warranted.[16] In 1959

15. The Gore-Holifield bill, introduced in 1956, sought authorization for an expenditure by the AEC of $400 million for the construction of demonstration power plants. (See *Civilian Atomic Power Acceleration Program,* Hearings, Joint Committee on Atomic Energy, 84th Cong., 2nd Sess., June 28, 1956.) The bill passed the Senate but was defeated in the House. Since then some members of the Joint Committee have, with mixed success, made repeated efforts to increase AEC funds for construction of demonstration plants.

16. Frank K. Pittman, Director, Division of Reactor Development, AEC, remarks for presentation at the Second Joint Conference on Nuclear Power, U. S.–Japan Atomic Industrial Forums, Tokyo, December 6, 1961 (AEC Release S-26-1961).

some private utilities met this by joining with equipment manufacturers in suggesting construction subsidies for privately owned demonstration plants.[17] This indicated that private resources committed to this end had almost reached their limit—in the absence of much greater government assistance, or of direct subsidies. But it also raised doubts about the reasons for continuing to encourage nuclear power development in the United States. (Shared private and public responsibility for power reactor programs is discussed in greater detail in Chapter 4.)

The Grounds for Fear of Federal Public Power

The Eisenhower administration's sensitivity to private-power economic doctrine prompts further explanation of the arguments on which it was based. Private power had several reasons to fear federal "encroachment" through nuclear power after 1954. All fissionable material in the United States, however produced, was government owned. Foreign policy commitments were used as an argument for a more aggressive federal program than could be justified by immediate domestic needs. The fact that Congress reaffirmed the traditional status of public power in the preference provision of the 1954 act appeared to private power to nullify the prohibition against federal sale of by-product power commercially. Private utilities also sensed the institutional hazards of heavy, sustained public financial support of power reactor research and development, particularly if private investment could not maintain a commensurate scale. This conflict, it might be noted, has not been confined to the United States.

The historical origins of local and federal government operations in electric power are indelibly impressed on the minds of private utility executives. For the lesson of history is quite plain: there is no way of predicting by what route further government (or cooperative) "encroachment" in electric power generation and distribution may come. The original preference clause, which appeared in the Reclamation Act of 1906, applied to municipal plants. It was later broadened to include cooperatives. The TVA Act of 1933 emphasized flood control and navigation, with hydropower as a by-product. Today, however, four fifths of TVA's plant is for electric power generation and three fourths of the power is generated in steam plants. Since passage of the Rural

17. See statement by Willis Gale, Chairman, Commonwealth Edison Co., in *Development, Growth and State of the Atomic Energy Industry*, Hearings, Joint Committee on Atomic Energy, 1959, pp. 439–41. (Hearings under this title have been held annually since 1955 by the Joint Committee under Sec. 202 of the Atomic Energy Act of 1954. They are referred to hereafter as "Section 202 Hearings.")

Electrification Act, establishing the REA in 1936 to finance power lines and rural stations, 96 per cent of the farms have been electrified. The private companies are now concerned that many rural cooperatives are serving suburban loads in formerly rural areas.

With all these precedents private utilities naturally fear further "encroachment," particularly in the field of nuclear power.[18] Under these circumstances the question arises whether reactor development can be effectively administered and planned and can balance the debilitating and stimulating influences of the controversy. This was not possible during the first six years of the act and the controversy has continued to be a factor in the formation of nuclear power policy under the Kennedy administration.

In emphasizing the relevance of the private-vs.-public-power controversy, one need not contend that nuclear power policy has revolved around it. Equally important, possibly, was the evident haste in passing the basic legislation, which in turn hindered an orderly transition from a degree of "government monopoly" to a degree of "private enterprise." The choice of public and private means for achieving this end, accepted by Republican and Democratic administrations, has proved repeatedly to be linked with the private-vs.-public-power issue. A recent example was the administration's inability in 1961 to secure congressional approval of funds to add electric generating facilities to the New Production Reactor being built at the AEC's installation at Hanford, Washington. In 1962, however, the proposal by a group of sixteen Washington state public utility districts to finance the addition of and to operate these generating facilities was authorized by the Congress—over the objections of the same interests that had rejected the federal plan a year before.

Institutional Issues[19]

There are also several "institutional" issues imbedded in the 1954 statute. The first—"an anomalous carry-over from the past"[20]—is the continued government ownership and "purchase" of all fissionable materials, even though they are produced in licensed, privately owned reactors. Not unexpectedly the public financial burden, the administrative complexities of this arrangement and private industry's natural abhorrence of government ownership have led to the question of modification, at an appropriate time. The

18. J. W. McAfee, President, Union Electric Company, "The Threat of Government Operations—Our Common Problem," *EEI Bulletin*, December 1958.

19. For detailed discussion of the issues summarized here see Chapter 5.

20. Palfrey, *op. cit.*

major remaining bulwark of the present policy, the supposed need for having an additional degree of protection in public control of weapons material, has begun to erode. Actually, government ownership as such—in the face of private production—provides scant additional security not already assured by licensing, accountability and inspection. Meanwhile, however, private reactor operators find that government ownership and price setting coincide with their immediate economic interests.

A second example of tension on institutional matters is found in the much-debated patent provisions. These were motivated by seemingly conflicting desires: to prevent a patent monopoly by any of the major AEC contractors and to encourage private development. Most of the reactor technology developed by 1959 had been acquired under contract or other arrangements with the government, hence any overhauling of existing policies had a serious public interest argument to overcome. Why should private rights be granted in inventions "bought," so to speak, by government research and development funds? No strong pressure to effect a change favoring more liberal patent policies had become evident by 1959 and in that year the compulsory licensing of certain patents was reviewed and sustained for another five-year period.[21]

A further source of controversy has been the statutory terms surrounding the AEC's responsibility for providing government materials and services. The AEC has been guided, on the one hand, by "no subsidy" and "fair value" standards but, on the other, it should set terms that encourage research and development as well as promote private production of materials and services. Faced with conflicting criteria, the AEC long followed a pricing policy that placed a high premium on recovering "full costs" and avoiding frequent change. As the period of commercial feasibility approaches, however, the conflicting private interests of operators, of materials and service suppliers, of equipment manufacturers and of foreign customers will probably compel critical examination of price schedules and their present, scarcely revealed basis.[22]

Foreign Policy Issues

The administration of the foreign program has been less sensitive to economic controversy, but there have been problems, ranging from such specific details

21. *Atomic Energy Patents*, Hearings, Subcommittee on Legislation, Joint Committee on Atomic Energy, 86th Cong., 1st Sess., 1959.

22. See Philip Mullenbach, "Government Pricing and Civilian Reactor Technology," *Science and Resources: Prospects and Implications of Technological Advance*, Henry Jarrett (ed.), Resources for the Future, Washington, 1959.

as how United States suppliers could secure patents abroad, in view of the limitations on such rights at home, to the broad question of whether American foreign assistance was to be provided mainly through bilateral agreements or through the International Atomic Energy Agency. The most awkward problem has been how to reconcile the technical and economic realities of lagging power reactor development at home with the hopes and promises held out to industrializing countries under the long-standing atoms-for-peace program.

The President's UN Address

When President Eisenhower addressed the General Assembly of the United Nations on "Atomic Power for Peace," on December 8, 1953, he expressed the United States intention to make a break from the "hopeless finality of a belief that two atomic colossi are doomed malevolently to eye each other indefinitely across a trembling world" and to find an acceptable solution to the armaments race by adapting nuclear energy to peaceful use.

"Peaceful power from atomic energy," he said, "is no dream of the future. That capability, already proved, is here—now—today." Were sufficient amounts of fissionable material made available to develop scientific and engineering ideas, "this capability would rapidly be transformed into universal, efficient, and economic usage." President Eisenhower proposed that nations contribute from their stockpiles to an international atomic energy agency to be set up under the aegis of the United Nations. An important responsibility of the agency, he suggested, would be to devise methods for making these contributions useful for peaceful pursuits and "a special purpose would be to provide abundant electrical energy in the power-starved areas of the world." He further indicated that he was prepared to ask congressional approval of a plan that would provide all the material needed to encourage appropriate investigations, begin reducing the world's atomic stockpiles and open a new channel of peaceful discussion between the East and the West.

This imaginative and idealistic appeal for a new approach to the problem of atomic energy in a divided world was enthusiastically received by most free nations, simply because it encouraged new hope for the future. In the United States the statement provided momentum for the movement by industry and the executive branch for major amendments to the McMahon-Douglas Act. The amendments, incorporated in the 1954 act, permitted the declassification and exchange of technical information and, subject to the approval of Congress, permitted the United States to make cooperative arrangements with other countries for the development of atomic energy. This fundamental change in foreign policy reinforced the equally important shift in domestic policy that permitted a larger measure of private development. It is doubtful that either could have come to fruition without the other, though the participation of private enterprise received earlier and more persistent attention in the controversial hearings in 1953 and debate in 1954.

Dubious Economic Premises

Though seemingly less controversial, the economic issues in the formation of United States foreign nuclear power policy have not been wholly dissimilar from the domestic issues outlined above. Should the United States attempt to meet foreign government competition in export markets with subsidies to manufacturers? Should the United States keep foreign assistance on a government-to-government basis? Similarly, several foreign policy issues have had their origin in unfounded initial premises about the immediate economic prospects for nuclear power. For example, there were exaggerated and misleading implications in the President's statement that nuclear power had been demonstrated technically (in the *Nautilus* and experimental units) and that this capability could be converted rapidly to economic use to meet the needs of "power-starved" areas.[23] There are, as shown in Chapter 6, no areas in the world that can be so described. Also, at the time of President Eisenhower's address it was the judgment of the AEC that achieving competitive nuclear power would require a large, sustained effort by industry and government over many years.[24] The expectation that peaceful development can soon begin

23. Former members of the U. S. Atomic Energy Commission have reported that the President's statement was prepared in the Executive Office and presented without benefit of consultation with the Commission.

24. At the time of the President's statement the staff of the AEC was engaged in preparing, at the formal request of Chairman Sterling Cole of the Joint Committee on Atomic Energy (July 31, 1953), reports on the technical program and on the economic prospects for nuclear power. The first report, "The Five-Year Power Reactor Development Program," submitted to the Joint Committee March 12, 1954, indicated that the probability of achieving competitive nuclear power was "good," and that this could be accomplished "within a decade or two," if the goal were "pursued with vigor." (See *Report of the Subcommittee on Research and Development on the Five-Year Power Reactor Development Program Proposed by the Atomic Energy Commission*, Joint Committee on Atomic Energy, 83rd Cong., 2nd Sess., March 1954, p. 8.) The second report, submitted June 2, 1954, in considering the time schedule for realization of economic nuclear power, indicated that achieving competitive costs in the United States "may be a matter of 10 to 20 years" and that the "solution of the long and difficult problems standing in the way of economical nuclear power cannot be safely disassociated from the assistance industry is prepared to give." (See "Probable Course of Industrial Development of Economic Nuclear Power," in AEC, *Major Activities in the Atomic Energy Programs, January–June 1954* (Semiannual Report), July 1954, Appendix 8.)

to diminish the destructive power of atomic stockpiles has also proved unrealistic, in the light of the great existing nuclear productive capacity.[25] Far more effective methods will have to be found to meet this problem than unwarranted reliance on small, potential diversions for civilian power uses.

Notwithstanding numerous unsupportable economic and technical premises in the original statement of the Eisenhower administration's foreign nuclear power policy, the United States launched into a cooperative program with other nations that presupposed a more rapid domestic development program than it was able to accomplish. This aggressive program of negotiating agreements led, by the end of 1961, to thirty-eight bilateral agreements for atomic research, fourteen bilateral agreements for nuclear power, the full encouragement of the European Atomic Energy Community (Euratom), the offering of 65,000 kilograms of nuclear fuel for use in reactors abroad and also to the initiative taken in establishing the International Atomic Energy Agency.

Other Issues

Some other economic issues in foreign nuclear power policy have been politically less controversial. Which of the various methods being followed by the AEC and the Department of State for promoting the peaceful uses of nuclear energy—bilateral, regional and multilateral—will, in each situation, best serve the interests of United States foreign policy and the economic needs of other countries? How much emphasis on nuclear power is justifiable in relation to economic and technical assistance as a whole? What should be the nation's economic policy for meeting possible nuclear "penetration" by the USSR in the uncommitted nations? Considering the more urgent needs of Japan and parts of Western Europe, how much effort should be devoted to the industrial nations and how much to the less developed economies, where early introduction of nuclear power appears less warranted economically?

The bilateral, regional and multilateral approaches being used by the AEC parallel those being used in the technical and foreign economic assistance programs administered by the ICA (which became AID, the Agency for International Development, in late 1961). Some observers, such as the U. S. Chamber of Commerce, feel that bilateral arrangements maintain the best

25. This doctrine has persisted in policy statements since 1953. In his message to Prime Minister Nehru of India, December 15, 1957, responding to Nehru's public appeal for disarmament on November 28, 1957, President Eisenhower noted that the United States had proposed the transfer to peaceful uses of fissionable material now tied up in stocks of nuclear weapons. "We believe," he said, "this is the way to a true reduction of the nuclear threat and to an increase in confidence among nations." ("Text of Eisenhower Cable," *New York Times*, December 16, 1957.)

control of the aid and assure clear identification of the source. Others, such as former Secretary of State Dulles, have held that assistance through multilateral arrangements, such as the IAEA, under the United Nations, might well accomplish foreign policy objectives and avoid the drawbacks of the donor-recipient relationship.[26] Each of these approaches is of value in a balanced foreign program. These questions are discussed in detail in Chapter 8.

The fact that the economic benefits of nuclear power have been less immediate than most other forms of conventional economic and technical assistance has been generally accepted. Nuclear power thus has required especially careful evaluation in the allocation of resources and the provision of assistance. Government support of exports of nuclear power equipment and supplies, beyond the customary forms of assistance, as through the Export-Import Bank, could hardly be justified on economic grounds. This has not, of course, excluded the possibility of special government-to-government assistance during the developmental phase, as through Euratom.

Short- vs. Long-Term Foreign Benefits

The economic benefits of nuclear power, except in Japan and much of Western Europe, have been properly looked on as applying only in special situations and over a long term—beyond 1975–1980. The increasing costs of coal production and the overhanging threat to imported energy supplies—despite the North African discoveries of oil and the transport of liquefied natural gas—have been sufficiently imposing to indicate a need for special assistance to Japan and Western Europe.[27] Obviously promising was the possibility of matching the United States need for demonstration reactors with the need of these industrial nations for an alternative energy source. This was brought about through government-to-government financial arrangements, rather than by capital subsidies, which former Joint Committee Chairman Sterling Cole had suggested.

While widely varying forms of cooperation were considered, the first was the joint arrangement between Euratom and the United States to build a few demonstration reactors of American design by 1965. Policy leaders well realized that European utility executives, like American, required proof of the

26. Statement of John Foster Dulles, *Statute of the International Atomic Energy Agency*, Hearings, Committee on Foreign Relations, 85th Cong., 1st Sess., 1957.

27. The nations of Western Europe differ widely in regard to adequacy of energy supply, but the chief countries considered as "energy deficient" and likely on economic grounds to turn toward nuclear power are Belgium, Denmark, Great Britain, Italy, the Netherlands, Spain and Sweden.

technical and competitive feasibility of nuclear power plants. In the absence of strong government promotion the utilities in Western Europe would be disposed to meet additional load requirements with conventional fuel and thus vitiate a major purpose of Euratom—to reduce growing dependence on unassured overseas sources of oil and on high-cost domestic fuel requiring subsidies.

However, in 1960 Robert McKinney, adviser to the Joint Committee on Atomic Energy, concluded that, owing to the surplus of conventional fuel in Western Europe, the North African oil discoveries and the reduced level of fuel prices, competitive nuclear power in the near future was no longer to be considered an achievable objective. Therefore, he recommended that the U. S. program of cooperation with the countries of Western Europe in nuclear power drop the short-view objective, yielding only marginally useful reactor projects, and that the program be reoriented toward greater laboratory cooperation and the long-term goal of very low-cost nuclear power through development of highly advanced reactor concepts.[28]

Nuclear Power and the Developing Countries

How nuclear energy might best be introduced in the developing economies has remained a difficult economic and political problem.[29] Early in the atoms-for-peace program the question arose whether nuclear energy—and nuclear power in particular—might prove a useful tool, among others, to help counteract communist economic penetration of the uncommitted nations.[30] The issue has not had to be drawn in concrete terms, however, for the Soviet Union up to mid-1962 had shown no disposition to include nuclear power plants in its bundle of exportable capital items—except for overtures to India. Deterrents to aggressive use of nuclear power as an instrument of Soviet foreign policy

28. Robert McKinney, *Review of the International Atomic Policies and Programs of the United States,* report to the Joint Committee on Atomic Energy, 86th Cong., 2nd Sess., October 1960 (referred to hereafter as the McKinney Review), Vol. 1.

29. See, for example, the series of case studies by the NPA, *Productive Uses of Nuclear Energy,* Washington, 1956–57; also, UN, *Economic Applications of Atomic Energy: Power Generation and Industrial and Agricultural Uses,* Report of the Secretary-General, New York, 1957.

30. For some time Joint Committee members feared that the USSR might be the first nation to supply a power reactor in south or southeast Asia. In 1958 India announced that its first power reactor would come from the United Kingdom and in 1960 called for proposals from any country interested in supplying a natural uranium power reactor. Earlier the Soviet Union had offered to build a large power reactor for India near Bombay, but on condition that no international bids would be invited. In 1962 the International General Electric Co., a division of General Electric Co., was selected by the government of India to construct a 380,000-kw. nuclear power station 60 miles north of Bombay at a cost of $100 million.

may exist for some years, though hardly indefinitely. Hence, there may be a transient opportunity for the free nations to take advantage of a gap in the arsenal of Soviet devices for extending its influence.

In this situation one extreme view held that, because of United States nuclear capacity, the nation should take the initiative in establishing a massive worldwide type of "Marshall Plan" for nuclear energy.[31] The notion failed to win support and the formation of the International Atomic Energy Agency doubtless helped, in a more practical fashion, to satisfy the need expressed.

Thus far several semi-industrialized and uncommitted nations have received the benefits of bilateral research agreements, but they have not had any special nuclear assistance from the United States, the United Kingdom or the Soviet Union in moving ahead with nuclear power programs.[32] Almost all these emerging economies have been watching and waiting for the demonstration of nuclear power development by the atomic leaders, and have been expecting to rely on more or less conventional commercial relations with the free nations having nuclear capacity and, more remotely, on the potentialities of the International Atomic Energy Agency. Were the policy of the Soviet Union to shift toward extensive use of nuclear power as an instrument of foreign policy, the State Department would then need to consider whether major reliance on the IAEA and on customary commercial relationships could supply sufficient bases of foreign policy for these areas. By early 1962 the IAEA had been unable, for a variety of reasons, to demonstrate its capabilities in this respect.

Inconsistency of Foreign and Domestic Policies

That the nation and the rest of the world had received a distorted view of the economic promise of nuclear power under the atoms-for-peace program was soon apparent to a number of officials in the State Department. As early as 1955 the State Department began, and has consistently continued, to deemphasize nuclear power and to favor atomic research activities. While the AEC went ahead with bilateral foreign negotiations on a wide scale, the responsible officials of the Department of State were pursuing a much less enthusiastic

31. John Jay Hopkins, "Unatom: A Plan for the Development of a United Atomic Treaty Organization of Free World Nations," an address to the Third International Conference of Manufacturers, National Association of Manufacturers, New York, November 29, 1956.

32. Only India, among the underdeveloped countries, had embarked on a nuclear power program as of the end of 1961, though Brazil and Israel appeared about ready to do so.

course.[33] In time the inconsistency between the actions of the Executive Office and the AEC, on the one hand, and of the State Department, on the other, became unmistakable. Former AEC Commissioner Henry DeWolf Smyth in October 1956 noted that in the three years following the President's address to the United Nations the principles of the program had been reaffirmed but hardly put into effect and that there appeared to be "a discrepancy between our statements and our actions."[34] He held that the AEC policy of expecting private industry to assume the major responsibility for reactor construction might be reasonable if only domestic considerations were involved. As they were not, he urged a more ambitious approach, including continued government construction of full-scale, power-producing reactors, when technically justified. As he put it:

> We cannot simultaneously make "atoms for peace" a major part of our foreign policy and atoms for private industry a controlling part of our domestic policy. However desirable it may be to get the Government out of the nuclear power business, it is more important to back our announced foreign policy with a vigorous and fast-moving program of reactor development and construction.

Former AEC Commissioner Thomas E. Murray, also concerned by the inconsistency of foreign and domestic policies, stated that while "pushing atoms for war" the national efforts supporting atoms for peace were "cautious and niggardly." The Eisenhower administration, he said, interpreted the 1954 legislative changes as justifying "a slackening of government efforts" and "prematurely abdicated to private industry the primary responsibility for building large power reactors." The "fear of public power" and the private-vs.-public-power conflict, he felt, had needlessly dominated the policies of the private power industry and the AEC in the development of nuclear power.[35]

The State Department remained silent on the inconsistency between domestic and foreign policies. One may assume that the Department policy makers, in effect, believed that foreign policy objectives did not justify extraordinary measures over and above the customary commercial development of

33. See, for example, addresses by Ambassador Morehead Patterson, U. S. Representative for International Atomic Energy Agency Negotiations, at the opening of the School of Nuclear Science and Engineering, Argonne National Laboratory, Lemont, Ill., March 13, 1955, and at the Atomic Industrial Forum, San Francisco, Calif., April 4, 1955. (Both in *Atoms for Peace Manual*, Joint Committee on Atomic Energy, Senate Document No. 55, 84th Cong., 1st Sess., June 21, 1955, pp. 353–56 and pp. 360–66.)

34. "Nuclear Power and Foreign Policy," *Foreign Affairs*, October 1956, pp. 1–16. The quotation which follows is from p. 15.

35. *Nuclear Policy for War and Peace*, World Publishing, Cleveland, Ohio, 1960, Chaps. 6 and 7.

a new technology. Indeed, throughout the Eisenhower administration there was no statement by the Department outlining its policy position on nuclear power—despite repeated requests by the Joint Committee. The Department found it expedient to let the AEC "do the talking" on the atoms-for-peace program—except on Euratom. However, in May 1962 the Smyth Committee prepared for the Department a policy statement recommending strong U. S. support of the International Atomic Energy Agency.[36]

Special Interest Attitudes

While one must consider any "special interest" view with caution, statements of representatives of industry, labor and the private and public utility systems on nuclear energy policy have shown less than the usual resort to hackneyed phrases. Some novelty has crept in, prompted in part by the challenge of nuclear energy and by the desire to take a broad, national position.

American Business

In recent years the U. S. Chamber of Commerce has made a noticeable shift toward recognition of the foreign policy implications of the domestic development program.

In 1956 and 1957 its Committee on Commercial Uses of Atomic Energy[37] issued policy statements which emphasized the necessity for avoiding any growth of public power. The committee called for development by private enterprise, declassification of the technology as far as compatible with security and relaxation of patent restrictions. It favored government assistance to industry where necessary and opposed giving preference to public power systems in the sale of power from government-owned reactors.

In 1958 and 1959, however, the Chamber of Commerce changed its former policy position by explicitly recognizing the need for international leadership, stating that "some domestic activities must be keyed to maintaining this leadership."[38] For example, pending restoration of normal patent rights, American industry should be permitted, the committee recommended, "to

36. U. S. Department of State, *Report of the Advisory Committee on U. S. Policy toward the International Atomic Energy Agency*, Washington, May 19, 1962.

37. L. M. Smith, Vice Chairman of the Board, Alabama Power Co., was chairman of the committee, consisting of thirty-six representatives of business. See U. S. Chamber of Commerce, *Policy Declarations on Natural Resources*, Washington, 1957.

38. U. S. Chamber of Commerce, *Policy on Atomic Energy*, Washington, January 31, 1959.

obtain adequate patent protection in foreign countries." The committee indicated preference for U. S. support of bilateral arrangements rather than of arrangements through the International Atomic Energy Agency. Construction of large-scale power reactors "should not be attempted unless justified by the status of the technology developed through prior research efforts." The effects on private industry of any program or policy undertaken for reasons of foreign policy should be fully considered. The Chamber of Commerce still opposed commercial power production in government plants and the preference clause in the sale of power from experimental plants. In 1961 it reiterated the desire to increase the role of private industry in all phases of the government's atomic energy program.[39]

Private Electric Utilities

Since 1954 the private electric utilities have expressed continuous concern that the nation's nuclear power program might go too fast and might take a course jeopardizing investor-owned systems. In annual statements before the Joint Committee[40] the Edison Electric Institute has also recognized the importance of foreign policy considerations, expressed mainly in terms of America's fortifying its position of technical leadership. The EEI has always been opposed to the public-power preference provisions of the act as being discriminatory and has urged the Committee to avoid building government-owned plants. It has also held that private industry should carry a substantial part of the expenses of research and development, including the construction of full-scale demonstration plants, if the construction is justified by prior technological advances and there is reasonable assurance that the power will be competitive. As the problems of reactor development have multiplied, the institute has urged increased government aid to private utility systems.

Being sensitive to the need for public approval, the EEI has invariably included in its annual presentation a listing of the power reactor projects being undertaken by private industry to show how well the industry is fulfilling the promises made in 1954. The early 1962 status of reactor projects owned by private utilities is shown in Table 1-1. Estimated expenditures by electric utility companies for nuclear power development have risen from $37.4 million in 1957 to a peak of $106.1 million in 1960; it is projected that they will decline to $33.1 million in 1963.[41]

39. Task Force on Increasing the Role of Private Industry, Release, Washington, March 21, 1961.
40. See Section 202 Hearings, 1955–1962.
41. Section 202 Hearings, 1961, p. 416; and 1962, p. 509.

TABLE **1-1**

Status of Nuclear Power Reactors Built or Planned by Private Utilities, February 1962

Status of plants	Number	Net size (megawatts)	Estimated cost to utilities (millions)	Year of initia operation
Total	13	1,943	$489[a]	
In operation	2	330	80	1960–61
Under design or construction	9	938	409	1962–1965
In planning	2	675-725	...	1965–1967

a. Excludes cost of two projects in planning.

Source: Section 202 Hearings, 1962, pp. 502, 505, 508 (EEI data).

Public Power

The American Public Power Association makes recommendations annually for development of nuclear power.[42] Its 1956 statement emphasized that in large part existing technology had been publicly created and that these resources should be used to promote the general welfare. The government should encourage free competition, prevent monopoly and provide no subsidies to selected groups, unless the results of the work are made available for the benefit of all. It should regulate atomic activities "with scrupulous care and impartiality to protect at all times the public health and safety." The association favored continuing the compulsory licensing of patents and government ownership of fissionable materials. It also recommended that, in addition to giving assistance in the construction and operation of demonstration plants by both private and consumer-owned utilities, the AEC should construct and operate demonstration plants of various types and sizes. Running through the recommendations was repeated support of full public disclosure, consistent with national security, of such matters as the nature and cost of federal assistance and the prices of services and facilities provided by the government. The APPA has also urged that the AEC support developmental projects sponsored by municipal and rural cooperative systems and strengthen the program for small reactor development.

The association's position has reflected primary preoccupation with government control of private enterprise development of nuclear energy and with

42. See *Public Power:* "Federal Atomic Power Policy," January 1957, pp. 15–18; and "Resolutions Adopted at Convention" (New Orleans, May 8, 1958), June 1958, pp. 29–33.

assuring maintenance of the preferential right customary with hydroelectric power. In addition, however, the APPA has annually expressed its belief that a strong federal program is essential to support of the international program.

Organized Labor

The views of organized labor have been expressed in the AFL-CIO resolutions on atomic energy at annual conventions,[43] which have urged full U. S. participation in the International Atomic Energy Agency, support of Euratom and encouragement of regional arrangements under the UN. Emphasizing the importance of rapid development of peaceful uses, the AFL-CIO has called for particular attention to a sound labor-management relations program, effective health and safety standards, fair workmen's compensation and a voluntary manpower training program, to be established with the advice of a labor-management advisory committee to the AEC.

Labor has customarily tried to avoid taking sides in the private-vs.-public-power controversy and has favored rapid development by both government and private enterprise. One labor leader suggested that "private enterprise cannot reasonably be expected to shoulder so much of the burden" in the development phase.[44] The 1955 resolution of the AFL-CIO convention declared that "federal policy must prevent the development of monopoly in any aspect of this new industry," and "should encourage development of power using all possible sources of energy with both public and private ownership." Organized labor also strongly supported the Gore-Holifield bill and has continually urged government plants to accelerate development. A significant feature of labor's position has been explicit recognition of the worldwide scope of nuclear energy, and the need for vigorous support of Euratom.

Public Interest Groups

The three-year study by the National Planning Association, 1954–1957, and its policy recommendations were unique in the fact that the twenty-member special policy committee consisted of individuals selected from industry, labor, agriculture and the professions.[45] The thirteen-point recommendations

43. AFL-CIO, Washington: "1955 Convention Resolutions on Atomic Energy and Power," Publication No. 17; and "Resolutions Committee Report No. 3 to the Second Constitutional Convention, Atlantic City, 1957," pp. 10–13.

44. Walter P. Reuther (President, United Automobile Workers), "Atoms for Peace: A Separate Opinion on Certain Aspects of the Report of the Panel on the Peaceful Uses of Atomic Energy to the Joint Congressional Committee on Atomic Energy," Washington, January 25, 1956.

45. NPA, *Productive Uses of Nuclear Energy: Summary of Findings—Policy Suggestions for the Future*, Washington, September 1957.

of the committee, grouped by the domestic and foreign aspects, emphasized the importance of an accelerated nuclear power program based on greater private and public investment in demonstration reactors. They noted the encouraging economic prospects for the nonpower applications of nuclear energy and recommended that the AEC periodically provide, on a uniform and comparable basis, unclassified reports on the cost of generating nuclear power in experimental reactors. The committee recommended that the Joint Committee on Atomic Energy examine the special problems of waste disposal and of workmen's compensation and that the AEC establish an electric utility advisory committee consisting of public and private power representatives.

The committee recommended full support of the International Atomic Energy Agency, encouragement of Euratom and a strengthening of the U. S. program of regional research and training centers abroad. The committee also recommended additional emphasis on reactor types holding special promise for countries with foreign exchange problems and limited resources. Noting the serious economic obstacles facing U. S. business abroad, the committee recommended that the federal government take special steps to encourage industry in establishing joint arrangements and branch plants abroad.

A notable feature of the NPA 1957 policy report was explicit recognition that the U. S. reactor program at home was inadequate, considering emerging nuclear power needs in Western Europe and Japan, for example, to which American industry should be expected to contribute.

The Twelfth American Assembly of Columbia University in the fall of 1957 examined U. S. policy in atomic energy development. In the report of the sixty-odd participants, invited from a wide variety of fields, the primary issue of economic policy was related to the need for federal leadership in atomic development:[46]

> There is urgent need for a thorough review of the United States atomic power program. Such a review should lead to a clear formulation of the program's objectives in terms of the national power needs of the United States in the long run as well as the immediate requirements of United States foreign policy. . . .
> In recommendations which were taken into account in the drafting of the Atomic Energy Act of 1954, it was hoped that private industry could assume a more substantial role in the development of atomic power reactors. In the light of what has been learned since that time about the technical complexity and the cost of the program and the greater need for international actions, it is now apparent that

46. *Atoms for Power: United States Policy in Atomic Energy Development*, Columbia University Press, New York, 1957, pp. 158–59.

at this time there is a larger need for government support and leadership. The desired rate of progress calls for the AEC to assume more positive leadership and direction.

The statement noted that domestic needs did not call for numerous power reactors, whereas the demands of various foreign industrialized economies for competitive nuclear power were urgently felt. Domestically, the chief issues were a satisfactory distribution of development costs between the government and private enterprise and the appropriate distribution of development functions by private and public groups. A majority favored government assistance to private industry, perhaps by direct construction subsidy as well as by government-financed research and development and favorably priced materials and services. The minority preferred that the government itself should construct large and small plants for demonstration purposes. The assembly recognized that the domestic development program might be accelerated by full U. S. cooperation with the industrial nations in Western Europe and Japan.

The conference helped crystallize the belief among leaders in public policy formation that U. S. support of Euratom was a timely, highly desirable way to achieve foreign and domestic policy objectives.

Toward Compatible Foreign and Domestic Policies

By the end of 1957 the need for reconciliation between the U. S. foreign and domestic programs and policies had been revealed. Shortly after the policy statements by the National Planning Association and the American Assembly appeared, Congressman Sterling Cole, the former Chairman of the Joint Committee, upon becoming the Director General of the International Atomic Energy Agency, set forth his views on the main issues.[47] He urged the AEC and the Department of State to prepare a clear statement of the overseas objectives which an expanded development program should meet. He called on the AEC to prepare a new, expanded, government-sponsored reactor program and a formula for federal subsidies for development projects, recognizing the requirements of international and military responsibilities and that the costs and risks were too great for private capital alone. Finally, he suggested that the Joint Committee appoint a broadly constituted advisory panel to review the AEC proposals and to prepare its own independent statement of objectives of the nation's nuclear power program.

47. Remarks before the Lockheed Management Club of Georgia, Marietta, Ga., November 12, 1957.

At the same time his successor to the chairmanship of the Joint Committee, Congressman Carl T. Durham, reiterated his earlier suggestion of a ten-year demonstration program to follow the existing five-year program, established in 1954.[48] He noted the confusion about national objectives and policies and the inadequacy of the program for maintaining world leadership in reactor technology. In 1958 the Cole and Durham proposals led to formation of an advisory panel to the Joint Committee and issuance of an important staff document setting forth economic and policy objectives.[49] From this emerged the AEC's ten-year development plan—still the basic guideline.[50]

The joint arrangement with Euratom in 1958 had been the first major step toward compatibility of foreign and domestic nuclear power policies and programs. The explicit statement joining foreign and domestic objectives and linking short- and long-term goals provided the second major step toward reconciliation.[51] Early in 1960 the AEC stated the five objectives of the ten-year program as follows: to reduce the cost of nuclear power (in large plants) to levels competitive with conventional power in high-energy-cost areas of the United States in ten years (or about 1968); to assist friendly nations now having high energy costs to achieve competitive levels with nuclear power in five to ten years; to support a continuing long-range program to achieve low-cost power and widen the economic benefits; to maintain the U. S. position of leadership in civilian reactor technology; and, finally, to recognize the long-term importance of developing breeder-type reactors for both the uranium-238–plutonium and the thorium–uranium-233 fuel cycles.

The interweaving of foreign and domestic nuclear development programs has been seen in the problems confronting both the Euratom and United States demonstration programs. Since fuel prices in much of Western Europe and in Japan have been somewhat higher than in the United States, those areas have offered greater immediate scope for construction of high-cost demonstration reactors. Necessarily, domestic experience, based on smaller prototypes, first had to establish the reliability of operating characteristics. It

48. Letter to Honorable Lewis L. Strauss, Chairman, U. S. Atomic Energy Commission, November 27, 1957.

49. Joint Committee on Atomic Energy, *Proposed Expanded Civilian Nuclear Power Program*, 85th Cong., 2nd Sess., August 1958.

50. See *AEC Authorizing Legislation, Fiscal Year 1961*, Hearings, Subcommittee on Legislation, Joint Committee on Atomic Energy, 86th Cong., 2nd Sess., 1960, Appendix II, pp. 474 ff.

51. AEC Chairman J. A. McCone in early 1959 stated before the Joint Committee on Atomic Energy that the objectives of the nuclear power program called for short- and long-term cost reductions for plants appropriate to local conditions in the United States and other countries (Section 202 Hearings, 1959). A brief statement of the ten-year program may be found in the Section 202 Hearings for 1960, pp. 122–38.

would have been economically unsound and morally questionable for the United States to encourage construction of full-scale reactors abroad that had not first been proven by domestic prototypes.[52]

A possibility long existed that emphasis on "exportable" reactor technology might curtail diversified development of some eight or more reactor designs and related fuel cycles. In fact, in 1957 the AEC's Director of Reactor Development suggested concentrating on water-cooled or -moderated reactors, which might have required slowing down—though not discontinuing—the effort on more advanced types of reactors that seemed to offer greater long-term prospects of very low-cost power.[53] The AEC did not accept the proposal, but the issue of narrowing the program has remained alive.

Until 1960 it was a commonly accepted doctrine that United States participation in the foreign market would help sustain the developmental reactor program during the long period before widespread commercial adoption in the United States. Yet, by the end of 1960 it became clear that this help would be more restricted than had been assumed.[54] The issue of federal assistance for reactor development at home, it was seen, could not be solved by unqualified reliance on emerging foreign requirements.

Therefore, when the Kennedy administration became responsible for the program in January 1961, it was clear that a reassessment of the domestic and foreign programs was necessary. While compatibility had increased in the preceding three years, many problems still confronted the AEC and the State Department. For example, the preoccupation of the atoms-for-peace program with enriched uranium reactor systems presupposed economical ways of using by-product plutonium as reactor fuel. Yet, the domestic development program could provide no assurance in 1961 that the technology of recovering and recycling plutonium would soon prove economically feasible. Should the joint reactor research program with Euratom be extended or terminated? Should short-term, marginally useful reactor systems be subordinated to reactor projects that seemed to hold out greater hope for very low-cost nuclear power in the long run? These and many other techno-economic issues confronted the new administration early in 1961.

52. Doubts about the safety and reliability of a full-scale power reactor for which prototype experience is lacking could prove an obstacle in foreign relations and cooperation. Consider, as a domestic parallel the legal objections raised to the fast breeder reactor constructed near Detroit, Mich., by the Detroit Edison Co. and associated companies. (See Chapter 5 for further discussion.)

53. See two addresses by W. Kenneth Davis: at the Atomic Industrial Forum, New York, October 30, 1957; and at the Fast Reactor Information Meeting, Chicago, November 20, 1957.

54. Cf. Chauncey Starr, "Economic Incentives for the Equipment Manufacturer," Fourth Annual Conference, Atomic Industrial Forum, New York, October 28–31, 1957.

CHAPTER 2

Reactor Technology and Economic Policies

Development of the productive uses of nuclear energy has not been occurring in a laboratory vacuum, but has been fitfully pushed and pulled by changing public and private policies. Economic policies and civilian reactor technology have necessarily been cognate, here and in other countries. Relevant factors in examining these interrelations are the emphasis on nuclear electric power as against other atomic energy applications, the economic features of the various reactor systems, the cost estimates and the nature of the gap between current technology and future competitive nuclear power.

Peaceful Applications[1]

Within a nuclear reactor the controlled fission process yields neutrons and related forms of radiation, fission products and heat. Neutrons, over and above those needed to carry on the chain reaction, are chiefly of value for

---

1. For background, a variety of sources designed for the nontechnical reader are now available. In particular, see Selig Hecht, *Explaining the Atom*, Viking, New York, rev. ed., 1954; Gordon Dean, *Report on the Atom*, Knopf, New York, 2nd ed., 1957; Gerald Wendt, *The Prospects of Nuclear Power and Technology*, Van Nostrand, Princeton, 1957; Samuel Glasstone, *Sourcebook on Atomic Energy*, Van Nostrand, New York, 1950; AEC, *Atomic Energy Facts*, Washington, 1957; Donald J. Hughes, *On Nuclear Energy*, Harvard University Press, Cambridge, 1957; and Battelle Memorial Institute, "The Applications of Atomic Energy Other Than Central-Station Power Generation," in *Background Material*, McKinney Review, Vol. 5, pp. 1697–1897.

producing fissionable isotopes; and in so-called "production" reactors, as well as in breeders or converters, they are used to produce plutonium from uranium-238 or uranium-233 from thorium. The fission products, sometimes unimaginatively referred to as radioactive waste, may be treated and particular radioisotopes separated for useful purposes. Heat, customarily thought of as the primary reactor product, may be used for generating electric power; for propulsion of naval vessels and, ultimately, space satellites; and for space heating and process heat at low or high temperature.

The Emphasis on Electric Power

The public and private investment each year in the development of nuclear electric power has been several times that devoted to all other civilian applications of nuclear energy, briefly reviewed below. The origins of the private and governmental preoccupation with nuclear power have been primarily economic and institutional, rather than technical. Also, nuclear power development has required capital investment that dwarfs the rather small amounts needed for isotopes, fission products, or low-temperature, process-heat reactors. Furthermore, the manner of developing nuclear electric power promptly became enmeshed in the long-standing private-vs.-public-power controversy, thus focusing on nuclear electric power a degree of attention not given to the other uses of nuclear energy. Finally, nuclear power was early expected to help ameliorate the economic and strategic risks confronting the energy-importing industrial nations, a consideration that rendered the early achievement of practical nuclear power more important than the development of other uses. The priority given to the development of nuclear electric power does not minimize the potential economic effects of the nonpower applications of nuclear energy. Indeed, for such uses as tools of research or as new devices for assisting industrial production the nonpower applications may, in the long run, have an impact exceeding that of electric power generation or ship propulsion. They do not, however, cost so much to develop nor involve such sensitive issues of economic policy.

Isotopes

Radioactive and stable isotopes, produced in nuclear reactors or in particle accelerators, have been widely used in biology, medicine and industry as tools of research or production. The most widespread industrial uses are in radiography and in gauging thickness and density. The AEC has very crudely estimated the cost-saving benefits of radioisotopes in industry at one third of a billion dollars annually.[2]

High-Level Radiation

High-intensity radiation may be produced by many sources, including spent fuel elements, separated fission product gases, particle accelerators and X-ray machines. Such high-intensity radiation, sometimes known as ionizing radiation, which is not available in quantity from the commoner radioactive isotopes, may find economic use in food processing and preservation, and in initiating chemical processes as a substitute for heat or pressure. With some interesting exceptions, such as the sterilization of surgical sutures and cross-linking of polyethylene to increase its strength, these applications are still in their infancy. The role of high-intensity radiation in industry has been surveyed and some investigators feel that it has only moderately promising prospects,[3] while there are others who feel that high-intensity radiation may prove more "revolutionary" than most uses of atomic energy. This type of radiation may in some circumstances be a joint product with power in a fission reactor, though some investigators consider particle accelerators the more economical source.[4]

Space Heating and Industrial Process Heat

The uses of low-temperature reactor heat for processing in the paper and pulp, food and chemicals industries have been explored in several economic studies, but no heat demonstration projects have yet been undertaken by industry in the United States and the AEC in 1961 decided not to proceed with a demonstration plant. Since the low temperatures of less than 1,000° F. can be achieved with current reactor technology, several observers have made a case for early application in high-fuel-cost areas. The major immediate

2. AEC Commissioner W. F. Libby, address at the University of Oregon, January 15, 1958; UN, *Economic Applications of Atomic Energy: Power Generation and Industrial and Agricultural Uses*, Report of the Secretary-General, New York, 1957, p. 20; the National Industrial Conference Board in 1959 prepared a more detailed analysis indicating substantially smaller dollar benefits (AEC Press Release TI-120, Washington, April 9, 1959).

3. S. E. Eaton and Michael Michaelis, *Radiation: A Tool for Industry*, Arthur D. Little, Cambridge, Mass., 1959. Also, Battelle Memorial Institute, *op. cit.*

4. The design of an AEC-owned power plant of 75,000 kilowatts capacity, built at Hallam, Nebraska, in the system of the Consumers Public Power District, was modified by the contractor, North American Aviation, Inc., to include a facility for preserving and sterilizing food by exposure to the radiation of the liquid sodium coolant.

obstacle has been the question of scale; few low-temperature industrial operations would require more than small reactors, hence the economies of scale are unattractive. In 1959 the AEC entered into a cooperative program with the Department of the Interior to develop an experimental plant for converting saline water to fresh water by utilizing steam from a reactor. A 40,000-kilowatt reactor and a one-million-gallon-per-day conversion plant were to have been located near San Diego, California, but in 1960 Interior abandoned the reactor portion, owing to the delays in selecting an acceptable site. In the spring of 1962, however, the AEC sought congressional authorization for a proposal by a company producing pulp and paper in Michigan (a high-cost fuel area) to operate a government-assisted, organic-moderated reactor (50 tmw.), the steam from which would be used partly for electricity generation and partly for process heat.

The technology of reactors has not yet advanced sufficiently to produce high-temperature process heat, although Los Alamos Scientific Laboratory is experimenting with ultrahigh temperatures. High-temperature applications account for a large part of total process heat consumption in industry and the quantity required at a plant is often large enough to warrant a reactor of efficient size. An important market is possible—provided high temperatures can be attained. The AEC has been engaged in a long-term joint program with the Interior Department to develop a high-temperature process heat reactor for the gasification of coal. Temperatures of 2,500° F. or more are the objective, but the AEC considers the feasibility questionable and has limited its emphasis.

The prospects for nuclear reactor heat in space heating appear to be unpromising, owing to the limited industrial requirement and the large capital investment required in conducting the heat to a wide area. Swedish scientists and engineers who studied reactors particularly for space-heating purposes in 1958 suggested reactors for power and district heating jointly.[5]

Nuclear Propulsion

Nuclear propulsion of manned aircraft is still, technically speaking, too distant to consider seriously for civilian or even military purposes. Such is not

5. G. Cederwall, "The Swedish Nuclear Energy Program," *Peaceful Uses of Atomic Energy: Proceedings of the Second International Conference on the Peaceful Uses of Atomic Energy, Geneva, 1–13 September, 1958*, UN, New York, 1958 (referred to hereafter as *Proceedings*, Second Geneva Conference), Vol. 1, pp. 154–56. Other useful sources on process and space heating: G. Perazich, *Nuclear Process Heat in Industry*, NPA, Washington, September 1958; and AEC, *Process Heat Generation and Consumption, 1939 to 1967*, Washington, January 1958.

the case with nuclear propulsion of surface ships and submarines—and, per-haps, of railroad locomotives, which may be a possibility within the next couple of decades.[6] A drawback to the development of nuclear-powered locomotives, and perhaps of nuclear-powered aircraft, is that they represent significant public hazards. Also, in the United States at least, the load condi-tions and length of haul are not conducive to economic application of nuclear-powered locomotives. There seems to be little need for such locomotives in Western Europe, where many lines are electrified. In contrast, conditions in the Soviet Union do suggest a potential long-term place for nuclear-powered locomotives: a general shortage of fuel, broad gauge tracks (permitting less constraint on reactor design), long hauls and, in some instances, high density of load.

The possibility of perfecting nuclear ship propulsion for commercial pur-poses within the next two decades holds out an economic prospect that is attracting attention in Italy, Japan, France, West Germany, Norway, the United Kingdom and the USSR.[7] The primary reasons for this interest are the demonstrated technical feasibility of nuclear ship propulsion in the United States naval program and the desire to be free from dependence on oiling stations.[8]

Economic analyses have suggested that ore carriers and tankers, as well as small ships on long trade routes, may offer the most promising opportunities for the use of nuclear power in merchant ship propulsion. Only two nonmili-tary nuclear vessels, the NS *Savannah* in the United States and the icebreaker *Lenin* in the Soviet Union, have been constructed. The hazards represented by nuclear ship operation raise special questions of indemnification and insur-ance similar to, but certainly more acute than, questions raised by nuclear power plants on land. The institutional and economic problems are indeed difficult and may outweigh the operational advantages demonstrated by nuclear-propelled military vessels.

6. Cf. L. B. Borst and others, *An Atomic Locomotive: A Feasibility Study*, University of Utah, Salt Lake City, 1954.

7. A major difference between the first and second international conferences on the peaceful uses of atomic energy, held in Geneva in 1955 and 1958, was reflected in the large number of papers on nuclear ship propulsion submitted at the second conference by countries engaged heavily in shipping. See *Proceedings*, 1955 and 1958.

8. For a sampling of the extensive literature on the economics of nuclear ship propulsion, see the following: D. L. Conklin and others, *Economics of Nuclear and Conventional Merchant Ships*, AEC, Washington, June 30, 1958; Walter H. Zinn and R. P. Godwin, "The Use of Nuclear Energy for Purposes Other Than the Generation of Electricity," *Proceedings*, Second Geneva Conference, Vol. 8, p. 107; and AEC, *Power Reactor Technology*, *Quarterly Technical Progress Review* (pre-pared for the AEC by General Nuclear Engineering Corp.), Washington, March 1959, pp. 1–6.

Peaceful Uses of Nuclear Explosions [9]

Atomic bomb scientists in the Manhattan Project early became intrigued by the possibilities of "containing" a fission explosion in connection with the problem of how to prevent the loss of fissionable material in case the high explosive failed to initiate the nuclear reaction. The idea of testing the first weapon assembly in a large steel tank led to construction of the container, which was accidentally wrecked in the process of testing with conventional high explosives. Later, Soviet statements following their first atom bomb test in 1949 indicated nuclear explosives had been used for moving earth, though no evidence of such use was provided then or later. Several years ago the AEC undertook a series of underground shots of nuclear assemblies as part of Project Plowshare. These were suspended between 1958 and the fall of 1961, when the USSR resumed weapon tests. The first experimental detonation, Project Gnome, in December 1961, has encouraged the AEC laboratory at Livermore, California, to undertake economic analyses of peaceful applications—canal excavation, recovery of oil from oil sands, mining by block-caving, among others.

The potential applications of nuclear explosions are varied, but reservations have been expressed as to their probable economic benefits. [10] Craters made in construction of harbors or canals may remain too radioactive to work in for a long period, an intolerable economic burden in some cases. The production of power by use of nuclear explosions in underground chambers may be handicapped by the cost of constructing and lining the chambers, although recent studies suggest the possibilities of using unlined salt domes.

In crushing rock for mining low-grade ores, the use of thermonuclear (hydrogen) explosions in the range of 100 kilotons (TNT equivalent) appears to offer cost savings—offset in part, however, by radioactivity. An example might be in certain mining operations in Chile, where a massive overburden of waste rock must be broken and moved to reach the ore body. Arrangements for experimental explosions to recover oil from oil shale have been under negotiation between the AEC and the oil industry for some time. Promising as this application appears to be, the fact that an alternative method of

9. See, among others, W. F. Libby, "Toward Peaceful Uses of the Atom," *Science and Resources*, Resources for the Future, Washington, 1959; Frederick Reines, "The Peaceful Nuclear Explosion," *Bulletin of Atomic Scientists*, March 1959, p. 118; H. Zodtner, ed., *Industrial Uses of Nuclear Explosives*, University of California Radiation Laboratory, Berkeley, September 1958 (UCRL-5253); and AEC, *Major Activities in the Atomic Energy Programs, January–December 1961* (Annual Report), Washington, January 1962, pp. 208–19; and Ralph Sanders, *Project Plowshare*, Public Affairs Press, Washington, 1962.

10. Reines, *op. cit.*

Figure 2-1   Schematic Nuclear Fuel Cycle

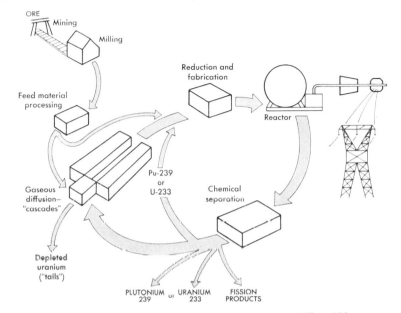

Source: Adapted from AEC, *Atomic Energy Facts,* Washington, 1957, p. 108.

recovery of oil from tar sands and oil shales has already been developed—at costs only slightly higher than the recovery of oil from wells—means that the economic benefit would not be so great as originally thought.

The Supply of Nuclear Fuel

The free world supply of uranium and thorium, while known to be large compared with fossil fuels, is finite and is unevenly, though widely, distributed among the nations.[11] The efficiency of fuel utilization already achieved and that reasonably in prospect are pertinent technical and economic considerations in judging the energy value of nuclear source materials.

The energy equivalent of uranium and thorium in the earth's crust is estimated to be many times that of all fossil fuels. The scaling calculations in Table 2–1 show potential energy production from uranium as a function of increasing technical progress and increasing annual rates of free world production. Only a few years ago free world uranium production was roughly 10,000 short tons a year and it was probably feasible then to utilize only about

11. AEC, "Energy from Uranium and Coal Reserves," Washington, May 1960 (TID 8207).

TABLE **2-1**

Approximate Heat Value of Varying Annual Rates of Free World Uranium Output

Assumed per cent of U utilization[a]	Megawatt-days per short ton of natural U[a]	Heat value (BTU X 10^{15}) with U output (short tons) of—[b]				
		10,000	20,000	30,000	40,000	50,000
"Present" technology—low utilization						
0.3	2,500	2.05	4.1	6.2	8.2	10.3
0.6	5,000	4.1	8.2	12.3	16.4	20.5
"Near-term" technology—with fuel recycle						
1.2	10,000	8.2	16.4	24.6	32.8	41.0
1.8	15,000	12.3	24.6	36.9	49.2	61.5
2.4	20,000	16.4	32.8	49.2	65.6	82.0
"Highly advanced" technology—breeding						
20.0	170,000	139.4	278.8	418.2	557.6	697.0
30.0	250,000	205.0	410.0	615.0	820.0	1025.0
40.0	340,000	278.8	557.6	836.4	1115.2	1394.0

a. 1 mw.-d. = 82 X 10^6 BTU. Mw.-d. per short ton X 1.18 X 10^{-4} = per cent U fissioned (low enrichment).

b. Uranium production capability is currently about 40,000 tons a year, at present production costs or lower. As a benchmark: total U. S. commercial energy consumption in 1960 was 44.9 X 10^{15} BTU. (See Table 3-1.)

Note: Apparent inconsistencies in the computations are due to rounding.

Source: AEC, Power Reactor Technology, Quarterly Technical Progress Review (prepared for the AEC by the General Nuclear Engineering Corp.), Washington, June 1959, pp. 1–12.

0.1 per cent of the potential energy available (natural uranium basis). At that level, if all the material were to be used in power reactors, the total energy produced (0.7 x 10^{15} BTU) would represent less than 2 per cent of total United States energy consumption. Since then fuel efficiency has risen to about 0.6 per cent utilization (5,000 megawatt-days per short ton) and may well go up to 1.2 per cent (10,000 megawatt-days per short ton). Annual uranium production in recent years has been about 40,000 tons, hence present technology could produce 16.4 x 10^{15} BTU, or almost one third of the annual United States energy consumption. This is a significant but not impressive magnitude.

If greatly advanced reactor and nuclear fuel technology involving high utilization (breeding) can be achieved, then 50,000 tons of uranium, for example, at 30 per cent utilization theoretically could produce 1.0×10^{18} BTU, about twenty-three times the 1960 rate of United States energy consumption. Moreover, such a rate of free world uranium production could be sustained for many years at no great increase above the recent cost of approximately $10.00 per pound. At the Second Geneva Conference, 1958, the AEC estimated reasonably assured reserves in known areas at 1 million tons and these might be doubled by new discoveries elsewhere.[12] But the matter does not end there, for the reserves of material recoverable at higher cost (above $10.00 per pound), in phosphates, shales and, ultimately, granite, are inestimably greater than economically recoverable reserves. At the extreme it has been demonstrated in the laboratory that the most common component of the earth's crust—ordinary igneous rock—could yield many millions of tons of uranium and thorium. This could, of course, be done only at very high cost (up to $600 per pound), but the energy obtained would be greater than the energy input required to process the rock. This means, among other things, that if the controlled release of energy from thermonuclear reactions does not ultimately prove possible as an inexhaustible source of power, then the widespread presence of physically recoverable uranium and thorium assures an energy supply that may be considered as practically infinite.[13]

Power Reactor Types

One of the chief economic problems of power reactor research is the multiplicity of choices among promising reactor types. At the First Geneva Conference, 1955, Weinberg noted that several hundred combinations of different nuclear fuels, fertile material, neutron energy and other characteristics were conceivable. Among these, he stated, perhaps a hundred reactor systems were not obviously impractical.[14] By the end of the Second Geneva Conference,

12. Based on Robert D. Nininger, "Geneva Conference Summary—Availability and Production of Source Materials," Fifth Annual Conference, Atomic Industrial Forum, Washington, November 10, 1958. Further details are given in Chapter 7.

13. Harrison Brown and L. T. Silver, "The Possibilities of Securing Long-Range Supplies of Uranium, Thorium and Other Substances from Igneous Rocks," *Peaceful Uses of Atomic Energy: Proceedings of the International Conference on the Peaceful Uses of Atomic Energy, Geneva, 8–20 August, 1955*, UN, New York, 1956 (referred to hereafter as *Proceedings*, First Geneva Conference), Vol. 8.

14. A. M. Weinberg, "Survey of Fuel Cycles and Reactor Types," *Proceedings*, First Geneva Conference, Vol. 3, p. 19.

1958, the range of most promising reactor types had been narrowed to about a dozen.

Many policies, such as those relating to the scale of effort and the forms of governmental assistance, have been determined in part by efforts to find the most promising reactor types and associated fuel cycles. In this process economics and technology have taken part, but the differences in viewpoint among reactor technicians and among national governments have been great. Scientists have stressed the desirability of "good neutron economy." Reactor engineers have stressed materials and thermal efficiency. National governments have been concerned with the use of indigenous resources and developing domestic technology and manufacturing. Individual reactor manufacturers have aimed to capitalize on their specialized experience under government contracts with a view to gaining a competitive advantage by using one or, at most, two reactor types. Hence, the spectrum of promising reactor types and fuel cycles has, on the one hand, introduced a salutary degree of flexibility of choice, as well as differentiation, among reactor operators, private and public. On the other hand, no company or government has had sufficient resources to attempt to develop the whole range of possibilities. The major reactor types (excluding mobile reactors, fissionable material production reactors and research reactors) that are being developed for central station power use here and in other countries are reviewed below.

Central station power reactors may be broadly classified, by the speed of neutrons, as fast reactors and thermal (slow) reactors.[15] In the thermal range, of which the early Manhattan District reactors at Chicago, Oak Ridge and later Hanford and Savannah River are examples, a further classification consists of heterogeneous and homogeneous types. The latter—still in an experimental stage—is an advanced design in which the coolant, fuel and moderator are mixed together as a fluid, whereas in a heterogeneous reactor each of these is customarily separate. Further, enriched fuel is necessary for fast reactors, but may also be desirable in thermal reactors, irrespective of application. Fast reactors require no material to "moderate" or slow down the neutron speed, but in thermal reactors the moderator may be ordinary water, heavy water, graphite or organic material. Also, the coolant, used to extract the heat from the core, may be gas (CO_2 or helium, for example), liquid metal (sodium) or natural or heavy water. The nuclear fuel may be in liquid, solid or slurry form.

15. Neutrons that have been slowed down to speeds of about 3,000 meters per second are described as thermal or slow neutrons, in contrast to fast neutrons, which at the instant of fission move at 15 million meters per second. Manson Benedict and Thomas H. Pigford, *Nuclear Chemical Engineering*, McGraw-Hill, New York, 1957, pp. 7–8.

Fuel Utilization

Another significant classification is made on the basis of the breeding or nonbreeding characteristics of a reactor—whether it produces more fissionable material than is consumed. On this criterion Weinberg has defined one group of reactors as being "high-utilization reactors" (or breeders), consisting of uranium-system fast-neutron breeders and of thorium-system thermal-neutron breeders. Both these systems, described as "advanced technology," will require much longer development than "low-utilization reactors" (or burners). Low-utilization reactors may be further classified as highly enriched, slightly enriched or unenriched burners. Most of the civilian reactor development effort thus far by this and other countries has been directed into the slightly enriched or unenriched burners.

A standing issue of reactor technology and economics, then, has been the division of investment and effort between the short-range burners and the long-range breeders. Table 2-1 indicates that, desirable as high utilization reactors may in time become, the potentialities of even the low-utilization reactors are important compared with total energy consumption. Reactor development programs may well continue, as they are now doing in the United States, the United Kingdom, the Soviet Union, France and Germany, to provide support for both current and advanced technologies.

Different Fuel Cycles

Technical and economic uncertainties relating to fuel and the fuel cycle have proved greater than those relating to the reactor itself. There has therefore been a strong disposition, notably in the United States, to concentrate first on fuel technology and to defer construction of prototype and full-scale demonstration plants until conspicuously warranted by progress with fuel testing in demonstration units.

The principal fissionable materials—uranium-233, uranium-235 and plutonium-239—have nuclear properties that deeply influence the technical and economic problems of reactor design. One of the primary characteristics of these materials is the relation between the number of neutrons produced per fission and the use (or loss) of these neutrons. Depending on the kind of fissionable material, an average of between 2.0 and 2.5 neutrons will be produced per fission. Since the chain reaction requires one neutron to sustain it, the remaining neutrons may be wasted or used productively, depending on the reactor design. Some fraction of the excess neutrons will be absorbed in the fuel (converting it into other isotopes), in the moderator, in the coolant, in

TABLE **2-2**

Characteristics of Nuclear Fuels: U235, U233 and Pu239

| | Neutrons produced per neutron captured | | | |
Fuel	Thermal reactor	Fast reactor	Radioactivity	Handling precautions
U235 (in natural U)	2.1	2.2	Weak gamma, and weak alpha from U234	None
U233 (from Th232)	2.3	2.5	Strong gamma and alpha	Remote handling, shielding
Pu239 (from U238)	2.0	2.6	Strong alpha	Remote handling

Source: A. Amorosi, Nuclear Engineering Handbook, McGraw-Hill, New York, 1958, p. 12–9.

the structural materials, or it will escape. However, reactor designers hope to keep the neutron economy at a level where the fertile material is converted to new fissionable material at ratios of more than 0.7 for thermal reactors and 1.0 or more for breeders.[16]

There is only one naturally occurring fissionable material—U235—but there are two naturally occurring fertile materials—Th232 and U238, which become converted to fissionable material after capturing a neutron. Thus, Th232 becomes, after decay of certain intermediate isotopes, U233; and U238, similarly, becomes Pu239. The comparative degree of technical interest in these fissionable materials is influenced strongly by the ratio of the neutrons produced per fission to the neutrons captured by the fuel and also by the radioactivity that may be associated with the fuel. (See Table 2-2.)

Each of the three major reactor fuels has its own disadvantages and advantages and these in turn affect the economic promise of each. For example, U235 has the great advantage of minimal associated radioactivity, whereas both U233 and Pu239 involve dangerous and costly difficulties in handling. On the other hand, the number of neutrons available beyond the one necessary for sustaining the chain reaction is so small in the case of U235

16. Reactor technicians use the term "breeder" in two different senses. In one case breeding involves the conversion of a fertile material (U238 or Th232) to a fissionable material when the original source of the neutrons is the same isotope as that which is produced; thus, fissioning Pu239 produces neutrons to breed new Pu239 by capture and decay reactions of U238. (The amount of new fissionable material may or may not exceed that consumed.) The second meaning of "breeding" is producing more fissionable material, regardless of kind, than is consumed. Unless otherwise indicated, this is the sense in which "breeding" is used in this study.

that use of this fuel for a breeder reactor is unpromising. The same is true of Pu239 in the thermal energy range. U233, however, is theoretically promising for breeding at both thermal and fast neutron speeds, but radioactivity problems in fuel handling are serious. Pu239 appears promising for breeding only in the fast neutron range, and it also is dangerously toxic if ingested. In general, the technology of thermal reactors is better understood than that of fast reactors, and the use of U235 as reactor fuel is better known than that of Pu239 and U233.

Certain economic implications of reactor technology should be evident. A nation possessing economically recoverable natural uranium ore not only has a practical base for trying to develop competitive nuclear power generation, but it also is in a position, for example, to plan ultimately for the breeding of plutonium to be used as fuel in fast reactors. Further, a nation may approach its ultimate objectives by progressive stages and need not commit itself to a single route. As shown in Chapter 7, the United Kingdom, Canada, India and the United States are following different routes, suggesting the diverse possibilities in this respect.

Competition among private reactor developers is also influenced by these diverse technological possibilities. The giant corporation is in an advantageous position, because it alone may have sufficient resources to weather the long, costly period of development from experimentation to prototype plant construction required to perfect even one reactor design and its associated fuel. Differentiation between competing companies has already taken the form of concentration on particular reactor systems.[17] In most instances a company's emphasis has been the result of research and development sponsored by the AEC in the national laboratories or by contract with the company. Indeed, the successful entry of new companies into the concentrated power supply business may be determined by the character and administration of the AEC's development program in support of particular power reactor concepts.

Major Reactor Concepts[18]

THE PRESSURIZED WATER REACTOR, operating with either natural or heavy water as moderator, gained its preeminence as the type first used for

17. For example, the boiling water reactor (using enriched uranium fuel) has become the primary orientation in central station development of the General Electric Co.; the pressurized water reactor, the almost exclusive design for submarine propulsion, has been emphasized by Westinghouse Electric Corporation; and Atomics International (of North American Aviation, Inc.) has concentrated on sodium graphite and organic-cooled designs.

18. This section is based on: AEC, Washington: *Atomic Energy Facts*, September 1957, pp. 75–105; *Technical Progress Reviews: Power Reactor Technology*, December 1958, Vol. 2, No. 1;

submarine propulsion and now used to the exclusion of others for that purpose. High-pressure vessels to house the core are necessary, although the use of pressure tubes may obviate the pressure vessel. Some question exists whether the pressurized water reactor (an example of which is the AEC-Duquesne demonstration reactor at Shippingport, Pennsylvania, the first atomic power plant in the United States) holds promise of being a low-cost producer, although experts reporting to the AEC (see Table 2–8) estimated its costs as low as most other types.

Figure 2-2   Power Reactor Diversification—National Differences in Types, 1961

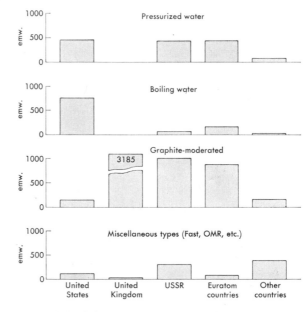

Source: Table 2-3.

THE BOILING WATER REACTOR, using natural or heavy water as moderator, seems to offer simplicity of construction and operation. The direct-cycle reactor permits the steam from the reactor vessel to pass to the turbine and condenser without a secondary heat exchange, though this may raise a maintenance and safety problem in radioactive carryover from the core vessel. The

Civilian Nuclear Power, Report of Ad Hoc Advisory Committee on Reactor Policies and Programs, January 2, 1959 (printed in Section 202 Hearings, 1959); *Civilian Power Reactor Program*, Part I, 1960; and Annual Report for 1961, pp. 75–111; also A. Amorosi, in *Nuclear Engineering Handbook*, McGraw-Hill, New York, 1958, Section 12.

boiling water, direct-cycle design has received special international recognition. It was selected in 1958 from among bids on several other designs submitted in international competition for construction of the 150-megawatt plant in southern Italy, the so-called "SENN Project," to be financed by the International Bank for Reconstruction and Development. This reactor type, like the pressurized water reactor, is well advanced and further development probably requires diminishing assistance from the AEC.

GRAPHITE-MODERATED REACTORS cover at least three classes of design, based on type of coolant—gas, water or sodium. The gas-cooled variety has been pushed furthest in the United Kingdom, where it early became the first-stage demonstration of practical, though not competitive, power in a full-scale plant. Gas-cooled, graphite-moderated reactors are economically attractive because they require only readily available materials. They can operate, at some disadvantage, with natural uranium and do not require special moderator materials, such as heavy water. The capital cost is high, which offsets the low fuel cost of operating with natural uranium. Gas-cooled technology was explored by the Manhattan Engineer District and discontinued later by the Atomic Energy Commission, but its promising potentialities for high-temperature operation (above 1,000° F.) have revived interest in the United States, leading to projects at Oak Ridge National Laboratory and at Peach Bottom, Pennsylvania. The water-cooled types of graphite-moderated reactors are descendants of the large MED and AEC plutonium-production reactors and benefit by slightly enriched uranium to overcome the neutron absorption of the surrounding materials. The Soviet Union has used this design for dual-purpose reactors. In 1959 the United States started a dual-purpose reactor of this type at the AEC installation in Hanford, Washington, but in 1961 the Congress rejected the AEC's request for funds to build the generating facilities required to convert the heat of the reactor to electric energy. In 1962 the Congress authorized a proposal by local public power groups to provide the generating facilities. The sodium-cooled, graphite-moderated reactor is of interest because it eliminates high pressure in the primary system and provides steam of fairly high temperature. The main technical problems concern the handling of sodium and the necessity for primary and secondary cooling circuits to prevent a dangerous sodium-water reaction in the steam generator.

ORGANIC-COOLED REACTORS use a hydrocarbon (terphenyl) as coolant and moderator and have advantages over pressurized water reactors, because of good steam quality, low vapor pressure, noncorrosive coolant and low-cost materials. The present drawbacks are the decomposition of the organic material under irradiation and heat and the low heat-transfer coefficient.

THE FAST BREEDER REACTOR, one of which is scheduled for completion in 1962 in the system of the Detroit Edison Co., near Detroit, is technically the most advanced type being constructed in full scale (90 to 100 electric megawatts). This reactor has faced a number of developmental problems. Some of these stem from the small core, which intensifies heat transfer difficulties; also, the physics of the core, including short neutron lifetime, makes reactor control harder. Economically most serious, perhaps, is the fuel cost. Since the fuel must be highly enriched (plutonium or U235), very high burn-up is a necessity to avoid frequent reprocessing of the fuel and excessive inventory charges. Whether or not the AEC will maintain the 4.75 per cent use charge on nuclear fuel, sustain the price of plutonium and continue to provide chemical processing and refabrication of radioactive material creates several uncertainties for this reactor design. The legal issue surrounding the AEC's issuance of a provisional construction permit for the reactor was resolved in June 1961 when the Supreme Court upheld the AEC's action and rejected the contention that the AEC's safety findings were inadequate. (See discussion of the so-called "PRDC case" in Chapter 5.)

THE AQUEOUS HOMOGENEOUS REACTOR is an advanced type of fluid-fuel design in which water (natural or heavy) and enriched fuel are mixed. The heat is generated directly in the coolant (and moderator), which is pumped to the heat exchanger and then back into the reactor tank. In this so-called "dream" cycle a small amount of the fluid fuel is continuously being removed, reprocessed and then returned. In the "single-region" type the fuel and fertile material are mixed; in the so-called "two-region" type the core consists chiefly of the fuel and a surrounding blanket is composed of fertile material. Owing to its high conversion ratio, the thorium-U233 cycle is preferred over the U238-U235 fuel cycle. (See Table 2–2.) The promising two-region reactor design presents technical problems—the corrosion of tank and piping and the precipitation of uranium, which leads to hot spots. The prospect that breeding in the thorium cycle can be achieved has improved, since the ratio of the total number of neutrons produced to the neutrons absorbed in fertile material ("eta," as it is termed) had been reasonably well established by 1960.[19]

19. See, for example, J. E. Evans and R. G. Fluharty, "Evaluation of Low-Energy Cross Section Data for U233," *Nuclear Science and Engineering*, July 1960, pp. 66–82. The value recommended for eta, at 2,200 meters per second, is $2.291 \pm .009$ (cf. Table 2–2).

Despite technical and economic obstacles to its development, interest in the homogeneous reactor has been great at the Oak Ridge National Laboratory, because this type provides an apparently simple fuel cycle (hence low cost) and it also offers the possibility of thermal breeding on the thorium-U233 fuel cycle. No full-scale power reactors of this type are now planned and the AEC in mid-1961 terminated further experiments on homogeneous types, but continued research on thorium utilization. The thorium-U233 cycle is of interest to both India and Brazil, which have large reserves of thorium but small uranium supplies.

In addition to the above, scientists and technicians are exploring a number of "advanced reactor" concepts, including such systems as molten plutonium, molten salt, pebble bed, among others.

National Proclivities

Each of the few countries seeking to develop nuclear power has been pursuing a characteristic route, which has been dictated more by the postwar history, the readily available resources and the special needs of the country than by a choice based strictly on technical and economic considerations. Only the United States has been able to devote substantial development effort to each of the reactor types just reviewed, but even in the United States some lines have been subordinated (e.g., gas-cooled and natural uranium). (The emphasis of each country's program is suggested by Table 2-3, listing the power reactor projects and design studies under way at the end of 1961.)

The United Kingdom has been pursuing two routes and time scales. For the short term it has concentrated on the gas-cooled, graphite-moderated, thermal reactor using natural uranium. For the long term the United Kingdom has explored the fast breeder type, the purpose of which is to produce power and plutonium in practical quantities for use in subsequent power reactors. This "beer-and-champagne" approach was adhered to (until early 1958), because the quantities of enriched uranium available as reactor fuel were small, owing to the prior claims of the military on the limited capacity for producing enriched uranium. In 1958, however, the British recognized the high-capital-cost disadvantage of natural uranium, gas-cooled reactors and expanded reactor research on high-temperature, gas-cooled systems requiring enriched uranium as fuel to secure increased burn-up and lower capital cost.

In Canada the primary interest has been in reactors utilizing heavy water as a moderator with natural uranium as fuel, a consequence of special Canadian circumstances and wartime history. During the war the Canadian Trail plant

TABLE **2-3**

Worldwide Central Station and Experimental Power Reactors, 1961

Name (and/or owner)	Location	Power output net (emw.)	Date critical
Central station power reactors			
Boiling water			
Pathfinder Atomic Power Plant (Northern States Power Co.)	Sioux Falls, S. Dak.	62	1962
Dresden (Commonwealth Edison Co.)	Morris, Ill.	185	1959
RWE (Rheinisch-Westfalisches Electrizitatswerk)	Kahl, Germany	15	1960
Ulyanovsk	Volga, USSR	50	1961
ERR (Elk River Reactor) (Rural Coop. Power Assn.)	Elk River, Minn.	22	. . .
Big Rock Point (Consumers Power Co.)	Charlevoix, Mich.	47.8	1962
Humboldt Bay (Pacific Gas & Electric Co.)	Humboldt Bay, Calif.	48.5	1962
JPDR (JAERI)	Tokai-Mura, Japan	11.7	1962
SENN (Società Elettronucleare Nazionale)	Garigliano River, Italy	150	1963
BONUS (Boiling Nuclear Superheater)	Punta Higuera, Puerto Rico	16.3	1963
Bodega Bay (Pacific Gas and Electric Co.)	Bodega Bay, Calif.	313	1965
La Crosse BWR (AEC and Dairyland Power Cooperative Assn.)	Genoa, Wis.	50	1965
Pressurized water			
Shippingport (AEC & Duquesne Light Co.)	Shippingport, Pa.	60	1957
Lenin icebreaker	USSR	180[a]	1959
VVER (210)	Voronezh, USSR	420[b]	1961
Nuclear merchant ship reactor (*Savannah*) (AEC & U. S. Maritime Administration)	U. S.	69[a]	1961
Yankee Atomic Electric Co.	Rowe, Mass.	141	1960
CEN (BR-3)	Mol, Belgium	11.5	1962
Atomkraftwerk I (VVER—7 prototype)	E. Berlin, East Germany	70	1962
Enrico Fermi (SELNI)	Northern Italy	165	. . .
Chooz (SENA)	Ardennes, Belgium	242	1965
Southern California Edison	U. S.	355	. . .
CETR (Consolidated Edison Thorium Reactor)	Indian Pt., N. Y.	255	1962
Heavy water			
NPD (AECL and Ontario Hydro)	Rolphton, Canada	19.3	1961
Douglas Point Generating Station (CANDU) (AECL)	Douglas Pt., Canada	202	1964

TABLE **2 - 3** (continued)

Name (and/or owner)	Location	Power output net (emw.)	Date critical
AGESTA-R3 (AB Atomenergi and State Power Board)	Stockholm, Sweden	10	1963
Carolinas-Virginia Tube Reactor (C.-V. Nuclear Power Associates)	Parr Shoals, S. C.	17	1962
KS-150	Bohunice, Czechoslovakia	150	1965
EL-4 (CEA/EDF), experimental	Monts d'Arrée, France	80	1964
Halden BHWR (IFA)	Halden, Norway	20[a]	1959
Ulyanovsk experimental BWR	Volga, USSR	35[a]	...
Graphite-moderated			
APS-1 (USSR)	Obninsk, USSR	5	1954
Calder Hall (UKAEA)	Calder Hall, England	152[c]	1956–58
G-1 (CEA)	Marcoule, France	5	1956
G-2, G-3 (CEA)	Marcoule, France	56	1958–59
Siberian power station	Troitsk, USSR	600[d]	1958
EDF-1 (Electricité de France)	Chinon, France	60	1961
Berkeley (CEGB)	Berkeley, England	274[b]	1961
Bradwell (CEGB)	Bradwell, England	300[b]	1961
Hunterston (SSEB)	W. Kilbride, Scotland	328[b]	...
Hinkley Point (CEGB)	Somerset, England	500[b]	1963
Trawsfynydd (CEGB)	North Wales	500[b]	1963
Dungeness (CEGB)	Dungeness, England	550[b]	1964
Latina (Società Italiana Meridianale per l'Energia Atomica, SIMEA)	Latina, Italy	200	1962
Tokai-Mura (Japan Atomic Power Co.)	Tokai-Mura, Japan	158	1965
Sizewell (CEGB)	Suffolk, England	580[b]	1965
EDF-2 (Electricité de France)	Chinon, France	170	1963
EDF-3 (Electricité de France)	Near Chinon, France	375	1965
Beloyarsk power station	Urals, USSR	400[c]	1961
HTGR (High-Temperature Gas-Cooled Reactor) (Philadelphia Electric Co.)	Peach Bottom, Pa.	40	1964
Hallam (AEC and Consumers Public Power District)	Hallam, Neb.	76	1962
Experimental power reactors			
Graphite-moderated			
AGR (Advanced Gas-Cooled Reactor) (UKAEA)	Windscale, England	28	1962
AVR (Arbeitsgemeinschaft Versuchs-Reaktor GmbH.)	Julich, Germany	15	1964
Dragon (OEEC High-Temperature Reactor Project)	Winfrith, England	20[a]	1963
UHTRE (AEC)	Los Alamos, N. Mex.	3[a]	1964
SRE (Sodium Reactor Experiment) (AEC and Atomics International, Inc.)	Santa Susana, Calif.	6.0	1957

TABLE **2-3** (continued)

Name (and/or owner)	Location	Power output net (emw.)	Date critical
EGCR (Experimental Gas-Cooled Reactor) (AEC)	ORNL, Tenn.	22.3	1962
MSRE (Molten Salt Reactor Experiment) (AEC)	ORNL, Tenn.	10[a]	1963
Light water (experimental)			
Portable Russian plant	Obninsk, USSR	2	1959
Saxton (Gen. Public Utilities Corp. subs.)	Saxton, Pa.	3.25	1961
EBWR (Experimental Boiling Water Reactor) (AEC)	Argonne, Ill.	100[a]	1956
VBWR (Vallecitos Boiling Water Reactor) (GE)	Pleasanton, Calif.	5	1957
VESR Superheat Reactor (ESADA)	Pleasanton, Calif.	12.5[a]	1962
Borax-5 (Boiling Reactor Experiment) (AEC)	NRTS, Idaho	2.65	1961
Fast (experimental)			
EBR-1 (Experimental Breeder Reactor) (AEC)	NRTS, Idaho	0.2	1951
S BR-5	Obninsk, USSR	5[a]	1959
DFR (UKAEA)	Dounreay, Scotland	15	1959
LAMPRE-1 (Los Alamos Molten Plutonium Reactor Experiment) (AEC)	Los Alamos, N. Mex.	1.0[a]	1961
FRCTF (Fast Core Test Fac.) (AEC)	Los Alamos, N. Mex.	20[a]	1964
EBR-2 (AEC)	NRTS, Idaho	16.5	1961
Enrico Fermi Atomic Power Plant (PRDC & Detroit Edison Co.)	Lagoona Beach, Mich.	60.9	1962
BN-50	Ulyanovsk, USSR	50	...
BN-250	USSR	250	...
Rapsodie (CEA)	Cadarache, France	10[a]	1963
Organic-moderated (experimental)			
OMRE (Organic-Moderated Reactor Experiment) (AEC)	NRTS, Idaho	16[a]	1957
Piqua (AEC and City of Piqua)	Piqua, Ohio	11.4	1962
EOCR (Experimental Organic-Cooled Reactor) (AEC)	NRTS, Idaho	40[a]	1962
PRO (CNEN)	Near Bologna, Italy	30[a]	1963

a. Thermal.   b. Two reactors.   c. Four reactors.   d. Six reactors.

Note: Minor differences in project descriptions between this table and others appearing later reflect different sources and dates of compilation. Also, authoritative data are not available, for example, for the USSR reactors (cf. Tables 7-5 and B-6.)

Source: "World Reactor Chart: 3rd Edition," *Nuclear Power*, Rowse Muir Publications, London, January 1962; and Section 202 Hearings, 1962, pp. 599 ff.

supplied some of the needs of the Manhattan District for heavy water, and Canadian scientists became familiar with the material's use for reactor purposes. Moreover, the Canadian output of natural uranium has become so large that an alternative to sales for weapon use has become essential. Success with long exposure of natural uranium fuel elements has led Canadian scientists to believe strongly that high burn-up in heavy water (or gas-cooled) reactors could make the recovery and recycling of plutonium as a reactor fuel unnecessary for many years.[20]

The distinctive features of the United States reactor development program are not only the diversity of reactor types being explored simultaneously but also the strong preference throughout the program for using enriched uranium fuels and natural water—boiling or pressurized. Both preferences are largely the result of ample supplies of enriched uranium in all degrees of concentration in U235, the large number of AEC laboratories engaged in reactor technology and the broad spectrum of military reactor requirements, which have pointed the way for civilian reactor development generally. Since 1957 the program has been further broadened to bring in, for example, the high-temperature, gas-cooled reactor, the heavy water–moderated reactor and plutonium-recycle fuel systems.

The Soviet Union, in its emphasis on water-cooled reactors and on diversified research, has come closer to the United States than to either Canada or the United Kingdom. An important feature, as indicated in Table 2–3, is that the Soviet Union has also stressed the progressive development of fast breeder technology.

The multiple objectives of the leading atomic nations in the development of atomic power have presented a dilemma for other countries considering introduction of still costly nuclear power. Each country may choose among a wide variety of types in order to meet the short- or long-term necessities indicated by its unique energy situation and peculiar national circumstances. However, a nation choosing one of the designs immediately available from the United Kingdom or the United States will find, unfortunately, only high-cost, demonstration plants. Where the economic pressure is urgent—as in Italy or Japan—the purchase of one of these may be justified as the price of getting a fast start. Yet, because nuclear power is noncompetitive, most countries have been waiting to see the outcome of demonstration reactors now being constructed elsewhere before making commitments.

20. See, for example, W. B. Lewis, "High Burn-up from Fixed Fuel," Atomic Energy of Canada, Limited, Chalk River, Ontario, November 27, 1957; and "Canada's Steps Toward Nuclear Power," *Proceedings*, Second Geneva Conference, Vol. 1, p. 53.

Estimated Costs of Nuclear Power

In view of the variety of reactor types and the lack of long operating experience, it is understandable that the avalanche of cost estimates appearing in the United States and abroad in the last ten years has provided an insecure, if not indeed dangerous, foundation for policy formation. This is especially true in relation to such matters as the scale and duration of efforts to close the gap between technically feasible and economically competitive nuclear power. Inadequate operating experience and reactor variety, however, have perhaps been no more important in explaining the diversity of cost estimates and the "miscalculation" of nuclear power's imminence than has the apparent subjectivity of most of these cost estimates in the literature. Wide differences of opinion have existed between proponents of different fuel and reactor systems, between foreign and domestic estimators, between buyers and sellers of equipment and between estimators in private and in government laboratories. Furthermore, variation from a common basis of practice—the "economic ground rules"—for cost estimating has added to confusion about the prospects of one reactor type as against another. "The simple truth," according to the former heads of the AEC's Reactor Development Division, "is that the assumptions of amortization period, interest rate, allotment of developmental costs, taxes, capitalization method, fuel life, power rating, etc., are much more determining than the choice of reactor type."[21] Finally, the cost estimates have displayed recurrent waves of optimism and pessimism.

The available cost estimates will remain unconvincing until a number of reactors of varying size and type have been constructed and operated in this country. Indeed, to cross the threshold of competitive feasibility in the United States, advisers to the AEC in 1959 indicated it would probably be necessary to build two, and perhaps more, prototypes in the same line of reactor type.[22]

The Competitive Cost Threshold: United States

A primary purpose of the AEC's 1959 reactor development program was to "reduce the cost of nuclear power to levels competitive with power from fossil fuels in high energy cost areas of this country within ten years." Though often used loosely, the term "competitive" acquires specific meaning if the appropriate conditions are stated. There is wide variation in conventional

21. W. Kenneth Davis, Louis H. Roddis, Jr., and C. Goodman, "Power Reactors: The Government View," *Nucleonics*, September 1957, p. 93.

22. *Report by the Ad Hoc Advisory Committee on Reactor Policies and Programs.*

steam-generating costs in the United States, probably wider than in any other industrial nation. The primary sources of variation are: the fixed charges applied to plant investment, generally 13 to 15 per cent for privately owned plants, 8 to 10 per cent for plants under public or cooperative ownership; the plant size, larger plants being less costly per unit of capacity;[23] and the cost of fuel, varying, usually according to the distance from its source, from 17 to 41 cents per million BTU. (See Table 2–4.)

The multiple influence of these institutional and economic factors can be seen by comparing generating costs of individual power plants in different sections of the country. (See Table 2–5.) For comparative purposes, the plants selected are in the general areas where demonstration nuclear power plants are being constructed or planned.

As seen in Table 2–4, nuclear power becomes marginally competitive with steam plants in the United States at costs ranging between 6.0 and 7.6 mills per kilowatt-hour (private financing assumed), depending on region. But to become widely competitive in the lower cost range, its costs would have to be cut below 6.0 mills per kilowatt-hour. There has been an understandable tendency for equipment suppliers to estimate foreseeable costs falling close to the competitive threshold. Yet, objective appraisal suggests, as shown in succeeding sections, that nuclear cost estimates based on technology in sight are not yet assuredly within these limits.

Review of the cost estimating literature (1946–1960) may help to reveal the unfortunate policy consequences of the transient and uncertain estimates.

The Thomas Report (1946)

When the 1954 Cole-Hickenlooper bill was being debated, there was no official Atomic Energy Commission statement of the estimated costs of generating nuclear power with which policy makers might gauge the difficulty of the economic barrier confronting private and public development. Two

23. Average investment costs for steam-electric units have been reported as follows (per kilowatt of capacity):

Plant capacity (megawatts)	Southern locations	Northern locations	Average
Less than 10	. . .	. . .	$252
10–25	$184	$227	207
25–50	169	206	181
50–100	142	162	151
More than 100	135	182	155

Figures are from the Federal Power Commission, as reported in *Nuclear Engineering Handbook*, McGraw-Hill, New York, 1958, Sec. 12, p. 93.

TABLE **2-4**

Range of United States Conventional Fuel Costs and Corresponding "Standard" Electric Generating Costs, 1961

Region	Fuel costs (per million BTU)	"Standard" generating costs (mills per KWH)[a]
U. S. range	$0.17–$0.41	5.2–7.6
New England	0.36– 0.41	7.1–7.6
Middle Atlantic	0.22– 0.41	5.7–7.6
East North Central	0.22– 0.31	5.7–6.6
West North Central	0.20– 0.26	5.5–6.1
South Atlantic	0.18– 0.35	5.3–7.0
East South Central	0.18– 0.26	5.3–6.1
West South Central	0.17– 0.25	5.2–6.0
Mountain	0.21– 0.40	5.6–7.5
Pacific	0.33– 0.36	6.8–7.1

a. Fuel costs computed on a low heat rate of 10,000 BTU per eKWH; added to these are operating and maintenance expenses of 0.5 mills per KWH and private financing fixed charges of 3.0 mills per KWH, or 13.5 per cent at high plant factor. Actual costs differ, of course, from these comparative standard costs.

Source: Based on National Coal Association, *Steam-Electric Plant Factors, 1961,* Washington, July 1962, Table 2.

classified reports, one in 1946 and the other in 1953, had been prepared by contractors during the postwar interval, but neither apparently had real influence on the views of the Congress or the Commission itself in 1953 and 1954. The first, the so-called "Thomas report," prepared rather hastily in 1946 at Oak Ridge under the Manhattan Engineer District,[24] served as one of the bases of the observations on civilian nuclear power prospects and control in the Acheson-Lilienthal report[25] and of the scientific information transmitted to the ill-fated United Nations Atomic Energy Commission. This tentative and impressionistic appraisal also became the unfortunate basis of estimated nuclear power costs used in pioneering economic studies on the

24. Charles A. Thomas and others, "Economics of Nuclear Power," Clinton Laboratory of the Manhattan Engineer District, Oak Ridge, Tenn., July 19, 1946 (Report CF 46-7-257, secret, declassified with deletions, February 12, 1958). The 1953 report is cited in footnote 32, p. 58.

25. U. S. Department of State, *The International Control of Atomic Energy, Scientific Information Transmitted to the United Nations Atomic Energy Commission, June 14, 1946–October 14, 1946,* Washington, pp. 125–27.

long-term impact of nuclear power on industrial location, growth and techniques.[26]

The detailed figures of the Thomas report, which was not declassified until 1958, and then not in its entirety, are no longer significant, but the general tenor of the report is revealing. In retrospect, it is evident that a most competent group of reactor scientists,[27] while advising the UN Atomic Energy Commission that "an extensive research and development program would be required to solve the problems which will arise" and that the "problems appear difficult but not insurmountable," were in fact unable to foresee the scale and depth of the problems in store. The answer to the question which the Thomas report sought to resolve—whether the estimated cost of nuclear power was "in such a range as to encourage development by industry"—was in the affirmative and set the tone for industry's attitude toward the prospects for years thereafter. It was emphasized that the cost estimates implied the successful solution of a number of difficult technical problems, but that "nuclear power would find favorable industrial application if obstacles are not placed in the path of its development."

Industry Participation Teams (1951–1953)

In 1950 Charles A. Thomas, an officer of Monsanto Chemical Co. and primary author of the Thomas report, proposed to the AEC that industry, with its own capital, might well design, construct and operate dual-purpose nuclear reactors for the production of weapon-grade plutonium and electric power. This led to the formation of a series of five study groups from industry, usually consisting of two firms each, invited by the AEC to make "initial surveys" of reactor technology, on a cleared basis and at the expense of the companies, to determine the prospects for engineering and technical feasibility of dual-purpose nuclear power. The groups concluded that "dual purpose reactors are technically feasible and could be operated in such a fashion that the plutonium credit would reduce the cost of power." But they also found that "no reactor could be constructed in the very near future which would be economic on the basis of power generation alone."[28] The value of plutonium

26. Sam Schurr and Jacob Marschak, *Economic Aspects of Atomic Power*, Princeton University Press, 1950; Walter Isard and Vincent Whitney, *Atomic Power: An Economic and Social Analysis*, Blackistone, New York, 1952.

27. The study was made, under the chairmanship of Charles A. Thomas, by the following members of the Clinton Laboratory staff: M. C. Leverett, C. R. McCullough, L. S. Nordheim, W. I. Thompson, A. M. Weinberg, E. P. Wigner and Gale Young.

28. AEC, *Reports to the U. S. Atomic Energy Commission on Nuclear Power Reactor Technology*, Washington, May 1953, p. 2.

TABLE 2-5

Conventional Electric Power Costs in General Area of Nuclear Power Plants in the United States, 1960[a]

Utility system and plant location	Capacity (mw.) (1)	Net power generated (billions of KWH) (2)	Plant factor (per cent) (3)	Plant investment (per kw.) (4)	Costs — Fixed charges — Rate (per cent) (5)	Costs — Fixed charges — Mills per KWH (6)	Costs — O. & M. (mills per KWH) (7)	Costs — Fuel — Mills per KWH (8)	Costs — Fuel — Cents per million BTU[b] (9)	Total (mills per KWH) (10)
Privately owned										
Commonwealth Edison, Stickney, Ill.	600.0	3.84	73	$208	13.5	4.4	.7	2.9	29.31	8.0
Consolidated Edison, Astoria, N. Y.	695.0	4.07	67	196	13.5	4.5	.8	3.6	36.35	8.9
Detroit Edison, St. Clair, Mich.	950.0	5.43	65	146	13.5	3.4	.5	2.8	30.50	6.7
Duquesne Light, Elrama, Pa.	447.5	2.6	...	189	13.5	4.4	.5	2.1	20.29	7.0
New England Power, Salem, Mass.	319.9	2.24	80	178	13.5	3.4	.7	3.5	37.10	7.6
Northern States Power, Sioux Falls, S. Dak.	45.0	.210	53	201	13.5	5.8	1.8	4.1	28.04	11.7

Pacific Gas & Electric, Humboldt Bay, Calif.	102.4	.37	42	159	13.5	5.9	.99	4.85	36.90	11.7
Pennsylvania Power & Light, Stroudsburg, Pa.	312.5	1.3	47	115	13.5	3.7	.87	3.8	33.17	8.4
South Carolina Generating, Aiken, S. C.	250.0	1.11	51	156	13.5	4.7	.51	2.97	29.41	8.3
Publicly owned										
City of Piqua, Piqua, Ohio	33.0	.098	49	105	8.0	2.8	1.9	4.4	...	9.2
Consumers Public Power District, Scottsbluff, Nebr.	15.0	.138	89	160	8.0	1.4	.7	2.6	...	4.7

a. Data for plants at Piqua and Scottsbluff are for 1961.   b. Of the major type of fuel consumed (coal, oil or gas).

Note: Discrepancies in addition are due to rounding.

Sources:

Cols. 1–4 and 7–10—For privately owned plants: FPC, Steam-Electric Plant Construction Cost and Annual Production Expenses, Thirteenth Annual Supplement. 1960, Washington, 1961. For publicly owned plants: data furnished by the two utility systems listed.

Col. 5—Assumed.

$$\text{Col. 6} \frac{\text{Cols. 5 X 4 X 1}}{\text{Col. 2}}$$

clearly was a crucial element in the early estimates of prospective nuclear power costs. Indeed, in the report of the Monsanto Chemical Co.–Union Electric Co. team it was held that in a dual-purpose reactor the heat in the steam should be considered free, for "the cost of the heat should be borne by the plutonium since it is an inevitable consequence of the formation of this material."[29] Without the credit from the weapon-value plutonium, it appeared that competitive nuclear power would be very difficult to achieve, and much development was "still required to make the costs of power low enough to interest private capital on a large scale."[30] By that time, however, the AEC had already adopted a power policy "to further the development of nuclear power plants which are economically independent of Government commitments to purchase weapons-grade plutonium."[31] The cost estimates themselves are therefore no longer relevant. They did, however, serve unmistakably to encourage industry's belief in the good prospects for nuclear power, although the policy decision to avoid making development contingent on weapon-value plutonium was an important reason that certain companies, such as Monsanto, lost interest in the program.

Project Dynamo (1953)

In view of numerous cost studies made in the AEC's national laboratories and by the five industry participation teams, the AEC in 1953 sought a more systematic approach to judging the economic prospects. It therefore contracted with the Massachusetts Institute of Technology to prepare estimates of nuclear power costs for thermal types of reactors and for producing power only (i.e., no weapon value for plutonium). This pioneering study, Project Dynamo,[32] set down estimates of cost for the long term, assuming a "situation which might prevail within the next decade or two," and which, after development, has led to a "self-supporting nuclear power industry" of possibly 10 million kilowatts of capacity, or fifty large reactors, representing 10 per cent of existing United States capacity. The significant policy contribution of the

29. *Ibid.*, p. 61.

30. For a comparative analysis of the cost estimates by the industry participation teams, see Theodore Stern, "Appraisal of Reactor Systems for Central-Station Nuclear Power Plants," *Chemical Engineering Symposium Series: Nuclear Engineering*, American Institute of Chemical Engineering, New York, 1954, Vol. 50, No. 11, Part I, p. 177.

31. Presented to the Joint Committee on Atomic Energy, May 26, 1953. See AEC, *Major Activities in the Atomic Energy Programs, January–June 1953*, (Semiannual Report), Washington, July 1953, p. 19.

32. AEC, unpublished report number MIT-5003 (extract), classification canceled May 25, 1954, available from AEC Technical Information Service, Oak Ridge, Tenn.

study was that the report held out the hope that nuclear power, after long development, might become competitive "without the crutch of weapon-grade plutonium sales," and that costs might ultimately reach levels as low as the United States average for conventional power. The project's results suggested that a substantial program of research, development and small experimental plant investigations would be necessary to avoid the serious risks of premature, full-scale plants. Hindsight now suggests that fuller appreciation by the Congress and the AEC of the great developmental effort required to achieve these cost levels might have led to a more realistic evaluation of policies a year later, during the debate on and passage of the 1954 act, a measure anticipating an unrealistic degree of private initiative and risk bearing for nuclear power development.

From Geneva I to Geneva II (1955–1958)

The AEC's Ad Hoc Advisory Committee in 1959 skeptically observed that a cost estimator's confidence in his figures usually varied inversely with the degree of actual technological experience.[33] The optimistic outlook for the cost of nuclear power reached its highest, and most misleading, level as a result of the data presented at the First Geneva Conference (1955), chiefly because little pertinent experience existed. Subsequent evaluation revealed that, according to the Geneva I estimates (particularly those in the United States papers), 4 to 5 mills per kilowatt-hour of nuclear power was not unreasonable to anticipate for a number of reactors, providing solutions were found to problems of obtaining high burn-up or low fuel-reprocessing costs, or both.[34]

The innocent enthusiasm for nuclear power's cost prospects continued for a brief time after the First Geneva Conference. Technical advisers to the McKinney Panel (1956)[35] provided "pessimistic" and "optimistic" projections of capital, fuel and maintenance expenses, but they thought it the better part of wisdom not to compute total costs per kilowatt-hour. Their figures, translated into unit costs, at 50 per cent plant factor and 10 per cent fixed charges, project a decline, optimistically, from 8.5 mills per kilowatt-hour in 1960 to 5.0 mills by 1980 and, pessimistically, from 10.3 mills to 5.9 mills in

33. *Op. cit.*

34. James A. Lane, "An Evaluation of Geneva and Post-Geneva Nuclear-Power Economic Data," *The Economics of Nuclear Power*, McGraw-Hill, New York, 1957, Series VIII, p. 173.

35. *Report of the Panel on the Impact of the Peaceful Uses of Atomic Energy* (Robert McKinney, Chairman), Joint Committee on Atomic Energy, 84th Cong., 2nd Sess., January 1956 (referred to hereafter as "McKinney Panel").

the same years. According to the pessimistic projection, practically no nuclear power plants would be competitively justified until 1975, but according to the optimistic projection nearly three fourths of the United States power increment would be nuclear.[36] In 1957 the AEC Director of Reactor Development, though he felt compelled to set down a more sober evaluation of cost estimates, still supported the view that nuclear power costs would fall rapidly to the marginally competitive level of 9 to 11 mills per kilowatt-hour by about 1965 and to 6 to 7 mills by 1980.[37]

By the end of 1957 the shift toward greater economic realism—some observers considered it pessimism—had finally set in, more than ten years after the Thomas report. The main reasons were the increased plant costs being reported by reactor projects and the continued uncertainties of fuel-cycle costs, in the absence of experience with the long fuel-element exposures required for low fuel expense.[38] Furthermore, in 1957 the results of independent appraisal (Project Size-up), carried out for the AEC on major British, Canadian and United States reactor types, disclosed that nuclear power costs, based on immediately foreseeable technology, would be substantially higher than United States average conventional power generating costs and somewhat higher than the competitive threshold.[39] The international comparisons made on Project Size-up disclosed that construction costs were as much as 50 per cent greater in the United States than in the United Kingdom.

By the Second Geneva Conference (1958) it had become clear to United States observers that, until actual prototype power reactor experience was available, the existing cost estimates would be unconvincing. The estimates, in fact, had already obscured the degree of technical advance required before electric utilities could consider nuclear power as an economic alternative. Geneva II, then, was singularly different from Geneva I. There were few specific cost estimates and these, in the main, showed sharp increases over those in 1955.

36. Richard A. Tybout, "The Economics of Nuclear Power," *American Economic Review*, May 1957, pp. 351–60, based on McKinney Panel, Vol. 2, pp. 8–30.

37. W. Kenneth Davis and Louis H. Roddis, Jr., "A Projection of Nuclear Power Costs," Fifth Annual Conference, National Industrial Conference Board, New York, 1957.

38. James A. Lane, "Cost Trends," Fourth Annual Conference, Atomic Industrial Forum, New York, October 1957, Paper No. 57.

39. The results were published in two reports prepared by David P. Herron and others for American Radiator and Standard Sanitary Corporation, under contract from the AEC: *Comparison of Calder Hall and PWR Reactor Types*, March 1957 (AECU 3398), and *An Evaluation of Heavy Water Reactors for Power*, October 1957 (ASAE S-3). They were distributed for the AEC by Office of Technical Services, U. S. Department of Commerce, Washington.

Some Implications of the Cost-Estimating History (1946–1958)

The path from naive optimism to more realistic evaluation of the cost prospects in 1958 paralleled, or led to, a number of changes in the view toward nuclear development policy and programs, here and abroad. In brief, a long, hard development period appeared to be certain in 1958; gradual improvement in technology, rather than any break-through, appeared to be the soundest assumption. To maintain the participation of private enterprise in reactor development, it would be necessary to provide substantial governmental assistance, perhaps a capital subsidy, to worth-while projects. The role of the federal program of direct development seemingly increased in relative importance, and the question of full-scale demonstration reactors appeared to be again deferred in favor of prototype construction.

The reactions of foreign countries to poorer cost prospects were mixed in 1958. In Japan and the Euratom nations plans to proceed with nuclear power continued, though with much less urgency than had been indicated in 1956. In other countries, except the three atomic leaders, the wisdom of a wait-and-see attitude was strongly confirmed. None of the economically developing countries, except India, was prepared to undertake nuclear power investment. Of great economic importance was the fact that the cost estimates, prepared on a variety of accounting bases for different reactor types and fuel cycles, indicated that, in general, no uniformity of nuclear power costs could be expected. Moreover, the prospect that nuclear fuel costs would become practically nil, as early cost studies and initial economic studies had indicated, clearly had to be postponed to the very distant future.

Recent Estimates (1958–1961)

Despite the understandable skepticism with which one should view all past estimates of nuclear power cost, the "best available" estimates remain indispensable guidelines for the private and public plans of development. The most convincing estimates are those derived from manufacturers' bids on full-scale projects, those prepared by potential buyers—the utility systems—and certain official estimates prepared by governments on rigorously consistent bases.

The three major sources of the best cost data are found in the official estimates used as a basis for the joint U. S.–Euratom agreement (1958), the successful bid by the International General Electric Co. (IGE) on the Italian SENN (Società Elettronucleare Nazionale) project (1958), and the series of estimates prepared for the AEC under the Civilian Power Reactor Program (1959). All are directed to large central station power reactors.

TABLE **2-6**

Comparison of Two Low Bids on SENN Project, 150-Megawatt Plant, 1958

	Boiling water enriched uranium (ER-1)	Gas-cooled natural uranium (GC-1)
Plant cost inferred per kw.	$330	$410
	Mills per KWH (80 per cent plant factor)	
Total	9.5–11.8	9.8–12.8
Fixed charges (at 10 and 15 per cent)	4.7–7.0	5.8–8.8
Fuel cycle equilibrium fueling	3.8	2.8
Operation and maintenance	1.0	1.2

Note: Assumptions are: Fixed charges consist of depreciation (straight-line, 20-year-life, 5 per cent per year); taxes and insurance, 2 per cent; balance, interest and return on equity. Fuel inventory carried at 7 per cent of initial value.

Source: IBRD, *Summary Report of the International Panel, Project ENSI*, Washington, March 1959 particularly Appendix C.

THE SENN BIDS. A primary purpose of the joint undertaking by the Government of Italy and the International Bank for Reconstruction and Development for a nuclear power plant to be built in southern Italy was to secure data on the relative costs of nuclear and conventional power. In 1957 SENN (also known as Project ENSI) invited firm price bids for this plant, a 130,000- to 150,000-kilowatt unit to be completed about 1963. The most promising bids were for a boiling water, enriched fuel reactor, tendered by the winning United States firm, International General Electric Co. (IGE), and for a gas-cooled, natural uranium–fueled reactor, tendered (presumably) by a British organization. The SENN bids revealed that in international competition the estimated total costs for the American enriched uranium, water-cooled reactors and for the British and French gas-cooled, natural uranium reactors were roughly in the same range. (See Table 2–6.)

These estimates could be considered the firmest available up to the middle of 1959, yet they were not wholly above skepticism born of experience. The commercial importance of winning this first competition may have led bidders to absorb costs, as was widely mentioned in the trade. This can be tested, in the IGE case, only by completion and operation of the plant, expected in 1964. In any case, the low SENN bids for both gas-cooled and enriched reactors place nuclear power costs close to alternative fossil fuel plants in southern

Italy. In 1958, when the bids were submitted, the fuel costs for an oil-fired plant were about 6.5 mills per kilowatt-hour (65 cents per million BTU). If plant costs are included, at an annual rate of 8 to 10 per cent of fixed charges (SENN is a government system), the conventional power costs are on the order of 9 to 9.5 mills per kilowatt-hour, about the same as the nuclear estimates.

THE EURATOM AGREEMENT. The 1958 cost estimates supporting the U. S.–Euratom agreement, summarized in Table 2–7, are important because they establish, first, the basis for the United States loan of capital to Euratom and,

TABLE **2-7**

Estimated Nuclear Power Costs in the Joint U. S.–Euratom Agreement, Pressurized Water Reactor Type (150 Megawatts)

	Nuclear (ca. 1963–1965)	Imported coal (1957)
Assumptions for fixed charges		
Cost per kw.	$350	$145
Interest rate (per cent)	6[a]	4.75
Interest during construction (per cent)	16	9.5
Amortization period (years)	15	30
Amortization rate (per cent)	10.3	6.3
Taxes and insurance (per cent)	3	—
Plant factor (per cent)	80	80
Cost (mills per KWH)	13.9	9.6
Fixed charges	7.7	1.5
Fuel-cycle costs	4.2[b]	6.8[c]
Operation and maintenance	2.0	1.0

a. One half of total construction cost financed in Europe at 8 per cent and one half at 4 per cent, giving average of 6 per cent for nuclear plant.

b. Enriched uranium fuel (3 per cent or less U235); inventory charge, 4 per cent; fabrication cost of stainless steel elements, $100 per kg. of uranium; AEC prices of enriched uranium and chemical processing assumed; credit for plutonium the published AEC fuel value, $12 per gram of metal less published charge of $1.50 per gram for conversion from nitrate to metal. Thus cycle costs are: fuel inventory, 0.6 mills; U235 burn-up, 2.3 mills; fabrication, 1.5 mills; chemical processing, 0.3 mills; conversion of UNH to UF_6, 0.1 mills; transport and insurance, 0.3 mills; plutonium credit, −0.9 mills; total, 4.2 mills per KWH.

c. Based on imported coal at $18.50 per metric ton delivered, or roughly $0.68 per million BTU. More recently, coal prices have been appreciably lower.

Source: Proposed Euratom Agreements, Hearings, Joint Committee on Atomic Energy, 85th Cong., 2nd Sess., July 1958, pp. 39–41.

TABLE 2-8

Estimated Current and Potential Generating Costs in Nuclear and Coal-Fired Plants, United States, 1960

| | Mills per KWH | | | | | | | | | | Construction completion date |
| Reactor type | Total | | Fixed charges | | Fuel-cycle cost | | Operation & maintenance | | Nuclear insurance | | |
	Current	Potential	Current	Potential	Current	Potential	Current	Potential	Current	Potential	
Pressurized water	9.28	7.80	5.05	4.40	3.38	2.56	0.59	0.59	0.26	0.25	1966
Boiling water	9.61	7.45	5.26	4.31	3.47	2.29	0.61	0.61	0.27	0.24	1967
Light water-moderated, superheat	...	6.71	...	3.91	...	1.96	...	0.61	...	0.23	1967
Organic-cooled	11.45	6.67	4.39	3.53	5.72	1.83	1.09	1.09	0.25	0.22	1967
Sodium graphite	11.22	7.42	6.11	4.47	4.12	2.00	0.07	0.65	0.29	0.25	1968
Gas-cooled (enriched fuel)	10.36	7.98	5.97	4.63	3.21	2.62	0.89	0.49	0.29	0.24	1968
Fast breeder	13.25	7.46	5.10	4.43	7.10	1.99	0.79	0.79	0.26	0.25	1969
Aqueous homogeneous	...	11.33	...	6.38	...	2.12	...	2.53	...	0.30	1970
Heavy water	12.50	8.20	7.05	5.80	4.22	1.21	0.91	0.91	0.32	0.28	1969
Gas-cooled (natural U)	11.89	...	7.60	...	3.35	...	0.61	...	...	0.33	...
Coal-fired plants											
35c per 10⁶ BTU fuel cost	7.0		3.31		3.32		0.36				
25c per 10⁶ BTU fuel cost	6.0		3.31		2.37		0.36				

Note: All estimates are based on plants of 300 emw. size—80 per cent capacity factor—14 per cent fixed charges. The power costs are based on the expected equilibrium fuel cycle 3 to 4 years after completion of construction.

Source: AEC, *Civilian Power Reactor Program*, Washington, 1960, Part II, p. 4.

second, the guarantee of nuclear fuel performance and cost made by the United States when it entered into the ten-year agreement. The spread between nuclear and conventional power costs was substantial, 13.9 mills as against 9.6 mills per kilowatt-hour (equivalent to about $4.5 million of increased costs per year for a plant of 150 megawatts). The so-called "standard" guaranteed fuel-cycle costs of 4.2 mills per kilowatt-hour were substantially lower than the fuel cost of imported coal, but these savings were more than offset by the heavier fixed charges of the nuclear plant. The higher costs represented the "price" of early Euratom development, the advantages of which were expected to go far beyond the economic potentialities alone.

CURRENT AEC COST ESTIMATES. Not until 1959 did the AEC make a comprehensive study of estimated costs, on a uniform and consistent basis, for the eight major reactor systems. Prepared in cooperation with the equipment manufacturers, the estimates were a major contribution of the AEC's ten-year Civilian Power Reactor Program. They revealed, as shown in Table 2–8, that "current" estimated costs of generation in large nuclear power plants are far higher than costs in coal-fired plants in high-fuel-cost areas, but that "potential costs"—that is, after cost reductions over the ten-year period—might well put several reactor types across the competitive threshold.

Figure 2-3   The Targets: Regional Electric Generating Costs, 1961

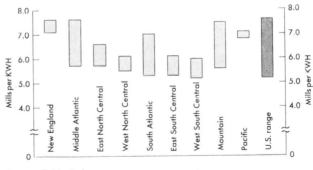

Source: Table 2-4.

The AEC estimates also suggested the long period of development required to achieve the "potential," and the appreciable degree of variability in the estimates that possible changes in the cost and policy assumptions might introduce. Among these are the effect of changes in the "buy-back" price of plutonium, the influence of purchasing as against leasing enriched uranium from the AEC and the effect of reductions in the price of enriched uranium that occurred in 1961 and in 1962.[40] Understandably, the electric utility systems of the United States and Western Europe (excluding the United Kingdom) have not been prepared, as yet, to make substantial investments in nuclear power plants on other than an experimental or demonstration basis. Indeed, the uncertainties of public policy and of technology have appeared to be greater than have the differences between the cost estimates for particular types and the gap between "current" and "potential" costs.

Closing the Gap Between Technical and Competitive Feasibility

Illusive as the cost estimates may be, they clearly show that a serious economic gap must be bridged before nuclear power can be judged and accepted by utility executives as competitive in the United States, even in the sections of the country with the highest fuel costs. In parts of Western Europe the corresponding gap is less formidable, but still real. As to the time perspective, the views of the utility industry, being more conservative than those of the Atomic Energy Commission or of equipment manufacturers, are especially pertinent. In 1958 the Edison Electric Institute Task Force[41] said it

> . . . believes that it will be possible to develop, design, construct and safely operate nuclear-electric power plants which can compete economically with fossil-fuel-fired plants, but that the day of generally competitive nuclear power in this country may be as much as 10 to 20 years away.

In the ten-year program the AEC attempted to measure the effort required, in prototype construction and research and development, to convert "current" estimated costs of nuclear power to "potential" costs in the United States by 1968–1970. The results are summarized in Table 2–9, showing anticipated reductions of total current costs (mills per kilowatt-hour), ranging from 16 per cent to 44 per cent, prototype construction aggregating $465 million for all eight types and the cost of research and development required before starting construction, ranging between $20 million and $160 million for particular

40. The first two are analyzed, on the basis of private financing, in AEC, *Civilian Power Reactor Program*, Washington, 1960, Appendix III. The IAEA has compared the cost estimates prepared by several countries in *Nuclear Power Costs*, Vienna, September 1961. The U235 price reductions in mid-1961 and mid-1962 are not reflected in the cost estimates cited in the present study. However, the generalized effects of the new price schedule under varying assumptions are indicated by nomograms presented by David P. Herron in "Rapid Estimation of Nuclear Power Costs," *Nucleonics*, August 1962, pp. 128–30.

41. EEI, *Status and Prospects of Nuclear Power: An Interim Survey, as of July 1958*, A Report of the Technical Appraisal Task Force on Nuclear Power to the Board of Directors of the Edison Electric Institute, New York, 1958, p. 3.

TABLE 2-9

Closing the Economic Gap between Current Estimated Costs of Nuclear Power and Potential Costs, United States, 1960

Reactor type	Projected cost reduction		Possible date of construction start on potential plant	Needed before plant construction		
				Research and development (millions)	Prototypes	
	Mills per KWH	Per cent			Number	Cost (millions)
Total				$577		$465
Enriched thermal converters[a]						
Pressurized water	1.5	16	Near future	20	None	—
Boiling water	2.1	22	1964–65	20	1	25
Organic-cooled	4.4	38	1965	40	1[b]	30
Sodium graphite	3.4	31	1965–66	82	1[b]	50
Gas-cooled	2.7	26	1966	100	1[c]	30
Natural uranium reactor[d]						
Heavy water	3.5	28	1967–68	80	1 or 2	175
Breeders[e]						
Fast breeder	5.8	44	1968–69	160	1	55
Aqueous homogeneous	—	—	1970–71	75	3[f]	100

a. Objective is competitive power as soon as possible.   b. 75 megawatt.   c. Under construction.
d. Objective is operation on natural uranium.   e. Objective is breeding with a reasonable doubling time.   f. 2 experimental; 1 prototype.

Source: AEC, *Power Reactor Technology, Quarterly Technical Progress Review* (prepared for the AEC by the General Nuclear Engineering Corp.), Washington, March 1960, pp. 1–12.

reactor types. These "price tags" seemed to confirm the wisdom of the AEC's emphasis on the enriched thermal converters.

Nuclear plant costs (dollars per kilowatt) are expected to be reduced, as a result of higher performance, because experience will help define the limits on heat transfer, corrosion and power density. The average heat flux (BTU per hour per square foot of core surface) may well be increased by a factor of two or more. Unit plant costs should drop as plant size increases, a factor the British are counting on heavily. On the other hand, repetitive production can help little in reducing capital costs, since the small volume of construction and continuing changes in design will stand in the way of mass production of components. The spreading of engineering design experience over a larger number of units will doubtless permit some equipment manufacturers to submit progressively lower bids.

Fuel-cycle costs are susceptible to a wide range of cost-reducing technical advances, and improving the fuel cycle therefore has been considered one of the most important objects of development. Higher thermal efficiencies and hence lower plant cost per thermal kilowatt may be achieved only if fuel elements can withstand higher temperatures, without too great sacrifice of the exposure level. Undoubtedly the major advance will come through increasing the exposure, since within certain limits this directly reduces all unit fuel costs. Credit has already been taken for major advances, since the thinking on the prospects for feasible exposure has moved progressively upward over the last several years from an average of roughly 5,000 megawatt-days (First Geneva Conference, 1955)[42] to 10,000 megawatt-days (Euratom) and to 13,000 megawatt-days per metric ton (SENN bid by IGE). Nevertheless, still higher estimates are not believed unreasonable.[43]

Furthermore, the conversion ratios (grams of new fissionable material formed per gram destroyed) may be substantially raised by better neutron economy, which will depend on numerous features of the reactor design and the fuel itself. If high conversion ratios can be achieved, as expected, then economical methods of using plutonium (or U233) as fuel will need to be found. This has appeared promising, but thus far not enough work has been done to be confident of the cost outcome. Finally, and bulking largest in

---

42. Enriched uranium basis; the estimates would be substantially lower computed on the basis of natural uranium equivalent. See Table 2–1, p. 38.

43. The economic significance of high utilization extends beyond the power reactor itself. For example, the greater the irradiation level of nuclear fuel the less need there will be for large processing plants to treat the irradiated fuel elements. The economies of scale in fuel processing may be unrealizable therefore. On the other hand, fuel processing costs may not be reduced unless large processing plants can be utilized and these may be justified only if irradiation levels of fuel remain low.

total fuel costs, is fuel fabrication, that is, shaping and jacketing the fissionable material. There is hope that volume production and simplified designs will greatly reduce the current estimated costs.

When these and many other "foreseeable" advances are translated into lower capital, fuel and operating costs, it appears that nuclear power may fall below marginal regional costs in the United States and well below those in parts of Western Europe or in Japan. For low-cost power in the United States, more drastic advances will be necessary. Among these, for example, are means of nuclear superheating within the reactor core, by using highly enriched uranium in water-cooled reactors; also, the development of high-temperature, high-pressure, gas-cooled reactors and perhaps reactors fueled with molten salts.

Finally, the ultimate development of true breeders in both the plutonium and U233 cycles might also provide low-cost power, though there is some doubt on this point for the reasons mentioned earlier. Setting a level on such "futuristic" generating costs has been viewed as sheer speculation and in recent years the effort has been avoided, in the concentration on costs of the "proven" reactor types. The last such estimate was by Walter H. Zinn, published in 1958, in which he projected costs for what were called "more-distant-future reactors," that is, a couple of decades hence, at a level of about 5 mills.[44]

That such costs in large plants might be feasible much sooner was implied in mid-1961 when the Pacific Gas and Electric Co., in conjunction with the General Electric Co., announced plans for building a 325–electric megawatt (gross) boiling water reactor at Bodega Bay, California, which would be competitive when completed in 1965. At 90 per cent load factor, the plant is expected to generate electricity at 5.7 mills per kilowatt-hour (private financing assumed) on its first core—compared with 5.77 mills for a conventional oil-fired plant, with oil at $2.25 per barrel (36¢ per million BTU).[45] Thus, the

44. His summary figures are as follows (mills per KWH):

Total	5.2
Fixed charges	4.8
Capital ($200 per kw., 15 per cent)	4.3
Fuel inventory (12 per cent)	0.5
Fuel fabrication and separation ($100 per kg.)	0.2
Fissionable material production	−0.3
Operating and maintenance	0.5

(*Nuclear Engineering Handbook*, McGraw-Hill, New York, 1958, Sec. 12, p. 109, Tables 8 and 9.) Other assumptions: specific power, 3,000–4,000 mw. heat per kg. of fissionable material; irradiation level, 20,000 mw.-days per metric ton; cost of nuclear fuel (pure), $10 per gram; thermal efficiency, 35 per cent; plant factor, 80 per cent.

45. *Electrical World*, March 19, 1962, pp. 66–67.

AEC's short-range objective of making it possible by 1968 for utility owners in high-energy-cost areas to elect large nuclear plants instead of conventional plants seemed about to be achieved.[46]

Sensing that the new estimates of competitive feasibility by industry and the AEC might again prove premature, Philip Sporn, former chief executive of the American Electric Power Company, early in 1962 cautioned policy makers that improvements in the conversion of conventional fuels made competitive costs "a moving target." His cost projections suggest that even by 1973–1978 and in high-cost fuel areas (40 cents per million BTU) it is probable that conventional generating costs (5.60 mills per KWH in large plants) will still be well below nuclear power costs of plants starting up then (6.17 to 6.89 mills per KWH).[46a]

Contrary views are held concerning the significance of these cost estimates for reactor development policy. One holds that competitive nuclear power in high-energy-cost areas is now assured and imminent, hence no additional federal measures for assisting development are necessary in order to achieve the AEC's short-range goal. The other, less optimistic view suggests that private utilities have been once more too hasty in claiming competitive nuclear power, and that substantial technical and institutional obstacles remain to be overcome, hence that sustained federal efforts, including government demonstration plants, continue to be necessary to assure success in meeting both the short- and long-range goals of the AEC program. Up to the present the Congress, the AEC and the electric utility industry have held the former view.

Whether marginal or low-cost nuclear power is achieved in the United States depends not on technology alone but also, as we shall see, on congressional and AEC economic policies designed to promote and regulate nuclear power development. In addition, certain social costs and economies that are external to the individual power reactor influence the technology and the cost estimates surveyed here.

Interaction of Economic Policies and Technology

Policy makers and reactor technicians long tended to take each other's work as "given," and proceeded accordingly in pursuing their own independent lines of responsibility. This early separateness, however, was weakened by the

46. Frank K. Pittman, Director, Division of Reactor Development, AEC, remarks for presentation at the Second Joint Conference on Nuclear Power, U. S.–Japan Atomic Industrial Forums, Tokyo, December 6, 1961 (AEC Release S.26–1961).

46a. Section 202 Hearings, 1962, pp. 688–92.

impact of a few critical economic "facts of life" coming to view as additional information about military and civilian aspects of nuclear energy became widely known in industry. The supply of natural uranium was revealed as being large, distributed worldwide and readily expandable at no increase in unit cost. The implications for the economics of nuclear power were clear: all nations had access to sources of nuclear fuel and "monopolization" or "domination" by one nation or a group of nations was not feasible, if any such motivation had indeed existed; moreover, the immediate need for breeder reactors was set down a notch in the scale of desirable objectives. The production rates and stockpiles of fissionable material for weapon purposes had grown rapidly to great size as a result of successive expansions of AEC capacity. The desirability of having civilian power reactors in the United States to serve as additional sources of weapon material was diminished, and hence the dual-purpose reactor lost its original attractiveness. This, among other reasons, led to the dropping of government support for dual-purpose reactor designs in favor of designs specifically for power production.[47] (The situation was reversed in the United Kingdom.) Finally, the cost of producing enriched uranium in the expanded gaseous diffusion cascades at Oak Ridge, Tennessee; Paducah, Kentucky; and Portsmouth, Ohio, was revealed to be not so high as to eliminate enriched uranium from consideration as fuel in civilian power reactors. The cost of U235 was not prohibitive, as had been initially assumed, and a broad range of technical and economic benefits from the use of enriched uranium came into view. The limits are not yet in sight.

Meanwhile, the Atomic Energy Commission has been establishing, under the guidelines of the 1954 act, administrative economic policies that also influence technical development, though perhaps less fundamentally or extensively than knowledge of the background technical facts just mentioned.

AEC Pricing Policies and Technology

The estimated costs of fuel cycle components reveal most clearly the potential effect of economic policy on reactor technology. A simplified diagram of the cyclical flow of reactor fuel is shown in Figure 2–1. The AEC's practice has been to provide, at a price, materials and services that are not commercially available: it provides enriched uranium on loan to reactor operators and receives a "use charge" of 4.75 per cent (increased from 4 per cent in mid-1961) on the value of the material outstanding; it charges a price

47. Perhaps equally important was the impact of the private-vs.-federal-public-power controversy which in 1961 blocked consideration on its merits of the generating facilities requested by the AEC for addition to the dual-purpose New Production Reactor at Hanford, Wash.

for the amount of U235 actually burned up and charges for the cost of reenriching the spent fuel to the level required by the reactor; it pays the reactor operator for any plutonium (or U233) produced in the irradiated fertile material (U238 or Th232); and, as the only present source of chemical processing services, the AEC charges the reactor operator for taking his irradiated fuel elements and chemically separating the remaining uranium, the plutonium and the fission products and for disposing of the waste materials.[48]

The scope of these administered prices in determining total fuel cost estimates is apparent: the net fuel burn-up charge represents about one fifth of the total, chemical processing roughly the same and the use charge on the inventory of fuel more than one tenth. Only fuel fabrication costs, representing roughly two fifths of the total, are directly unaffected. The AEC prices thus affect at least one half of total fuel costs. Changes in these discretionary charges, some of which were altered in 1961 and again in 1962, could well prove to be as important in determining fuel-cycle costs as the effect of improvements in technology and in the economies of commercial-scale production.

The AEC price practices have naturally influenced the direction of fuel and reactor technology. For example, the former schedule of charges for enriched uranium, in effect up to July 1961, apparently penalized enriched, as against natural, uranium reactors since the price of natural uranium declined appreciably after 1955.[49] Further, the new 4.75 per cent use charge established by the AEC in 1961 is still so low, compared with private charges on working capital or inventory, that an advantage accrues to certain fuel and reactor systems, such as the fast breeder, which initially require large inventories of nuclear fuel. However, when recycled plutonium has become economically useful as fuel, then the economics of the fast breeder reactor may become independent of the government's pricing system. Also, "low" chemical processing charges favor reactor systems, such as the fast breeder, which require frequent removal and processing of fuel elements, but they discourage the entry of private chemical processors and hence require continued government operation.[50]

As a final example, the so-called "buy-back" prices the AEC has set on the plutonium (and U233) produced in private reactors has an especially great

48. See Chapters 4 and 5 for critical evaluation of these prices and of pricing policy.

49. Average AEC prices for domestic production of uranium oxide (U_3O_8) decreased from $11.94 per pound in fiscal year 1956 to $8.19 in fiscal year 1962.

50. As is also true of commercial fuel fabrication, the economies of scale are exceedingly important. The AEC has reported that unit chemical processing costs would decrease by a factor of eight by increasing the plant throughput from 100 kg. per day to 8,000 kg. (UN, *Economic Applications of Atomic Energy: Power Generation and Industrial and Agricultural Uses*, Report of the Secretary-General, New York, 1957, p. 73.)

impact. The AEC has quoted a weapon-value, buy-back price, applicable until mid-1962, ranging from $30 to $45 per gram of plutonium, depending on the freedom of the desired Pu239 from isotopes which reduce the value of the material for weapons use.[51] Benedict and Pigford found that if plutonium is credited at $30 per gram, the lowest fuel-cycle costs are possible with natural uranium, heavy water reactors; but if plutonium is credited at a calculated fuel value of $12 per gram, as assumed in many fuel cycle analyses, the slightly enriched heavy water reactor shows the lowest fuel costs.[52] Most important, perhaps, maintaining a premium on weapon-value plutonium would tend to prevent development of economical ways of recycling plutonium in nuclear reactors.

Policy Support of Enriched Uranium Reactor Systems

The use of enriched uranium, obtained from the AEC's gaseous diffusion plants, was assumed for all uranium-fueled power reactors that were being built or were definitely planned in the United States up to 1959. The AEC's preference for enriched uranium reactor systems has been based partly on the low cost of enriching uranium. However, some reactor specialists of other countries, also seeking the benefits of enriched fuel, have concluded that it would be less costly in national resources to secure enriched reactor fuel by producing and separating plutonium than by building indigenous gaseous diffusion plants to enrich natural uranium.[53] While this is unlikely to be true in the United States (the relative costs are classified), it may well be correct for most other countries where the cost of power to run the cascades would be substantially higher and the plant scale would be much smaller than here.[54]

51. Thus, for 0 per cent of Pu240 the price was $45 per gram of Pu metal; at 4 per cent, $38; and at 8.6 per cent and over, $30. For the period July 1, 1962, through June 30, 1963, the domestic price is $30 per gram, regardless of isotopic composition. There are no AEC commitments for prices to be paid thereafter.

52. Manson Benedict and others, "Fuel Cycles in Single Region Thermal Power Reactors," *Proceedings*, Second Geneva Conference, Vol. 13, pp. 198–228.

53. See, for example, H. J. Bhabha, "The Role of Atomic Power in India and Its Immediate Possibilities," *Proceedings*, First Geneva Conference, Vol. 1, p. 107.

54. On the cost of producing enriched uranium in the United States, see Karl Cohen, "Charting a Course for Nuclear Power Development," *Nucleonics*, January 1958. For possible production in Western Europe see OEEC, "Brief Description of an Isotope Separation Plant," *Possibilities of Action in the Field of Nuclear Energy*, Paris, January 1956, Annex IV, p. 55. Cohen's estimate implies a power input of roughly 700,000 KWH per kg. of U235 (90 per cent enrichment), whereas the OEEC estimate implies 1,330,000 KWH per kg. Assuming the validity of this difference, in part a matter of plant scale, and recognizing that power costs in Western Europe are roughly twice those in the Ohio Valley, it is reasonable to assume that enriched uranium produced in Western European plants would cost perhaps twice that produced in the United States.

There are several reasons for the United States cost advantage. Power to run the cascades can be had at low cost, in part because new, efficient coal mines were opened to meet the needs of the expansion program in the early 1950's. Also, the private power plants were financed at interest rates close to "public" rates, since the AEC entered into long-term, virtually "no-risk" contracts with liberal termination provisions. The Securities and Exchange Commission permitted company financing to consist of 90 per cent bonds and 10 per cent equity (rather than the customary ratio of 60 per cent bonds and 40 per cent equity), thus lowering capital charges. Furthermore, the scale of AEC gaseous diffusion plants, producing primarily for military purposes, is many times that conceivable for plants producing predominantly for civilian nuclear power.[55]

The AEC's pricing standards for enriched uranium and for chemical processing, as well as the support being given research on the use of plutonium (and U233) as reactor fuel, seem certain to have strong influences on the direction of future technology and on the program choices other countries make if they enter reactor development.

Plutonium as Nuclear Fuel

The United States has been producing plutonium for weapons use since the latter part of World War II. Despite more than fifteen years of experience with the element, only within the last few years has substantial effort been directed toward finding ways of making plutonium useful as nuclear fuel in power reactors.[56] Plutonium might be used to enrich natural uranium in thermal reactors by "spiking" or blending, or in conjunction with enriched or depleted uranium. A provocative possibility exists of enriching the vast quantities of now useless depleted uranium stored in both the United States and the United Kingdom.[57] Additionally, and more frequently discussed in the literature, is the long-term objective of burning plutonium in fast breeder reactors. In either case reactor technologists still must learn how to fabricate and process irradiated plutonium economically.

55. The first gaseous diffusion plant suggested for Western Europe, for example, was one twentieth as large as the U235 capacity estimated for gaseous diffusion plants in the United States.

56. AEC, *Civilian Power Reactor Program*, Washington, 1960, Part II, p. 66. Through fiscal year 1959, $18.2 million had been spent on the plutonium recycle program.

57. Presumably, the advantage of enriching depleted material with fuel-grade plutonium will be determined mainly by the costs of separating plutonium from irradiated fuel. If these costs prove to be high, compared with the cost of enriched uranium, there may be little incentive for enriching fuel with plutonium.

The use of plutonium as a nuclear fuel will prove more difficult, technically and economically, than has the use of U235. The reasons are not far to seek. As suggested by the growing literature on plutonium metallurgy, the material is "nasty" to separate, to handle and to fabricate. Plutonium emits alpha particles and is highly toxic. Permissible activity levels, recommended internationally, allow an approximate concentration in air of only 10^{-10} grams per cubic meter.[58] If plutonium is swallowed or inhaled, it settles largely in the bone marrow, causing leukemia and cancer after an interval of some years. Consequently, laboratory and production operations call for remote handling, fabrication, transfer and storage to minimize airborne contamination. In addition, since plutonium is fissionable, a close control to prevent critical (explosive) assemblies of the metal—a few pounds, the exact amount varying with circumstances—must be maintained. Finally, reactor scientists need to know the influence of high isotopes on the behavior of plutonium as fuel. Still, it is on this material that the hopes of several nations depend for securing an alternative to uranium enriched with U235 in gaseous diffusion plants.

USE AND VALUE OF PLUTONIUM FOR ENRICHMENT. Lacking the large uranium enrichment capacity which the United States has, the United Kingdom has continued to study the use of plutonium for enriching its nuclear fuel. The British foresee the use of plutonium—first simply as replacement of U235—in the fuel by spiking or by blending with natural or depleted uranium. Later, perhaps, when larger quantities of plutonium become available, they may recycle the irradiated fuel in refabricated form. The value of enrichment plutonium in the gas-cooled, graphite reactor therefore is measured by the alternative cost of the number of atoms of U235 that can be replaced by one atom of plutonium, while maintaining the reactor's performance. The British computations, based on their accounting assumptions and costs of enriching uranium and reprocessing fuel, suggest a fuel value of $14.00 per gram, after allowing for the additional costs of handling plutonium.[59]

The benefit of this enriched fuel compared with natural uranium is measured by the increased reactivity obtained by permitting irradiation beyond the hoped-for 3,000 megawatt-days per ton, higher operating temperatures and

---

58. W. B. H. Lord and M. B. Waldron, "The Development of Handling Techniques for the Study of Plutonium Metal," *Journal of the British Nuclear Energy Conference*, October 1958.

59. N. L. Franklin and others, "Economics of Enrichment and Use of Plutonium and Uranium," *Proceedings*, Second Geneva Conference, Vol. 13, p. 273. This value is based on plutonium produced from natural uranium irradiated to 3,000 megawatt-days per ton.

smaller plant size (and cost) per unit of heat produced.[60] Through such enrichment and other advances the British foresee a reduction in the capital cost of their gas-cooled, graphite reactors from about $325 to $225 per electrical kilowatt.

WEAPON-VALUE PLUTONIUM. Under certain circumstances the operation and economics of nuclear power reactors are inseparable from the reactors' potentialities as producers of weapon material. Indeed, the fact that plutonium or U233 will be generated in virtually all reactors and that these materials, if in sufficient quantity, may be made into weapons is the starting point of the control problem for nuclear power reactors. Assuming that a country, following Britain's example, is motivated by the joint goal of nuclear power and weapons, it will be found that a dual-purpose reactor calls for a choice, that is, between designing primarily for power or for weapon material.

The degree of exposure given fuel elements will necessarily differ in the two cases. Fuel elements designed to produce weapon-grade plutonium (that is, containing a large proportion of the fissionable Pu239 and a small amount of Pu240 and Pu242) must be removed after relatively brief exposure, since the amount of Pu240 builds up quickly. Frequent refueling and frequent chemical separation become necessary, thus adding to the cost of the fuel cycle and hence the costs assignable to weapon-grade plutonium.

The economics of this dual-purpose reactor may be less significant than are the worldwide implications of the spawning of nuclear weapons production by peaceful nuclear power. To be sure, safeguards and controls on the diversion of nuclear fuels to military uses are invoked on "importing" countries who secure materials through the International Atomic Energy Agency or through bilateral agreements. But it is evident from the published technical data that there are no insurmountable obstacles to the production, in time, by most industrialized nations and perhaps by several semi-industrialized countries, of weapon quantities and grade of plutonium, without major reliance on foreign sources. Whether this possibility should put a brake on international assistance to nuclear power development is discussed in Chapter 8. At this point it is sufficient to suggest that a country's acquiring nuclear weapon capability is not contingent upon its first establishing nuclear power plants. Hence, holding back nuclear power assistance on the theory of delaying a dangerous spread of atomic weapons is debatable.

60. British calculations suggest that irradiation lifetimes around 3,000 megawatt-days per ton can be increased 10 per cent by increasing U235 content only 1 per cent; e.g., from 3,000 to 3,300 megawatt-days per ton by going from 0.71 to 0.717 per cent U235.

Social Costs and External Economies

Nuclear power development has been subject to the bipolar influences of potentially great social costs, on the one hand, and external economies, on the other. External economies, though immeasurable, flow from the vast atomic energy system of facilities and supplies brought into being by the war and the atom bomb program. An obvious economic example of these appears in the present civilian price of enriched uranium produced in AEC plants.

Whereas the external economies accruing to private and public development of nuclear power are real and discernible, the social costs of nuclear power are contingent and in fact unknowable. A potential social hazard exists wherever radioactivity exists, but the major hazard of nuclear power plant operation is customarily considered the "maximum credible accident"—the accidental destruction or malfunction of the reactor resulting in jeopardy to widely surrounding populations and property. This is the more obvious part of the nuclear hazard, to be sure, but fuel fabrication, handling and shipping, the processing of irradiated fuel, and waste disposal are also hazardous. Indeed, some experts have indicated that the hazards of escaping radioactive materials from fuel-reprocessing plants and the hazards of waste disposal may be as great over the long term as those of power reactor operation.[61] At this stage of development, however, the hazards of power reactor operation have had greater pertinence for planning private plant investment.

The maximum credible accident poses a thorny actuarial and financial question, since experience with power reactor operation has been brief and limited. The probability of a disaster is believed to be very small, but the resulting property damage could amount to several hundred million dollars, depending on the circumstances, not to mention personal injury and fatalities. By 1956 it was well established that the insurance industry was ready to provide reactor operators up to about $60 million coverage per installation for property damage and the same for liability protection. Because the amounts were far less than the risk represented by a conceivable, though improbable, reactor disaster, an effective appeal was made to the Congress for help in solving the problem by means of a combined program of private insurance and government indemnification.[62] Finally passed in 1957, the Anderson-Price amendment to the 1954 act provided up to $500 million of government

61. A. W. Murphy and others, *Financial Protection Against Atomic Hazards*, Atomic Industrial Forum, New York, January 1957, p. 13.

62. Defined as an agreement whereby one party agrees to recompense another for loss or damage sustained under certain circumstances. (*Ibid.*, p. 25.)

protection above the amount available privately for each nuclear incident. The AEC collects a fee, $30 per year per thousand kilowatts of thermal energy capacity, from each licensed reactor operator who secures this indemnification. Thus, in the interest of promoting private development, the federal government has assumed the major financial liability for the hazards of private reactor operation. Obviously, the potential social costs of reactor operation were not eliminated by this legislation, but the private costs of securing such liability protection were reduced and made manageable.

The nuclear power industry is therefore traversing the period of reactor demonstration with the combined advantages of great external economies and financial protection against the major foreseeable social costs of reactor operation. Whether "real" nuclear power costs in the forthcoming commercial phase can ever become free of these forms of public assistance, as the price system takes over allocation of resources, is a matter of conjecture.

CHAPTER **3**

U. S. Need
for Nuclear Power

Failure to achieve consensus on just how urgently competitive nuclear power is needed in the United States has long been a major obstacle to sound policy formation.[1] Much of the controversy over acceleration of reactor development through greater government effort and over the restraints on private efforts written into the act have been based on conflicting views of the applicability of "strict economics."

Each year, in the Section 202 Hearings held by the Joint Committee, representatives of the private utilities and of the producers of conventional fuel have insisted that no urgent demand for nuclear power exists in the United States and that government programs have been questionable. They have argued that ample reserves of low-cost fuels are available for many years of steadily expanding energy consumption. The case has been most persistently made and carefully documented by Philip Sporn, former head of a major private utility in the Ohio Valley which enjoys especially low fuel costs. Sporn in 1959 estimated that in 1975 nuclear power would probably provide no more than 7.5 per cent of total electric power produced and less than 2 per cent of total energy. On the basis of these estimates for 1975, Sporn concluded, there is "little justification for all the activity and all the national effort that is being given to this atomic program."[2] The real justification, in his view, is the

1. *Accelerating Civilian Reactor Program*, Hearings, Joint Committee on Atomic Energy, 84th Cong., 2nd Sess., May 1956.

2. Section 202 Hearings, 1959, p. 242.

belief that after 1975 conventional sources of energy might be unable to meet the demand.

The argument of "no urgent need" has been echoed by coal producers and, to a lesser degree, by domestic oil producers. The "leisurely" approach implied by this point of view has been criticized by public power advocates, by domestic uranium producers and, in guarded terms, by most equipment manufacturers, who foresee a dearth of commercial reactor business for some years to come. Review of the annual Section 202 Hearings suggests that the question of urgency of need for nuclear power in the United States necessarily involves a separation of short- and long-term considerations and a clear recognition of the effect of attempts by interest groups to influence public policy. In the short term, for example, the "urgency" of need cannot be considered apart from the emerging competitive rivalry of equipment manufacturers in a highly concentrated industry, nor from the overtones of the private-vs.-public-power controversy, nor from the response of electric utility systems in marginal fuel-cost areas to the pressure of rising fuel prices. In the long term, of course, the main strictly economic question is whether the reserves and the production capability of conventional fuels can be considered adequate to meet expanding consumption in the future at no appreciable increase in real price. But to arrive at useful interpretations, we "must import data outside the scope normally considered economic."[3]

As a Primary Energy Resource

The main economic issue is whether the United States can double or treble its annual energy consumption over the next few decades without major increases in costs. To answer this question we turn, selectively, to the voluminous statistical record and projections of U. S. energy consumption, production and resources.[4] Table 3–1 shows the distribution by primary energy source of total commercial energy consumption in 1960.

Energy Consumption Trends

From this tabulation we see that more than two thirds of U. S. primary energy demand is being supplied by petroleum and natural gas. The future supplies and requirements of these fuels will therefore be of outstanding importance in the aggregate future energy balance and prospective energy prices.

3. Adolf A. Berle, Jr., *Power Without Property*, Harcourt, Brace and World, New York, 1959, p. 21.

4. In particular see Sam H. Schurr, Bruce C. Netschert and others, *Energy in the American Economy, 1850–1975*, Resources for the Future, Washington, 1960.

TABLE **3-1**

Primary Energy Consumption, by Source, Selected Years, 1920–1960

Primary energy source	Total, 1960[a] (BTU X 10^12)	Commercial energy consumption				
		Percentage distribution				
		1920	1930	1940	1950	1960[a]
Total	44,864	100.0	100.0	100.0	100.0	100.0
Water power	1,766	3.9	3.5	3.9	4.7	3.9
Coal	10,357	78.4	61.2	52.4	37.8	23.1
Anthracite	429	11.0	7.7	5.2	3.0	1.0
Bituminous & lignite	9,928	67.4	53.5	47.2	34.8	22.1
Liquid fuels	32,741	17.7	35.3	43.7	57.5	73.0
Crude petroleum	18,616	13.3	25.4	31.3	37.2	41.5
Natural gas	14,125	4.4	9.9	12.4	20.3	31.5

a. Preliminary.

Source: U. S. Bureau of the Census, *Statistical Abstract of the United States, 1961*, Washington, p. 522.

Over the last few decades the oil and gas share of total primary energy consumption has risen sharply, while that of coal has dropped and that of hydroelectricity has remained steady. The relative growth of oil and gas consumption from 1920 to 1960 is suggested in Table 3–1.

The pattern of energy consumption by consuming group has also shifted with the associated growth of oil and gas supplies, as shown in Table 3–2.

One of the key features of energy supply and demand is interchangeability: three fourths of all heat and power consumed in 1960 could have been provided by any of the three major energy sources. The two chief fuel requirements which do not permit interchangeability are coke requirements of the metallurgical industries and liquid fuel requirements of internal combustion engines.[5] It is significant for the energy economy at large that nuclear energy

5. Nathaniel B. Guyol, "United States Energy Requirements in 1965," paper presented before the American Marketing Association, June 1957.

The rapidly declining share of energy consumption by railroads, shown in Table 3–2, has resulted from the substitution of diesel oil for coal after 1947, with accompanying great gains in efficiency of energy utilization. The growth of oil and gas consumption relative to coal has been due as much to the expansion of the market for fluid fuel as to direct displacement of coal (e.g., in home heating).

TABLE **3 - 2**

Primary Energy Consumption, by Consuming Group, 1947 and 1954

	Per cent of total primary energy consumption	
Consuming group	1947	1954
Total	100.0	100.0
Electric power generation	14.3	18.2
Industrial heat in manufacturing	23.4	24.6
Railroads	9.8	2.3
Ocean shipping	1.5	1.2
Military propulsion (Navy & Air Force)	0.4	2.6
Highway, aircraft, etc.	11.9	16.3
Residential and commercial	30.8	29.6
All other, nonfuel use, etc.	8.1	5.2

Source: Perry D. Teitelbaum, *Nuclear Energy and the U. S. Fuel Economy, 1955–1980*, NPA Washington, 1958, p. 42.

is entering primarily into a growing sector of energy consumption—electric power generation—where coal, oil, natural gas and hydropower are interchangeable.

Projected Energy Consumption and Fuel Reserves

In evaluating the economic justification of high fuel prices over the next couple of decades, one should project the scale of future requirements against estimated economically recoverable reserves and import potentialities. A variety of reasonably adequate methods is available for estimating energy requirements a decade or more in the future, but none can pretend to provide a conclusive judgment. In general, the leading energy specialists in this art have favored the use of segmental projections covering detailed kinds of energy and have carefully avoided the use of extrapolated growth rates for aggregate energy consumption. These various detailed projections to 1975 and 1980 differ, but their totals are sufficiently close to lend a degree of credibility to results arrived at by different methods.

A comparison of the major projections of primary energy consumption in 1975 and 1980 is shown in Table 3–3.

TABLE **3 - 3**

Projections of Primary Energy Consumption in 1975 and 1980[a]

	Amount in BTU X 10[15]				
		Base		Projection	Annual growth
Source	Year	Consumption	1975	1980	rate (per cent)
1. PMPC, 1952	1950	33.8	68	78.0[b]	2.8
2. McKinney Panel, 1956	1954	37.4	75	87.5	3.3
3. NPA, 1958	1955	40.3	70	80.0	2.8
4. Sporn, 1959	1957	41.9	72	84.0[b]	3.1
5. RFF, 1960	1955	39.7	75	87.0[b]	3.2

a. These estimates are not precisely comparable and are shown together to illustrate the narrow range of differences in implied energy consumption. For example, the RFF estimate assumes no nuclear energy and is "meant to be on the high end of a range of reasonable possibilities . . . ," whereas the NPA projection, assuming minimum impact of nuclear energy, is on the low end of the various possibilities.

b. Extrapolated from 1975 value.

Sources:

1. President's Materials Policy Commission, *Resources for Freedom,* Washington, 1952, Vol. I, p. 103.

2. McKinney Panel, Vol. 2, pp. 73–74.

3. Perry D. Teitelbaum, *Nuclear Energy and the U. S. Fuel Economy, 1955–1980,* NPA, Washington, 1958, p. 41.

4. *Energy Resources and Technology,* Hearings, Joint Economic Committee, 86th Cong., 1st Sess., October 1959, p. 78.

5. Sam H. Schurr, Bruce C. Netschert and others, *Energy in the American Economy, 1850–1975,* Resources for the Future, Washington, 1960, p. 239.

The differences in the projected rates of growth in energy consumption imply wide divergence in the projections beyond 1980. However, as pointed out above, the projected totals for 1980 are close enough together to provide a reasonable basis for judging the adequacy of production capacity and fuel resources.

These projections clearly indicate that, ignoring the possibility of extraordinary improvement in efficiency of energy use, the production rate for the basic fuels in 1980, in the aggregate, will have to be about double that of 1955. The projections also imply that annual consumption of each fuel individually will also be roughly double that of 1955. (See Table 3–4.)

TABLE **3 - 4**

Consumption of Major Fuels, 1955, and in 1980 as Implied by Projections of Primary Energy Consumption[a]

Source and year	Coal (short tons X 10⁶)	Crude oil (barrels X 10⁹)	Natural gas (cu. ft. X 10¹²)
1955	447	2.8	8.7
1980			
PMPC	817	5.8	18.0
McKinney Panel	950	5.3	21.0
NPA	851	6.2	18.0
RFF	880	6.1	24.0
		Per cent	
1980 as per cent of 1955 (range)	183–213	189–221	207–276

a. See Table 3–3.

Sources:
   1955—Sam H. Schurr and Bruce C. Netschert, *Energy in the American Economy, 1850–1975,* Resources for the Future, Washington, 1960, pp. 508–09.
   1980—See Table 3–3.

COAL. Coal reserves of the United States, as reported by the U.S. Geological Survey, are physically sufficient to meet the projected 1980 rates of coal consumption for several hundred years. In 1953 the Survey estimated economically recoverable coal reserves at 950 billion short tons, about one fourth of which, according to the U.S. Bureau of Mines in 1956, were recoverable at or near 1954 production costs.[6] The aggregate figure is a thousand times the highest projection of 1980 coal consumption, shown in Table 3–4, and what may be called the "constant-cost" fraction (237 billion short tons) is two hundred and fifty times the highest projected 1980 consumption. Seemingly, this is authoritative evidence of ample reserves at no increase in prospective production costs. Yet Eugene Ayres, one of the main exponents of the "depleted reserves" theory, has questioned the estimates and their implications by asserting that the amount of fuel-grade bituminous coal that can be mined at current costs is little more than one tenth that set down by the Bureau of Mines.[7] Nevertheless, even on the basis of this pessimistic estimate, the

   6. See U. S. Geological Survey, Department of the Interior, *Coal Resources of the United States,* Geological Survey Circular 293, Washington, 1953; and for U. S. Bureau of Mines estimates, McKinney Panel, Vol. 2, p. 74.
   7. "The Fuel Situation," *Scientific American,* October 1956, p. 47.

reserves at current cost would still be substantial (thirty times 1980 require-ments). In 1960 the Bureau of Mines reaffirmed its 1956 estimates of reserves available at substantially current costs. It also indicated, however, that expected improvements in technology would probably result in a very great increase in output by 1975—to a level approximating the lower range implied by the 1980 consumption projections shown in Table 3–4.[8] Schurr and Netschert were even more optimistic of the prospects, without an increase in costs.[9]

PETROLEUM. Crude oil resources are more problematical than coal re-sources, partly because there have been more assiduous specialists—and parties at interest—making estimates. Also, the estimates themselves carry sensitive public policy implications and interpretations—for import quotas and depletion allowances. An independent appraisal of the major estimates of oil and gas availability, made by Netschert, shows that at least in the period through 1975 the rate of production can be more than doubled, to about 6 billion barrels per year, without confronting reserve limitations that might lift production costs significantly above present levels.[10] This is about the same as the requirements projections, shown in Table 3–4, for 1980. Unfor-tunately, Netschert's study stops too soon for long-range analysis of energy questions, but one may infer from his computations that the United States in 1975 is unlikely to be right at the brink of rapidly declining crude produc-tion—though certain estimators (Eugene Ayres and M. King Hubbert, for example) believe that point may be reached by 1975 or very soon after.[11]

Netschert's survey indicates that even the lowest estimates of "ultimate reserves"—120 billion barrels—provide room for a few decades of production at the current rate, with some decades of additional supply potentially avail-able at no appreciable increase in constant-dollar costs. The 1960 estimates of the Bureau of Mines, however, indicate that a 50 per cent increase in price (from $3.00 to $4.50 per barrel), as well as expected advances in technology, would probably be necessary to achieve a doubling of domestic crude oil production by 1975.[12]

8. See McKinney Review, *Background Material*, Vol. 4, pp. 1517–20.

9. Schurr, Netschert and others, *op. cit.*, p. 343.

10. Bruce C. Netschert, *The Future Supply of Oil and Gas*, Resources for the Future, Washing-ton, 1958. This estimate was reaffirmed in 1960; see Schurr, Netschert and others, *op. cit.*, p. 386.

11. Ayres, *op. cit.*; and M. King Hubbert, "Nuclear Energy and the Fossil Fuels," *Drilling and Production Practice, 1956*, American Petroleum Institute, New York, 1957.

12. McKinney Review, *Background Material*, Vol. 4, p. 1533.

NATURAL GAS. Physical reserves of natural gas appear to be very large compared with current and prospective rates of consumption. Netschert's survey of the numerous estimates and his estimate of the minimum "resource base" indicate that many decades of gas supply remain. The principal question is the price at which it will become available. The estimated future supply of natural gas—recoverable at constant-dollar costs—falls in the wide range of 240 to 1,200 trillion cubic feet, against annual consumption of only 10 trillion cubic feet in 1955 and at least twice that by 1980. Netschert accepts the "availability estimate" of 22.5 trillion cubic feet in 1975 prepared by the American Gas Association.[13]

Cost-Price Relations

Ample reserves of fuel should permit increased rates of fuel production at relatively steady constant-dollar costs. But they cannot assure stable constant-dollar prices, for many factors other than domestic resources influence fuel prices paid by consumers. This is demonstrated historically by the relative price trends of coal, oil and natural gas. In his U. S. energy study Teitelbaum[14] found that the national average prices of fuel oil, most nearly competitive with nuclear energy for boiler fuel purposes, have shown no perceptible trend upward or downward since the beginning of the century. But the constant-dollar prices of bituminous coal rose significantly, at the rate of about 1.5 per cent annually up to 1947–48. Since then coal prices have declined slightly. Moreover, although natural gas prices declined sharply from 1920 to 1945, after World War II they began to rise at a rapid rate. The Teitelbaum study also shows, however, that the national averages obscure diverging trends in regional fuel prices. While the national average price of bituminous coal trended upwards to 1947, prices at the mine in most midwestern and western producing states were stable or declining.

Despite the ample reserves of coal, oil and natural gas, the record of rising real prices of coal (up to 1947–48) and gas compels examination of those elements of supply—other than geologic reserves—which may contribute to higher or lower prices during the next decade or two. In the boiler fuel market, where nuclear energy may be most directly competitive, coal is the predominant fuel on a national scale and fuel oil characteristically is often priced competitively with it (on an equivalent BTU basis, after allowance for some

13. Schurr, Netschert and others, *op. cit.*, p. 412.

14. Perry D. Teitelbaum, *Nuclear Energy and the U. S. Fuel Economy, 1955–1980*, NPA, Washington, 1958.

additional convenience in use of oil). Delivered natural gas prices are still below coal prices in most markets, but prices are moving rapidly upward, presumably toward parity with coal and fuel oil. Prospective coal prices, therefore, may be considered a key determinant of fuel prices generally.

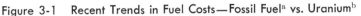

Figure 3-1   Recent Trends in Fuel Costs—Fossil Fuel[a] vs. Uranium[b]

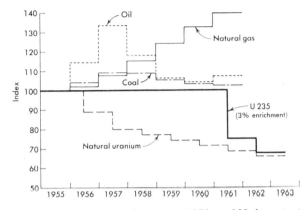

a. 1955 = 100.   b. Fiscal year 1956 = 100 for natural uranium and for U235 (3 per cent enrichment).

Sources: Tables 4-5 and 5-3; Steam-Electric Plant Factors, 1961. National Coal Association, Washington, 1962.

Teitelbaum notes that if coal production doubles by 1980, the principal offsets to a possible continuing gradual rise in the price of coal (at mine mouth) will be: the declining cost of transportation, the rapid increases in mechanized mining and strip mining and improved prospects for capital investment in larger producing units. An end is not foreseeable for any of these cost-reducing elements. Their implications for future coal prices are not clear. Some analysts predict that these elements will prevent an increase in real costs over the next few decades,[15] whereas others believe that the persistent upward trend in real prices may be only partly offset.[16] Future coal prices, therefore, are so shrouded in uncertainty that speculation about them seems only to mark out a wide range of possibilities.

15. See Schurr, Netschert and others, op. cit., Chap. 8.

16. Teitelbaum suggests that while average prices at the mine mouth may increase appreciably by 1980—"on the order of 25 per cent"—they will be offset slightly by decreased costs of transportation, yielding a net increase in national average delivered prices of "no more than 25 per cent, and probably . . . somewhat less," compared with 1955. (Teitelbaum, op. cit., pp. 27 and 31.) The Bureau of Mines also has implied an appreciable increase in real costs, if production is to about double by 1975. (McKinney Review, Background Material, Vol. 4, p. 1517.)

The same is true of future oil prices, especially in view of the uncertainty of the possible effects of varying degrees of restriction against importation of foreign oil and of production controls imposed at the state level. Those who project level real prices assume a continuance of historic trends—continued production proration and control of the industry through a mixture of monopolistic and competitive elements. The argument of those who foresee declining real prices is based in part on the fact that production costs in the Caribbean or the Middle East are much lower than in the United States and that sufficient imports may be admitted to force down real prices of oil. The independent U. S. petroleum producers are politically strong and, since they are buttressed by the national security argument for the necessity of maintaining domestic exploration of new reserves, despite the evidence that domestic resources are ample for several more decades, they may be able to prevent for a long period any major relaxation of import barriers.

The argument of those who foresee progressively rising oil prices stems from the disturbed political conditions prevailing in the Middle East, augmented by potential interference in this area by the Soviet Union. The taking over of the Suez Canal by Egypt in 1956 led (temporarily, to be sure) to higher oil prices, longer transport, industry-wide allocations, large shipments from the Western Hemisphere to Western Europe and so on. Also, the breaking of the historic fifty-fifty royalty arrangement with petroleum-producing countries by Italian and Japanese interests seeking oil production capability in the Middle East probably means that producing countries will demand a larger share of the royalties under other contracts, and that will spell higher prices.

Many other elements are involved, not the least of which is the combination of high capital investment (large overhead costs) and low operating costs of the industry, which has been a recurrent source of price competition in the battle for markets.[17] Indeed, the slackened demand situation of 1959–60, the breaking up of the long-standing price pattern into multiple basing points, the evidences of surplus shipping capacity, increasing competition of Soviet oil in Central and Western Europe and the imminence of competitive nuclear power may have set the stage for a long period of declining, rather than rising, world petroleum prices. Current development of the rich North African fields is reinforcing the probability of that decline.

Because seemingly rational economic arguments justifying a projection of rising or declining or level real fuel prices can be made, one is impelled to consider the question moot, barring, of course, a catastrophe in the Middle East,

17. Paul H. Frankel, *Essentials of Petroleum: A Key to Oil Economics*, Chapman and Hall, London, 1946.

TABLE **3 - 5**

Average Fuel Costs of Steam Electric Plants, by Region, 1961

Region	Average fuel cost per million BTU (cents)			Percentage distribution of BTUs of fuel consumed			Net generation (KWH X 10⁹)
	Coal	Oil	Gas	Coal	Oil	Gas	
U. S. total	25.8	35.5	25.1	65	8	27	631.6
New England	36.2	37.7	36.3	63	34	3	25.2
Middle Atlantic	29.9	36.2	37.7	78	14	8	101.0
East North Central	25.0		26.4	96	—	4	161.9
West North Central	26.2		22.8	45	—	55	38.9
South Atlantic	25.8	35.2	32.5	78	9	13	99.5
East South Central	19.7		25.4	92	—	8	71.7
West South Central			19.0	—	—	100	62.8
Mountain	19.6	25.6	28.5	30	7	63	16.8
Pacific		32.6	35.2	—	27	73	54.0

Source: National Coal Association, *Steam-Electric Plant Factors, 1961*, Twelfth Edition, Washington, July 1962, Table 2.

and proceed on the historical price record. However, this assumption ignores the role of public policies, such as import quotas on oil, the indicated preference of the Congress for a relaxation of natural gas price regulation and the failure to fulfill programs for recovering oil from shale.

Regional Differences in Fuel Prices

Despite steady reductions in the cost of transporting fuel and energy, some regional differences in fuel prices are likely to persist, since no revolutionary improvement in overland energy transport is in prospect.[18] At present nuclear energy is the only development that might sharply lessen these geographic differences. Regional differences are far greater, indeed, than any anticipated national increase in fuel prices over the next couple of decades. In the formation of economic policy for nuclear power, then, regional differences in conventional fuel prices may well be a more pertinent consideration than the debatable eventuality of rising prices nationally.

18. Significant reductions in energy transport costs should result from specialized application of such technical advances as pipeline or belt conveyance of coal in slurry form, progressively higher electric energy transmission voltages and shipment of compressed natural gas by specially constructed tankers.

Regional differences in fuel prices in the United States are shown in Table 3–5, which covers the fuel consumed by all electric utilities reporting to the Federal Power Commission. In New England—the most striking case of high energy prices—coal prices are nearly double those in the East South Central region, fuel oil prices are slightly higher than in other regions which use appreciable amounts of oil in generating electricity, and gas prices are almost double those in the gas-producing West South Central states. Where the three fuels meet competitively in sections remote from the sources of supply, as in New England, energy prices tend to be roughly equivalent on a BTU basis.

Alternative Primary Energy Sources

The question held in abeyance thus far is whether, in the unlikely event of a marked increase in fuel prices, alternative energy sources might become economic in the United States to restrain further price increases. The recovery of shale oil, the relaxation of import restrictions, the transport of liquefied natural gas by ship and the competitive entry of nuclear power in high-cost fuel areas seem to be the major immediately foreseeable possibilities.

Production of oil from shale, while still not out of the pilot-plant stage in Colorado, is economically feasible in Western Europe. The estimated cost in Colorado is in some dispute, though the range of difference is not large. On the basis of the highest cost estimate, that of the National Petroleum Council (1957), it appears that a reduction of roughly one fourth in delivered price (19 cents per gallon) would be required to bring gasoline from shale oil down to a level (14 to 15 cents) competitive with gasoline produced in southern California, the market considered most logical for a shale oil plant in Colorado.[19] A marked increase in West Coast crude oil prices would be necessary to make large-scale shale oil production attractive. This might well restrain further crude oil price increases. Other strong deterrents to commercial shale oil operations are the large excess crude production capacity in the United States, the unfavorable location of the oil shale deposits, water supply problems and the availability of imported crude at less than $3.00 per barrel.[20] The obstacles, politically, to an early abandonment of import controls can be described as formidable.

In the next ten years nuclear energy in marginal-cost areas can provide at best only slight restraint on potentially rising conventional fuel prices. The number of nuclear plants and the quantity of displaced fuel are certain

19. Schurr, Netschert and others, *op. cit.*, p. 388.
20. McKinney Review, *Background Material*, Vol. 4, p. 1541.

to be small in this period. The real question is whether nuclear power might become strictly competitive, after the first stage of developmental and demonstration plants, and hence provide a large, if not indeed the major, fraction of the growth in power production in marginal-cost areas. If nuclear power makes this transition successfully, then the degree of restraint on rising fuel prices will be suggested by the amount of conventional fuel it can hope to displace. This, as shown later, has been estimated at less than 10 per cent of national energy consumption by 1980 but a much larger fraction in the marginal-cost areas. If technical progress permits, nuclear energy, like shale oil and imports of oil, may therefore represent an additional price-restraining feature. At present, however, the range of uncertainty in prospective nuclear power costs is greater than the potential fuel price increases; there is also a possibility that real fuel prices may decline. If present energy policies are maintained, however, the chances of such a decline are greatly reduced.

National Energy Policies

The year 1954 stands out in the history of the nation's evolving energy policies. It was in 1954 that the new atomic energy act came into being, providing a new relation between industry and government in development of the peaceful power of the atom. It was also the year of the "Phillips case" (347 U. S. 672), determining that the FPC had authority and responsibility for regulating the prices of natural gas sold in the field by independent producers. The Eisenhower administration also decided in that year, as a matter of policy, that responsibility for developing economic processes for recovering oil from shale should be transferred from the Bureau of Mines to private industry. Further, a policy committee of the Cabinet, established in 1954, later found that imports of foreign crude petroleum endangered the national security and called for "voluntary" import controls—which, with little metamorphosis, became mandatory quotas in 1959. The large number of coal producers, meanwhile, unhampered by serious state or federal controls— though highly sensitive to the rate-making powers of the Interstate Commerce Commission—continued the course of strong competition, whereas the production of domestic crude oil, long under stringent state controls, was subject to proration, originally established in the name of "conservation." In reviewing the events of 1954, one is struck by the divergence and inconsistency of fuels policy and wonders at the failure of private and public groups to consider seriously the strong recommendation of the Paley Commission—only two years earlier—that steps be taken to establish a comprehensive national energy policy.[21]

How did these diverse and divergent energy policies, private and public, affect the determination of urgency of need for nuclear energy? (The converse question, the effect of nuclear energy on energy policy generally, has been intimated by the limited role it is expected to play during the next decade or two.) Though competitive nuclear energy, when achieved, may help in the formation of wise public policies designed to reduce real prices of fuel, no one supposes it can be decisive. Nevertheless, as shown in Chapter 4, uranium is unique in that it is the only primary energy source that will assuredly be lower in real price twenty years hence than at present. It is important, therefore, to examine national policies for conventional fuel, with special emphasis on real price prospects for each fuel.

Of the total energy used in 1980, petroleum is expected to provide 40 to 45 per cent, coal about 25 per cent, natural gas 25 to 30 per cent and nuclear energy and hydro the small remainder. Petroleum and natural gas, then, representing more than two thirds of total consumption now and in 1980, must bear closest examination. The presumption, requiring careful evaluation, is that notwithstanding the nation's great reserves of coal, oil and natural gas, our energy policies—private and public—are such that they counteract the long-run economic tendency toward constant or declining real prices of conventional fuel. National average real prices of energy have risen over the last few decades and present policies, if continued, will serve to sustain increases and prevent decreases in the foreseeable future.

Petroleum: National Defense and Economic Policy

The major explicit elements of petroleum policy consist of: mandatory import quotas on petroleum and certain refined products; the practice in certain states of "conserving" petroleum reserves through "proration," or restriction of production from the wells; and the federal government's decision to turn over to private business the problems of producing fluid fuels from oil shale, tar sands and coal.

The first two policies prevent economically available supplies of crude from having their full effect upon oil prices; the third makes the prospect of the development of alternative fluid fuels dependent on favorable business conditions. These policies all involve controversial questions, on which competing suppliers of fuels differ strongly.

21. President's Materials Policy Commission, *Resources for Freedom*, Washington, 1952, Vol. I, pp. 129–30.

OIL IMPORT QUOTAS. The present quotas on imports of crude oil and certain oil products are an outgrowth of the February 1955 report of the President's Advisory Committee on Energy Supplies and Resources Policy, established July 30, 1954.[22] The committee noted that since World War II the importation of crude oil and residual fuel oil had increased substantially and in 1954 supplied a significant fraction of the U. S. market for fuels. Tacitly assuming the probability of a long war, the committee held that, if imports should exceed significantly the 1954 proportion of one tenth of domestic production, the "domestic fuels situation could be so impaired as to endanger the orderly industrial growth which assures the military and civilian supplies and reserves that are necessary to the national defense." The President thereupon asked a special Cabinet committee to investigate crude oil imports to examine the question whether an adjustment of the imports could be accomplished voluntarily. In 1957 the special Cabinet committee found that national security required a limitation on imports. It recommended that unless the importing companies complied "voluntarily" with the allocation plan proposed, the President should find that there was a threat to the national security under Section 7 of the Trade Agreements Extension Act of 1955. The initial plan, approved by the President, covered a slight reduction in imports into all areas except District V (Pacific Coast). In 1958 District V was also included. In March 1959 the President found the voluntary quotas insufficient protection of the national security and made the quotas mandatory on crude oil and certain refined products in order to "preserve to the greatest extent possible a vigorous, healthy petroleum industry in the United States."

The controversy over import quotas, no less bitter than that over nuclear energy development, is largely between the domestic "independent" and the international "major" oil companies.[23] The chief arguments of each make the issue pertinent to nuclear power development policies and to prospective energy prices.

In general, the independents want protection against low-cost oil, especially from the Middle East. The independents urge that, while conservation is an element of good national policy, reserves are sufficient to protect the national security and, indeed, meet a larger share of domestic consumption than is permitted by present import quotas.

22. "Report on Energy Supplies and Resources Policy," Release by the Press Secretary to the President, The White House, February 26, 1955.

23. See, for example, Sebastian Raciti, *The Oil Import Problem, Studies in Industrial Economics*, Number 6, Fordham University Press, New York (no date).

The major companies, operating both inside and outside the United States, want to ship more oil to the United States. They argue that prospective domestic consumption rates cannot be met by domestic output, without an impracticable increase in drilling at increasingly high costs.[24]

The Eisenhower administration's justification for the import controls thus rested on an assumed relation to national security. This reasoning is by no means clear in the present controversy, since both majors and independents seem to agree that imports in some relation to future domestic capacity and growing consumption are economically necessary. But it is held that domestic oil exploration and production may represent a "special case," deserving protection on security grounds.[25] The theory presupposes the necessity for a "protective reserve," identified in some quarters as the difference between current Western Hemisphere production (since little is actually imported from the Middle East) and what could be produced in a war that would cut off sea traffic for a lengthy period.

Critical economic analysis of the series of special committee reports leads one to believe that the committee fully accepted the necessity of a protective reserve for national security reasons, that it found that severe trade restrictions were necessary to protect the high-cost domestic oil industry and that it assumed that the resulting maintenance of high U. S. oil prices was a justifiable cost to incur compared with the cost of alternative methods of assuring national security. Stockpiling or storing of foreign crude oil for military requirements was dismissed as "impracticable"; withholding of certain new discoveries from production was found "contrary to the principles of free enterprise"; and no consideration was reported as having been given to production of oil from shale.[26] Finally, the special committee disposed of the key argument in favor of more imports—that greater imports would permit conservation of domestic resources—by indicating that domestic exploration would decline sharply with "no assurance of an adequate market"; that ultimate petroleum reserves could not be established without a continuing high rate of exploration; and that an emergency cutting the United States off from foreign sources would result in long delays and in large private and public expenditures to restore the industry on a "crash" basis.

24. The Chase Manhattan Bank, *Future Growth of the World Petroleum Industry*, New York, 1958, p. 25 ff.

25. J. M. Letiche, "United States Foreign Trade Policy," *American Economic Review*, December 1958, p. 962. (Letiche does not support such a view, however.)

26. "Petroleum Imports," Report to the President by the Special Committee to Investigate Crude Oil Imports, July 29, 1957 (printed for government distribution by the Office of Defense Mobilization, now the Office of Emergency Planning, Washington).

Apparently, the real argument has been about measures to protect the domestic oil industry rather than about measures to protect national security. If the security of the Western World is paramount, then the real danger is not that of a long world war, but of loss of access to Middle Eastern oil required by Western Europe. There are, it should be emphasized, alternative possibilities for reducing the vulnerability of the free world as a whole. Among them are private and public measures necessary to perfect the processes for recovering oil from both shale and tar sands, to provide supertankers required to bypass the Suez Canal and to establish—outside the Middle East—alternative, new sources of petroleum, such as North Africa. A combination of such measures for general free world security might well do more to protect the United States and with less burden on the economy than the high-cost device of import quotas.[27]

As to the relation of these high-cost policies to nuclear power prospects, maintenance of the quotas would encourage the introduction of nuclear energy in marginal fuel-cost areas, whereas their discontinuance might be a deterrent. The pertinence of nuclear energy development to America's foreign trade policy, particularly for fuels, is discussed further in Chapter 10.

PRORATION OF OIL PRODUCTION. Just as "national security" was used as an excuse for import quotas in 1959, so too, many years earlier, "conservation" served as an excuse for production quotas imposed by state regulatory bodies to avoid great overproduction resulting from both the important discoveries and worldwide depression of the early 1930s. Texas, Oklahoma, Louisiana, New Mexico and Kansas regulate production by some form of proration—in Texas the allowable days of production have been reduced steadily since 1948, to one third of full-time capacity in 1961.[28]

Stabilization of prices has been an important motive of domestic producers in adhering to proration and demanding limitation of imports. Both policies

27. One test of the efficacy of import quotas to preserve domestic production capacity is the extent to which output can be expanded in an emergency situation. The record is not reassuring: following the 1956 closing of the Suez Canal, domestic crude production scarcely changed, although exports from the United States and other parts of the Western Hemisphere rose sharply to fill part of the supply gap in Western Europe.

28. Aside from marketing considerations, proration stems from certain physical facts: oil and gas being liquids are "migratory"; they are also under pressure in most cases and hence flow toward points of reduced pressure; further, large quantities of oil and gas may become unrecoverable through unwise development of a field. Since a landowner possesses all minerals under his property, oil strikes in the early days led to drilling races, to the dissipation of field pressures, to reduction of recoverable oil and to market gluts breaking the so-called "industry price structure." Since proration was instituted in the 1930s, producers have been able to eliminate chaotic conditions. Since that time, too, the price of domestic oil moved continuously upward until about 1957, when imported oil became the principal threat to the price structure.

contribute, too, to the national policy of maintaining the high rate of discovery and development of petroleum in the United States. The long-standing tax subsidy—the 27.5 per cent depletion allowance for oil and gas producers—also has contributed importantly.

The major elements of national oil policy—state proration, extraordinary depletion allowances and import quotas—make for a mutually reinforcing "closed system" as long as reserves exist. The circularity is evident: the proration system has led to progressively less production from present wells, leading to more strenuous discovery and development efforts to secure new production "allowables" and maintain former rates of output and income, which in turn are sustained by protected domestic prices and by extraordinary depletion allowances, designed to encourage expenditures for further exploration and development. The end of this system of massive subsidy and excessive drilling is not in sight, primarily because national security considerations have been identified with production capability of the United States rather than of the free world and because the resource base is sufficiently great to permit more than optimum exploration and development for several years. Such policies mean that substantially lower prices for oil are unreasonable to assume, notwithstanding large, growing proven reserves and ample supplies of oil in the Western Hemisphere. They therefore increase the probability of the introduction of nuclear power in areas dependent on oil for power generation—New England and the Pacific Coast, among others.

Federal Regulation of Natural Gas Prices

In 1954 the Supreme Court, in the case of *Phillips Petroleum Co. v. Wisconsin* (347 U. S. 672), held that the Congress under the Natural Gas Act (52 Stat., 1938, as amended) had intended to give the Federal Power Commission jurisdiction over companies (such as Phillips) which sell gas in the state where it is produced to companies operating pipelines in interstate commerce. Hitherto the Federal Power Commission had generally acted in the belief that such sales were exempt from the Natural Gas Act, which stated ambiguously that the statute should apply, on the one hand, to the transportation and sale of natural gas in interstate commerce but not, on the other, to "the production or gathering of natural gas" (Section 717, a).

The issue, in simplified terms, has come down to a struggle between natural gas producers, who contend that vigorous federal regulation would destroy the incentive to develop new reserves, and the consumers of natural gas, composed mainly of gas distributing utilities, who long ago accepted federal regulation of gas transportation and distribution. Since gas production is closely associated with crude oil production, the events affecting the oil industry in recent years have also influenced the gas utilities and industrial consumers. Both before and after the Phillips case the price of gas to pipeline operators and distributors rose rapidly, chiefly because old contracts expired and the new ones made usually contained escalator clauses. In 1955 Congress passed the Harris-Fulbright bill, which doubtless would have permitted field prices to rise even faster had President Eisenhower not felt compelled to veto the bill.[29] The continuous rise of gas prices in the future, it is contended by consumers, could be slowed by federal regulation of field prices under present statutes. In the absence of federal regulation, gas prices presumably would rise to a limit roughly established by the alternative delivered cost of coal or oil, varying with the place.

The Federal Power Commission has authorized independent gas producers to raise prices, where, in its opinion, the circumstances have warranted increases.[30] Rising prices for gas, under regulation, are occurring and may continue until competitive parity with oil or coal is reached.

Plausible Scope for Nuclear Power, 1965–1980

The thrust of inadequate energy policy, the leverage of geographic price differences in conventional fuels, the rapid growth of electric energy consumption and the confidently expected decline in nuclear power cost provide the major footings for projections of nuclear power capacity in the United States over the next two decades. Indeed, the strength of the economic case for encouraging nuclear power development must be evaluated largely by the contribution it can be expected to make in the energy economy. "Urgency of need" for nuclear power should be judged, therefore, mainly by the speed with which it can become competitive and provide sizable increments to expanding generating capacity in the United States. This is essentially a matter of comparative cost of generation.

29. H. R. 6645, as amended, 84th Cong., 1st Sess.; S. 1853, 84th Cong., 1st Sess.

30. In one case the FPC authorized William T. Burton Industries, Inc., of Sulphur, La., to sell gas to United Gas Pipe Line Company of Shreveport, La., at 22.55 cents per thousand cubic feet, overruling the staff recommendation of 18 cents. Commissioner William R. Connole dissented, noting that the price was higher than any price on file in the area and more than twice the average rate being paid by United Gas Pipe Line Co. in Louisiana. He recommended that, in order to stem the tide of rising prices, new sales be permitted only at prices shown to be required by the public convenience and necessity. (FPC, Release No. 9885, Washington, June 16, 1958.)

Projected U. S. Electric Power Consumption

Electric energy consumption in the United States is growing at roughly twice the rate of primary energy consumption.[31] However, over the last thirty years remarkable technical improvements in furnace-boiler and turbogenerator systems have cut the average amount of fuel required per kilowatt-hour from 2 pounds of coal equivalent (25,175 BTU) in 1920 to well under one pound (10,356 BTU) in 1960. During the next couple of decades the heat rate per kilowatt-hour may decline to 7,000 BTU for the best stations and to 9,150 BTU for the average. Moderate increases in boiler fuel prices may therefore continue for some time to be offset by technical advances. Moreover, the trend in constant-dollar capital costs of conventional plant seems to be downward.[32] Thus, the competition of the best conventional stations with nuclear power plants is unlikely to lessen.

The speed of nuclear power's introduction will also be partly dependent on the growth in consumption of electric energy. Some recent projections are summarized in Table 3–6. There are significant differences in the projected rates to 1980—far greater differences, indeed, than in the projections of total primary energy consumption, discussed earlier. Only projections in the upper and lower ranges need be considered to establish the probable limits of primary energy requirements for electric power.

According to the highest projection of electric energy consumption, that of the *Electrical World*, if 5 per cent is deducted for hydropower and an average heat rate of 9,150 BTU per kilowatt-hour is assumed, the 1980 total fuel requirement will be roughly 31×10^{15} BTU. This fuel requirement is 36 per cent of total primary energy consumption projected for 1980 by the Bureau of Mines. (See Table 3–3, p. 83, source 2.)

On the other hand, if we use the much lower projection of the National Planning Association, the corresponding primary energy requirement in 1980 will be 15.5×10^{15} BTU, or roughly 19 per cent of the NPA projection of total primary energy requirements. Considering that some 18 per cent of total primary energy in 1954 went into electric power generation, we can see that

31. Nelson and Keagy estimate that mineral fuels for electric generation have increased from only 3.6 per cent of total primary energy consumption in 1920 to 12.8 per cent in 1955. (Harlan W. Nelson and W. R. Keagy, Jr., "The Economic Background for the Competitive Development of Nuclear Power," Second Nuclear Engineering and Science Conference, American Society of Mechanical Engineers, New York, March 11–14, 1957.) Schurr, Netschert and others (*op. cit.*, p. 239) in 1960 made a corresponding estimate of 19.3 per cent for 1955 and projected that this would rise to 24.2 per cent in 1975.

32. See "12th Steam Station Cost Survey," *Electrical World*, October 2, 1961.

predictions as to nuclear power capacity are greatly influenced by the particular assumptions of growth rate in consumption of electricity and improvement in the heat rate, aside from questions of relative fuel prices. Thus, the
fuel requirement for electric power generation in 1980 may well range between 2.2 and 4.3 times the actual 1954 requirement. From the preceding

Figure 3-2   Growth of U. S. Energy Consumption and Electric Power
             Generation

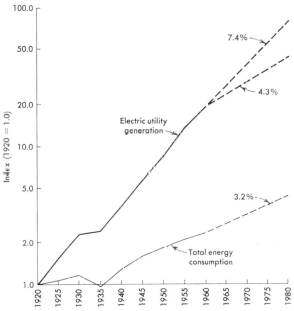

Sources: Energy consumption and electric power generation, 1920–
1960—U. S. Bureau of the Census, Washington: *Historical Statistics of
the United States, Colonial Times to 1957,* 1960, p. 506; and *Statistical Abstract of the United States,* 1961, **pp. 522 and 523.** Projections
to 1980—Tables 3-3 and 3-6.

discussion of economically recoverable energy reserves, it can be seen that a
doubling of fuel production for all purposes appears quite feasible over two
decades. Yet a quadrupling of production for electric energy alone has
prompted concern; spokesmen for the electric utility industry have expressed
doubt that output can be expanded so greatly without increases in real
prices.[33]

33. Philip Sporn indicated that while a doubling of current coal production by 1975 appeared
possible, he was gravely concerned about meeting the growth in fossil fuel requirements after 1975.
(Section 202 Hearings, 1959.)

TABLE **3 - 6**

Projections of Electric Energy Consumption, 1970, 1975 and 1980

			Annual consumption in KWH X 10^9			
		Base		Projected consumption		Annual growth rate (per cent)
Source of projection	Year	Consumption	1970	1975	1980	
1. PMPC, 1952	1950	389	1,070[a]	1,400	1,800[a]	5.25
2. McKinney Panel, 1956[b]						
Low	1954	478	1,150	1,380	1,650	4.9
High			1,470	2,010	2,770	7.0
3. NPA, 1958[c]	1955	625	1,279	1,523	1,795	4.3
4. Sporn, 1959[d]	1957	631	1,450[a]	2,000	2,750[a]	6.6
5. RFF, 1960	1955	633	1,475[a]	1,966	2,590[a]	5.8
6. Electrical World, 1961[e]	1960	806	1,661	2,370	3,372	7.4
7. FPC, 1962[f]	1960	763	1,564	2,139	2,866	6.9

a. Estimated by interpolation or extrapolation.

b. Converted from capacity data; utility plants only.

c. All utility and industrial plants.

d. Electric utility generation.

e. Total electric industry output, excluding Alaska and Hawaii.

f. Electric utilities only; energy requirements; Alaska and Hawaii included.

Sources:

1. President's Materials Policy Commission, *Resources for Freedom,* Washington, June 1952, Vol. I, p. 11.

2. McKinney Panel, Vol. 2, pp. 24–30.

3. Perry D. Teitelbaum, *Nuclear Energy and the U. S. Fuel Economy, 1955–1980,* NPA, Washington, 1958, p. 155.

4. Philip Sporn, statement in *Energy Resources and Technology,* Hearings, Joint Economic Committee, 86th Cong., 1st Sess., October 1959, p. 77. (Sporn reaffirmed this projection in 1961.)

5. Sam H. Schurr, Bruce C. Netschert and others, *Energy in the American Economy, 1850–1975,* Resources for the Future, Washington, 1960, p. 238.

6. "Twelfth Annual Electric Industry Forecast," *Electrical World,* September 18, 1961, pp. 105 ff.

7. FPC, Release No. 11,829, Washington, January 30, 1962.

Sources to Table 3-7 continued

8. Keith L. Harms, Supplement II to the Report of the Ad Hoc Committee on Atomic Policy of the Atomic Industrial Forum, Inc., New York, March 1962. (Several other cases on different assumptions with respect to total generating capacity, increasing fossil fuel prices and lease or ownership of nuclear fuel are also covered by this study.)

TABLE **3-7**

Projections of Nuclear Power Capacity in the United States, Selected Years, 1965–1980

Source of projection	Nuclear capacity, end of year (thousands of mw.)				Nuclear as per cent of total generation[a]	
	1965	1970	1975	1980	1975	1980
1. AEC staff, 1954						
Case 1			21.0		10	
Case 2			5.0		2	
2. McKinney Panel, 1956						
Series I (optimistic)	4.0	12.3	48.0	137.0	11	23
Series II (pessimistic)	2.9	7.2	22.6	54.3	7.5	15
3. Davis-Roddis (AEC staff), 1957	4.0	22.6	88.9	227.2	18	32
4. NPA, 1958	1.9	8.5	28.0	57.6	8	21
5. Lane (ORNL), 1959		11.0		78.0	...	...
6. Sporn, 1959[b]			25.0	60.0	7	...
7. Starr, 1960[b]			8.0	30.0	...	...
8. Atomic Industrial Forum, 1962						
Case 5		1.0		66.0		
Case 8				10.0		

a. The percentages are not directly comparable, since the estimates of total electricity generation were made on different bases.

b. Data are converted from kilowatt-hours per year.

Sources:

1. AEC, *Major Activities in the Atomic Energy Programs, January–June 1954* (Semiannual Report), Washington, July 1954, Appendix 8.

2. McKinney Panel, *Background Material*, Vol. 2, p. 27.

3. W. Kenneth Davis and Louis H. Roddis, Jr., "A Projection of Nuclear Power Costs," NICB, Fifth Annual Conference on Atomic Energy, New York, March 1957.

4. Perry D. Teitelbaum, *Nuclear Energy and the U. S. Fuel Economy, 1955–1980*, NPA, Washington, 1958, Table 5, p. 59, and Appendix 8.

5. James A. Lane, "Economics of Nuclear Power," *Annual Review of Nuclear Science*, Annual Reviews, Palo Alto, Calif., 1959, Vol. 9, p. 478.

6. Philip Sporn, statement in *Energy Resources and Technology*, Hearings, Joint Economic Committee, 86th Cong., 1st Sess., October 1959, pp. 49 ff.

7. Chauncey Starr, Section 202 Hearings, 1960, pp. 295 ff.

Sources continued on opposite page.

Projections of Nuclear Power Capacity

The major responsible estimates of future nuclear power capacity, shown in Table 3–7, reveal the wave of enthusiasm that overtook "official" views after 1953. Shortly before the 1954 act was passed, the AEC staff suggested that nuclear power capacity might range between 5,000 and 21,000 megawatts in 1975, yet only three years later, at the peak of optimism, W. K. Davis and L. H. Roddis, also members of the AEC staff, projected 89,000 megawatts. More realistic estimates were made in 1958 by the National Planning Association and in 1959 by James A. Lane of the Oak Ridge National Laboratory. Only the Davis-Roddis projections suggest that nuclear power can make more than a modest contribution to electric power supplies during the next couple of decades.

Institutional Incentives

As an urgent domestic need for nuclear energy has not been established, other motivations necessarily account for the extraordinary private and public effort devoted to it since 1954. Foremost undoubtedly—aside from foreign policy considerations—has been the rivalry of private and public power. Another factor has been the keen rivalry between established companies and newcomers in electric equipment manufacture. In addition, fuel prices after World War II for a time threatened to outrun the improvements in plant efficiency and led utilities to consider alternative sources of energy.

Rivalry of Private and Public Power

Most public and governmental groups that have examined nuclear power policy questions in recent years have shied away from overtly considering the influence on the development of nuclear power of the private-vs.-public-power controversy,[34] or have hoped to insulate the issue by suggesting that it should be considered "irrelevant"[35] or have appealed for a truce between the two groups to permit an unimpeded nuclear power program.[36] Most members of the Joint Committee have studiously avoided making proposals that might raise or exacerbate the issue. Evidently, however, the issue will not subside

34. See, for example, the McKinney Panel, Vol. 1.

35. NPA, *Productive Uses of Nuclear Energy: Summary of Findings—Policy Suggestions for the Future*, Washington, September 1957, p. 5.

36. *Atoms for Power: United States Policy in Atomic Energy Development*, Columbia University Press, New York, 1957, pp. 154–55.

and may be expected to continue as a pervasive influence on nuclear power development. This was illustrated in the 1961 hearings on, and rejection of, the AEC proposal to produce electric power from the New Production Reactor built by the AEC at Hanford, Washington. There were, to be sure, valid differences on the merits of the project, but these were subordinated by the views of those who chose to make the question primarily an issue of public power.

As mentioned in Chapter 1, each group fears that the manner in which nuclear power is introduced may undermine its position. Both sides have cause for disquiet. Private power has seen public power grow from 5 per cent to 24 per cent of total U. S. generation since 1933. On the other hand, public power has witnessed the loss of municipal plants through purchase by surrounding private utilities and has been subjected to a concerted campaign of antagonistic advertising in the name of investor-owned utilities.

Perhaps the most critical event in this conflict was the Dixon-Yates proposal initiated by the Executive Office in 1953 to have a new privately owned plant of 450,000-kilowatt capacity serve the AEC and thus release in the Memphis, Tennessee, area that amount of power the AEC was buying from the TVA. The proposal was widely interpreted as an attack on the TVA service area. However, as construction was being started on the private plant under the AEC contract, the city of Memphis decided to proceed with a municipal plant. The AEC canceled the contract in 1955 but did not reimburse the private group for costs incurred because there was a question of a possible conflict of interest on the part of an individual who served both as a consultant to the Bureau of the Budget on the matter and as an employee of the company expected to handle the bond financing. Public power groups, and others, felt justified in inferring a possible broader "conflict of interest" within the government and feared that the administration would use nuclear power development to aid private power interests.[37]

How the controversy has impinged on the development of nuclear power cannot be directly discerned, but it is intimated by the overtones of the Dixon-Yates proposal. Probably one of the most important aspects of the con-

---

37. A most revealing history of the proposal, from its inception in 1953 to the U. S. Supreme Court writ in 1961 upholding the AEC's cancellation of the contract on the ground of a conflict of interest, is given in Lewis L. Strauss, *Men and Decisions*, Doubleday, New York, 1962, Chap. 15.

The misgivings of public power systems were epitomized by Gordon R. Clapp in 1957 when he cited "the AEC's incredible performance in promoting and underwriting the Dixon-Yates scheme" and declared that henceforth the AEC "will be suspect in its treatment of the relative merits among conflicting views concerning the scope, methods and means to be pursued in a reactor program . . ." (NPA, *Productive Uses of Nuclear Energy: Summary of Findings—Policy Suggestions for the Future*, Washington, September 1957, p. 5.)

troversy has been that the existence of public power has served as a spur to private utilities to develop progressive reactor programs in order to avoid being left out.[38] This compulsion to "fill the vacuum" that would otherwise be occupied by public power is a leading reason for the comparatively large investment program of the electric utilities in nuclear power.[39] Candid comments to the press by industry representatives attending the First Geneva Conference (1955) record the motivation characteristic of many private utilities.[40]

The public power sector has likewise been apprehensive lest the emphasis given to private development of atomic power by the 1954 act and the AEC's administration of the program might result in a failure to meet the legitimate needs of public power groups, particularly for small- and medium-sized plants. Indeed, it was public power's appeal for a demonstration of small plants that prompted the AEC to undertake the "second round," emphasizing small reactors. Since then the AEC has been careful, under continuing Joint Committee pressure, to recognize the legitimate participation of nonfederal public power in the reactor demonstration program.[41]

The private-vs.-public-power controversy has not only compelled the private utilities to proceed when they would not have done so on economic grounds. It has also prevented any large-scale federal power construction. It has been one of the dominating economic influences on the recent pace and direction of nuclear power development in the United States. In the light of the limited domestic need for nuclear power, this controversy has been instrumental, fortuitously, in broadening the nuclear power program in a manner that may help generally to achieve foreign policy objectives, outlined in Chapter 8.

The possibility of federal power's preempting the field has been used as a convenient lever by the AEC to bring private utilities and industry into

38. The force of the issue is wider than the electric utilities and includes some equipment manufacturers. For example, speaking before the Edison Electric Institute, Ralph J. Cordiner, Chairman, General Electric Co., identified it as a critical area in future public policy: "Will atomic energy provide a second chance for those who want to see investor-owned electric utilities wither away, replaced by federal power plants?" (Address before the Twenty-Sixth Annual Convention of the Edison Electric Institute, Boston, June 9, 1958.)

39. Expenditures by electric utility companies for nuclear power development through 1961 were estimated by the Edison Electric Institute at $433 million and expenditures of $520 million were projected through 1963. (Section 202 Hearings, 1962, p. 509.)

40. See issues of the *Wall Street Journal* during and soon after the First Geneva Conference, August 8–20, 1955, especially that of August 22, 1955, reporting that their "primary motive is to stake this out as an area of private rather than public power."

41. See remarks of AEC Commissioner Harold S. Vance, "Atomic Energy Commission Basic Philosophy," Idaho Falls, Idaho, October 2, 1957, p. 3 (AEC Release).

specific demonstration projects. Private groups have understood that failure to present proposals acceptable to the AEC, the Comptroller General and the Joint Committee would mean that the AEC would have to consider federal construction of the projects. Under the circumstances private utilities have chosen to participate, largely with heavy AEC assistance, to be sure.

Private power's fear of public development has not been expressed to the same degree by other sectors of industry. Aside from the private utilities and private power groups, the so-called "atomic energy industry" may be said to consist of three elements: the manufacturers of atomic products and equipment; architect-engineering-construction-consulting concerns; universities and research institutions. While all have many economic interests in common, it is clear from polls of industry opinion that on some questions of economic policy the private utilities and the other segments have characteristically different views. For example, in a poll of opinion in January 1958 the utility segment showed less interest in expanding the power development program or in formalizing a new national program than did the other segments of the industry.[42] This departure from the industry norm is undoubtedly due to fear of public "encroachment."

Competition among Reactor Equipment Manufacturers

The supplying of nuclear materials and equipment is a highly competitive field composed of several large, established suppliers and many new entrants, large and small.[43] While there are hundreds of companies offering equipment and services, only a few companies are yet prepared to offer complete nuclear power reactors. Concentration is high.[44] But even among these few, the AEC's experience of the last few years indicates strong competition for the limited existing market in the United States. The power reactor industry may well be described as a sick "infant industry"—composed mainly of industrial giants. The industry consists both of old giants in turbogenerator or furnace-boiler fields and of enterprises which have a diversity of special skills and resources acquired during or after World War II, but which do not yet have established sales relations with the private utilities.

42. Atomic Industrial Forum, *Forum Memo*, February 1958, pp. 16–18. Of the utility respondents, 50 per cent favored no new formalized national atomic power program and 47 per cent believed the program should be expanded, whereas two thirds of all respondents believed the program should be both expanded and formalized. In almost all other respects the utility systems conformed to the preferences of the industry as a whole.

43. See "Buyers' Guide," *Nucleonics*, August 1962, p. 270.

44. Richard A. Tybout, *The Reactor Supply Industry*, Bureau of Business Research, Ohio State University, Columbus, 1960, Chap. 5.

For convenience, the two groups are identified in the lists below, derived from the *Nucleonics International Buyers' Guide* (1957–1962, inclusive), which gives most of the suppliers of nuclear power reactors:

Old-timers	Newcomers
Allis-Chalmers Mfg. Co.	ACF Industries, Inc. (absorbed by Allis-Chalmers, 1959)
Babcock and Wilcox Co.	
Combustion Engineering, Inc.	Aerojet-General Nucleonics
General Electric Co.	Alco Products, Inc.
Westinghouse Electric Corp.	American Machine & Foundry Co.
	American Radiator and Standard Sanitary Corp.
	General Dynamics Corp.
	General Nuclear Engineering Corp. (merged into Combustion Engineering, 1959)
	Lockheed Nuclear Products
	Martin Co.
	North American Aviation, Inc.
	Nuclear Development Corp. of America (merged into United Nuclear Corp.)
	United Nuclear Corp.
	Vitro Corp. of America

Interestingly, this classification suggests that the existence of a well-established trade position in equipment for conventional power stations is no guarantee of an unobstructed route to a corresponding trade position in nuclear power plants. The newcomers, in some instances equipped with large financial resources, are challenging the dominant position of the old-timers. Many of the challengers, however, have shown a lack of "survival power." In 1958 and 1959 a number of companies sharply curtailed their nuclear power activities (American Machine and Foundry Co.) or withdrew entirely (ACF Industries, Inc. and Bell Aircraft Co.). Still, the competitive rivalry among the remaining companies is sufficiently strong that none has a secure and dominant position. Any advantage that one company may have usually arises from previous contract work in development of a particular reactor design.

In order to gain a foothold in the market, several companies in both categories have been prepared to help pay the cost of the "first" reactor project undertaken jointly with a utility, or on contract with the AEC. In some instances this "price of admission," as it has been called among equipment manufacturers, has been high. For example, though General Electric's contribution to the Dresden, Illinois, plant of the Commonwealth Edison Co. has not been disclosed, it has been reported to be in the tens of millions.

Without this competitive willingness to contribute, the utilities might have been less inclined to commit such large capital sums to developmental projects—but not much less inclined, for capital formation occurs readily in large, publicly regulated private utilities, which are in a position to secure rate adjustments.

Industrial Cooperation and Forms of Organization

On both the national and international levels the competitive development of nuclear power has prompted a variety of forms of cooperation between industrial firms. These joint undertakings have arisen from the need to spread the costs of development, to combine complementary specialties and to distribute technology among interested companies. In the United States the principal forms of joint undertakings have been among the private utilities, some agreements involving as many as fifty companies each.[45] Among U. S. manufacturers of nuclear power equipment there has been much less use of joint undertakings in the domestic field. In the United Kingdom, however, the manufacturers are grouped into several consortia, in which each participant provides a complementary specialty.

In the United States electric utilities have found it desirable for the first time to expend large sums in developing a new technology. Heretofore the equipment manufacturers have carried on the research and engineering that have resulted in the steady and striking advances in fuel and thermal efficiencies marking the last few decades. Direct utility support of research and development may now have become a permanent industry pattern.

Another notable feature in the United States is that such industries as aluminum, iron and steel, etc., which require heat and power in large quantities, have been conspicuously uninterested in nuclear energy, despite the fact that these industries together use more energy than do the electric utilities. Since the energy-intensive industries are characteristically located where energy costs are lowest, one may infer that they will wait to see whether, in the long term, nuclear energy can reach comparable low costs.

The equipment manufacturers, seeking to develop the seemingly more promising foreign market, are entering into joint arrangements with foreign concerns, particularly in Western Europe, that are similar to those already established in electronics. The export of American technology is being accomplished by cross-licensing, by overseas subsidiary manufacturing and engineer-

45. All but a very small fraction of the private utilities in the United States are participants in nuclear power projects. (*Edison Electric Institute Bulletin*, March 1958, pp. 75–79.)

ing companies in which foreign concerns hold a large or equal interest or by other instruments, the essential feature being large utilization of foreign technical capabilities. One purpose is to offset the rather unpromising prospects for the export of comparatively high-cost United States equipment.

Such limited integration of U. S. companies as has occurred has been on horizontal rather than vertical lines. Thus far, only two companies (United Nuclear Corp. and the Vitro Corp.) have attempted to extend their activities over the entire chain of operations from the mining of ore to the manufacture and processing of fuel and the design and construction of reactors. Horizontal integration, rather than vertical, often results, perhaps because work in nuclear power is so costly that even the largest company has generally preferred nuclear activities which are closely allied to its existing work.[46] Also, there has been little expectation that vertical integration would provide any clear competitive advantages or cost savings. The antimonopoly and patent restraints of the statute, discussed in Chapter 5, help to assure competition. Yet, these are probably less significant than the inherent diversity and specialization of the industry as it emerges from the purely experimental phase.

GROWTH OF REACTOR ENTERPRISE. Many aspects of atomic energy, notably radioisotopes, electronic instruments and uranium mining, have led to the formation of numerous new enterprises, many of them rather small. Development of power reactor technology, however, has generally occurred by extension of existing giant corporations, able to supply the heavy investment required to develop reactor concepts to possible commercial usefulness. Such "commodity extension" represents, as in other similar historic examples (radio, television, plastics, etc.), a stage of corporate expansion in which "competition becomes a rivalry among organizations as well as a rivalry for particular markets."[47] What is occurring, then, is a competitive struggle in which the combatants are well established, financially powerful corporate giants, rather than new, small enterprises appearing with the emergence of nuclear power.

46. For example, General Mills decided to confine its activities to remote-handling equipment, in which it already had demonstrated its commercial capability, and fuel element fabrication, since this appeared most logically related to its conventional technical work. There is also evidence that companies which have chosen more ambitious participation, including the construction of full-scale nuclear power plants, though they have had no prior experience in power-plant engineering and construction, have been compelled to withdraw or reduce the scale of their activities in nuclear energy by concentrating on a more limited sector (e.g., AMF Atomics, a subsidiary of American Machine and Foundry Co., withdrew from large power reactor development).

47. Alfred R. Oxenfeldt, *New Firms and Free Enterprise*, American Council on Public Affairs, Washington, 1943, p. 48.

For public policy formation this fact may be important. It suggests that corporate strength may prove just as vital an element of survival power as technical excellence in determining the outcome of competition among the few. Also, it means that the forms of public assistance to private research and development, the form of patent controls established and the selection of contractors or subcontractors for particular reactor studies or projects by the AEC are all pertinent to the competitive posture of each major and minor equipment supplier in the field.

THE MERGER MOVEMENT (1958–1960). A variety of circumstances in nuclear development has led, during the last few years, to the merger of new, independent nuclear equipment suppliers with long-established companies.[48] While these mergers have reduced the number of companies in the business, the initial effect has been to broaden the scope of competition among the large power equipment suppliers. For example, the acquisition of General Nuclear Engineering Corp. by Combustion Engineering, Inc., meant that the latter, a leading supplier of boiler equipment, came into direct competition for the first time with General Electric and Westinghouse in supplying utility systems. General Nuclear, too, gained entry to the electric utility business that it would otherwise have had to win by fighting its way in against the dominant industry suppliers.

A further example: in 1959 Allis-Chalmers Manufacturing Co. acquired the nuclear engineering division of ACF Industries, Inc., a newcomer. A spokesman for ACF Industries said the division had been sold because "future rewards in the commercial reactor field will accrue principally to companies dominant in the power equipment industry."

Were it not for constraining public policy, set forth in the Atomic Energy Act, the major power equipment companies might well increase their present dominant positions by way of nuclear power development. Indeed, the concentrated structure of suppliers to the electric utilities underlies much of the public and congressional concern with the need for maintaining competition and avoiding further concentration. Three major manufacturers of turbo-generators—General Electric, Westinghouse, and Allis-Chalmers—account for all but a small part of the market; and low-cost foreign suppliers plus Department of Justice antitrust action are the major sources of competitive

---

48. Recent illustrations: General Nuclear Engineering Corp. acquired by Combustion Engineering, Inc.; merger of Sylvania Electric Products with General Telephone and Electronics Corp.; Metals and Controls Corp. merged with Texas Instruments (*Nucleonics*, February 1959, pp. 22–23.)

restraint on rising prices. These U. S. companies have a large new market to win (and none to lose) by developing nuclear power reactors to supply steam in place of conventional furnaces and boilers. On the other hand, the three dominant furnace-and-boiler manufacturers—Babcock and Wilcox, Combustion Engineering and Foster-Wheeler—realize that to survive they must develop and market nuclear power reactors and compete with the turbo-generator companies and, perhaps, with the newcomers in the field of nuclear power equipment.

Speculation about the outcome of this triangular contest of generator companies, steam producers and newcomers to the nuclear power equipment field is not idle. For a number of newcomers have already failed to survive and also the furnace-and-boiler manufacturers have been less successful thus far in securing power reactor contracts, here and abroad, than have the leading electrical equipment manufacturers. A long-drawn-out period of development would tax the survival power of the newcomers and steam generator manufacturers relatively more than that of the electrical equipment manufacturers. Failure to achieve competitive nuclear power soon, and by a broadly competitive industry, may lead to greater industrial concentration than now exists. The policy issue thereby raised is not too remote for practical consideration. Recent appeals for greater private patent privileges have stressed, as partial justification, the protection such privileges would give the small manufacturer who lacks an assured competitive position. This question is discussed further in Chapter 5.

Conclusion

Economic justification for a large, costly, accelerated nuclear power development program, such as that now engaging the United States, cannot be found in the present or prospective energy resources position of the United States. No other industrial nation is so favorably endowed. Rapidly rising energy and power demands can be met from conventional sources during the next couple of decades, and probably longer, at real costs not significantly higher than present costs. Among the various energy resources only petroleum reserves raise a question of domestic availability over the next few decades, and this issue has been gravely distorted by intrusion of badly defined national security considerations. The issue appears suspiciously like the age-old one of foreign competition in domestic markets, with national security arguments a convenient cloak. To a degree, the field for early use of nuclear power is being opened by policies artificially raising conventional energy prices rather than by physical need.

The private-vs.-public-power controversy has been the main cause of the interest of private utilities in power reactor projects. This motive is reinforced by the existence of strong political forces pressing toward higher fuel prices despite plentiful reserves. Further, the competitive structure of the power supply business has led the established manufacturers to make large investments in facilities. These actions have recently brought the leaders to a point of no return. Continued government assistance, pending more distant commercial feasibility, has become a necessary condition for recovering the investment already made. To understand how private utilities—probably much against their better judgment—and power equipment suppliers have become so heavily dependent on government assistance and subsidies to "stay in the game," it is necessary to assess the scale of federal resources and reactor development programs that are now available to achieve policy objectives and sustain a heavily committed industry.

CHAPTER **4**

U.S. Programs and Resources

A striking feature of the atom bomb project was the fact that, despite the prosecution of the war, the Manhattan District had at its disposal all the resources it could possibly need. Several years later, under the AEC, the same was true of the hydrogen bomb and plant expansion programs undertaken when the United States learned that the Soviet Union had the atom bomb and, more disquieting, had already made a start toward thermonuclear (hydrogen) weapons. Since about 1954 the civilian nuclear power program has also been well supplied with technical and material resources, though on a much smaller scale, to be sure. Policies have been the main restraint.

By 1960 an extraordinary economic situation had arisen: the vastly expanded nuclear resource base—in uranium output, fissionable material production, chemical processing facilities and nuclear energy laboratories—had become so great and the claims of civilian applications had proved to be so small that, as military stockpiles grew, a huge surplus of nuclear capacity appeared probable until 1970 at least.

Any major decline in military requirements over the next several years would raise serious questions about whether or not development of nuclear power should be strongly pushed to avoid intolerable waste of existing capacity. A policy issue for the present administration is whether the nation's nuclear power development programs have been and now are commensurate with national resources and with national objectives. Also it is necessary to judge

113

Figure 4-1   Energy Value of U. S. Fuel Reserves[a]

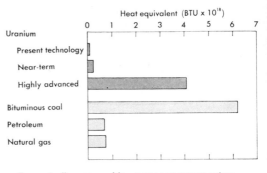

a. Economically recoverable at or near current prices.

Source: Table 4-3.

what the economic consequences of an early nuclear peace, or reduced international tension, might be for civilian nuclear power; whether prompt acceleration of reactor development could fill the gap of unused nuclear capacity; and to what extent AEC facilities could be shifted to private industry for civilian applications.[1]

Men, Money, Materials

The resource base of U. S. nuclear power effort is made up of: the materials production chain, from uranium mine to the stockpile of weapon components; the research and development personnel, facilities and activities of the AEC and its contractors; and the financial programs of the AEC and industry. Crude, yet sufficient, estimates of this resource base are available and do not infringe on restricted data. Statistics on the production of uranium, electric energy consumption and published estimates of fissionable material production are adequate for general economic analysis of policy questions. Similarly, research and development efforts can be gauged by numbers of scientific and technical workers. Moreover, the AEC's numerous programs can be reasonably well described by way of congressional appropriations and their allocation for operating and construction purposes.

1. We need hardly emphasize that description of the AEC's materials procurement and production and the research and development on types of military power reactors is hampered for security reasons by lack of unclassified information. Also, in the private sector, an atomic "industry" has not really developed, hence measurements of activity by the participating companies are still crude and fragmentary. Notwithstanding these obstacles, the available data seem sufficient to permit broad judgments of the atomic energy resource base and the current, comparative scale of reactor effort, public and private.

AEC Expenditures

The oft-mentioned $2 billion gambled on the atomic bomb project in World War II seems small now by current standards. By mid-1961 the atomic energy program represented a total investment of $26 billion—nine tenths of it committed since the war. Operating costs in fiscal year 1961 were $2.6 billion and construction costs were $433 million—one third the peak reached in 1954, when the AEC's expansion of gaseous diffusion capacity and production reactors was fully underway. The growth in AEC expenditures has been rapid, though they were less than 5 per cent of total expenditures on major national security programs in recent years. The size of the resultant weapon stockpile remains classified, of course, but the plant and equipment investment that made it possible is fully reported. In mid-1961 total plant investment was $7.7 billion, of which $2.4 billion was in gaseous diffusion plants for enriching uranium, $1.7 billion in materials production reactors and chemical separation plants, $869 million in weapon production and storage facilities and $1.8 billion in research facilities—$986 million in laboratories alone.[2]

The major nonmilitary AEC laboratories are listed in Table 4 1. The long-term utilization of these installations, with their scientific and technical personnel and their accumulation of science and technology, is an important problem of the immediate future, particularly as it relates to the question of the potential infringement of public activity on private opportunity. (See Chapter 10.)

Uranium and Thorium

Until the technology of thorium-U233 reactors is more fully established, the domestic reserves of thorium will remain of much less significance than those of uranium.[3] As a result of successful cooperative effort between industry and the AEC it has been possible to estimate uranium reserves with a relatively high degree of accuracy. Moreover, the supply curve as a function of cost is reasonably well known.[4]

2. AEC, *Major Activities in the Atomic Energy Programs, January–December 1961* (Annual Report), Washington, January 1962, pp. 501–40.

3. Exploration for domestic thorium ores has been less extensive than for uranium; while low-cost, known reserves are reasonably well established, they are still less than one tenth those of uranium—20,000 tons against 240,000 tons. The implication, one that has perhaps constrained thorium-U233 development, is that foreign supplies would be necessary for any large number of power reactors requiring thorium. (James A. Lane, "Economics of Nuclear Power," *Annual Review of Nuclear Science*, Annual Reviews, Palo Alto, Calif., 1959, p. 480.) In 1960 the AEC reaffirmed the estimate of 20,000 tons of ThO_2 in reserves recoverable at $10 per pound or less. (McKinney Review, *Background Material*, Vol. 4, pp. 1609–12.)

4. AEC, *Energy from Uranium and Coal Reserves*, Washington, May 1960, pp. 2–3.

TABLE **4 - 1**

Major Nonmilitary AEC Laboratories and Research Facilities[a]

Name, major operating contractor and location	Value of plant and equipment (millions) (1)	Scientific and engineering personnel (2)	Total staff (3)
Lawrence Radiation Laboratory, University of California, Livermore and Berkeley, Calif.	$163.7	1,624	5,800
Reactor and research facilities, Atomics International Div., North American Aviation, Inc., Canoga Park, Calif.	32.7	...	...
National Reactor Testing Station, Idaho			
Argonne National Laboratory	37.8		
General Electric Co.	58.9		
Phillips Petroleum Co.	192.1	210[b]	...
Westinghouse Electric Corp.	61.8		
Other	17.1		
Argonne National Laboratory, University of Chicago, Lemont, Ill.	214.0	844	3,600
Ames Laboratory, Iowa State University of Science and Technology, Ames, Iowa	15.8	233	423
Brookhaven National Laboratory, Associated Universities, Inc., Upton, Long Island, N. Y.	159.3	440	1,800
Knolls Atomic Power Laboratory, General Electric Co., Schenectady and West Milton, N. Y.	113.4	475[b]	2,180
University of Rochester Atomic Energy Project, University of Rochester, Rochester, N. Y.	5.7	100[b]	...
Bettis Atomic Power Laboratory, Westinghouse Electric Corp., Pittsburgh, Pa.	54.3	525[b]	3,600
Oak Ridge National Laboratory, Union Carbide Nuclear Co., Oak Ridge, Tenn.	209.7	1,562[b]	5,000

a. Includes completed plant, projects under construction and authorized projects as of June 30, 1961. The facilities are in most instances predominantly nonmilitary, but not exclusively so.

b. Data (from *Atomic Energy Facts*) as of March 31, 1956.

Sources:

Col. 1—AEC, *Major Activities in the Atomic Energy Programs, January–December 1961* (Annual Report), Washington, January, 1962, pp. 534 ff.

Cols. 2 and 3—*The Future Role of the Atomic Energy Commission Laboratories*, Joint Committee on Atomic Energy, 86th Cong., 2nd Sess., 1960, p. 156; and AEC, *Atomic Energy Facts*, Washington, 1957, pp. 37–47.

TABLE **4-2**

Energy Value of Low-Cost U. S. Uranium at Varying Rates of Utilization

| | Heat value measured in BTU X 10^{15} | | |
Utilization (megawatt-days per short ton of U)[a]	Known reserves of low-cost U (200,000 short tons)[b]	AEC receipts of domestic U in fiscal year 1962 (15,000 short tons)	"Years" of energy reserves[c]
"Present" technology—low utilization			
2,500	41	3	5
5,000	82	6	9
"Near-term" technology—with fuel recycle			
15,000	246	18	28
20,000	328	24	37
"Highly advanced" technology—breeding			
250,000	4,100	300	460

a. 1 megawatt-day $= 82$ X 10^6 BTU.

b. Reasonably assured reserves, recoverable at $8 to $10 per pound, 240,000 short tons of U_3O_8. U_3O_8 converted to U at 0.85.

c. Based on benchmark of current energy consumption by electric power plants: total U. S. energy consumption in 1960, 44.9 X 10^{15} BTU X .20 (the approximate fraction consumed as electricity) = 8.9 X 10^{15} BTU.

Sources: AEC, Energy from Uranium and Coal Reserves, Washington, May 1960: and AEC, Raw Materials Program, Hearings, Subcommittee on Raw Materials, Joint Committee on Atomic Energy, 87th Cong., 1st Sess., 1961, pp. 153–57.

"Economically recoverable reserves," defined as uranium oxide (U_3O_8) that can be mined and concentrated at $10 or less per pound, are estimated at almost 240,000 short tons. In world perspective these reserves are large, though not quite so large as those of Canada and South Africa. However, the AEC has estimated that, at these costs, known and inferred reserves may well be doubled by allowing for extension of existing ore zones and the probable discovery of new ore bodies in present or adjacent mineralized districts. Beyond this are the high-cost reserves, consisting of uranium in phosphates, shale and lignite, recoverable at costs up to $50 per pound, which would boost recoverable reserves to tenfold the current estimates.

Considering the available estimates of uranium requirements, the reserves are adequate for any nuclear power industry that is reasonably likely to develop over many decades.[5] The key question is not whether the reserves are adequate, but rather how efficiently reactor technology is able to use the low-cost material and, if need be at some future date, the slightly higher cost reserves. Indeed, whether material can be defined as "economically recoverable" depends rather more on how much energy can be extracted from it than on the cost of producing it.[6]

The estimated energy equivalents of uranium reserves demonstrate the crucial role of advances in nuclear fuel technology. Many theoretical examples of the great energy value of uranium assume a high degree of burn-up, but to achieve this objective is proving a difficult technical problem, considering the unrelenting economic constraints of competitive conventional fuel costs. In fact, before the known reserves of low-cost uranium can become a large addition to domestic energy supplies, great improvements in fuel technology need to be achieved. This is seen in Table 4–2, in which known U. S. reserves and 1962 production of uranium (equivalent to 15,000 short tons) have been converted into their heat value at various levels of fuel technology. For example, at the "current" level of technology 0.6 per cent of the uranium (roughly 5,000 megawatt-days per ton) can be burned; thus the heat value of 1962 uranium production was 6×10^{15} BTU. This was only 13 per cent of the heat value of total U. S. commercial energy consumption in 1960, and represents a small contribution, compared with coal, oil or gas.[7] However, if the degree of utilization can be increased greatly, by the recycle of by-product fuel and ultimately by breeding, the uranium output required to meet any foreseeable demand would represent only a small annual drain on the resource base and on economically recoverable uranium.

Clearly the game is hardly worth the candle unless the heat equivalent of our uranium reserves can be made to compare favorably with reserves of coal, oil and natural gas. The figures in Table 4–3 show that on the basis of "present" technology low-cost U. S. uranium reserves are small compared to oil or gas and quite insignificant compared to bituminous coal. In policy perspective, then, a primary reason for a vigorous reactor development program is to achieve an efficient use of uranium resources.

5. R. A. Laubenstein and Chauncey Starr, "The Availability of Uranium for a Nuclear Power Industry," Section 202 Hearings, 1960, pp. 660–76.

6. Walter H. Zinn reports, for example, that a doubling of fuel burn-up would permit a vast expansion of estimates of economically recoverable reserves, since it would make possible the use of uranium of twice the cost without affecting total nuclear power costs. (*Energy Resources and Technology*, Hearings, Joint Economic Committee, 86th Cong., 1st Sess., October 1959, pp.277–83.)

7. This is, of course, an oversimplified comparison; both recovered U235 and by-product plutonium would be significant additions to the energy value of natural uranium output.

TABLE **4 - 3**

Rough Comparison of Heat Equivalent of "Economically Recoverable" U. S. Reserves[a] of Uranium, Coal, Oil and Natural Gas

Fuel	Estimated "economically recoverable" reserves[a]	Heat equivalent (BTU X 10^{15})
Total, fossil fuels		7,650
Coal (bituminous)	237 billion short tons	6,200
Petroleum and liquid hydrocarbons	120 billion barrels	700
Natural gas	725 trillion cubic feet	750
Uranium	200,000 short tons	
Present technology		82
Near-term		246
Highly advanced		4,100

a. Reserves available at or near current prices.

Sources:
  Coal, petroleum and natural gas—McKinney Panel, Vol. 2, p. 74 (coal) and p. 94 (petroleum and natural gas).
  Uranium—Table 4–2 this study.

Uranium Supplies and Requirements

Available estimates of uranium consumption during the next two decades indicate that, even if progress in fuel efficiency should be disappointing, present U. S. uranium production capacity (about 18,000 tons of U_3O_8 a year) will certainly prove to be substantially greater than reasonably conceivable civilian requirements.

A careful estimate by the National Planning Association (1957) suggested that nuclear energy might contribute as much as 9 per cent of total U. S. energy consumption in 1980, or about 7 x 10^{15} BTU.[8] This would be approximately equal to the energy equivalent of the 18,000 tons of U_3O_8 produced in 1962, assuming 0.6 per cent utilization. However, it is unreasonable to project no technical progress in twenty years. By 1980 about 2.4 per cent burn-up rate (or 20,000 megawatt-days per ton) should be possible with fuel recycle, which would cut the uranium requirement roughly by three fourths (ignoring the growth in inventory needs). This suggests, rather crudely, that the probable

8. Perry D. Teitelbaum, *Nuclear Energy and the U. S. Fuel Economy, 1955–1980*, NPA, Washington, 1958, p. 57.

TABLE **4-4**

Projections of Natural Uranium Requirements, U. S. Civilian Nuclear Energy Plants, 1960–1980

	Short tons of $U_3 O_8$			
	AEC staff, 1955		AECL Canada, 1959	Lane (ORNL), 1959
	Optimistic	Conservative		
1960	1,310	350	1,150	
1965	2,550	685	3,850	
1970	22,100	5,925	9,000	2,400
1975	41,000	11,000		
1980				12,000

Sources:

AEC staff—McKinney Panel, Vol. 2, pp. 113–25.

AECL—S. W. Clarkson, *Uranium in the Western World*, Atomic Energy of Canada, Ltd., July 1959 (AECL No. 858).

Lane (ORNL)— J. A. Lane, "Economics of Nuclear Power," *Annual Review of Nuclear Science*, Annual Reviews, Palo Alto, Calif., 1959, Vol. 9, p. 479, Table IV.

rate of growth in civilian nuclear energy consumption, together with the probable technical progress, will be hardly likely to require the present rate of uranium production within the next decade or two. Civilian uranium requirements based on three other projections are compared in Table 4–4. The estimates of James A. Lane (ORNL) suggest that less than one seventh of present U. S. uranium capacity may be required for civilian purposes in 1970. Therefore, any major slackening of military requirements or of civilian reactor development, or the two together, would place the domestic uranium industry in most serious straits. The impact on other uranium-producing countries, particularly Canada, would be still greater after 1966, when their sales contracts with the United States expire.

AEC Procurement and Uranium Prices

Roughly 85 per cent of free world uranium produced up to 1960 was purchased by the United States and most of the balance went to the United Kingdom.[9] Moreover, the prices were largely determined by what the AEC would pay in order to meet military requirements. The average price has

9. *Atomic Energy Appropriations for 1958*, Hearings, Subcommittee of the House Committee on Appropriations, 85th Cong., 1st Sess., 1957, p. 47.

Figure 4-2   AEC Purchases of Natural Uranium

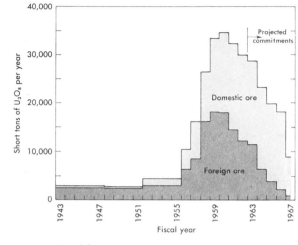

Source: Table 4-6.

tended to rise through the years until recently. Perhaps its lowest level pre-
vailed during World War II and for a time thereafter, when the Belgian Congo
Shinkolobwe mine was the most important source for the United States and
the Combined Development Agency. The AEC has clearly been paying incentive prices, certainly much higher than is necessary now to meet civilian requirements. Each AEC contract carries a unique price schedule under a
multiple price system, and the prices are not so high as they might be had
still higher cost sources been brought into production, such as, for example,
Florida phosphate at roughly $35 to $45 per pound of U_3O_8. Recently the
AEC has been paying $7.87 per pound for U. S. uranium oxide, $9.74 for
Canadian and $11.36 for overseas material. (See Table 4-5.) In the main the
domestic ore has been far richer (4.5 pounds of U_3O_8 per ton of ore) than the
Canadian (2.2 pounds per ton). Overseas ore, averaging only 0.7 pound per
ton, reflects the uranium that is a by-product of gold mining in South Africa.

The higher yield and lower cost of domestic ore and uranium has provided
major justification for the AEC's cutting foreign purchase commitments far
more drastically than the domestic, in the face of reduced uranium requirements for military production. (See Table 4-6.) This has softened the blow for
domestic mills and most of the mines, but has compelled foreign operators—
particularly the Canadian—to face the prospect of drastic curtailment likely
to result from a diminished military demand in the mid-1960s, long before
a substantial civilian demand can appear. One of the seldom-recognized, but

TABLE **4 - 5**

AEC Expenditures for Uranium (U_3O_8) and Average Prices Paid per Pound, by Source, Fiscal Years 1956–1963

Fiscal year	United States	Canada	Overseas	Total or average
		Expenditures (millions)		
1956	$101.3	$136.9		$238.2
1957	161.3	72.6	122.6	356.6
1958	196.0	204.1	156.5	556.6
1959	280.7	293.6	110.3	684.6
1960	293.4	296.8	109.9	700.0
1961	303.2	223.7	100.2	627.0
1962[a]	282.0	155.2	100.9	538.1
1963[a]	272.5	134.4	95.4	502.2
		Unit price per pound		
1956	$11.96	$10.94		$11.35
1957	10.64	10.78	11.78	11.03
1958	9.57	10.77	11.76	10.55
1959	9.26	10.87	11.84	10.27
1960	8.85	11.04	12.01	10.12
1961	8.54	10.91	11.78	9.72
1962[a]	8.19	10.02	11.54	9.18
1963[a]	7.87	9.74	11.36	8.84

a. Estimated.

Sources:

Fiscal years 1956 and 1957—AEC, *Financial Report*, Washington, 1957 and 1958.

Fiscal years 1958–1963—Annual hearings on atomic energy appropriations before the Subcommittee of the House Committee on Appropriations.

clear, reasons for accelerating reactor development is the need to support an orderly transition in the uranium production industry.

The curtailment in the AEC's foreign procurement has left producers of uranium in the rest of the free world without a continuing, substantial market.[10] And at the moment there is no substantial civilian market in sight to relieve the bleakness of the prospect until 1970, and probably later. Under

10. Current and immediately prospective uranium production rates are far above the "capacity" requirements of production reactors and gaseous diffusion plants. The requirements may be crudely estimated at 10,000 to 15,000 tons of U_3O_8. This is broadly deduced from the fact that the level of production activity at AEC facilities, measured by the annual rate of electric power consumption, has remained about at the level prevailing in 1955 and 1956, after the plant expansion

TABLE **4-6**

AEC Annual Purchases of Uranium, 1943–1960, and Annual Purchase Commitments, 1961 to Mid-1967, by Source

	Short tons of U_3O_8		
Fiscal year	Domestic	Foreign	Total
		Actual	
1943–1947 average	360	2,540	2,900
1948–1951 average	295	2,430	2,725
1952–1955 average	1,350	2,945	4,295
1956	4,200	6,240	10,440
1957	7,580	8,580	16,160
1958	10,250	16,130	26,380
1959	15,160	18,170	33,330
1960	16,566	18,015	34,581
		Projected purchase commitments	
1961	17,760	14,500	32,260
1962	17,820	12,105	29,925
1963	17,300	11,300	28,600
1964	16,900	6,210	23,110
1965	16,000	3,805	19,805
1966	16,000	2,100	18,100
1967 (first half)	8,000	800	8,800

Sources:

Actual—AEC Release B-166, Washington, September 23, 1959; *Public Works Appropriations for 1962, Hearings, Subcommittee of the House Committee on Appropriations, 87th Cong., 1st Sess., 1961, p. 1044.*

Projected—*AEC Raw Materials Program, Hearings, Subcommittee on Raw Materials, Joint Committee on Atomic Energy, 87th Cong., 1st Sess., 1961, p. 157.*

Footnote 10 continued
program was fully completed. Uranium procurement then was reported at 10,440 tons (in fiscal year 1956). Therefore, with AEC procurement, domestic and foreign, recently at more than 35,000 tons annually, a huge surplus of uranium procurement and of U_3O_8 production capacity therefore exists to meet any conceivable expansion of military requirements as well as of civilian nuclear power capacity.

A crude computation shows that the projected 17,000 tons of U_3O_8 per year domestic procurement by the AEC in the mid-1960s is sufficient to supply the nuclear fuel required for approximately 145 million kw. of power capacity—or about two thirds of present total generating capacity in the United States. (Calculation: assume 6,000 mw.-days per ton of U metal, 0.85 ton U per ton of U_3O_8, 35 per cent thermal efficiency and 5,000 hours per year plant factor. Then, 0.85 x 17,000 tons U_3O_8 x 6 x 10^3 mw.-days per ton x 24 x 10^3 tKWH x 0.35 efficiency for 5,000 hours = 145 x 10^6 ekw. at 57 per cent average plant factor.)

the circumstances the world price of uranium may decline drastically—from the fiscal year 1963 range of $7.87 to $11.36 per pound (see Table 4–5) to something like $5 or $6 per pound after the mid-1960s, when accelerated plant amortization will permit uranium prices which exclude plant costs.[11] The decline in the prices paid after 1955 and the prospect of further reduction were among the factors that encouraged the AEC to reduce sharply the prices of enriched uranium in 1961. That action also helped to avoid putting U. S. reactor technology at a disadvantage compared with natural uranium reactors. A unique feature of uranium fuel is the strong probability that its price, contrary to that of all other energy sources, will decline sharply over the next decade. Thus, looking at economically recoverable reserves and prospective prices, the United States possesses in its uranium a tremendous resource base, assuming the expected technical advances, and one that will be available at decreasing cost for many years.

Fissionable Material Production Capacity

In fiscal year 1962 the United States spent $538 million for uranium procurement at home and abroad, and almost $527 million for the production of nuclear materials—chiefly enriched uranium and plutonium. Together these represented one half of the AEC's total operating expenses in that year. Expenditures for fissionable material, however, fail to reflect the scale of activity, as does the consumption of electric energy—which for several years has exceeded 5 per cent of total U. S. power consumption. Most of the 57 billion KWH of power consumed by the AEC in 1960 at a cost of roughly 3.8 mills per KWH, was used by the uranium enrichment plants at Oak Ridge (Tennessee), Paducah (Kentucky) and Portsmouth (Ohio).[12] With the plant expansion

11. In fiscal year 1965 the AEC is scheduled to pay the following "contract prices" per pound for U_3O_8: domestic, $8.02; Canadian, $10.35; overseas, $12.00. (Section 202 Hearings, 1960, p. 275.) Current prices have already declined below those projected.

12. FPC, "Electric Energy Purchased, Generated and Used in Major Atomic Energy Commission Installations," Washington, 1960 (multilith).

Part of the uranium supply goes to the production reactors for the synthesis of plutonium and part goes to the gaseous diffusion plants for the separation of U235 from U238. The diffusion plant is, in effect, a series of screens through which the gaseous uranium is pumped to separate the heavier atoms from the lighter. It is possible to get a desired output of enriched uranium, within certain limits, by feeding in more natural uranium or applying more separation effort (power for pumping) to a smaller amount of uranium. The primary considerations, therefore, are the relative costs of additional power and of additional natural uranium. There is some freedom of choice, therefore, in the manner of meeting requirements for U235. Natural uranium requirements for sustained operation of the plants could be set much lower than procurement schedules suggest.

For example, the July 1957 testimony of AEC General Manager Fields and the staff of the AEC suggested that, with existing plant capacity, additional U235 might be secured more economically by using additional power, considering the amount and cost of uranium that was then available (*Atomic Energy Appropriations for 1958*, p. 67).

program following the Soviet atom bomb test, the AEC consumption of power rose from only 5.5 billion KWH in 1951 to a peak of 60.7 billion KWH in 1956.

In terms of energy resources, however, the "value" of fissionable material production capacity must be judged in physical units of output, rather than in dollars or in the use of electric power for processing.

Reactor Fuel Availability

If present fissionable material production plants were, in due course, to be devoted to peaceful ends, what might the current capacity produce? Actual capacity to produce enriched uranium and plutonium in weapon grades is highly classified. However, crude estimates, sufficient to indicate the order of magnitude involved, have been made by qualified scientists. These estimates serve to indicate a huge capacity to produce nuclear fuel for both military and peaceful purposes.

The AEC's annual capability in enriched uranium has been estimated by Karl Cohen, on the basis of published information, at roughly 70,000 kilograms of U235 in 90 per cent enriched material.[13] This is equivalent to approximately 17,000 short tons of uranium enriched to 1.5 per cent, a concentration commonly assumed for reactor fuel. The most optimistic projections of enriched fuel requirements (inventory plus burn-up) in the United States and Western Europe during the 1960s amount to only a fraction of AEC capacity. Not until after 1980 does it appear that 17,000 tons annually might prove insufficient to meet expanding civilian requirements.

In contrast, the AEC's plutonium production capacity is at present of only incidental significance, for, lacking appropriate technology, this material is potentially—but not yet actually—useful as power reactor fuel. But since plutonium-burning technology is being developed, it can be expected in time to complement the use of enriched uranium.

The AEC's plutonium output may be estimated as not less than several thousand kilograms yearly. Public information indicates that the United States has thirteen operable materials production reactors (excluding the New Production Reactor)—eight graphite-moderated, at Hanford, Washington; and five heavy water–moderated, on the Savannah River, South Carolina.[14] In the absence of specific data on their heat output one may use the average

13. "Charting a Course for Nuclear Power Development," *Nucleonics*, January 1958, pp. 66–70.

14. AEC, *Major Activities in the Atomic Energy Programs, January–December, 1961*, (Annual Report), Washington, January 1962, p. 478.

figure of 1,000 megawatts per reactor, reported in the published literature.[15] The conversion ratios (units of fissionable material produced to those destroyed) for most thermal light water reactors fall around 0.8;[16] also, very roughly one gram of fissionable material is burned in producing one megawatt-day (heat). Therefore, on these skeleton assumptions the plutonium production rate may be crudely estimated as being at least 4,000 kilograms annually.[17]

These estimates, crude as they are, provide quantitative insight into a number of pertinent questions concerning nuclear fuel supplies and the respective importance of U235 and plutonium as energy sources directly controlled by the government.

The AEC capacity for highly enriched uranium is many times greater than for plutonium, hence government pricing policies for nuclear fuel are determined more by costs of producing U235 than by public or private output of plutonium.[18] Obviously, on technical and economic grounds, the foreseeable civilian demand for nuclear fuel would not justify expanding government-owned capacity for producing plutonium.

U. S. enriched uranium capacity is apparently so great compared to the capacities of the United Kingdom and the USSR[19] that the United States has an advantage, civilian and military, in supplying friendly foreign countries with nuclear fuel (and weapon material, if desirable).

Production of nuclear weapons at the indicated rate of tens of thousands annually[20] should soon raise such questions as the marginal utility of further

15. See, for example, Sylvania-Corning Nuclear Corp., *Nuclear Fuels: Key to Reactor Performance*, Bayside, N. Y., 1958, p. 9. The average may be somewhat higher, since the average cost of the Savannah River reactors was 55 per cent more than that of the Hanford reactors. A capacity of 2,000 megawatts per reactor for Savannah has been estimated by Marvin Kalkstein and Winthrop Smith, "An Estimate of the Nuclear Stockpile from Unclassified Sources," *Arms Reduction: Program and Issues* (David H. Frisch, ed.), Twentieth Century Fund, New York, 1961, p. 92.

16. *Nuclear Engineering Handbook*, McGraw-Hill, New York, 1958, p. 12–23, Table 11.

17. Computation: 13 reactors @ 1,000 tmw. = 13,000 tmw. capacity
    13,000 tmw. x 360 days = 4.7 x 10^6 mw.-days
    Burn-up: 1 gr. U235 = 1 mw.-day = 4.7 x 10^6 gr. U235
    Conversion U235 to Pu: @ 0.8 = 3,800 kg. Pu

Kalkstein and Smith, *op. cit.*, have made a somewhat higher estimate, 5,400 kg. annually, reflecting the much higher assumed power level for the Savannah River reactors.

18. Note that fuel-grade plutonium produced in privately owned nuclear power plants will in time approach the roughly estimated rate of weapon-grade plutonium being produced in AEC reactors. In 1959 AEC projected plutonium output of domestic power reactors fueled with U. S. enriched uranium as totaling 3,300 kg. in 1968. (*AEC Authorizing Legislation, Fiscal Year 1960*, Hearings, Subcommittee on Legislation, Joint Committee on Atomic Energy, 86th Cong., 1st Sess., 1959, p. 680.)

19. See *The Manchester Guardian*, February 27, 1956.

20. On the conjecture that 5 to 10 kg. of fissionable material are required for a nuclear weapon. NPA, *The Nth Country Problem and Arms Control*, A Statement by the NPA Special Project Committee on Security through Arms Control, Washington, January 1960, p. 4.

stockpiling and possible "higher uses" of such vast resources and expenditures. In this long phase of "nuclear plenty," it is necessary to ask when civilian needs might begin to supplement military requirements as a use for these resources.

Finally, allocation by the President of 165,000 kilograms of U235 for domestic and overseas civilian use is within production capacity for both military and civilian purposes, since the need will be spread over several years.

As to plutonium, certain inferences for civilian power are clear: Plutonium has no assured economic use as fuel. Furthermore, present weapon-grade plutonium production is large, in terms of implied numbers of weapons, even though it is small compared with estimated U235 output. It is also large when compared with immediately foreseeable by-product plutonium production in civilian power reactors. (Roughly 10 million electric kilowatts of nuclear power capacity, not expected until 1975, would be required to produce corresponding quantities of plutonium.) Finally, the AEC may well consider the economic desirability of meeting a substantial part of its long-term military requirements for plutonium from the by-product output in civilian reactors. The AEC's cost of producing plutonium, as prime product, in its own reactors is clearly far higher than the cost when produced as joint product with electric power.[21]

The Power Reactor Program

The major economic influences that have determined the structure of the U. S. program have been the confused mixture of private and public efforts, the extraordinary variety of commercially promising reactor concepts, the tendency of major manufacturers to secure product differentiation by concentrating on particular reactor types and the early subordination of civilian to military development. A few key figures should suffice, at this point, to illustrate these relationships.[22]

As of June 30, 1961, the AEC had invested $2.5 billion in research and development activities associated with reactor development and had committed

21. The current fuel-value price of $9.50 per gr. of plutonium, based on its value as an alternative to U235, is far less than the AEC's cost of production as indicated by weapon-grade prices. It represents a price that had already been reduced sharply (from $12.00 per gr.), along with reduction in mid-1961 of the excessive prices set on enriched uranium. See Chapter 5 for fuller discussion of pricing policy. Following the U235 price reduction in mid-1962 the AEC placed the near-term value of fuel-grade plutonium at "not less than $8.00 per gram."

22. The figures are derived mainly from AEC, *Major Activities in the Atomic Energy Programs, January–December 1961* (Annual Report), Washington, January 1962, pp. 501–40. See also Section 202 Hearings, 1962, pp. 501–40.

TABLE **4-7**

Cost Summary, AEC Reactor Development Program, Cumulative Through June 30, 1961

Purpose	Research and development costs[a]		Total authorized capital costs	
	Amount (millions)	Per cent	Amount (millions)	Per cent
Total	$2,463.6	100.0	$784.1	100.0
Civilian	470.9	19.1	202.3	25.8
Civilian nuclear power	457.1	18.5	181.9	23.2
Merchant ships	13.8	.6	20.4	2.6
Military	1,341.9	54.5	350.5	44.7
Army	45.4	1.8	12.3	1.6
Aircraft	472.4	19.2	54.1	6.9
Missile propulsion	132.1	5.4	39.6	5.0
Naval	650.3	26.4	238.0	30.4
Auxiliary power[b]	41.7	1.7	6.5	.8
General nuclear technology and support[c]	650.8	26.4	231.3	29.5

a. Includes AEC depreciation charges.

b. Satellite and small power sources.

c. Costs are believed to be divided about equally between military and civilian effort.

Source: AEC, *Major Activities in the Atomic Energy Programs, January-December 1961* (Annual Report), Washington, January 1962, p. 509.

or authorized $0.8 billion more for construction, while private industry had undertaken the construction of privately financed projects at an estimated cost of $300 million. In addition, private industry was contributing some $245 million to "cooperative power reactor projects," mainly for construction. Thus, government and private industry have been deeply committed in a mixed relationship that is, strictly, neither "private" nor "public," as these terms are customarily used.

Despite strong incentives for concentrating on only a few types of reactor technology, the AEC at the end of 1961 was still supporting eight lines of civilian power reactors, each entailing tens of millions of dollars in research and development and construction. In each of these concepts a particular company had a predominant interest. Thus, multifarious technology has combined with corporate competition and the luxury of large resources to maintain a broad development program.

Figure 4-3   Distribution of Effort, AEC Nuclear Power Development, through June 30, 1961

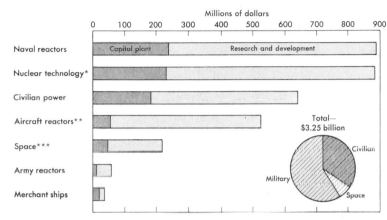

*Probably less than one half for civilian nuclear power.   ** Aircraft Nuclear Propulsion Program discontinued in 1961.   *** Satellite and small power sources; missile and space propulsion.

Source: AEC, Annual Report for 1961, p. 509.

Reflecting the cold-war orientation of the atomic energy program, nearly two thirds of all research and development and construction costs of the AEC reactor program, to June 30, 1961, were committed to military categories. (See Table 4–7.) This seeming neglect of the civilian program caused unpublicized resentment among a number of reactor manufacturers who had been hurt by the lack of new business. They felt that civilian development was being needlessly constrained by excessive "noninterference" policies based on unfounded fears of hampering the naval reactor and missile programs.[23] In fact, however, the expenditure program for civilian development was held in check not by competing military needs but by the AEC's policy (1954–1960) of having the electric utilities, rather than the government, decide what development plants to build.

23. The fear that an accelerated civilian program might hurt the emerging missile program was implied in the findings and recommendations of the McKinney Panel, 1956. (See in particular the section on manpower, pp. 117 ff., Vol. 1.)

Civilian Nuclear Power in Retrospect

Reactor technology for peaceful uses, as it exists today in the United States but not in the United Kingdom, began with the graphite-moderated reactors for production of weapon-grade plutonium and was continued to the pressurized water reactors, fueled with enriched uranium, for submarine propulsion. Later, as the influence of military application diminished, a multiplicity of technically feasible reactor concepts, uncovered even before the end of the war, became the subject of intensive development.[24]

In addition to natural uranium, graphite-moderated reactors, scientists of the Manhattan Engineer District, during its wartime operations, explored the possibilities of various other reactors. But none of these investigations could be pressed during the MED days, beyond experimental units. The state of the technology scarcely warranted more than "paper" studies of design and fuel concepts. Nevertheless, an extensive knowledge of reactor design and fuel technology was accumulated. Indeed, "by the end of the war there had been built, operated, or studied by people within the United States atomic energy program nearly every kind of reactor that anyone has ever thought of, then or since."[25]

Immediately after the war the MED elected to pursue the wartime research on power reactors by establishing programs to develop a gas-cooled pile for central station power, nuclear propulsion of naval vessels and nuclear energy propulsion for aircraft (NEPA). When the AEC took over, on January 1, 1947, the formidable problems confronting each of these programs were soon recognized. The first project was canceled and the other two were reduced to "holding" operations. In fact, the AEC was so preoccupied with the problems of fissionable materials and of weapon production that it did not have even an outline of a reactor program until 1948.

In the main the AEC civilian reactor development activities in this period were of a third order of urgency. Not until private industry in 1950 and the Joint Committee in 1952 began to urge wider outside participation in reactor development was a notable change made in the program—one that presaged the new Atomic Energy Act of 1954.

In 1951 the AEC invited industry to conduct studies of the technical and economic feasibility of dual-purpose reactors to produce both power and

24. This brief historical section draws on the illuminating, nontechnical review of power development by Oliver Townsend, "The Atomic Power Program in the United States," *Atoms for Power: United States Policy in Atomic Energy Development*, The American Assembly, Columbia University, New York, 1957.

25. *Ibid.*, pp. 45–46.

weapon-grade plutonium. At the start of the so-called "industry participation program," four industry groups[26] took part and submitted studies suggesting some optimism about overcoming the technical and cost obstacles to nuclear power. In 1952 more than twenty-five additional groups were making feasibility studies and a number recommended that the AEC join with industry in the development and construction of dual-purpose reactors.

Premature though the study groups now appear, they compelled fresh congressional and AEC appraisal of reactor development and the degree of industry participation. This led, in 1953, to AEC formulation of a policy for reactor development that did not depend on government purchases of plutonium and that called for major modification of the 1946 McMahon Act, to allow private ownership and operation of reactors under suitable safeguards. While the Commission was prepared, in terms of policy, to launch a substantial civilian power program in 1953, the funds were not available to proceed. Early in 1953 the new administration eliminated the funds for the aircraft carrier reactor and the nuclear-powered aircraft. The military requirements were withdrawn by the Department of Defense, and the National Security Council disapproved the funds for the proposed sodium-graphite experimental reactor on the assumption that the private utility industry was prepared to develop nuclear power. At this point the Joint Committee on Atomic Energy intervened, as it has many times during the AEC's history, to permit the AEC to continue the work on the pressurized water reactor for central station generation and the development work on sodium graphite.

In 1953 the Joint Committee, recognizing the indefiniteness of the reactor development effort, virtually demanded (and in February 1954 received) from the AEC the first formal statement of the Commission's reactor development program.[27] It was a five-year, five-reactor program covering the period 1954 through 1958 and included: a pressurized water reactor (formerly the aircraft carrier reactor dropped by the Department of Defense) being developed by Westinghouse; an experimental boiling water reactor, developed at Argonne to explore the direct circulation of heat produced by the reactor; a sodium-cooled, graphite reactor, developed by North American; an advanced experimental breeder reactor, scaled up from the one first generating power at the Reactor Testing Station in Idaho in 1951; and an advanced experimental

26. Detroit Edison and Dow Chemical; Commonwealth Edison and Northern Illinois Public Service; Monsanto Chemical and Union Electric; and Pacific Gas and Electric and the Bechtel Corporation.

27. *Report of the Subcommittee on Research and Development on the Five-Year Power Reactor Development Program Proposed by the Atomic Energy Commission*, Joint Committee on Atomic Energy, 83rd Cong., 2nd Sess., March 1954.

homogeneous reactor, scaled up from that operated at Oak Ridge in 1953. Since its "command" formulation in 1954, the AEC's experimental program has been augmented by numerous other reactor experiments, already mentioned in Chapter 2.

Following the 1954 five-year reactor development program the AEC established the "power demonstration program" in 1955, inviting both the private and public sectors to submit proposals for joint development projects (see section on "Cooperative Power Reactor Projects," below). At the same time two utility groups proposed to go ahead independently, and both have since completed full-scale reactors—the Dresden Station in Morris, Illinois, owned by Commonwealth Edison Co.; and the Indian Point Unit in Buchanan, New York, owned by Consolidated Edison Co. of New York.

Meanwhile, navy and other military power reactors have come into use on a growing and impressive scale. Besides the two original submarines, the *Nautilus* (1954) and the *Seawolf* (1956), more than sixty-four submarines and other vessels have been constructed or are being built (end of 1961). Development of aircraft propulsion reactors for the Air Force has been much more difficult; plans for a flying test were repeatedly postponed and in 1961 were shelved. A number of reactors, too, have been developed for specialized army use, such as, in the Arctic and Antarctic, on the Distant Early Warning line and for propulsion of land vehicles. Also, the Maritime Commission has pushed through to completion the construction of a nuclear-powered merchant ship, the *Savannah* (1961). Virtually all these power reactors are of the pressurized water type. Finally, the AEC has underway a number of nuclear rocket and space propulsion experiments, and the greatest increases in AEC expenditures for power reactor development over the next few years are planned in these applications.

Implications of the History

Even from so brief a history of reactor development as this, some implications and conclusions are clear:

The civilian power "program" was long lacking in clear direction and motivation and did not get substantial administration support until almost a decade after World War II. Also, while giving full weight to the technical and economic obstacles encountered, one is struck by the slow progress of the civilian program as contrasted with the manifest success of the naval propulsion program, where institutional considerations have been absent.

The general research and development resources of the AEC laboratories have been so great that it has been possible and seemingly desirable to explore a large number of reactor designs—in widely varying degrees, to be sure. Spreading financial and technical resources among eight or more reactor designs has, until very recently, resulted in insufficient attention to long-term designs that may be especially promising, for example, in foreign economies. Among these are reactors using natural uranium, plutonium or thorium and also gas-cooled reactors. Belatedly, the AEC recognized that the diversity of approaches was not, in fact, providing a systematic coverage of the major possibilities—perhaps understandable considering the scores of promising, technically feasible reactor designs. At the same time, in plans for building prototype and full-scale reactors, excessive reliance may have been placed on the technology already developed successfully for naval propulsion.

The technical obstacles apparent when the 1954 act was passed have proved more difficult than expected. Solving the problems of neutron economy, of heat transfer and removal, of reactor control and of chemical processing of fuel, including waste disposal, is still difficult—as in 1954.[28] Seemingly, too, the period of prototype construction and experimentation before full-scale demonstration of most of the reactor concepts can be successfully undertaken has proved longer than expected.

Finally, a few reactor types (boiling water and pressurized water) have now been brought to the stage of full-scale demonstration, and much more operating experience should be forthcoming during the next few years. However, plant demonstration has fallen behind the state of reactor technology, according to the AEC. Progress toward prototype demonstration of other and more advanced reactor systems—pebble bed, molten salt, etc.—is considered important by reactor scientists, since it may take a considerably longer period before the cost characteristics of these can be known.

Shared Private and Public Responsibility

In the cooperative effort of industry and government, set up in 1954, the AEC was expected to furnish most of the basic technology and pilot-plant testing. It was hoped that industry would build larger prototype plants, but the AEC offered certain financial assistance, if necessary. The private utility industry was expected to build full-scale plants on its own with no direct government assistance or subsidy. In practice these lines of shared responsibility became mixed, yet the basic distinctions remained. The private and governmental expenditure rates best reveal both the scale and the blurred division of labor.

28. See Henry DeWolf Smyth, "The Development of Nuclear Power for Peaceful Purposes," remarks before the American Institute of Chemical Engineers, Washington, March 9, 1954, for an outline of the general problems confronting power reactor development at that time.

THE AEC GENERAL RESEARCH ACTIVITIES. Most of the nation's reactor technology is still based at AEC installations—the experimental reactor sites and the national laboratories.[29] By June 30, 1961, the AEC had invested $651 million in "general" reactor development (military and civilian) and this represented one fourth of all its reactor research and development costs. (See Table 4–7.) Under the heading of "general" are included the laboratory efforts that cannot be readily associated with specific reactor concepts. Among them are such thorny research topics as reactor fuels and materials development, reactor safety, fuel element reprocessing systems and waste storage and disposal systems. To be sure, substantial industrial effort has been directed toward this work, but the major responsibility and initiative have been with the AEC laboratories.

Figure 4-4   AEC Cooperative Power Reactor Program—Shared Costs, to June 30, 1961

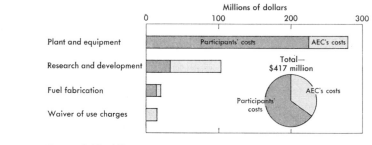

Source: Table 4-9.

EXPERIMENTAL POWER REACTOR PROJECTS. Except for two experimental plants—a General Electric plant at Pleasanton, California, and a Saxton Nuclear Corporation plant at Saxton, Pennsylvania—all of the experimental power units have been built as government-owned projects—under contracts with industry or the universities—rather than on government force-account. A major "experiment" is the full-scale pressurized water reactor, built by Westinghouse Electric Corp. at Shippingport, Pennsylvania, for the AEC and the Duquesne Light Co. The latter gave $5 million toward the construction of the reactor, provided the nonnuclear facilities and buys the reactor heat. Other government-owned experimental projects, all smaller than Shippingport, are shown in Table 4–8. The cost of each experimental facility except

29. In fiscal year 1961 the distribution of AEC reactor development funds, totaling $425 million, was as follows: to industry, $113 million; AEC laboratories, $303 million; and the small balance was to universities and other nonprofit organizations (AEC, Annual Report for 1961, p. 32).

TABLE **4 - 8**

AEC Experimental Civilian Power Projects (Government-Owned), February 1962

Name, contractor and location	Net power output (ekw.)	Start-up dates		Total costs—1962 estimate (millions)
		First criticality	At design power	
Built				
EBR-1, Argonne National Laboratory, NRTS, Idaho Falls, Idaho	150	1949	1951	$2.7
EBWR, Argonne National Laboratory, Lemont, Ill.	4,000	1956	1957	5.9
SRE, Atomics International, Inc., Santa Susana, Calif.	6,000	1957	. . .	7.6
OMRE, Atomics International, Inc., Reactor Testing Station, Idaho	16,000[a]	1957	1957	2.6
Shippingport Atomic Power Station, Duquesne Light Co., Shippingport, Pa.	60,000	1957	. . .	75.2
PRTR, General Electric Co., Hanford, Wash.	70,000[a]	1960	. . .	. . .
LAMPRE, Los Alamos Scientific Laboratory, Los Alamos, N. Mex.	1,000[a]	1960	. . .	. . .
Being built				
HWCTR, E. I. du Pont de Nemours & Co., Savannah River, S. C.	61,000[a]	1962	. . .	. . .
EBR-2, Argonne National Laboratory, NRTS, Idaho Falls, Idaho	16,500	1961	1962	65.6
Borax V, Argonne National Laboratory, NRTS, Idaho Falls, Idaho	2,650	1962	1962	3.6
EOCR, Atomics International, Inc., NRTS, Idaho Falls, Idaho	40,000[a]	1962	1963	14.1
EGCR, Kaiser Engineers—ACF Industries, Inc., Oak Ridge, Tenn.	22,300	1963	1964	72.8
MSRE, Oak Ridge National Laboratory, Oak Ridge, Tenn.	5,000[a]- 10,000[a]	1964	. . .	. . .

a. Thermal kilowatts.

Sources: AEC, *Major Activities in the Atomic Energy Programs, January-December 1961* (Annual Report), Washington, January 1962, pp. 457 ff.; Section 202 Hearings, 1962, pp. 585 ff,

TABLE **4 - 9**

AEC Cooperative Power Reactor Projects, Summary of Cost Participation, June 30, 1961[a]

	Millions		
	Total	AEC assistance[b]	Participants' costs
Total estimated costs	$417.2	$146.2	$271.0
Per cent of total	100.0	35.0	65.0
Research and development	$102.8	$70.4	$32.4
Plant, equipment and land	280.2	55.8	224.4
Fuel fabrication	19.6	5.4	14.2
Waiver of use charges	14.6	14.6	—

a. Total estimated costs of projects approved under the cooperative program as of June 30, 1961 (ten projects totaling 526, 473 ekw.). The cumulative expenditures for these projects through June 30, 1961 were: AEC assistance, $102.5 million; participants', $181.7 million. Data for privately and publicly owned projects are shown separately in Table 4-10, as of February 1962.

b. Includes estimated costs for five years after reactor operation begins.

Source: AEC, *Major Activities in the Atomic Energy Programs, January-December 1961* (Annual Report), Washington, January 1962, pp. 510–11.

Shippingport has been small in comparison with the cost of the usual prototype. Moreover, the AEC experimental program has been judged successful in advancing the art, as well as in revealing major technical problems, such as the corrosion encountered in the homogeneous fluid fuel reactor (HRE-2) at Oak Ridge National Laboratory.

COOPERATIVE POWER REACTOR PROJECTS. Tables 4–9 and 4–10 summarize the expenditures for cooperative arrangements that were established under the first three "rounds" of the power reactor demonstration program. Supporters of the AEC have defended the program as a far-sighted method of providing government assistance and avoiding federal nuclear power. Critics have struck at the lack of progress and the interminable negotiations that have marked an overly complicated relationship. Detached evaluation indicates that both views are justified. The cooperative program did succeed in bypassing federal power generation and encouraged private development—though it did so at a penalty, in delay and in ultimate cost. The program is described as

TABLE **4 - 10**

The AEC Cooperative Power Reactor Demonstration Program, February 1962

Project	Net capacity (ekw.)	Start-up dates		Estimated costs (millions)		
		First criticality	At design power	Total	AEC costs	Partici-pants' costs
First round						
Yankee Atomic Electric Co., Rowe, Mass.	141,000	Aug. 1960	June 1961	$46.0	$5.0	$40.9
Consumers Public Power District, Hallam, Nebr.	76,000	June 1962	Aug. 1962	70.1	49.5	20.6
Power Reactor Development Co., Lagoona Beach, Mich.	60,900	Fall 1962	May 1963	89.5	3.6	85.9
Second round						
Rural Cooperative Power Assn., Elk River, Minn.	22,000	. . .	. . .	12.4	10.8	1.6
City of Piqua, Piqua, Ohio	11,400	July 1962	Sept. 1962	13.5	13.3	.1
Puerto Rico Water Re-sources Authority, Punta Higuera, P. R.	16,300	July 1963	Aug. 1963	17.0	12.9	4.1
Third round						
Carolinas-Virginia Nuclear Power Assn., Parr, S. C.	16,900	Aug. 1962	Nov. 1962	33.2	10.1	23.0
Consumers Power Co., Big Rock Point, Mich.	47,800	Sept. 1962	Oct. 1962	32.7	3.2	29.5
Northern States Power Co., Sioux Falls, S. D.	62,000	Nov. 1962	Mar. 1963	33.6	7.5	26.1
Philadelphia Electric Co., Peach Bottom, Pa.	40,000	June 1964	Dec. 1964	49.6	12.5	37.1

Sources: AEC, *Major Activities in the Atomic Energy Programs, January-December 1961* (Annual Report), Washington, January 1962, pp. 457 ff.; Section 202 Hearings, 1962, pp. 585 ff.

a success by the private electric utility industry, but a failure by groups that have urged an accelerated attack and have been less constrained by federal power considerations. The AEC has also held that the program saved substantial public funds through greater private investment.[30] However, the schedule of original and current starting dates shows that long delays have hampered most of the projects. Furthermore, the cooperative program has

TABLE **4-11**

Estimated Expenditures of Privately Owned Electric Utility Companies for Nuclear Power Projects Through 1963

	Millions			
Year	Cumulative	Total	Expenditures on specific projects[a]	Other expenditures[b]
1957 and earlier	$79.8	$79.8	$73.0	$6.8
1958	134.8	55.0	50.3	4.7
1959	236.6	101.8	98.5	3.3
1960	342.7	106.1	103.1	3.0
1961	432.8	90.1	84.1	6.0
1962	487.4	54.6	47.9	6.7
1963	520.5	33.1	27.0	6.1

a. Expenditures for research, development and construction of plants under construction or under contract or in contract negotiation. These projects include fifteen plants. Operating expenditures are excluded.

b. Expenditures of twelve utility study groups not associated with specific projects.

Source: Statement of Edison Electric Institute submitted to the Joint Committee on Atomic Energy, giving the estimated expenditures on twenty-seven power reactor projects and study groups, in which 131 utilities are participants (Section 202 Hearings, 1962, p. 509).

proved an administratively awkward instrument for giving public power systems participation in nuclear power development. Indeed, the demand for this after the program's first round compelled the AEC to provide a second round, emphasizing smaller reactors useful in cooperative and municipal systems. Yet, it proved necessary for the Joint Committee to intervene to have some of these projects initiated and others saved from cancellation.

30. Because the participants' estimated costs in these projects ($271 million) represent two thirds of the total, groups outside the AEC—private and public—may be said to have contributed significantly to the nation's program.

PRIVATELY OWNED PLANTS. Directly or indirectly about two thirds of the privately owned electric utilities of the country have taken part in the nuclear power development program. Their expenditures for participation in the program are shown in Table 4–11. While the private effort has been widely spread among companies, the number of privately financed power demonstration projects has not been large. In February 1962 private industry had

TABLE **4 - 12**

Privately Owned and Financed Nuclear Power Projects, February 1962

Owner and location	Net capacity (ekw.)	Date essentially complete	Estimated costs[a] (millions)
Total	809,750		$298.9
Consolidated Edison Co. of New York, Inc., Indian Point, N. Y.	255,000	Apr. 1962	129.5
Saxton Nuclear Experimental Corp., Saxton, Pa.	3,250	Sept. 1961	6.8
General Electric Co. and others,			
Pleasanton, Calif. (boiling water reactor)	5,000	1957	3.0
Pleasanton, Calif. (superheat reactor)	—	Sept. 1962	9.9
Commonwealth Edison Co., Morris, Ill.	185,000	Sept. 1959	60.9
Pacific Gas & Electric Co.,			
Humboldt Bay, Calif.	48,500	July 1962	22.4
Bodega Bay, Calif.	313,000	Fall 1965	66.4

a. Research and development costs plus construction, as reported by the companies; in one instance, the Dresden plant (Morris, Ill.), full costs are understood not to have been reported by the manufacturer (General Electric Co.).

Sources: AEC, *Major Activities in the Atomic Energy Programs, January-December 1961* (Annual Report), Washington, January 1962, pp. 457 ff.; and Section 202 Hearings, 1962, pp. 589, 605-07.

seven development plants underway (see Table 4–12), none of which had received direct financial assistance from the AEC.[31]

The $299 million spent or being spent for these seven plants is, of course, not included in Tables 4–9 and 4–10, covering the AEC cooperative projects.

31. Such private investments do receive certain forms of public assistance, including tax advantages (rapid amortization), utility rate making, public indemnification and guaranteed "purchase" of plutonium.

The sum private industry had committed to nuclear power plants early in 1962 was roughly $540 million, representing some 1,178,000 kilowatts of capacity. These are large numbers in absolute terms, but in 1962 the utilities were investing a total of over $4 billion a year for expansion of conventional facilities. On the other hand, their expenditure on nuclear development has been many

Figure 4-5   Expenditures of AEC[a] and Private Utilities[b] for Reactor Development

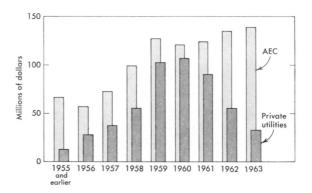

a. Civilian power programs plus one half the expenditures for general nuclear technology and safety. Excludes expenditures for plant and equipment. (Fiscal years.) Includes cooperative programs and (before fiscal year 1962) reactor safety.   b. Expenditures for research, development and construction. (Calendar years.)

Sources: AEC—AEC, Financial Report (annual, for fiscal years 1959–1961), Washington; and Atomic Energy Appropriations for 1963, Hearings, Subcommittee of the House Committee on Appropriations, 87th Cong., 2nd Sess., 1962. Private utilities—EEI data, Section 202 Hearings, 1962. 1962 and 1963 figures—estimated.

times larger than their usual expenditure on new technology which they have felt posed no threat from federal public power. Yet, the fact is that private utilities, eight years after passage of the 1954 act, had constructed only two full-scale plants without heavy government assistance, and these two were among the very first announced. The evidence raises the question whether the private utilities are prepared even at this late date to make the large investments called for by full-scale nuclear power.

Nuclear Resources: The Specter of Unused Capacity

Military Requirements—How Long?

In military terms the United States is often described as enjoying a period of "nuclear plenty," that is, it has productive capacity to meet the most ambitious and varied military requirements for nuclear and thermonuclear weapons.[32] This fact led, some years ago, to discussion of the possibility that the weapon stockpile had become sufficiently large and diversified to represent overwhelming "deterrence" through its ability to destroy all conceivable targets. This view of "strategic saturation" failed, however, to anticipate the changes in strategic and tactical doctrines that have since occurred, in part as a result of the USSR's rapid technical progress with nuclear and thermonuclear weapons, rockets and missiles.[33]

Several major developments that seem likely to increase or maintain large military requirements for atomic weapons for possibly several years are taking place simultaneously. The dispersion of weapons to scores of points inside and outside the continental United States—to the NATO countries and to naval vessels—is perhaps the leading development. Also involved is the growing importance of low-yield weapons for a variety of tactical applications; these call for more fissionable material per unit of yield than do the large, megaton weapons. In addition, an all nuclear-powered navy may soon create a demand by way of initial inventories for nuclear reactors, though the amount of fissionable material consumed annually will probably not be large.

Finally, the proliferation of types of nuclear weapons for offensive and defensive purposes has continued at a rapid pace. Besides the wide range of weapons developed in the early years of the program, the United States has had for several years, according to former AEC Chairman Gordon Dean, "warheads for atomic cannon; bombs that can be delivered from submarines, surface vessels, and small planes; and warheads for guided missiles of the ground-to-air, air-to-air and ground-to-ground types."[34] The concept that

---

32. Military requirements for fissionable material, it should be understood, are not directly related to any specific number of weapons. In response to queries of the House Appropriations Committee as to the demand of the armed services the answer, typical of the Commission's standard reply, was given by Commissioner Floberg in testimony in 1959: "Our demand is for all that we can produce, Mr. Taber. It is an open-end requirement in that sense." *The Supplemental Appropriation Bill*, Hearings, House Subcommittee on Appropriations, 86th Cong., 1st Sess., 1959, p. 1173.

33. See, among others, H. A. Kissinger, *Nuclear Weapons and Foreign Policy*, Harpers, New York, 1957, p. 125.

34. Gordon Dean, *Report on the Atom*, 2nd ed., Knopf, New York, 1957, p. 326.

there must be a saturation point for stockpiled strategic atomic weapons, owing to the limited number of targets, therefore has certainly been undermined—though not destroyed.[35]

No doubt the reworking of components of earlier nuclear weapons which are now obsolete should supplement current output of fissionable material. Moreover, the reported technical "simplicity" of producing thermonuclear weapons suggests that the supply of fissionable materials can now go much further in meeting very large requirements than it would have formerly.[36]

The conclusion of such speculation is apparent: production for military purposes may continue for several years. Yet, either through international negotiation with the USSR or through the rapidly diminishing marginal utility of additional stocks, the United States will probably sometime during the 1960s confront the serious question of the desirability of continuing to produce fissionable material for unneeded, or only marginally useful, weapons.

Some Economic Consequences of an Early Nuclear Peace

The duration of AEC procurement contracts for natural uranium, particularly from Canada, provides a partial view of the potential consequences of an early nuclear peace—say, before 1970—that would halt or greatly reduce production of weapons. For Canada there evidently will be no substantial alternative market when AEC procurement contracts terminate in 1966.[37] The prospect for producers in the United States, when contracts terminate in the latter part of the 1960s, is less painful, but any major fall in production rates would raise problems.

35. In making a distinction between large and small nuclear weapons, that is, weapons of mass destruction and weapons of discriminating military use in small-scale situations, former AEC Commissioner Thomas E. Murray said, "The first military fact is that the United States is entirely capable of giving full substance to the absolute strategy of deterrence and retaliation that looks to the prevention of all-out nuclear war or a massive surprise attack. The United States already has in its stockpile enough or more than enough megatonnage to render uninhabitable the communist world and the free world and all the rest of the world. . . ." (Statement before the Subcommittee on Agreements for Cooperation, Joint Committee on Atomic Energy, 85th Cong., 2nd Sess., April 17, 1958.)

36. Were military requirements to be defined as full use of existing productive capabilities, then the "requirements" concept would seem to be meaningless. For example, toward the end of World War II the capacity to produce, rather than a given procurement target, came to be the accepted criterion. However, it is now accepted doctrine that, in the event of all-out war, nuclear strength will be measured by force in being and not by potentially available industrial capacity. Hence, there may be a strong disposition to maintain maximum stocks of nuclear and thermonuclear weapons almost indefinitely, since it is recognized that production capacity would represent no additional advantage whatsoever, once the nation was at war.

37. S. W. Clarkson, *Uranium in the Western World*, Atomic Energy of Canada, Ltd., July 1959 (AECL No. 858). Procurement by the United Kingdom will help, of course.

Recent discussions and proposals looking toward limiting the testing of atomic weapons have frequently coupled limitation of testing with decreasing production of fissionable materials and weapons. To understand how released military capacity might find use for civilian purposes, specific steps in the production chain should be examined.

At one extreme, for example, the plutonium production reactors at Hanford and at Savannah River would have practically no immediate civilian use, since the technology for burning plutonium economically is still to be developed. On the other hand, AEC-owned facilities for chemically separating irradiated fuel, if they should become surplus, might be used to handle civilian fuel on appropriate terms. The AEC is prepared to perform the chemical separation service, because no private enterprise has been ready to undertake it at acceptable prices. These AEC facilities might ultimately be leased or sold to private operators.[38] Fuel element fabrication capacity, on the other hand, is likely to be of little use for civilian purposes, since privately owned facilities have already been established to meet the specialized requirements of both military and civilian power reactors.

The civilian usefulness of the huge facilities for the production of enriched uranium will depend on the course of reactor technology. Central station power reactors probably will be fueled almost entirely with slightly enriched uranium in the United States, whereas abroad some will be fueled with natural uranium and some with slightly enriched uranium, at least during the next decade or so. After that the initial inventory requirement of enriched material for the expected rapid growth in power reactor capacity, especially in Europe, may draw heavily on U. S. enriched uranium production capacity, unless by that time demand for enriched uranium produced in the United States is displaced by demand for that produced in European plants, possibly by some newer technique such as the German centrifuge process. Thus, if any substantial cutback in United States U235 production were made during the next decade, civilian requirements—judged by the projections in Chapter 3—would be insufficient to take up the slack.[39]

Such speculation may appear fraught with too great uncertainties to be fruitful. Nevertheless, one can foresee the shape of the impact of possible "nuclear peace" by 1970, for example, well enough to justify evaluation of current nuclear power policies. Assuming a realistic scale of development, as

38. General Electric, the prime contractor at Hanford, has suggested that a multifirm lease of the AEC processing plant there be considered. (*Nucleonics*, February 1962, p. 19.)

39. Probably the production plants can adjust to a reduced load at the least economic loss by using a greater input of natural uranium feed and smaller input of power, since the price of raw uranium is expected to be falling and surplus power will have a ready market.

projected by either Lane or the National Planning Association (see Table 3–7), one may conclude that the following economic developments are sufficiently probable in the last half of the decade to prompt careful policy consideration:

First, uranium production capacity in the United States would be far in excess of civilian and reduced military requirements, thus raising the question of a new balance of supply and requirements, presumably at lower prices, or of subsidizing the producers.

Second, the short-term demand for enriched uranium is likely to fall drastically, and some of the gaseous diffusion plants will have to be placed in stand-by unless large new markets can be found, presumably abroad.

Third, fuel-grade plutonium will have little, if any, market in civilian power plants until after a long process of technical development.

Fourth, the AEC and the industrial laboratories will come more into competition as they turn more to reactor technology. This has already created business demands for limiting the activities of government laboratories—demands that require policy decisions by the present administration, and possibly by the Congress.

Some of the economic criteria for wise choice of policies in each of these cases are readily apparent. The low cost of U. S. uranium production invites low prices that will permit only the low-cost producers to continue alive and consumers to benefit. The short-term solution to excess fissionable material capacity is, mainly, to cut prices close to marginal cost, i.e., current operating cost, since most government-owned plants will have been substantially depreciated and amortized by 1970. The emerging competition between private and public research in nuclear energy should be examined carefully in the light of the principle that research on the frontier requires much duplication and varied approaches. Moreover, experience has indicated that the more "basic" the research the more dependent it is on educational institutions.

The cost conditions of a "civilian-oriented" production chain are likely to be quite different from those prevailing today when military requirements are dominant. This suggests that a new form of national accounting may be called for, reflecting, for example, the writing off of "military" plants from the cost accounts governing civilian prices. The full amortization by 1965–1970 of virtually all plants now in the AEC production chain could influence the terms on which civilian nuclear energy passes from experimental to economic use. Before that time the domestic and foreign ore-concentrating mills will have been written off, for under the terms of AEC procurement contracts the price schedules in most cases permit amortization within five years. The same is true of the privately owned feed material plants constructed to supply the AEC.

As to the unique government facilities—the gaseous diffusion cascades, chemical separation plants and so on—that may have by-product civilian uses in the absence of private plants, there is a strong probability that these too will have been fully amortized under the AEC's accounting system. This bookkeeping may make it easier to adopt policies liberating civilian development from the burden of paying for past military operations, probably resulting in even lower prices than those which resulted from the reduction made in July 1961 and again a year later. (The pricing issue is explored further in Chapter 5.)

Transferring Functions and Facilities to Private Industry

The first stage of the AEC's long-standing program of expanding the role of private industry was to transfer functions, rather than facilities, out of government into private hands. This was accomplished mainly through government service contracts for such functions as: the conversion of uranium hexafluoride into, or from, uranium metal; the recovery of uranium in scrap; the fabrication of fuel elements; and certain other activities which are now available as commercial services. Commercial sources for certain materials (thorium, natural uranium metal and compounds, and small quantities of heavy water) have also been established. The AEC chose to follow a policy of restricting its own role as supplier and of providing materials and services, but only when they were not "reasonably available commercially."[40] An important step in this process was taken in May 1958 when the Commission announced its decision to allow private operators of uranium mills to sell uranium concentrate (U_3O_8) on the commercial markets.

The AEC remains, however, the sole supplier of fissionable material, heavy water in quantity and chemical reprocessing of spent fuel. Thus, the huge production facilities of the AEC remain, in a real sense, the great barrier to full private operation of the atomic energy industry, and it seems unlikely that these plants in the foreseeable future can be turned over to private ownership. Only a small fraction of the production plants now devoted primarily to weapon purposes can be shifted to private ownership, even though their present operation is by private contractors. A massive resource problem thus would be posed by a major reduction of weapon requirements before 1965–1970.

Whether the nation's economic policies for nuclear power development have been well designed to cope with such prospective surplus capacity, while also providing for orderly transition to private participation, is still to be determined.

40. AEC Release, A-231, Washington, September 5, 1958.

CHAPTER **5**

Economic Policies

The Atomic Energy Act of 1954

Described as establishing a "new government-industry relationship," the new statute—passed after intense but rather brief hearings and debate—represented in economic perspective an extraordinary bundle of ambiguous compromises, awkward contradictions and errors in drafting. A technically and economically premature statute was accepted on the tacit assumption that more good than harm would result from getting started early on a novel and complex regulatory problem. Yet under the 1954 act neither industry nor the AEC has acted forcefully and with full effect. Industry won a mandate it could not fulfill. The AEC had to assume multiple and often conflicting roles. The new relationship compelled the AEC to act at the same time as "partner, employer, promoter, rival and policeman. . . ."[1]

The 1954 act protected the interests of the private utilities, but also maintained the preference long accorded to public power. It called for a return to more normal private patent rights in civilian technology, but hedged this action with compulsory licensing and other restraints. It seemingly forbade subsidies to private commercial plants, yet left the way open for many forms of indirect subsidy and government assistance. Intended to be a set of guidelines, the act provided the AEC little firm guidance.

It proved to be essentially a regulatory statute. As one expert quickly pointed out, "It provides only the general framework within which Government decisions affecting private industry will be made. Congress did not solve

1. John G. Palfrey, "Atomic Energy: A New Experiment in Government-Industry Relations," *Columbia Law Review*, March 1956, p. 391.

overnight the problem of opening up atomic energy to industry . . . It is the AEC which must decide the questions of policy that will determine how far and how fast business can go."[2] The agency has done so in the framework of the long-standing congressional conflict over federal power policy.

Effects of the Private-vs.-Public-Power Controversy[3]

The pervasive influence of the power controversy makes it important to know what major power policies were adopted in the 1954 act.[4] The AEC was prohibited from selling or distributing energy for commercial use, except incidentally from production facilities and "experimental" plants, broadly defined. In disposing of the energy from such plants, the AEC was required to give preference to public bodies and cooperatives and to electric utilities in high-cost power areas. Furthermore, federal agencies, such as the Tennessee Valley Authority and Bonneville Power Administration, were specifically not precluded from securing commercial licenses for reactors if they were otherwise qualified. Also, when granting commercial licenses for reactors, the AEC was required to give preference to public bodies, cooperatives and high-cost power areas, if there were conflicting applications. Finally, any commercial licensee who might sell power from his reactor in interstate commerce became subject to the regulatory provisions of the Federal Power Act. The Atomic Energy Act thus expressed a mixture of views concerning the conflicting roles of public and private power that has had long antecedents.

With each passing year the AEC has grown more sensitive to the administrative implications of the private-vs.-public-power controversy. The electric utility advisory committee appointed by the Commission in 1951 consisted of representatives from both private and public utility systems. The Commission, in its first statement of policy on the development of nuclear power in 1953, expressed the conviction that progress would be advanced through participation in the program by "qualified and interested groups outside the Commission." That participation was not restricted to "industry" reflected an emerging awareness of the controversy. By 1955 the AEC had learned by experience that the terms of the "first round" invitation (1953) failed to meet the special

2. G. F. Trowbridge, "The Atomic Energy Act of 1954," *Atomic Energy—The New Industrial Frontier*, Atomic Industrial Forum, New York, October 1955.

3. See also the discussion in Chapter 1, outlining the origin of the controversy and its relevance for national policies for nuclear power, and in Chapter 3, describing the rivalry as a special source of economic motivation for rapid private nuclear power development.

4. See H. S. Marks and G. F. Trowbridge, *Framework for Atomic Industry: A Commentary on the Atomic Energy Act of 1954*, Bureau of National Affairs, Washington, 1955, Chap. 5.

needs of public power systems, and it took care thereafter to make invitations applicable to both public and private utilities. On the other hand, the Eisenhower administration was adamant in opposition to federally owned and operated prototype or demonstration plants, though not to smaller experimental reactors. This left the federal power-producing agencies, such as TVA, with only nominal participation in power reactor development.

The willingness of the AEC during the Eisenhower administration to extend progressively greater assistance to private utilities was based, in part, on the desire to avoid "federal atomic power." The evidence on this issue, and on the conflict within the Commission, is manifest by the comments of retiring Commissioners over the last several years. Former Commissioner Smyth's concise appraisal, in 1956, was that however desirable it might be to get the government out of nuclear power it was more important to support announced U. S. foreign policy with a vigorous program of reactor development and construction. Former Commissioner Zuckert, looking at the issue in the aftermath of the Dixon-Yates proposal (which he consistently opposed) indicated in 1956 that the defeated Gore-Holifield bill, which would have provided $400 million for reactor construction by the government in cooperation with industry, represented an opportunity, not a threat, to industry, and would have relieved the nation of its dependence on the limited investment capabilities of the regulated utility industry.[5] But the most outspoken critic of the Commission's doctrinaire policy was former Commissioner Murray.

In 1957 Murray, convinced that AEC development programs were inadequate, warned that the fear of an atomic TVA was distorting the program by leaving "responsibility for designing and constructing large reactors to private industry." The government, he added, "cannot relinquish the responsibility for constructing large-scale reactors," and "as a result of the policies we have pursued, the state of our reactor industry permits us to render but limited assistance to Euratom" and fulfill "the promises we have made to nations abroad . . . We certainly could have been better prepared to meet them."[6] Murray's proposal for a $300 million large-scale reactor construction program was not accepted by the majority of the Commission or the Congress.

The AEC's opposition during the Eisenhower administration to federal prototypes was defended on several grounds:

First, public power systems comprise only about one fourth of total generating capacity. (See Table 5–1.) Equally important, public power consists

5. Arnold Kramish and Eugene M. Zuckert, *Atomic Energy for Your Business*, McKay, New York, 1956, p. 183.
6. Section 202 Hearings, 1957, Part I, pp. 56 ff.

mainly of federally owned and operated low-cost hydro and steam systems and locally owned systems with relatively small power plants. Compared with the private sector, which depends mainly on large, steam-generating stations, many of which are in high-cost fuel areas, the public systems appeared inherently less attractive ignition points for the introduction of nuclear power.

TABLE **5 - 1**

U. S. Electric Utility Generating Capacity and Energy Generated, by Type of Utility Ownership, 1961[a]

Prime mover	Total[b]	Private	Public[c]
Generating capacity (thousands of kw.)[a]	180,119	136,399	43,720
Hydro	35,480	13,522	21,958
Steam	141,720	122,186	19,534
Internal combustion	2,919	691	2,228
Production (millions of KWH)[a]	791,975	604,817	187,158
Hydro	151,797	56,004	95,793
Steam } Internal combustion }	640,178	548,813	91,365

a. Generating capacity is as of December 31, 1961 (preliminary); production is for year 1961.

b. Excludes manufacturing and industrial establishments and electrified railways producing largely for their own use, for which preliminary figures for December 31, 1961, and year 1961 are, respectively:

Capacity (thousand kw.)	17,804	Generation (million KWH)	86,555
Hydro	723	Hydro	3,377
Fuel	17,081	Fuel	83,178

c. Includes cooperatively owned.

Source: U. S. Federal Power Commission, Washington.

Second, national policy for hydroelectric power development was viewed as not providing a useful parallel for nuclear power development. Government ownership of fissionable material, unlike the government's interest in the falling water of navigable streams, was regarded by the AEC as a short-run necessity that would in time give way to private ownership, under suitable controls. Furthermore, the hydro potential of a stream is limited, and hence the time-honored preference granted to municipal and other public groups had an economic justification. Nuclear fuel, by contrast, was known to be so plentiful in relation to foreseeable civilian needs that the application of public power preferences was looked upon as unjustified.[7] Federal water power policy provided no encouragement to the AEC to undertake more than minimum participation of public power in the development program. The Atomic Energy Act of 1954 made it impossible for either private or public power to exclude the other from nuclear power development. But in the absence of statutory policy standards as to the role of the two, the AEC was compelled to do no more than avoid overt favoritism.

Furthermore, the steam-generating plants of the TVA represented a warning to the AEC and private power that the growth of federal power generation could not always be foreseen and had no necessary limit. TVA's first steam-generating plants, it is recalled, received congressional sanction "through the back door," that is, by the appropriation route rather than by formal hearings, debate and original legislation. Neither the AEC nor private utilities had any desire to run the risk of an unlimited federal nuclear power system.

In addition, if the AEC were to build plants at other than its own installations, where it could consume the power in AEC operations, the power would have to be sold under the statutory preference provision. Even though a private utility owns a demonstration plant, if the utility enters into cooperative arrangements with the AEC for assistance, the local public power system (if any) might claim preferential access to the power generated.[8]

Finally, a federal construction program would involve proper allocation of public funds and technical assistance between private and public projects. One utility executive suggested that total federal aid for demonstration reactor construction be divided according to the ratio of private and public power generation in the country.[9] This problem has not proved a serious one, however.

The expedient policy of extending progressively greater help to privately owned projects seemed to the majority of the Commission during the Eisenhower administration to hold less danger than the construction of plants by the AEC.

There the issue stood until mid-1961 when bitter debate arose over adding $95 million of electric generating facilities to the new plutonium production

7. For a brief review of some of the possible parallels in water power legislation and nuclear power legislation, see statement of the FPC before the Joint Committee on Atomic Energy, *Hearings on S. 3323 and H. R. 8862, To Amend the Atomic Energy Act of 1946*, 83rd Cong., 2nd Sess., 1954, Part II, pp. 1127–29.

8. The government-owned plant in the Duquesne Power Co. system at Shippingport, Pa., was undertaken before the 1954 act became effective. The output of this plant presumably is not subject to the preference provision, though the issue has never been raised. The Shippingport plant is therefore considered an anomaly that cannot be repeated under the 1954 act.

9. Statement of Willis Gale, Chairman, Commonwealth Edison Co., Section 202 Hearings, 1958, pp. 522–24.

reactor being built at the AEC's installation at Hanford, Washington. Despite the facts that the AEC, the Federal Power Commission and the Bonneville Power Administration supported the economic merit of adding 400 megawatts of generating facilities[10] and that the power was available for sale to nonpreference customers,[11] the proposal was rejected by the House of Representatives—over the majority approval of the Joint Committee and a majority of the Senate. The debate hinged on the issue of private-vs.-federal-public power, rather than on the economic merits. The outcome removed all doubts about the pertinence of this controversy for government-owned, nuclear power demonstration plants. It left the Kennedy administration less scope in which to secure the construction of full-scale power reactors, needed to keep pace with advances in reactor technology.[12] At the beginning of 1962 three avenues were open: to propose a large program of federal construction, subject to possible repetition of the previous debates on the Gore-Holifield bill and the New Production Reactor; to propose construction subsidies or other expanded financial aids to private utilities; or to wait for the private utilities to undertake construction—the policy throughout the preceding seven years. The Kennedy administration rejected the first, accepted the second, but hoped that the private utilities might still come forward with full-scale demonstration plants. Whether or not they will do so remains the key question.

Institutional Constraints on Private Development

Private development of reactor technology was strongly encouraged by the character of the act as well as by the AEC's interpretation of it. Certain legal restraints were written into the act and these could not be avoided by the AEC, although, as pointed out below, they have not seriously impeded the pace of reactor development. They permit private development to occur within vaguely defined boundaries designed to protect the public interest and to maintain healthy, free competition.[13] The three provisions of the act charac-

10. *Power Conversion Studies—Hanford New Production Reactor,* Joint Committee on Atomic Energy, 87th Cong., 1st Sess., March 1961.

11. *AEC Authorizing Legislation, Fiscal Year 1962,* Hearings, Subcommittee on Legislation, Joint Committee on Atomic Energy, 87th Cong., 1st Sess., 1961, pp. 294–98.

12. Testimony of AEC Director of Reactor Development. *Ibid.* pp. 185–86.

13. Although the pertinent policy declaration of the act is to "strengthen free competition in private enterprise," the antitrust and patent provisions of the act are not so affirmatively stated; they appear rather more as boundary lines, suitable in the context of atomic energy's unique history and the nation's antitrust legislation. They provide a means of avoiding, in a new setting, the concentration of economic power and industrial relationships inconsistent with antitrust objec-

terized here as "institutional" are the government ownership of special nuclear materials, the provisions placing nuclear enterprises under the anti-trust laws and the restrictions on securing private patents.

The Anomaly of Government Ownership of Fissionable Material

A striking feature of the 1954 act is the seeming inconsistency between the extreme measures provided for encouraging private development and the provision requiring public ownership of the essential fuel required for and produced in privately owned reactors (Section 52). No controversy and, indeed, little discussion arose when the Joint Committee and the Congress accepted this "socialist island" in a sea of private enterprise. Until early 1961 there was little question of the wisdom of government ownership.[14]

The fact is that uncritically examined national security considerations, and not the economic merits, prompted conservatives and liberals alike to reject the concept of private ownership. Yet, careful review of the legislative history reveals that no real link between national security and government ownership was ever explicitly established on the public record; instead the link was accepted, largely unexamined, as an article of faith and doctrine.[15]

The consequences of such a major institutional anachronism are meshed with almost all aspects of the AEC's measures for assisting and accelerating industrial development of nuclear power. Indeed, government ownership of fissionable material necessitated administrative devices for getting enriched uranium into private hands at a reasonable use charge, and for carrying out the corollary provision of the act (in Section 52), which directs the AEC to pay a fair price to any person lawfully producing fissionable material.

tives. But they cannot "strengthen" free competition. Such strengthening, as shown in Chapters 3 and 4, is more likely to come as a consequence of the diversity of reactor concepts, the "lasting" power of new entrants in the power equipment business and the decisions of the AEC to maintain or limit the wide scope of reactor research.

14. In 1953 the AEC evidently favored a policy of private ownership of nuclear fuel, provided public control was maintained, but did not urge this view. See letter of Gordon Dean, former AEC Chairman, in *Atomic Power Development and Private Enterprise*, Hearings, Joint Committee on Atomic Energy, 83rd Cong., 1st Sess., 1953, p. 56. In May 1961, when it reduced the prices of enriched uranium, the AEC stated that it was considering the desirability of recommending the elimination of the statutory requirement (AEC Release, D-138, Washington, May 29, 1961).

15. AEC, *Legislative History of the Atomic Energy Act of 1954*, Washington, 1955, Vol. 2, pp. 1746, 1851 and 2238. The administration's original recommendations proposed private ownership of fissionable material, but the Joint Committee rejected this. Much later, in 1956, the McKinney Panel made definite the case for government ownership: "Retention of title to this material which could be used for atomic weapons permits the Federal Government to have more absolute control. Federal jurisdiction is made secure against State interference, recovery of material in wartime or emergency is expedited, and the United States is able to continue working toward international atomic controls with greater flexibility." (Vol. 1, p. 130.)

To be sure, the AEC's administration of these provisions has made government ownership profitable for industry. The advantage of the original low 4 per cent use charge—raised to 4.75 per cent in 1961—on enriched uranium is apparent, and this has been reinforced by the AEC's setting plutonium prices, temporarily, well above the fuel value of the material. In the future, furthermore, even if the use charge should be increased substantially and the buying price for plutonium should be set no higher than its estimated fuel value, future fuel-cycle costs would probably be lower with government than with private ownership of fuel.[16] The main indirect effect of private ownership would be termination of the AEC's guaranteed market for by-product plutonium from privately owned power plants.

Presumably industry will not find private ownership of fuel profitable, and hence attractive, until the recycling of plutonium can be proved economically competitive,[17] the weapon demand for plutonium falls to a point where the government no longer wants to buy civilian reactor output of the metal or fuel use charges are drastically increased in relation to other elements of fuel-cycle costs.

At some point, however—and aside from narrow cost calculations—the bookkeeping imposed on the AEC and industry by government ownership of fuel may become burdensome. Perhaps more important, it should become apparent in due course that proper accountability for fissionable material and precautions against diversions can be as effectively administered under private as under government ownership. Suitable safeguards are already available in the AEC's system of control of source and fissionable material.

Evidently erosion of government ownership will begin when private profit is taken out of continued public ownership; then national security will be based on regulated possession of fissionable material rather than on mere absentee title. Until 1959 the Commission had no specific problem that might justify requesting a change in the basic statute. In 1959, however, criticism of the AEC's pricing policy did create a setting conducive to reevaluation of continuing government ownership, and the lowering of U235 prices in 1961 raised

16. The AEC staff has estimated that under private ownership fuel-cycle costs for seven reactor types would be increased by 3 to 14 per cent, since private ownership would necessitate a private utility's capitalizing the fuel inventory at about 12 per cent, nearly three times the AEC lease charge. (AEC, *Civilian Power Reactor Program*, Washington, 1960, Part II, p. 96.)

17. Conversely, it could be argued that, in the short run, as long as the AEC stands ready to pay high prices for plutonium from privately owned reactors there will be much less incentive for recycling this fuel and, hence, for private ownership. The AEC's clear intention to pay no more, in the long run, for by-product plutonium or U233 than the price of U235 as nuclear fuel is indicated by the language of the AEC's 1958 proposed revision of Sec. 55 on acquisition. See *AEC Authorizing Legislation, Fiscal Year 1959*, Hearings, Subcommittee on Legislation, Joint Committee on Atomic Energy, 85th Cong., 2nd Sess., 1958, pp. 434–35.

the issue again. To be sure, private ownership of fissionable material would increase the cost of generating nuclear power and would delay its becoming competitive. The AEC and private industry more recently, therefore, have tended to defer the time when it may be desirable to consider private ownership.[18]

Antitrust Policies and the Competitive Setting [19]

Drafters of the 1954 act were aware that in prescribing patent and antitrust rules for nuclear energy they were treating a novel situation. However, while they broke new ground on patent policy, on antitrust matters they appeared singularly bound by precedent. They simply applied the existing antitrust laws and requested the AEC and the Attorney General to work together in enforcing them.[20] The legislative history suggests that fear was prevalent of the predominant advantage the early contractors—more aggressively called "the insiders"—enjoyed over new and usually smaller entrants into the competitive race.[21] The antitrust provisions were largely irrelevant to the competitive conditions prevailing during the long developmental phase.[22]

The major nuclear equipment suppliers, as outlined in Chapter 3, are a few, well-established, giant companies who have for years been dominant in such fields as electronics, power supply and electrical equipment. The two principal suppliers, General Electric and Westinghouse, were themselves AEC contractors and their established position was not seriously affected by the act. However, the patent provisions were considered "preventive measures" to assure new entrants an opportunity to compete, at not too great a disadvantage with early entrants.[23] The early rush to enter the field has not been re-

18. Section 202 Hearings, 1962, pp. 95–107, 509–12.

19. See also discussion in Chapter 3.

20. For careful reviews see Ephraim Jacobs and Donald F. Melchior, "Antitrust Aspects of the Atomic Energy Industry," *The George Washington Law Review*, April 1957, pp. 508–34; also address of Bennett Boskey, "Antitrust Enforcement by the Atomic Energy Commission," American Bar Association, Section of Antitrust Law, St. Louis, Mo., August 8, 1961.

21. W. A. Adams and H. M. Gray, *Monopoly in America*, Macmillan, New York, 1955, Chap. 7.

22. Moreover, they may have been applied ineffectively. Some experts think that, since action by the Attorney General is called for only with respect to commercial licenses (granted under Sec. 103) and not licenses for research and development activities (under Sec. 104), which, however, can be "commercial" activities, the benefits of Department of Justice guidance and possible rectification of any unwholesome tendencies in the present long developmental phase are lacking. Other experts dismiss this reasoning by declaring that the AEC might well seek the advice and possible action of the Attorney General before such tendencies could become fixed.

23. The importance of a preventive patent policy, in place of "remedial litigation," for assuring competition was emphasized by former Attorney General Herbert Brownell in "Atomic Energy and Free Enterprise," an address before the New York State Bar Association, January 24, 1957.

warded by expanding business opportunities, but rather has necessitated mounting investments with scant prospect of early returns. Under such conditions the outcome for free competition depends hardly at all on remote antitrust restraints, but rather on the AEC's growing assistance to industry and on the financial staying power of the remaining competitors. As mentioned, the longer the delay in nuclear power's becoming profitable, the greater the tendency for the nuclear power industry to be dominated by the conventional power and electrical equipment industry.

The AEC is directed to report promptly to the Attorney General "any utilization of special nuclear material or atomic energy which appears to violate or tend toward the violation" of any antitrust laws or to restrict free competition in private enterprise (Section 105, c). This obligation for affirmative action on the part of the AEC and the Attorney General should be sufficient to thwart any tendencies toward monopolistic restraints, if they can be recognized as such. There is nothing in the act or the legislative history, however, that requires the AEC to use atomic energy as a device for changing existing competitive conditions in the highly concentrated power and electrical equipment supply industry. However, as indicated in Chapter 3, suppliers of boiler equipment who have entered the power reactor field are now in direct competition with the electrical equipment manufacturers. Since these companies have great resources, it may be concluded that nuclear energy will probably heighten the degree of competition between suppliers to utility systems, provided the period of development is not excessively long.

ENTRY OF NEW UTILITY EQUIPMENT SUPPLIERS. Long-established suppliers of steam and electrical equipment to the utility industry have been confronted with the new, emerging competition of reactor manufacturers who are trying to establish a position in the market. Roughly four fifths of the market for utility equipment has been in the private systems and the balance in the public sector. The existence of the public systems evidently has made the entry of new suppliers who are prepared to furnish nuclear power reactors easier than it might otherwise have been. Indeed, most of the newcomers have made their entry by joining with local public power systems in reactor projects. Conversely, the major established suppliers of electric utilities have seldom gone outside the privately owned utilities to undertake power reactor projects.

Whatever the reasons for the phenomenon, the pairing of "new" suppliers mainly with public power groups and of "established" suppliers almost exclusively with private power is unmistakable. (See Table 5–2.)

TABLE **5 - 2**

Established and New Equipment Suppliers for Civilian Nuclear Power Projects, by Type of Utility Ownership, 1961

Equipment supplier	Project	
	System and plant location	Type of utility ownership
Established suppliers		
Allis-Chalmers Manufacturing Co.	Dairyland Power Cooperative, Genoa, Wis.	Cooperative
	Northern States Power Co.— Sioux Falls, S. Dak.	Private
Babcock & Wilcox Co.	Consolidated Edison Co.— Indian Point, N. Y.	Private
General Electric Co.	Commonwealth Edison (Dresden Plant)—Morris, Ill.	Private
	Consumers Power Co. Big Rock Point, Mich.	Private
	Pacific Gas & Electric Co.— Humboldt Bay, Calif.	Private
Westinghouse Electric Corp.	Carolinas-Virginia Nuclear Power Assoc., Inc.—Parr, S. C.	Private
	Duquesne Light Co.— Shippingport, Pa.	Private
	Southern California Edison— Southern California	Private
	Yankee Atomic Electric Co.— Rowe, Mass.	Private
New suppliers		
ACF Industries, Inc. (nuclear division merged into Allis-Chalmers above)	Rural Cooperative Power Association —Elk River, Minn.	Cooperative
General Dynamics Corp.	Philadelphia Electric Co., Peach Bottom, Pa.	Private
General Nuclear Engineering Co. (merged into Combustion Engineering)	Puerto Rico Water Resources Authority, Punta Higuera, P. R.	Public
North American Aviation, Inc. (Atomics International)	City of Piqua, Ohio—Piqua, Ohio	Municipal
	Consumers Public Power District— Hallam, Neb.	Public

Source: AEC, *Major Activities in the Atomic Energy Programs, January-December 1961* (Annual Report), Washington, January 1962, pp. 461–62.

The heavy reliance on private industry for large-scale demonstration projects since 1954 may have increased the concentration of the reactor industry, that is, of those few very large firms able to buy the "admission tickets." The basis for this judgment comes from the industry itself. One company in 1957 found the stakes too high and asked for relief from a fixed price arrangement under the AEC's cooperative demonstration program.[24]

MULTIPLICITY OF REACTOR DESIGNS AND INDUSTRIAL CONCENTRATION. The heavy cost of developing a new reactor design and the substantial number of promising reactor types have led to specialization by the various equipment manufacturers, which made improbable the early emergence of one or two manufacturers to positions of monopolistic domination. The situation could arise, however, if one type should prove to be the best—for example, the water reactors. The possibility that a newcomer to the field of power equipment might develop a superior new reactor design has been a minor restraint on major manufacturers. Thus far, the emergence of power reactor technology seems to have taken a form that holds some promise of wide industrial dispersion rather than concentration, but the experience is still too brief to judge the outcome.

Until the AEC grants facilities licenses for numbers of commercial reactors, antitrust enforcement may receive little attention from policy makers. Circumstances may soon arise, however, which will require the AEC and the Attorney General to give closer study to the avoidance of further concentration in this already concentrated industry. Before issuing numerous facilities licenses for commercial power reactors the AEC will be compelled to seek the advice of the Attorney General as to whether or not such licenses would "tend to create or maintain a situation inconsistent with the antitrust laws." Nevertheless, there is no evidence that the AEC consulted the Attorney General before issuing, under Section 104, facilities licenses already granted for the

24. Morehead Patterson, Chairman of the American Machine and Foundry Co., noting the purpose of the statute—to strengthen free competition—stated in a letter to the Joint Committee on Atomic Energy, September 18, 1957: " 'Buying in' to a development project through a cost-absorbing proposal impossible for competitors of lesser resources, with a view to future recovery of losses, is not in keeping with the spirit of the law. . . . I believe it is of the utmost importance to the progress of the Commission's program that all of the developmental projects be financed on a basis of full consideration of the requirement for a sustained effort over a period of many years. Otherwise, it will not be possible for American industry, perhaps with the exception of a few of its giants, to continue at high levels the developmental effort that is clearly called for if America is to maintain its position in the field of atomic energy." (*Review of Proposals Under Power Demonstration Program*, Hearings, Subcommittee on Legislation, Joint Committee on Atomic Energy, 85th Cong., 1st Sess. September 17, 1957, pp. 14–15.)

research and development type; nor apparently, has the AEC examined the data at hand to determine under what circumstances it should have been, or should in the future be, prepared to seek the advice of the Attorney General.[25] The AEC has, of course, been alerted to the antitrust problem by the 1961 prosecutions against manufacturers of electrical equipment, some of whom are also major manufacturers of nuclear power reactors (for example, Allis-Chalmers, General Electric and Westinghouse).

Patents: Battleground of Private and Public Interest

An inventor's seventeen-year right to his patent is a property right authorized by the Constitution as one means of promoting "the progress of science and the useful arts." In atomic energy the system of qualified private patent rights also represents a form of regulation of information that is designed both to promote competition and to protect the public interest. The McMahon Act did permit certain private patent rights, but it also abolished these rights on discoveries which were useful in the production of nuclear weapons or in the production of fissionable material; for other applications patents remained open questions.[26] The 1954 statute preserved the prohibition on patents of nuclear weapons, but outside this area the right to obtain patents was enlarged, though with qualifications.

In general, the patent provisions of the 1954 act represent an awkward policy containing two opposing points of view. One is that the patent system should be used primarily to provide incentive for private efforts toward technical progress; the other view is that the granting of private patents should not become a contributing means for a few companies, already contractors of the AEC, to win an unfair advantage over competitors and hence promote monopoly. In practice, the law has been more an irritant to industry than a serious constraint on invention. Yet, patent policy has remained one of the most controversial and least understood features of both the 1946 and 1954 statutes.

Most of the public argument over patent policy has been rather confused and lacking in clear purpose. Even experienced legislators and members

---

25. Boskey, *op. cit.*

26. The provisions in the McMahon Act were interpreted as meaning that such "other" discoveries might be patented. However, the terms of contracts with AEC contractors greatly restricted their right to secure private patents and "as a practical matter, the Government got the right to keep nearly all inventions by contract, and usually exercised the right to keep them." (Marks and Trowbridge, *op. cit.*, p. 27.) In recent years the AEC has issued several hundred nonexclusive royalty-free licenses on these inventions.

of the Joint Committee on Atomic Energy proved unable to foresee in 1954 the consequences of hastily improvised compromises.[27] Congress was unable to provide clear guidance to the AEC in applying the patent provisions—that is, whether they were to be primarily a means of promoting industry participation or regulating it.

The patent chapter of the 1954 act, probably the most painful legal constraint on industry's incentive to undertake atomic development, illustrates the problems of legislating long before sound technical and economic assumptions could be made. In the heat of the 1954 congressional hearings and debate, for example, the Chairman of the Joint Committee, the knowledgeable W. Sterling Cole, stated unequivocally, "compulsory licensing is not creeping socialism; it is socialism run rampant."[28] Yet, this provision was written into the law and five years later, at the end of the compulsory licensing period in 1959, the AEC recommended and secured congressional extension of this reserve authority for another five years. The AEC's main case—evidently persuasive, since there was scarcely any opposition in the Joint Committee— was that it "believed that the possibility for preferred positions still exists." The AEC cited the clinching fact that at the time (1959) 90 per cent of the inventions reported under Commission contracts were reported by only fourteen prime contractors.[29]

Furthermore, the AEC made it clear that it joined in the Attorney General's 1947 statement that, as basic policy, government contracts for research and development should entitle the government to all rights to inventions produced in the performance of the contract. This was a bitter pill for the manufacturers who had hoped, by 1959, to secure private patent rights, subject only to royalty-free licenses for the government. Finally, the AEC concurred in the view, stated by Congressman Holifield, that the major contractors could have received patents that would have given them "almost a monopoly position in the industry," if the generous patent practice of the Department of Defense, for example, had been employed instead.

---

27. Joint Committee Chairman Cole supported inclusion of Section 152 (Inventions Conceived During Commission Contracts) to provide public safeguards for private patents and, in part, to spike the argument of those contending for compulsory licensing. But "too much was written into" Section 152 "under the pressure of zealously trying to protect the normal American patent system" and it has become a greater restraint than the limited compulsory licensing provisions. (W. Sterling Cole, "Patenting Nuclear Developments," *Nucleonics*, April 1955, pp. 31–35.)

28. "Separate Views on Patents," *Amending the Atomic Energy Act of 1946, As Amended, and for Other Purposes*, Joint Committee on Atomic Energy, 83rd Cong., 2nd Sess., July 1954, p. 99.

29. *Atomic Energy Patents*, Hearings, Subcommittee on Legislation, Joint Committee on Atomic Energy, 86th Cong., 1st Sess., 1959, p. 23. Nine industrial companies accounted for most of the 90 per cent.

The General Setting

Certain drawbacks of the U. S. patent system have been clearly indicated,[30] and it has proved desirable under antitrust laws to maintain public surveillance over the effect of patents on competition.[31]

In nuclear energy technology this bipolar aspect of patent policy—incentive to innovation balanced by restraints on monopolistic tendencies—has appeared more significant than in most other technical fields. Until recently nearly all the patentable inventions in the nuclear energy field have been made by the government or its contractors. Many of the innovations were "born classified" and the "know-how" associated with the advance was accessible mainly to companies operating as AEC contractors, and to a lesser extent to those holding access permits. Thus, more recent increments resulting from wholly private, unassisted effort have permitted only limited scope for a company to secure an important patent position. In analyzing the competitive problems involved, one must start with the provisions of the act itself and then examine the administrative freedom the AEC has, if it wishes, to modify the more restrictive features.[32]

At the outset, it should be made clear that private industry did receive important freedom to patent under the 1954 act and has taken advantage of that new opportunity, despite objections to the policy restraints. The Joint Committee hearings in 1959 revealed that in the field of atomic energy a sharp increase in the number of privately owned patents and patent applications occurred after 1954. Patent statistics are a notoriously weak basis for judging the rate or depth of technical progress. Yet, the data available thus far show that the increase in patent activity has been due almost entirely to private

30. See, in particular, the series of studies of the U. S. patent system prepared for the Subcommittee on Patents, Trademarks and Copyrights, Committee on the Judiciary, U. S. Senate, 1958 and 1959.

31. For example, there is the 1959 court decision against the Radio Corporation of America for monopolistic use of its dominant patent position in radio purpose apparatus. Historically, it is worth noting that the use of a patentee's monopoly in an invention to frustrate the intention of the Sherman Act (1890) brought about the Clayton Act (1914), although the RCA case was prosecuted under the former. Also, General Electric and Westinghouse, who were silent during the 1959 reexamination of the patent provisions in the Atomic Energy Act, were named among the co-conspirators of RCA. (See Indictment filed by Department of Justice, No. 155–107, February 21, 1958, U. S. District Court, Southern District of New York, *U. S. v. Radio Corporation of America*.)

32. While the value of patents for building a monopolistic position seems clear, the incentive to further research and invention thereafter is not so easily demonstrated. That the patent incentive at this later stage may be buried deep among many others is suggested in the study by Seymour Melman, *The Impact of the Patent System on Research*, made for the Subcommittee on Patents, Trademarks and Copyrights of the Committee on the Judiciary, U. S. Senate, 85th Cong., 2nd Sess., 1958.

applications and issuances—not to governmental activity. Thus, supporters of the present policy of the act have been prompted to say that "industry has not been stifled." At the same time it is apparent that the AEC has retained in the public sphere patents on most of the basic reactor types.[33]

Inventions Conceived Under Commission Contracts (Section 152)

The act, as amended, states that any invention made under any contract, subcontract or arrangement entered into with or for the benefit of the AEC shall be the property of the AEC. It also provides, however, that the AEC may waive its claim under such circumstances as it "may deem appropriate." Despite strong and repeated requests from industry, the AEC has used the advance waiver only sparingly—in part because of the lack of statutory criteria.[34] Consequently, the massive inventory of knowledge accumulated at the national laboratories, at other AEC installations and at contractor's facilities has been held in government control. AEC contractors have proposed that the agency waive its rights and adhere to a practice similar to that of the Defense Department, which permits the contractor to secure certain patent rights subject to giving the government a nonexclusive license (Sec. IX of the Armed Services Procurement Regulations). Variations of this proposal are examined later in this section. At the end of 1958 the AEC reported that 1,737 public patents were available for licensing—a very crude index of the substantial base on which other innovators in and out of the atomic energy field may build.[35] Only a few public patents covering basic reactor types had

33. The statistics of filings and issuances up to 1958 are given in *Selected Materials on Atomic Energy Patents*, Joint Committee on Atomic Energy, 86th Cong., 1st Sess., March 1959, Vol. 1, pp. 46–126. For example, in fiscal year 1957, 925 applications were filed, of which 719 were private, 121 were U. S. government and 85 were "other government." In fiscal year 1952 only 255 were filed—135 private, 113 U. S. government and 7 other government. Also, patents issued in fiscal year 1957 numbered 246, compared with 109 in fiscal year 1952. In the field of reactors alone, the AEC in 1957 filed 56 applications and others 237, but in the same year the 38 awards were all to the AEC, and none to others. Moreover, the AEC in 1959 held the basic patents on almost all the various reactor types (major exception: organic-moderated, on which no patents had been issued.) Of applications filed abroad, the AEC reported 327 in 1958 (to November 21), whereas AEC contractors reported only 7 applications in foreign countries.

34. The AEC has exercised the advance waiver authority in connection with inventions resulting from: the sale or distribution of isotopes; use of AEC gamma irradiation facilities; exercise of access permits; and grants to educational institutions and training programs. There is ample room clearly for the AEC to enlarge the area, subject to advance waivers. (*Ibid.*, p. 4.)

35. Many patents owned by the government are not applicable merely to atomic energy; their scope is far greater. The first five patents listed by the AEC in January 1959, each of them by a foreign innovator, covered the following: pump for gaseous working fluids; method of coating surfaces with boron; sealed insulator bushing; balance; and a pulse scaling system. (*Major Activities in the Atomic Energy Programs, July–December 1958* (Semiannual Report), Washington, January 1959, Appendix 5, p. 235.)

been issued to the AEC up to April 1959. They include, for example, three boiling water reactors, one pressurized water, one fast breeder, nine homogeneous, fifteen gas-cooled and six sodium-cooled. Many of these public patents were applied for as long as ten or fifteen years earlier. Yet, information on each of these types has long been declassified and technology has developed to the prototype stage in most cases.

Compulsory Licensing Provisions (Section 153)

The compulsory licensing provision is an attempt to prevent the blocking of a useful improvement because an essential component is patented and the patentee refuses a license. The AEC may require an owner to issue a license on a reasonable royalty to a particular applicant, if the AEC finds the proposed use of the patent is of primary importance to the furtherance of technical progress.[36]

The AEC's authority to compel licensing, applicable to any patent for which application was filed before September 1, 1959 (later extended to September 1, 1964), is carefully circumscribed. Hence, many patent authorities have viewed this as only a limited deviation from patent custom and one which the AEC may never have to use. In effect it provides a safeguard, or reserve power, that would be employed only under most unusual circumstances. It seems to offset partially the inequality of opportunity prevailing in the early phase of development and "its mere presence in the law is a safety valve which may prevent abusive or unhealthy conditions from being created as this industry emerges from the cocoon of secrecy and government monopoly."[37] The cocoon stage has proved much longer than was assumed in 1954. It was to be expected, therefore, that the Congress would extend this limited compulsory licensing authority in 1959. It did so—without repeating the heated controversy of 1954 or the earlier controversy when the 1946 act was passed.

Other Patent Provisions

Other patent provisions are noncontroversial and need be mentioned only in passing to the broader question of the AEC's administration of patent policy. The patent award system, which comes from the 1946 act, provides

36. Paralleling the antitrust provisions, the act also makes explicit (Sec. 158) that if a patent is used intentionally in a manner to violate the antitrust laws, the court that finds this so may require the patent owner to license the patent to any other licensee who may demonstrate a need for it. The reasons are fairly obvious.

37. Bennett Boskey, "Some Patent Aspects of Atomic Power Development," *Law and Contemporary Problems*, Duke University, Winter 1956, p. 121.

(Section 157,b,3) that any person making a useful nuclear invention or discovery may apply for and receive an award. This incentive is in addition to the right of obtaining a patent, and some authorities consider it could be an equally attractive incentive, particularly for the small inventor or company, who may find securing a patent entails a long and difficult process of uncertain outcome. Thus far, however, the AEC has made little use of awards for inventions or discoveries in the civilian aspects of nuclear energy.

Under the 1954 act (Section 151c, as amended) an inventor must within 180 days either apply for a patent or report the invention to the AEC. Failure to do so may disqualify the inventor for an award and possibly subject him to more serious legal action. The purpose of this provision was to keep the AEC informed of the developing technology and to prevent companies from deliberately holding back information and thus narrowing the base for further advances by others.

AEC Administration of Patent Policy

One might reasonably conclude that the AEC has regarded patent administration more as a means of avoiding monopoly than as an incentive for a few giant corporations that still appear to hold "an undue advantage." Furthermore, the 1959 Joint Committee hearings, and industry's singularly muted appeal for liberalization of patent policy, did not change the 1954 legislative decisions. In 1959 the Congress merely extended for another five years the period of patents subject to compulsory licensing. In order to improve the competitive position of U. S. industry abroad, the AEC in 1960 adopted a policy of authorizing its contractors to file for foreign patents and retain substantive rights under specified terms.

Patent problems of nuclear power are not greatly different from those of the American patent system generally. The small inventor has seldom been able to secure an appreciable return on innovations. Proposals therefore have been made to provide government awards to inventors. Moreover, substantial, and perhaps growing, numbers of patents apparently are filed, not with the positive purpose of profitable use of the inventions but rather as a defensive measure to foreclose competitors who might invent something similar. Evidently, in the large modern corporation the customary public purpose of patents may have been lost in the context of monopolistic competition. Proposals have also been made, in order to allow defensive patents without blocking use by others, to permit patent publication without the inventor's asserting any exclusive rights.

Nuclear energy patent provisions have little direct relation to the original purpose of the patent laws—to protect the rights of the individual inventor. Broad, costly research and experimentation must be carried on over many years before profitable nuclear power is available for private operators. Patents may be no more than an incident in this multifarious process and may, indeed, provide little additional incentive. This partial atrophy of a basic social institution has not been overlooked by the legislative policy makers. "The patent laws," it has been said by a member of the staff of the Senate Subcommittee on Patents, "are written in terms of a stimulus to invent, whereas, today, the greatest expense and therefore the greatest need for stimulus is often connected with innovation or exploitation after the invention has been made."[38] This observation is indeed applicable to nuclear power development.

Against this background one may better evaluate the major proposals for changing atomic energy patent policies and their administration by the AEC. Both patent authorities and representatives of industry have suggested, for example, that within the framework of existing legislation the AEC should: follow the Department of Defense in allowing certain private patent rights to contractors; expand the practice of waiving in advance its rights to inventions made by private groups working for it; facilitate the filing for patents in foreign countries, as it did in 1960, and also permit contractors more freedom to file abroad than at home; and enlarge its grant of awards for inventions and discoveries.[39]

The first two proposals would diverge from the intent of the act and the Kennedy administration's policy position.[40] Over the last few years, therefore, industry has been trying to find a formula that would harmonize the corporate, government and public interests. One equipment manufacturer, Chauncey Starr, a "newcomer" to the power supply business, in 1958 expressed concern that competitive strength rested with the established, big companies and suggested that industry be permitted to retain title to all proprietary information developed under government contract, with royalty-free licensing to the government and compulsory licensing to other concerns

38. John C. Stedman, "Legislative Proposals for the U. S. Patent System," Atomic Industrial Forum, Washington, November 11, 1958.

39. See transcript of the hearings on patent policy held by the legal staff, AEC, Washington, April 15, 1958, particularly the testimony of Bennett Boskey; also, "Memorandum of Subcommittee on Patents, Copyrights and Proprietary Information, Atomic Industrial Forum, June 4, 1958," transmitted to the AEC and contained in *Selected Materials on Atomic Energy Patents*, Vol. I.

40. Representatives of the Department of Justice in early 1962 testified in favor of the AEC-NASA policy and urged a uniform patent policy favoring government retention of title.

at reasonable royalty on a nondiscriminatory basis.[41] The AEC and the Joint Committee, however, have preferred to leave the field open for all to build on, rather than to encourage any exclusive patent positions at an early stage.

There is no device for judging the incentive that might be provided by private patent rights. In any case, the immediate effect of the argument for private patent rights is weakened by the fact that only a limited commercial demand for power reactors is likely to arise in the United States soon. Meanwhile, the pace of technical advance will depend largely on AEC assistance and direct reactor programs, here and abroad. At most a patent position might encourage particular manufacturers to stay in the field a little longer by giving the newcomer's technology a protection that an established equipment supplier could not take over.[42]

One might say, as did Starr, that government retention of patent rights makes it easier for the largest companies to dominate the smaller companies trying to enter the field. A little more experience may reveal whether this is true.

There are no easy answers to such economic questions as these. The AEC and the Joint Committee in 1959 chose to abide by the 1954 solutions and compromises, awkward though they had proved to be.

The AEC as Price Administrator

When the 1954 act was passed, the AEC had already gained experience in setting prices for its materials and services. For many years the AEC had in effect an extensive program of cost accounting, including plant depreciation, that provided an indispensable base for setting prices on such materials as radioactive isotopes. Also, the "industry participation program" had compelled the AEC in 1951 and 1952 to furnish guideline prices and charges that industry teams could use in their "paper studies" of early reactor concepts. The incongruity and vagueness of the price criteria that are now apparent in the 1954 act thus represented no real obstacle to the AEC in establishing prices.

41. Chauncey Starr, Atomics International Division, North American Aviation, Inc., "The Manufacturer Looks At Proprietary Rights in Atomic Energy," address before Federal Bar Association, November 25, 1958, Washington.

42. This is more than a theory. Atomics International, Inc. (subsidiary of North American Aviation) has been responsible under AEC contracts for developing the organic-moderated reactor. This company cannot, under the act and the AEC's administration of it, acquire private patent rights to this reactor type or the associated technology. Therefore, any of its major competitors (e.g., Westinghouse) who lacks a promising reactor design to develop can enter the field and through greater financial and other resources, take over the organic-moderated reactor as its primary bid for commercial power.

The principal AEC prices cover enriched uranium, including use and burn-up charges, the prices paid by the AEC for plutonium and U233 produced, and the charges made for chemical processing of irradiated fuel. For these varied prices the act provides the AEC with divergent guidance. In supplying fissionable material to domestic operators of reactors under Sections 53,c and 53,d, the AEC may make a "reasonable charge" or waive the charge, if the use is for research and development and other constructive purposes of the act. For commercial licensees the "reasonable charge" is to reflect consideration of six criteria—cost of production, use of the material, extent the particular use aids development, energy value of the material in the particular use, adherence to uniform and nondiscriminatory treatment and the production cost to the AEC or the "average fair price" paid for production by others, whichever is lower. For fissionable material—plutonium and U233 —produced by others, the AEC shall pay a "fair price." In setting this price, under Section 56, the agency is to take into consideration the value of the material for its intended use by the AEC and give equitable weight to its cost if produced by the AEC. Such "guaranteed prices" may be set for a period of not over seven years. For other materials or services (under Section 161,m) the AEC shall establish nondiscriminatory prices that in its opinion "will provide reasonable compensation to the Government for such material or services and will not discourage the development of sources of supply independent of the Commission."

AEC Stated Price Policy

Amid this hodgepodge of criteria the AEC fell back on its own historical production costs as a point of departure, and has attempted to consider all prices as parts of an interrelated system, affecting total nuclear power costs in a consistent manner. Nevertheless, key AEC prices have tended to be inflated by the principle of recovering full costs of production, including imputed capital costs, AEC overhead and return on investment.[43]

The AEC also has given special weight to stability of its prices so as to permit long-range planning by industry, domestic and foreign. The primary guideline of the AEC is stated as follows:[44]

> In general, it is the policy of the Commission to supply the materials and services needed by industry only to the extent that they are unavailable commercially. Wherever practicable, the Government intends to reduce or eliminate its sales and

43. See AEC statement to Joint Committee on Atomic Energy, Section 202 Hearings, 1957, Part 1, p. 107.
44. AEC, *Atomic Energy Facts*, Washington, 1957, p. 12.

services as industrial sources become available. Prices and charges are based upon the principle of the recovery of full costs and include direct and indirect expenses (including depreciation) plus an added factor to cover overhead, interest on investment, process improvement, and expenses not subject to absolute determination.

Since actual AEC costs are classified, it is not possible to evaluate the extent to which prices and charges based on them are "fair" or "reasonable." Hence, a remarkable inconsistency in nuclear power information exists. Reactor technology and production methods for plutonium and U233 are "open" information, whereas the economics of nuclear fuel is, strictly speaking, unknowable, because the basic cost data are classified for national security reasons.[45] AEC's fixed prices have generally been accepted on faith, but growing criticism of the U235 price schedule contributed to the downward revision in 1961. The revision affected virtually all aspects of fuel-cycle economics.

The following four categories of prices or charges are predominant in the characteristic nuclear fuel cycle:

First, there are the prices of the source materials—natural uranium, depleted uranium and thorium. These prices are all presumably based on "full recovery of costs," but are known to have varied widely, especially the price of natural uranium, the cost of which to the AEC has declined by one third in recent years.[46] In fact, the 1961 reduction in U235 prices was made possible by the $8 per pound price of natural uranium, established for the domestic procurement program, April 1, 1962, to December 31, 1966. Uranium prices may well decline further when accelerated plant amortization results in complete write-off of the concentrating mills. AEC procurement prices paid for U_3O_8, recently approximating $7.90 per pound for domestic material, $9.75 for Canadian and about $11.35 for overseas, may decline after 1966 to $5 or $6 per pound.[47]

Second, there is the price charged for burning U235 contained in enriched uranium and the "rental," or use charge, placed on the value of the enriched material that is received from the government and held by the reactor opera-

45. To overcome this limitation the AEC in 1959 invited the Atomic Industrial Forum to examine, on a classified basis, the economics underlying the AEC enriched uranium prices. (See footnote 49.)

46. As early as 1959 the international panel that examined the bids on Italian Project ENSI made a point of showing how the existing schedule of U235 prices would be reduced by a 36 per cent drop in the price of natural uranium. The 1954 schedule would thereby be reduced 30 per cent at 1 per cent enrichment of U235, on down to 18 per cent at 90 per cent U235 content. The 1961 revision of U235 prices represented about an equivalent decrease. (IBRD, *Summary Report of the International Panel—Project ENSI*, Washington, 1959, p. 23.)

47. Jesse C. Johnson, Director, Division of Raw Materials, Remarks at the Colorado Mining Association Convention, Denver, March 17, 1962 (AEC Press Release No. S-5-62).

tor. Effective July 1, 1961, the AEC raised the use charge from 4 per cent to 4.75 per cent, and reduced the base prices for enriched (and depleted) uranium by amounts ranging between 20 per cent for highly enriched (90 per cent) and 34 per cent for slightly enriched (1 per cent) uranium. However, when the AEC reduced the prices of U235 again in 1962, it did not raise the use charge—though that might reasonably have been expected, pending private ownership.

Figure 5-1   Reductions in AEC Charges for Enriched Uranium

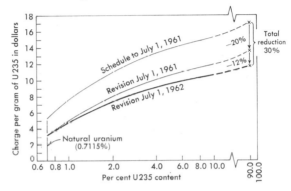

Sources: Federal Register, May 30, 1961 and May 29, 1962.

The policy supporting the AEC's 4 per cent use charge, up to July 1, 1961, is beclouded, since the agency did not report publicly the reasons for its choice at the time. Explanations long after the fact suggest that the AEC staff tried to set a use charge that was about equal to what the government was then paying for money. In any case, the 4 per cent use charge had long been an anachronism; before it was established, AEC studies of nuclear power costs (for example, Project Dynamo in 1953) had consistently used a 12 per cent use charge. In 1961 it was evident that the 4 per cent figure was low compared with the corresponding fuel inventory charges paid by electric utilities and with the prevailing rate of interest on government borrowing. The low use charge was widely recognized and accepted as a major form of subsidy.

The price schedule for enriched uranium in effect until July 1, 1961, was perhaps the most carefully constructed of the AEC prices. The operation of the gaseous diffusion cascades was well known and the relation between "tails" concentration, feed material input and so-called separative effort had been well established according to "ideal cascade theory."[48] While the theory

48. Manson Benedict and Thomas H. Pigford, *Nuclear Chemical Engineering*, McGraw-Hill, New York, 1957, pp. 396–404.

of pricing was evidently sound, based on physical principles, doubts arose in 1959 whether the costs imputed to separative work and the quoted price of enriched uranium were any longer valid.[49] After 1955 the cost of natural uranium feed dropped sharply, the efficiency of the cascades increased, the charges for plant depreciation apparently were greater than necessary and that catchall consisting of indirect expenses, overhead, interest on investment, process improvement and expenses not subject to absolute determination was apparently rather heavily weighted.[50] The industry was aware of the implications these factors held for possible future downward adjustment of U235 prices, but the AEC, when announcing the 1961 price schedule, explained that the downward adjustment was based only on the reduced cost of natural uranium and that the base charges representing the cost of separative work remained the same.[51] However, in July 1962 the AEC reduced the base prices again, this time to reflect (all or a part of?) the lower cost of separative work.

The third category of prices consists of prices the AEC pays for plutonium and U233 produced in licensed facilities, and guarantees to pay for seven years, under Section 56. The prices set for plutonium have been a constant source of confusion and bickering in Joint Committee hearings, partly because the AEC has been unable to state publicly what its price policy is actually based on, partly because the cost of producing weapon-grade plutonium has been classified and partly because no clear distinction has been made between fuel-grade material and plutonium that can still be used in weapons, though it is not of the lowest Pu240 content. To cap it all, the power costs of the Power Reactor Development Co.'s fast breeder reactor were especially sensitive to the price of by-product plutonium. As a consequence, Joint Committee critics of AEC policy for years were suspicious—and indeed believed—that the AEC's plutonium prices contained a subsidy, as did the original 4 per cent use charge.

The confusion in pricing plutonium is demonstrated by the conflicting actions the AEC has taken, since passage of the act, to set guaranteed prices

49. In 1959 an ad hoc committee of the Atomic Industrial Forum examined, on a classified basis, the AEC cost-price structure for enriched uranium fuel. The committee found, upon reviewing the AEC data, that the prices contained no subsidy and, on the contrary, were already so high that in the future a "decrease might be warranted." Also, published prices were sufficiently high that no increase would be necessary were weapon production requirements to decline, thus implying partial operation of existing plants for nonweapon purposes. (*Forum Memo*, December 1959, pp. 27–28.)

50. Philip Mullenbach, "Government Pricing and Civilian Reactor Technology," *Science and Resources: Prospects and Implications of Technological Advance*, Henry Jarrett (ed.), Resources for the Future, Washington, 1959, pp. 172–83.

51. AEC Release, D-138, Washington, May 29, 1961.

for plutonium. In January 1955 the prices were established on a classified basis, for a seven-year period ending in mid-1962, because, as was true of U235 prices, it was believed they might reveal U. S. production rates of fissionable material. In November 1956, however, the AEC set unclassified prices, for one additional year (to mid-1963), for plutonium at $12 per gram and U233 at $15 per gram, which represent their respective "fuel values" as compared with U235. Then in May 1957 it announced that the guaranteed prices for plutonium (presumably weapon grade) delivered before mid-1962 would range from $30 to $45 per gram, depending inversely upon the amount of Pu240 contained. And from mid-1962 to mid-1963 the price would be $30 per gram, regardless of the amount of Pu240. (The price of U233 remained the same throughout these seemingly divergent actions.) When the U235 prices were reduced in 1961, the AEC stated that while there were no price commitments for plutonium or U233 after June 30, 1963, it might well pay fuel-value prices that would be 20 per cent below former values, or a reduction from $12 to $9.50 per gram of plutonium (metal) and from $15 to $12 per gram of U233.

Lacking a firm basis for estimating future AEC prices, the nuclear power industry has generally assumed that in time the fuel value of plutonium ($12 per gram as metal and $9.50 as nitrate) would prevail. Under the 1962 price schedule for U235 it has been assumed that the fuel-value price might fall as low as $8.00 per gram (nitrate form), or to roughly 70 per cent of the price of highly enriched uranium (over 90 per cent).

The established prices of plutonium and U233 are related to those of U235 in an effort by the AEC to equalize approximately the "cost of heat" from the three fuels.[52] Obviously, then, as long as the price of U235 remains in doubt the so-called guaranteed prices of plutonium and U233 will also remain in doubt.

52. They may be calculated according to the following ratios: Assuming the nuclear constants of nonfission capture cross section to fission cross section (a) for U235 = .18; for U233 = .10; and Pu239 = .52, then price (Pr) for plutonium and for U233 may be calculated from the July 1, 1961, price of U235, at 90 per cent enrichment, as follows:

$$PrPu239 = \frac{PrU235 \ (1 + a \ U235)}{(1 + a \ Pu239)} \times \frac{\text{Atomic mass U235}}{\text{Atomic mass Pu239}}$$

$$= \frac{\$13.65 \times 1.18}{1.52} \times \frac{235}{239}$$

$$= \$10.45 \text{ per gram}$$

$$PrU233 = \frac{\$13.65 \times 1.18}{1.10} \times \frac{235}{233}$$

$$= \$14.65 \text{ per gram}$$

(Nuclear constants from Walter H. Zinn, *Nuclear Engineering Handbook*, McGraw-Hill, New York, 1958, p. 12–78; and equations from Manson Benedict, personal communication. For another approach, see M. C. Edlund, "Pricing Bred Reactor Fuel," *Nucleonics*, August 1960, p. 64.)

The fourth category of prices consists of the AEC prices for heavy water, isotopes and irradiated fuel elements—and its charge for processing irradiated fuel elements for the recovery of plutonium and remaining U235. The AEC has no visible pricing policy with respect to these materials and services. While its general policy of recovering full costs is said to be applicable,[53] sometimes a higher price has been set by the AEC to encourage commercial sources, in keeping with the intentions of the act.

On the other hand, heavy water (D_2O) was priced in the mid-1950s at $28 per pound—far less than the $80 per pound assumed in comparative reactor studies before the 1954 act. Since the AEC had great excess capacity for producing heavy water after the Savannah River reactors were completed, and the price was "low" by most private standards, no commercial sources in the United States were expected soon. Similarly, despite AEC "encouragement" to industry, the charges for chemically processing spent fuel were set by the AEC at levels that would be possible only with substantial tonnages, hence providing economies of scale that are not expected commercially for some years.

Evaluation of AEC Pricing Practices

The judgment that the prices of U235 (until July 1962) may have been too high—compared with real costs—rests not only on still further reduction of prices of uranium concentrates but on certain practical economic considerations. Average costs—rather than incremental costs—were the original basis of the AEC accounting cost both of feed material input and of separative work performed. The requirement for low enrichment material for civilian purposes was small, and probably will remain so for several years, compared with the "top" product for military purposes. Therefore, because military requirements could be met with less than full operation of all cascade capacity, it would have been economically sound to price the civilian product on incremental costs, rather than on average costs of raw material plus power plus fixed charges for the plant. (In the absence of published data, however, it is impossible to judge whether this refinement would have significantly altered the present price schedule.)[54]

53. Section 202 Hearings, 1957, Part 1, p. 107.

54. Moreover, the AEC apparently avoided any theory of discounting to a present-worth basis, or failed to consider its merits, when considering the cost and value of future output of enriched uranium for military and civilian requirements, respectively. Instead, the AEC apparently assumed a "zero time preference," that is, future output for weapons was considered, for all practical purposes, just as valuable as output today. Because future output for use in weapons may be assumed to have sharply diminishing value on a discounted present-worth basis, it might be proper to assign proportionately greater fixed costs to weapon requirements now, and thus less to future civilian requirements. Again, in the absence of sufficient public information, one can only cite the issue that is raised.

TABLE **5 - 3**

AEC Prices for Enriched Uranium: Effect of Assumed Reductions in Cost of Natural Uranium (C_F) and in Imputed Cost of Separative Work (C_s)

Basis	Per cent of enrichment				
	1.0	2.0	3.0	50.0	90.0
	Price per gram of U235 content				
Original schedule (C_F = $39.27 per kg. of U; C_s = $37.29 per kg. of U)	$7.58	$11.00	$12.52	$16.76	$17.07
Adjusted for lower C_F (C_F = $25.00 per kg. of U; C_s = $37.29 per kg. of U)	5.24	8.30	9.69	13.70	14.00
Adjusted for lower C_s (C_F = $39.27 per kg. of U; C_s = $26.00 per kg. of U)[a]	6.70	9.70	11.00	14.80	15.00
Adjusted for both lower C_F and lower C_s (C_F = $25.00 per kg. of U; C_s = $26.00 per kg. of U)	4.80	7.15	8.05	10.90	11.45
Revised schedule, July 1, 1961[b]	4.99	8.00	9.37	13.35	13.65
Revised schedule, July 1, 1962[c]	4.77	7.33	8.48	11.76	12.01
			Per cent		
Per cent reduction from original price schedule	37.1	33.4	32.3	29.8	29.6

a. C_s = $26.00 represents roughly a one-third reduction in the imputed cost of separative work ($37.29) under ideal cascade conditions.

b. Reflects a reduction of 40 per cent in natural uranium cost and none in cost of separative work.

c. Reflects an unstated amount of reduction in the cost of separative work and no additional reduction in the cost of uranium.

Sources:

Original price schedule—For the cost constants that best fit the AEC price scale see Manson Benedict and Thomas H. Pigford, *Nuclear Chemical Engineering*, McGraw-Hill, New York, pp. 403–04. The price scale is available in, among other places, AEC, *Atomic Energy Facts*, Washington, September 1957, p. 14.

Adjustment for lower C_F—See IBRD, *Summary Report of the International Panel: Project ENSI*, Washington, March 1959, Appendix E, p. 23. Schedule assumed a 36 per cent reduction in natural uranium costs.

Adjustment for lower C_s—Statement of Manson Benedict on government policy regarding pricing and ownership of nuclear fuels, Section 202 Hearings, 1962, pp. 560–62.

Values for enrichments other than 90 per cent in adjustments for lower C_s and in adjustments for both lower C_F and lower C_s are interpolated from generalized price scales for mixtures of U235 and U238 in D. P. Herron and others, "Fuel Cycles for Nuclear Power Reactors," *Proceedings*, Second Geneva Conference, Vol. 13.

Revised schedule, July 1, 1961—*Federal Register*, May 30, 1961.

Revised schedule, July 1, 1962—*Federal Register*, May 29, 1962.

Experience of the last five years has also indicated that fixed and variable costs may be less than were originally assumed. The cost of electric power—a major variable item—has remained approximately the same, but other charges and costs have apparently diminished.[55] New additions to cascade capacity have increased efficiency and improvements in processing have occurred; charges for depreciation and maintenance have proved to be less, based on AEC financial reports, than had previously been said to be necessary; and properly assignable "overhead" costs of the AEC now appear to be less than was originally assumed.[56]

The overstatement—extreme before July 1, 1961, and to a lesser extent thereafter—of AEC prices for enriched uranium is suggested by Table 5–3, showing the combined effect on the original price schedule of both lower natural uranium prices and lower imputed costs of the AEC's unit of separative work. This analysis indicates that for 2 per cent enriched material, a common fuel, a remarkable downward adjustment in the original price scale (from $11.00 per gram of U235) would have resulted from either a lower natural uranium feed cost or lower imputed cost of separative work. The lower feed cost assumed—down 36 per cent—gives a price of $8.30, 25 per cent less than the original scale. The lower indicated imputed cost of separative work ($26.00 per kilogram of uranium) would yield a price of $9.70 or 12 per cent less than scale. Both lower natural uranium prices and lower imputed costs of separative work would give a cost of only $7.15, or 35 per cent below scale. In 1961, when the AEC revised the schedule and allowed for a 40 per cent reduction in natural uranium costs, the decline in the price of 2 per cent enrichment was 27 per cent. A further reduction was made in 1962 to reflect lower processing costs, and the resultant decline in the price of 2 per cent enrichment was 33 per cent from the original schedule.

Still lower natural uranium prices are in prospect and gaseous diffusion plants will soon be fully amortized. In the absence of public disclosure of full cost data, the validity of the AEC's price policy for enriched uranium can be questioned only superficially and the detailed argument cannot be carried to

55. Robert E. Wilson, AEC Commissioner, remarks at the Second Joint Conference on Nuclear Power, U. S.–Japan Atomic Industrial Forums, Tokyo, December 5, 1961 (AEC Release No. S-27-61).

56. For example, Karl Cohen, in attempting to reconstruct the basic AEC cost of enriched uranium, used AEC sources for assuming a plant depreciation rate of 10 per cent and an allowance of 15 per cent for AEC overhead. ("Charting a Course for Nuclear Power Development," *Nucleonics*, January 1958, p. 66.) Yet, in contrast, the AEC is currently reporting depreciation charges at 4 per cent on production facilities (AEC, *Financial Report for Fiscal Year 1961*, Washington, 1961) and AEC expenses for administration of communities, program direction, security investigations and all other costs not separately identified do not exceed 4 per cent of total AEC operating expenses (excluding raw material procurement).

a conclusion. In any event, the new schedule has resulted in more reasonable prices for U235 and has rectified the former lack of consistency between the prices of natural uranium and slightly enriched uranium which had been distorting both the technology and economics of nuclear power.

With lower prices for U235 in 1961 it became feasible for the AEC to raise the use charge slightly, by 0.75 per cent, though not to the level—about 10 per cent—customarily applied to inventories of private utilities. At the same time the fuel values of plutonium and U233 could be established with greater confidence and at commensurately lower levels. Manifestly, the AEC's former "two-price system" for plutonium was untenable. For, with the fuel-value price of plutonium reduced by about one fifth, from $12.00 to $9.50 per gram, in consonance with the lower price for U235, the necessity for recycling plutonium had become evident.[57] Further downward adjustments in the prices of U235 may be possible: if there are further reductions in the price of natural uranium; if, as seems probable, further reductions in the cost of separative work occur; and when complete amortization of the older gaseous diffusion plants takes place.

Public Assistance for Private Development

In the 1954 act the Congress tried to make clear that it intended to permit no subsidy of private business. However, the act qualified this—rather ambiguously—by providing for government assistance (funds, materials and services) in the construction or operation of facilities required for conducting research and development under contract arrangements with the AEC (Section 169). Despite the "no subsidy" injunction, the AEC has had wide latitude in providing financial and other assistance to private concerns that engage in atomic development.

From "Assistance" to "Subsidy"

The AEC's support of private development often has left in doubt whether industry or the federal government should take primary responsibility for reactor progress during the costly early stages. It has also raised questions as to

---

57. The economic argument for fuel-value pricing may have received insufficient attention, for it was obvious that a "high" price for plutonium was attractive to all segments of the industry: uranium producers foresaw a larger market for natural uranium converters; reactor equipment manufacturers foresaw a greater chance of competitive generating costs; equipment exporters foresaw an important selling point abroad; and chemical processors foresaw a better market for plutonium separation services.

the tendency toward more extreme forms of government assistance—from waiver of fuel-use charges to proposals for capital grants or reimbursement of design costs. The growing incompatibility of the limited resources of the electric utility industry and the activity expected of it have led to the AEC's reluctantly assuming progressively greater initiative.

In the "first round" cooperative program in January 1955 the AEC offered to pay for developing the project, but not for construction. In the "second round" the AEC assumed most of the construction costs for publicly owned projects and most of the costs other than construction (i.e., research and development) for both publicly and privately owned projects. In 1959 AEC Chairman McCone suggested offering up to 50 per cent of capital costs for acceptable prototype projects. Were responses to AEC invitations to prove unsatisfactory, "the Commission would construct such plants on its own sites and generate power for its own use."[58] In 1962 the AEC Commissioners suggested that reactor design costs be reimbursed.[59]

There is a long tradition of government subsidies for industries—for example, the railroads, shipping and, more recently, aviation. Indirect or "concealed" subsidies, including airmail contracts, municipal airports and radio beacons, were especially important for aviation. Leaders of the nuclear energy industry have argued that such help is a necessary condition of successful private development.

Government aid as an alternative to government ownership and operation of nuclear power plants has had the closest attention of the Joint Committee and of the AEC during the last few years.[60] Construction subsidies—forbidden by the 1954 act—were the last resort of the Eisenhower administration's insistence on keeping the federal government out of nuclear power generation. The list of expedients was long, indeed, and the line between "private" and "public" development was almost obliterated. Some of the economic implications are now manifest.

Rate Base of Private Power Projects

The public construction costs saved by having private utilities build the plants was one of the AEC's arguments against federal construction. Early in 1962 the Edison Electric Institute estimated that the private utilities had invested about $400 million in fifteen nuclear power plants and associated re-

58. *AEC Authorizing Legislation, Fiscal Year 1960*, p. 143.

59. Section 202 Hearings, pp. 49 ff.

60. In 1962 the Chairman of the Joint Committee requested the AEC to submit data preparatory to Committee study of subsidies and assistance. (Section 202 Hearings, pp. 107–08.)

search and development work. However, as the public power groups have pointed out, there are compensatory factors that substantially reduce the burden on the private investor and shift it to others. A canvass of state regulatory commissions by Richard A. Tybout in 1957 revealed that most allow utilities to charge research expenses, but Untereiner found the precedents for allowing higher capital costs in the rate base were inconclusive.[61] Furthermore, private utilities have received accelerated amortization certificates, issued by the Office of Defense Mobilization, which greatly reduce the tax liability and, in effect, provide an "interest-free loan" on their total investments.[62] Construction costs paid out by the private utility are largely reimbursed over the years by taxpayers and consumers. In any case, the stockholder does not carry the full burden of added risks or costs of nuclear power plant.

Facilities Licensing by the AEC

The AEC's responsibility for licensing the construction of nuclear power plants has been complicated by the fact that the act itself provides help and encouragement to industry in undertaking nuclear projects, and at the same time requires strict government control to protect the public health and safety. The conflict between these two ends became apparent when the Commission in 1956 issued a provisional construction permit to the Power Reactor Development Co. (PRDC), despite the questions raised by the AEC Reactor Safeguards Committee, whose report was at first withheld, then released. The reactor proposed was a fast breeder, a highly advanced type, and granting a construction license required more than usual consideration.[63]

This case heightened the apparent conflict between control and assistance to private industry.[64] By this action the AEC in effect decided not to delay de-

61. *Atomic Power and Energy Resource Planning*, Bureau of Business Research, Ohio State University, 1958, Table 17, p. 74; Ray E. Untereiner, *State Regulation and the Future of Nuclear Power*, AEC, Washington, 1960.

62. National Rural Cooperative Association, *1958 Power Facts Handbook*, Washington, pp. 128–42.

63. The construction permit issued to the PRDC in August 1956 was provisional in that conversion to a license depended on satisfactorily showing that the final design would give reasonable assurance that the health and safety of the public would not be adversely affected by its operation. Furthermore, expiration would occur within one year if the PRDC failed to provide data required for the AEC to approve the findings of financial qualifications specified by the act. The permit was essentially the same as permits previously granted to Commonwealth Edison and Consolidated Edison.

64. For an analysis of the AEC's licensing responsibilities and actions see *A Study of AEC Procedures and Organization in the Licensing of Reactor Facilities*, Joint Committee on Atomic Energy, 85th Cong., 1st Sess., April 1957.

velopment of this advanced type of reactor to permit fuller exploration of safety questions, but to rely on advances in knowledge during the course of construction to provide the necessary data. Moreover, the AEC decided to encourage industry to undertake a full-scale plant of highly advanced design, rather than to confine it to a less risky, proven type. Finally, the AEC may have been accepting a less than optimum choice of reactor location and design in its effort to seize the opportunity to enlist a private concern. The clear alternative was to build the reactor at a remote location, as individual members of the Commission had suggested.

The AEC's role as both promoter and regulator of reactor development also raised the issue of the agency's capacity for objective evaluation. Considering the circumstances, it was of public importance that a petition for intervention filed by three labor unions in October 1956 was granted, permitting judicial review of the PRDC license. This event soon led the AEC to make numerous procedural changes that greatly improved the reconciliation of the agency's dual responsibility for both promotion and control.[65] In effect, the AEC concluded that in future it would not act first and then wait for reactions, but would instead provide notice of intent and allow time for demurral by interested parties.

After lengthy hearings on the PRDC case the Commission in December 1958 issued an order affirming and amending the original permit. In 1960 the U. S. Court of Appeals denied the validity of the permit, but in June 1961 the U. S. Supreme Court reversed the ruling and upheld the action of the AEC.[66]

The general economic implications of the case, less vital than the procedural improvements the AEC adopted during the interim,[67] are not easily identified but are nonetheless significant. First, public safety has become the predominant consideration in the AEC's licensing policy.[68] Therefore, the electric utility undertaking a reactor project can be expected to assure itself early in the developmental phase that the reactor can be shown to be safe, or the company risks heavy losses on research through failure to secure a permit. Safety, therefore, has also become a first consideration of designers working on advanced reactor concepts. Second, the PRDC case made it almost a certainty

65. Among other things these include: issuance of proposed licensing actions with opportunity for hearing, if requested; publication of a reactor hazards evaluation by the AEC staff prior to action; the separation of AEC staff engaged in public hearings on permits, the licensing staff and the promotional staff.

66. *Power Reactor Development Co. v. IUE*, 367 U. S. 396, June 12, 1961.

67. For an account of the administrative lessons see James L. Morrisson and B. John Garrick, "What We Learned From the PRDC Case," *Nucleonics*, July 1959, pp. 60–63.

68. AEC, *Opinion and Initial Decision, In the Matter of Power Reactor Development Company, Docket No. F-16*, Washington, December 10, 1958.

that the electric utility industry will be wary of highly advanced reactor types; and, as a corollary, the AEC may have to take the initiative in such projects and may find it hard to interest private industry without special subsidies. The cost of designing adequate safety features—such as a containment sphere—is likely to remain a significant element.

TABLE **5 - 4**

AEC Estimates of Plutonium Output of Nuclear Power Plants Supplied with U. S. Enriched Uranium, 1960–1968

Year	Nuclear capacity (mw.)		Plutonium output (kg.)		Financial commitment (millions) for domestic Pu at	
					$9.50 per gram	$30.00 per gram
	Domestic (1)	Foreign (2)	Domestic (3)	Foreign (4)	(5)	(6)
1960	500	40				
1961	700	240				
1962	720	600	200	50	$1.9	$6.0
1963	940	1,600	500	200	4.7	15.0
1964	1,300	2,200	900	600	8.5	27.0
1965	1,900	3,000	1,300	1,500	12.3	39.0
1966	2,400	4,000	1,700	2,700	16.1	51.0
1967			2,400	4,200	22.0	72.0
1968			3,300	6,400	31.4	99.0

Sources:
    Cols. 1–4—Letter from AEC to Joint Committee, March 1959, in AEC *Authorizing Legislation, Fiscal Year 1960,* Hearings, Joint Committee on Atomic Energy, 86th Cong., 1st Sess., 1959, p. 680.
    Cols. 5–6—Computed by author: $9.50 = fuel value; $30.00 = weapon value.

The Plutonium "Buy-Back" Commitment: Indirect Subsidy?

The volume of fissionable material the government may "buy" in coming years and the prices it may pay could also be important in terms of public assistance to the electric industry and of growing financial commitments by the government. The gross commitment for plutonium could conceivably run into hundreds of millions over a period of years;[69] the net commitment, however, would be largely reduced by sales and use charges on government sup-

69. James L. Morrisson, *Vanderbilt Law Review,* December 1958, p. 204. However, such AEC "purchases" of plutonium might well be sold or leased at a later date to utility systems, assuming competitive prices.

plied U235 in fuel. Nevertheless, the gross amount is the pertinent consideration when examining the scale of financial commitment to industry.

The AEC can be expected to reduce the buy-back prices for plutonium as
rapidly as technical progress and changes in U235 prices permit. Indeed, it has
long been within the AEC's discretion to set "low," though "fair," plutonium
prices that would encourage reactor operators to recycle their own plutonium
rather than turn it back to the government.[70] Moreover, if private ownership
of nuclear fuel were to be permitted, the fuel value totals shown in Table 5–4
would lose their significance as a measure of public subsidy.

It would be sheer speculation to attempt to estimate the total future financial
commitment implied by the terms of Sections 52 (ownership) and 56 (fair
price). The joint agreement between the United States and Euratom, for example, provides that the United States may purchase by-product plutonium,
if Euratom itself does not wish to retain it for future peaceful uses. In the
Euratom Cooperation Act of 1958 Congress authorized the AEC to acquire
up to 4,100 kilograms of plutonium (to be used only for peaceful purposes)
produced under the joint program for a period of no more than ten years. At
the original AEC fuel-value price for plutonium ($12 per gram) this repre-
sented a contingent commitment of nearly $50 million up to 1975. This, how-
ever, would be less than Euratom's estimated payments to the United States
for enriched uranium.[71]

In the short term, to 1970, the total fuel value of by-product plutonium in
the United States cannot be large, as is suggested by the projections in Table
5–4. Assuming the probable slow growth of nuclear power, the present seven-
year guarantee of "weapon-value" plutonium prices could by 1968 provide
almost $70 million of additional revenue to reactor operators in the United
States. However, the AEC made clear (in its decision on the PRDC case and
elsewhere) that reactor operators have no basis for assuming premium prices
for plutonium beyond the present seven-year price guarantee, that is, until
June 30, 1963. This was reaffirmed in 1962.[72]

Indirect Assistance: Economies of Scale

A variety of other subsidies has become imbedded in the hypertrophied
program of government assistance. Perhaps the greatest, and usually over-

70. Operators of breeder reactors, in which the fuel would be subject to frequent reprocessing,
may be expected to oppose a "low" price for plutonium (or U233), since the cost of generating
power in these systems will be more sensitive to the buy-back price than is the generating cost in
converter reactors.

71. See *Proposed Euratom Agreements*, Hearings, Joint Committee on Atomic Energy, 85th
Cong., 2nd Sess., July 1958, p. 31.

72. Section 202 Hearings, p. 108.

looked, form of public assistance comes from the large economies of scale that mark the government's nuclear energy facilities. In some cases these economies have been passed on to the reactor operators through lower prices or charges than could be secured from privately owned, commercial sources. Principal among these are the price of U235 and heavy water and provision of facilities for storing radioactive wastes. On the other hand, the charges for chemical processing of spent fuel are derived from a hypothetical plant that industry might build, hence the established charges are greater than the AEC costs and are not directly related to the AEC scale of operation.

Such an extraordinary multiplicity and depth of economic assistance to private development deserves more than casual evaluation, for the period of intensive development may still require a decade. But because of their great variety, it has become virtually impossible for private or public groups to judge the wisdom, quantitatively or qualitatively, of the direct and indirect forms of public assistance. Continuous evaluation is necessary for formulating wise public policy.

Judging the Reasonableness of Government Assistance

Private and public investments in research and development lack tidy standards of reasonableness to guide policy makers in planning a sensibly scaled effort, given acceptable national objectives. No neat relation exists between augmented research results and additional expenditures for different reactor types. Nonquantitative criteria useful in judging the quality and balance of the development program are more tractable. For this purpose a number of criteria are pertinent:[73] for example, whether sufficient support is being given to technical advances as they appear; whether the program avoids exacerbation of the private-vs.-public-power controversy; and whether military and civilian development efforts are in reasonable balance. These and others will be examined.

Balance of Effort Among Reactor Concepts

Until late 1959 the AEC encouraged work on almost all promising reactor concepts,[74] since there was no way of knowing the most promising approaches

73. See Perry D. Teitelbaum and Philip Mullenbach, "The Development of Nuclear Energy," *Federal Expenditure Policy for Economic Growth and Stability*, Joint Economic Committee, 85th Cong., 1st Sess., November 5, 1957, pp. 726 ff.

74. The shift toward a more concentrated approach occurred as a result of the "Report by the Ad Hoc Advisory Committee on Reactor Policies and Programs," January 2, 1959. (Section 202 Hearings, 1959, pp. 510–37.)

to competitive nuclear power in the long run. On the other hand, spreading the effort diluted the available resources and the AEC was inordinately pulled by the seeming initial technical success of the so-called "proven types"— pressurized water, boiling water and sodium-graphite reactors—all of them requiring enriched material. Since each of these types was picked up by particular reactor manufacturers, one might well have expected that the AEC would orient its direct activity more in favor of long-term approaches. These would include, for example: the fast breeder; the homogeneous; the high-temperature, gas-cooled; and the heavy water–moderated, natural uranium reactors. But the AEC was slow to do so. In particular, support of plutonium recycle technology was seriously delinquent. In fact, while the expenditure program until late 1959 seemed to emphasize breadth, it inexplicably "missed" promising reactor concepts.

The Scale of Construction Efforts

For reasons of foreign policy, "acceleration" has generally been accepted as desirable in nuclear power development, and yet, as indicated in Chapter 4, expenditures for civilian reactor development have increased no faster than those for military reactors or for other major research and development programs sponsored by the government. On the other hand, public expenditures for civilian power reactor construction were held in check as a result of the Eisenhower administration's effort to assign this responsibility to the reluctant private utility industry. The growth of private commitments for nuclear power plants thus was expected to parallel the heavy public research expenditures of the AEC. The two cannot be considered separately.[75] (See Figure 4–5, p. 140.)

While public expenditures can be sustained and presumably justified for several years more, there is doubt that private utilities can long continue the construction of high-cost prototypes or full-scale demonstration plants. Therefore, whether the future scale of private nuclear plant construction is commensurate with that of government research may well be a continuing source of controversy. At the end of 1961 the AEC technical staff clearly indicated that prototype and full-scale demonstration plants were not proceeding at a pace consistent with the advances in reactor technology, and Joint Com-

75. In the "cooperative arrangements program," the value of AEC assistance represents only a fraction of the contractor's investment. One might well conclude that for each dollar of public assistance the AEC has succeeded in attracting several dollars of private investment, almost entirely in plant. (See Table 4–10, p. 137.)

mittee Chairman Holifield in 1962 deplored the lack of "new starts" by private utilities after 1961.[76]

Relationship of U. S. Development to Foreign Requirements

As has been shown, natural uranium systems, plutonium recycle and the thorium-U233 cycle—all of unique interest to friendly foreign countries—have generally been given less attention than research on the historic and proven types using enriched uranium and water. The U. S. program has demonstrated international leadership in achieving such major technical advances as the boiling water reactor, recently of interest to the United Kingdom and the USSR. But it has proved slow in pressing the fast breeder reactor, the high-temperature, gas-cooled reactor or the thorium-U233 fuel cycle. To be sure, other countries have had no greater success with these advanced systems. The USSR has probably devoted a greater share of its resources to the fast breeder, yet it has not, apparently, accomplished a fast breeder approaching that of the Fermi reactor (PRDC).[77] International competition to achieve "technical leadership" is highly unpredictable, as the leading atomic nations broaden or narrow their present power reactor programs.[78]

Balance between Power Reactor Research and Related Research

The nation's resources of technical personnel and fissionable material are ample for adequate military and civilian nuclear programs.[79] Expenditures are much larger, however, for military than for civilian power reactor development, and the gap between military and civilian reactors may be widening. Today there is question whether strictly competitive nuclear power, acceptable to electric utilities in the United States, is not more remote than a nuclear-propelled missile or satellite.

In comparison with the resources dedicated to military reactors, the civilian nuclear power program cannot be judged excessive. On the other hand, the

76. Frank K. Pittman, Director, Division of Reactor Development, AEC, remarks for presentation at the Second Joint Conference on Nuclear Power, U. S.–Japan Atomic Industrial Forums, Tokyo, December 6, 1961 (AEC Release S-26-1961); Section 202 Hearings, 1962, pp. 6–22.

77. See Chapter 7; and V. S. Emelyanov, "The Future of Atomic Energy in the USSR," *Proceedings*, Second Geneva Conference, Vol. 1.

78. Reference here is to central station nuclear power. Were military applications to be included, then technical leadership in airplane propulsion, nuclear-powered satellites, and so on would be far more impressive evidence of leadership than such mundane accomplishments as an economically competitive fast breeder, for example.

79. Atomic Industrial Forum, *Engineering Manpower Requirements for the Atomic Industry*, New York, September 1957.

civilian program is large compared with other government-sponsored civilian research programs (except space travel and exploration), accounting as it does for a sizable part of all federal expenditures for civilian research and development.[80] With outer space research, controlled thermonuclear reactions and nuclear power, the nation has indeed entered a new era of huge federal commitments for research and development. In none of these programs are narrowly defined economic considerations the determining factor, though in relation to the nuclear power program they demand great attention.

Benefit-Cost Ratio of the Nuclear Power Program

A commonly accepted standard of the comparative economic value of public investment, notably in water development projects, has been the ratio of measurable economic benefits from a specific project to the public investment or other costs involved.[81]

A similar benefit-cost analysis of nuclear power development might help to indicate whether the scale of development cost has possibly outrun the foreseeable discounted benefits of nuclear power to the nation. One starts such an exercise, however, with skepticism.[82] The national return on research investment extends outside pecuniary measurements and includes such intangible but massive elements as foreign policy objectives. Hence, social return and research cost cannot be considered commensurate in applying strict benefit-cost ratios to nuclear energy and other broad programs.

An exploratory benefit-cost analysis by E. F. Renshaw in the United States, using alternative nuclear power growth projections by Mayer and by Davis and Roddis, suggests that during the period 1956–1980 the cumulative savings from nuclear power might be between two and six times the cumulative federal expenditures for research and development plus the excess cost of noncompetitive demonstration plants.[83] However, the results of a more refined study, begun in 1961 by the Ad Hoc Committee on Atomic Policy of the Atomic Industrial Forum, suggested a more favorable outlook and made a tentative

80. National Science Foundation, *Federal Funds for Science (X)*, Washington, 1962.

81. See, for example, Otto Eckstein, *Water Resource Development*, Harvard University Press, Cambridge, 1958; and Roland McKeon, *Efficiency in Government Through Systems Analysis*, Wiley, New York, 1958.

82. A British expert who has tried states that, while it appears theoretically possible to set limits on the total amount of development work worth doing by estimating the aggregate national savings to be achieved by nuclear power production, the calculations in practice prove not only exceedingly complex but also critically dependent upon such widely varying, subjective assumptions as the future real rate of interest. Furthermore, the derived benefits of research on such a new technology are hardly measurable. J. A. Jukes, "Economics of Nuclear Power," *Proceedings*, Second Geneva Conference, Vol. 13, p. 499.

83. "Atomic Power Research and Social Return," University of Chicago Office of Agricultural Economics Research, February 4, 1958, Paper No. 5801.

finding that a total public and private investment of $2 billion, 1962–1969, did not appear unreasonable in relation to the expected benefits as measured by generating cost savings over 30 years. Assuming 4 per cent interest for "present worth" calculations, the study suggested that savings in generating costs to the year 2000 might be on the order of ten times the investment commitment.[84]

Compared with similar analyses for other public investments, such as water development and agricultural research, these benefit-cost ratios for nuclear power are hardly impressive. Though not conclusive, they do carry useful implications for both policy formation and the direction of federal assistance. Obviously, owing to the small ratio of economic benefits to costs, it is particularly wasteful of public and private resources to construct nuclear plants in other than high-cost fuel areas.[85] Further, all indirect forms of financial assistance, such as rapid tax amortization, excessive valuation of plutonium production, provision of liability insurance and the like, should be reckoned in the investment. Adding these indirect costs to the direct would result in eliminating a significant fraction of the foreseeable net savings. Finally, however intriguing benefit-cost analyses may appear generally, the problems of estimating both elements in nuclear power development are inseparable. The vast uncertainty of the underlying projections renders the benefit-cost comparisons of little value in view of overriding foreign and domestic policy considerations.

It must be emphasized that benefit-cost ratios for nuclear power are hopelessly inadequate measures of whether public research resources are being dedicated to their "highest use," as judged by alternative possibilities. The fact that only trivial sums are being devoted to such purposes as salt-water conversion, hydrogenation or gasification of coal, recovery of oil from shale or tar sands and many other desirable programs does not dictate a substantial reduction in nuclear power expenditures. Rather, it prompts a reexamination of the benefit-cost ratios of these other programs.

Effects on the Private-vs.-Public-Power Controversy

Accommodation of this controversy has ranked high in legislative and executive consideration of the numerous devices proposed for accelerating reactor development. In general, members of the Joint Committee have

84. Section 202 Hearings, 1962, p. 462–81.

85. It was economic nonsense, for example, to construct the government-owned pressurized water reactor in one of the lowest fuel-cost areas of the east; the site was the fortuitous result of the offer of the Duquesne Light Co. to contribute a small part (6 per cent) of plant cost and its offer of somewhat more favorable terms than other interested utilities offered for the purchase of heat.

attempted to insulate or neutralize the effects of the controversy, for example, by avoiding sterile discussion of the merits of exclusive private or public nuclear power development. That has not been an issue.

Passage of the 1954 act made it clear that neither public nor private power should be permitted to preempt the field. While agreement on this principle provided some measure of constraint, it was unable to influence the incidence of particular government actions on the two sectors. For example, the AEC fuel-value price for by-product plutonium is presumably neutral in its effect on private and public plants, but the incidence of the 4.75 per cent fuel-use charge is not, because private utilities generally cannot secure financing at such a low rate of interest, whereas public power groups generally can—and often for less. Moreover, the return on the rate base is normally 6 per cent or higher for private utilities.

Similarly, while the prices for enriched uranium and for processing irradiated fuel are presumably neutral, the incidence of the "no subsidy" provision of the act may not be. Under the cooperative arrangements program the AEC (through Joint Committee persuasion) contracted to build and own the plants of public power groups, whereas the assistance to private utilities excluded construction subsidies.[86] In Table 4–9 we can see that AEC construction assistance to public groups totaled $56 million as of June 30, 1961, equivalent to one third the value of all forms of AEC assistance to both private and public power systems in the cooperative arrangements program. Clearly, the kinds of AEC assistance are so varied that it may be hopeless to expect "equal" treatment of the two contending sectors.

With the founding of Euratom and the IAEA, it became evident that the formation of domestic economic policies—for government assistance, pricing and private ownership of nuclear fuel and patent rights—also necessarily impinged upon the prospects for U. S. participation in nuclear power development elsewhere in the world.

86. However, it is of interest that two government-owned power reactors were built in private electric utility systems—the Shippingport, Pa., plant in the Duquesne Light Co. and the SRE plant in the Southern California Edison Co. (Santa Susana, Calif.).

CHAPTER **6**

Foreign Need: The Strategic Economic Factors

Conflicting views about where nuclear power should be applied first—in the highly industrialized countries or in the countries in the early stages of industrializing—have become a source of international tension. The conflict marked the Second Geneva Conference and has plagued the International Atomic Energy Agency.[1] Though generalizations about such highly diverse economies are dangerous, the growing literature on the role of nuclear power in various countries provides a perspective that deserves brief introductory comment.[2]

1. The reasons that nuclear power should come first to the industrialized nations and then to the countries in the process of economic development, after they have "gone through a preliminary stage of industrialization in the old way," were stated at the opening session of the Second Geneva Conference by its President, Professor Francis Perrin (France), September 1, 1958. Dr. H. J. Bhabha (India) presented a contrary view, which is developed later in this chapter.

2. Leading examples are the area case studies in the NPA series, *The Productive Uses of Nuclear Energy*, Washington: Michael Sapir and Sam J. Van Hyning, *The Outlook for Nuclear Power in Japan*, 1956; Stefan H. Robock, *Nuclear Power and Economic Development in Brazil*, 1957; H. H. Landsberg and G. Perazich, *Nuclear Power and Economic Development in Israel*, 1957; Norman L. Gold, *Regional Economic Development and Nuclear Power in India*, 1957; I. M. D. Little and P. N. Rosenstein-Rodan, *Nuclear Power and Italy's Energy Position*, 1957; A. Mayne, *Prospects for Nuclear Energy in Puerto Rico*, 1958; and Maurice D. Kilbridge, *The Prospect for Nuclear Power in Pakistan*, 1958. Also see Bruce C. Netschert and Sam H. Schurr, *Atomic Energy Applications With Reference to Underdeveloped Countries*, Resources for the Future, Washington, 1957; International Atomic Energy Agency, Vienna: *Prospects of Nuclear Power in Finland*, Technical Report Series No. 2, 1960; and *Prospects of Nuclear Power in the Philippines*, Technical Report Series No. 3, 1961.

For the quite underdeveloped countries, reporting low, stagnant per capita incomes (including several countries in Africa and South Asia, but not India), the prospect that nuclear power stations will make any important contribution to economic development seems poor for many years to come. None of the available economic studies indicates that these countries are "power-starved," or that nuclear power would permit these countries to leap over major elements of development—similar to the introduction of air transport in opening remote areas lacking rail facilities—as was suggested by the early popular snap judgment that atomic power would be cheap as well as potentially abundant.

The leaders of the underdeveloped countries, however, as indicated by the papers at the Second Geneva Conference, seem to have become quite realistic in their views concerning the near- and long-term role of nuclear energy, particularly power. They generally recognize that the chances of breaking the chain of low productivity, underemployment, poverty, excessive population, poor public administration and political instability cannot be greatly improved by resorting to a new source of energy.[3]

Furthermore, for the countries in the process of industrializing—such as Brazil, India and Israel—nuclear power stations appear to hold promise of contributing economically, but only in a specialized, highly selective manner during the next couple of decades. After that the benefits could be more extensive, as limited domestic energy resources become more fully utilized under the impact of both population growth and expanding industrialization. Meanwhile, the programs of accelerated economic development that these countries are undertaking have not, in general, been seriously constrained by inadequate or unreasonably priced energy sources.[4] Competitive nuclear power during this interval might have a marginal influence favoring industrial development, not so much by way of slightly reducing the costs of production or encouraging more power-intensive production techniques, but rather by encouraging development of areas—enclaves—distant from energy sources. In certain regions costs of conventional fuel may be high, especially if heavy investment of additional capital is required for both production and transportation of fossil fuels (as in India and Pakistan). However, in most regions further analysis may suggest that indigenous energy sources—particularly

3. It should be emphasized, too, that other new energy sources—solar, wind, tidal—appear to be no more imminent in substantial economic effect than nuclear energy. See, for example, Department of Economic and Social Affairs, UN, *New Sources of Energy and Economic Development*, New York, 1957.

4. There is evidence, to be sure, that high regional electric power rates and small inefficient generating units have led to inordinate aggregations of capital at centers enjoying low power rates, as, for example, at Manila, Philippine Islands. (See IAEA, *Prospects of Nuclear Power in the Philippines*.)

hydro, as in India and Brazil—could meet the growing demand at little or no increase in real energy cost for many years to come. Indeed, for almost all the industrializing nations that have been subjected to evaluation, nuclear power stations during the next two decades are seen as most improbable sources of more than a small fraction of total power requirements.

Significant for United States foreign policy formation is the fact that some of the industrializing nations, such as India and Brazil, possess nuclear source materials (thorium particularly) which might be developed as a first step toward putting nuclear energy to the service of economic programs emphasizing the use of domestic resources.

Finally, several of the industrialized nations (the countries of Western Europe, Japan and the USSR, for example) have found that their national energy positions have deteriorated. Production of coal, the base fuel, has proved to be rather inflexible in Western Europe, not only because of labor immobility, but also through depletion of the most economically mined seams. Moreover, in some countries the hydro potential may soon be fully used. Hence, the annual growth in total energy consumption (perhaps less than 3 per cent) and the much more rapid growth in demand for electric power (6 to 7 per cent) has been met, except in recent recession years, in large part by imported coal or oil. Each of these countries, described as energy deficient, has been subject to uncertainty of terms and of assured supply. Shipping rates have varied widely and recurring Middle East oil crises have jeopardized both price and availability. Energy specialists of these countries believe that nuclear power's appearance has been most timely—despite more ample domestic fuel supplies since 1957. Yet, even with competitive nuclear power, the growth in total energy requirements over the next couple of decades is likely to leave an energy deficit to be met by imported fuel—oil notably— in Japan, the Euratom countries and the United Kingdom.

World Energy Prospects

Nuclear energy development poses the question whether, in the absence of nuclear energy or other new source, an "energy resource problem" may emerge during the next few decades. By way of definition, resources are considered available if they can be recovered at not more than about double present costs of production. Thus, the time perspective is not centuries, nor are all conventional energy resources, irrespective of cost, encompassed. These ground rules are emphasized because technology—in the production, use and transportation of energy—is certain to be greatly advanced by the end of the twentieth century and because the cost curve of energy supply, beyond the broadly defined range of "economically recoverable" reserves, is unknowable on present data. Moreover, it is unnecessary to forecast energy prospects far beyond, say, 1980 in examining the major policy issues confronting United States nuclear power development now and over the next decade.

Ample or Declining Reserves?

There are opposing views on whether the energy resources of the world—like those of the United States, discussed in Chapter 3—are ample for many decades, or whether the prospect is one of declining reserves and an incipient downturn in production rates, together with rising real prices. The conflict of opinion arises mainly from applying a different time perspective, from varying assessments of technical advances in mining and processing and from the sheer statistical inadequacy of economic and physical data on other than "proved" reserves.

The "declining reserves" school, represented by such experts as Eugene Ayres, M. King Hubbert and Harrison Brown,[5] is illustrated by the statement of Brown that "although the age of fossil fuels has barely begun, we can already see its end." They stress the fact that fuel reserves are finite and therefore impose restraints on production rates, which are seen to rise rapidly to a peak and then decline. They hold that changing the estimates of total reserves, within wide limits, cannot greatly shift the peak or terminal point of production. They foresee, for example, continued growth of energy consumption, particularly in the industrializing regions of South Asia and South America, where per capita reserves of fossil fuels are smaller than elsewhere and alternative energy forms, such as nuclear and solar energy, are thus called for, if the process of worldwide industrialization is to be carried through.

While these experts accept world reserves of recoverable coal as ample for several hundred years, they foresee that world oil production will reach a peak no later than the end of the twentieth century, and in the United States peak production may be expected by 1970 or 1980. Thereafter conventional sources of oil will be replaced by production of fluid fuel from shale, tar sands and coal. Their "short-term" view of the world energy problem implies that nuclear energy may be supplying most of the world's energy demands by the

5. Eugene Ayres, "The Fuel Situation," *Scientific American*, October 1956, pp. 43–49; M. King Hubbert, "Nuclear Energy and the Fossil Fuels," *Drilling and Production Practice, 1956*, American Petroleum Institute, New York, 1957; and Harrison Brown and others, *The Next Hundred Years*, Viking, New York, 1957, Chaps. 12 and 13.

middle of the twenty-first century. This is not because coal will have been used up, but rather because it will be in such demand for production of liquid fuel that nuclear energy will have become widely competitive for the whole range of high- and low-temperature purposes now served by coal.

Those who contend, on the other hand, that world (and United States) energy resources are ample for many decades of continued high industrial production base their case primarily on relatively high prospective recovery ratios, particularly for oil, on improved technology in exploration and production and on a larger resource base than heretofore estimated.[6]

In recent years many policy makers in the AEC, Congress and much of the equipment industry have implicitly accepted the debatable declining reserves theory, and hence the view that depletion of energy reserves, accompanied by increasing recovery costs, would compel wide application of nuclear power within the next few decades. At the same time, reactor scientists urging support of a breeder development program have emphasized the need for extending and conserving the energy value of available reserves of nuclear fuels as indispensable alternatives to dwindling domestic reserves of conventional fuels. The policy implications of the reserve data therefore require study.

The Shift to Oil and Gas

Throughout most of the present century world energy consumption has been shifting from coal and lignite to oil and natural gas, while the small share contributed by hydroelectric power has risen but slightly. (See Table 6–1.) First evident in the United States, where fluid fuels (defined as oil and natural gas) now represent more than two thirds of total energy consumption, the shift more recently has also been occurring in the United Kingdom and other industrial countries formerly almost exclusively dependent on coal. The end of this trend toward oil and natural gas is not yet in sight. Recent levels of world coal production have been little higher than two or three decades ago, whereas the output of oil and natural gas has trebled. This expanding role is the effect of competitive displacement of coal, as in railroad locomo-

6. U. S. Bureau of Mines, Department of the Interior: "Impact of the Peaceful Uses of Atomic Energy on the Coal, Oil and Natural Gas Industries," McKinney Panel, Vol. 2, pp. 68–69, "Resources of Coal, Petroleum, Natural Gas, Oil Shale, and Tar Sands in the United States and Allied and Neutral Countries," McKinney Review, Vol. 4, pp. 1507–50; Department of Economic and Social Affairs, UN, "Contribution of Nuclear Energy to Future World Power Needs," *Proceedings*, First Geneva Conference, Vol. 1; Lewis G. Weeks, "Fuel Reserves of the Future," *Bulletin of the American Association of Petroleum Geologists*, February 1958, pp. 431–41; Sam H. Schurr, Bruce C. Netschert and others, *Energy in the American Economy, 1850–1975*, Resources for the Future, Washington, 1960.

TABLE 6-1

Percentage Distribution of World Consumption of Commercial Energy by Energy Source, 1900–1960 and Projections for 1984

Year	Total	Coal and lignite	Oil and natural gas	Hydropower	Nuclear
1900	100.0	94.9	4.7	0.4	—
1910	100.0	92.9	6.8	0.3	—
1920	100.0	88.0	11.4	0.6	—
1930	100.0	78.3	20.6	1.1	—
1940	100.0	74.0	24.8	1.2	—
1950	100.0	61.1	37.3	1.6	—
1960	100.0	48.9	49.3	1.8	—
1984	100.0	28.0	56.0	2.0	14.0

Sources:

1900–1950—"World Energy Requirements in 1975 and 2000," *Proceedings,* First Geneva Conference, 1955, Vol. 1, p. 30.

1960 and 1984—N. B. Guyol, "World Energy and World Oil," *Petroleum Refiner,* January 1959, pp. 192–96.

tives in the United States, and of satisfying new needs for which coal is impractical, as in automobiles and trucks. Lower price, greater ease in handling and lower costs of transportation also explain the growth of fluid fuels.

The introduction of fluid fuel has brought a new degree of transportability for energy. Conventional forms of energy can be supplied now to virtually any point on the globe. While benefiting from great advances in energy transport, consumers of energy everywhere—especially in Western Europe—have become increasingly sensitive to the terms, conditions and reliability of fuel supplies obtained from distant sources. Major changes in transport or in fuel production affect the world fuel price pattern for both coal and oil and thus tend to affect domestic energy production throughout the world, as indicated by the closing of the Suez Canal in 1956 and subsequent surpluses of conventional fuels in Western Europe after 1957.

Similarly, in industrial nations which obtain a large share of their energy needs from domestically mined coal, consumers of fuel are concerned about the prospect for continued supplies at tolerable real prices. In the United States fears on this score have been dormant because the reserves of coal are huge, amenable to highly mechanized extraction and served by a reliable transport system. But in much of Western Europe the cost of coal mining, roughly twice that in the United States, has held out little promise of declining relative to the cost of imported fuel. Moreover, labor supply problems have become so severe that coal production cannot be expected to keep pace with changes in demand, though the indicated reserves represent adequate supply for generations.

Reserves of Coal, Oil and Gas

Estimates of world fuel resources have varied, depending on whether they are estimates of "proved," "probable" or "ultimate" reserves and whether they are estimated to be "economically recoverable" within some stated relation to current costs of production.[7] The subjective element in all such estimates should be evident.

World reserves of coal (excluding lignite)—proved and probable—were officially reported to the United Nations in 1955 to be about 3.7×10^{12} metric tons, representing an energy content of about 109×10^{18} British thermal units.[8] Others have made much higher estimates ranging up to 6×10^{12} metric tons. However, according to the U. S. Bureau of Mines, also in 1955, the "economically recoverable" reserves were estimated at 2.5×10^{12} metric tons, and the reserves recoverable "at or near present costs" at only 625×10^9 metric tons.[9] Upon reexamining the global estimates in 1960 the Bureau of Mines reported free world coal resources "of probable economic interest in the period from 1960 to 2000" at 580×10^9 metric tons—an amount not substantially less than the Bureau's 1955 estimate of reserves recoverable at or near present costs.[10] The 1960 figure is equivalent to nearly three hundred years' supply at the current rate of coal consumption. Some energy experts have therefore assumed that costs of coal production need not rise for a long time, although they have in fact risen historically in several countries, despite ample reserves.

World reserves of petroleum (and liquid hydrocarbons) are probably less well established than coal reserves. Petroleum reserves, however they may be estimated, are only a fraction of the energy equivalent of coal reserves and are

7. In addition, as discussed in Chapter 3, Netschert has proposed for oil and gas the still wider concept of the "resource base" and "availability" in the physical and technological sense; but this concept seems to hold as many pitfalls of subjectivity as the other concepts, though it does provide greater freedom for forecasting technical improvements in recovery rates. (See Bruce C. Netschert, *The Future Supply of Oil and Gas*, Resources for the Future, Washington, 1958.)

8. *Proceedings*, First Geneva Conference, Vol. 1, pp. 96–102.

9. McKinney Panel, Vol. 2, p. 75.

10. McKinney Review, *Background Material*, Vol. 4, pp. 1507–50.

also a much smaller multiple of current annual consumption than are coal reserves, hence the reasonableness of the estimates of petroleum reserves is more critical for the formation of energy policy.

Lewis J. Weeks made an estimate in 1958 of world ultimate petroleum reserves of 1,500 x 10^9 barrels, representing roughly 8.7 x 10^{18} BTU, or about 8 per cent of the energy equivalent of world coal reserves.[11] Proved petroleum reserves, however, as reported by the U. S. Bureau of Mines in 1956, were only 10 per cent of Weeks' ultimate reserve figure, and this quantity (158 x 10^9 barrels at the end of 1954) was sufficient to sustain production for only twelve years at the 1954 rate.[12] A much higher figure of economically recoverable petroleum was the Bureau of Mines estimate of "remaining reserves" at the end of 1954 at 716 x 10^9 barrels.[13] Even this figure appeared too low to the Bureau in 1960, when it estimated hydrocarbon liquids "in place in discovered deposits" at 1,030 x 10^9 barrels and ultimate "resources" in place in all deposits at 5,350 x 10^9 barrels.[14] Furthermore, the estimates made by the Bureau of Mines and others do not include the vast quantities of oil recoverable from discovered deposits of oil shale or tar sands, at somewhat higher costs of recovery. Crudely but conservatively estimated, these could be several times the proved reserve figures of Weeks and of the Bureau of Mines. One might reasonably infer, therefore, that world consumption of oil could continue to increase for some decades without encountering serious increases in real costs or limitations in physical supply.

World natural gas reserves are even more difficult to judge. Inferences about supplies at varying costs are virtually useless, in part because gas is found both with petroleum and alone in the ground. The U. S. Bureau of Mines estimates of ultimate world reserves in 1955 were based on the very rough guess, in the absence of accurate information, that U. S. reserves, judged to be at least 1,000 x 10^{12} cubic feet, were one fifth of the world total, thus giving 5.0 x 10^{15} cubic feet.[15] The results of a 1955 poll of the international petroleum industry (free world only) by Wallace Pratt revealed proved reserves of 344 x 10^{12} cubic feet and remaining economically recoverable resources of 3.7 x 10^{15} cubic

---

11. Weeks, *op. cit.*

12.   To the extent that the estimate of the U. S. Bureau of Mines is based on oil company data, its figure for "proved reserves" may be a misleadingly low measure of remaining reserves recoverable at about current costs and operating conditions. For a variety of reasons, among them taxation, petroleum companies do not find it practical to estimate more than a few years in advance.

13. McKinney Panel, Vol. 2, p. 84.

14. McKinney Review, Vol. 4, pp. 1529–50.

15. McKinney Panel, Vol. 2, p. 93.

TABLE **6-2**

Estimated Aggregate Energy Reserves and Resources of the Free World, 1960

	BTU X 10[18]		
		Resources in place	
Energy source	Proved recoverable reserves	In discovered deposits	In all deposits
Total	14.0	35.7	122.7
Coal (including lignite)	11.1	22.3	67.0
Liquid hydrocarbons	1.6	6.0	31.0
Natural gas	0.4	0.7	7.3
Oil shale	0.6	4.9	11.6
Tar sands	0.3	1.8	5.8

Sources: U. S. Bureau of Mines, Department of the Interior, "Resources of Coal, Petroleum, Natural Gas, Oil Shale, and Tar Sands in the United States and Allied and Neutral Countries," McKinney Review, Vol. 4, pp. 1507–50.

feet.[16] However, in 1960 the Bureau of Mines made new estimates indicating ultimate reserves on the order of 6.6 x 10[15] cubic feet.[17] The life of these reserves is indeterminate, since the rate of natural gas consumption outside the United States is unknown. Assuming United States consumption is about four fifths of the world total, then proved reserves alone represent many centuries of supply at current rates of use. Here, again, one might infer that substantial further increases in consumption could occur without major increases in real costs. Thus, the Bureau of Mines concluded that a possible "ceiling on the rate of oil and gas production worldwide is not yet in sight" and a peak in production "may not appear in the next 40 years."[18]

The U. S. Bureau of Mines, demonstrating considerable audacity, has aggregated these diverse estimates to give a global view of energy reserves and resources (1960). As can be seen from Table 6-2, total "resources in place in all deposits" are almost ten times "proved recoverable reserves." The figures showing resources "in place in discovered deposits" may be taken as more representative of economically recoverable reserves, during the next few decades, than "proved recoverable reserves."

16. *Ibid.*, p. 94.
17. McKinney Review, Vol. 4, pp. 1522–50.
18. *Ibid.*, p. 1535.

A United Nations canvass of governments in 1955 indicated that the under-developed hydroelectric resources of the world were roughly ten times the capacity of existing installations. However, since hydropower is regarded as a renewable resource of indefinite life,[19] energy experts have had a problem in trying to combine the hydro energy potential with aggregate world reserves of nonrenewable fuels. The United Nations staff arbitrarily chose to multiply the estimated annual capacity by 1,000, thus raising the reported energy from 4.7×10^{12} to 4.7×10^{15} electric kilowatt-hours, which is equivalent to 16×10^{18} BTU, a very sizable figure compared with reserves of petroleum or natural gas.[20] Lacking a common basis of measurement, others do not attempt such addition to fuel reserves, and instead elect to add the annual hydroelectric output—actual or projected—to other energy production, customarily by converting the electric energy to its thermal equivalent of fuel required in a steam generating station. Since the developed hydro capacity is only a fraction of the potential total, one may assume that worldwide expansion of hydropower could proceed at steady historical rates of growth for several decades, though probably at increasing cost and not to the limits of estimated capacity. In any case, the most important aspect for policy formation is the relatively small fraction of total energy supplied by hydro, except in a few mountainous areas. (See Table 6–1.)

An important feature of fuel reserves and hydro potential is their obviously uneven national and regional distribution, in both geographic and demographic terms. For example, on the basis of the United Nations 1955 figures the heavily populated and least industrialized areas of the world have the lowest per capita reserves of energy, as shown by the following index of per capita energy reserves in the major regions of the world:[21]

World	1.00
Africa	.71
North America	5.24
Central America	.16
South America	.31
Asia	.22
Europe	.99
USSR	3.72
Oceania	1.46

19. In fact some hydroelectric plants cannot be so regarded, unless an economical way of removing silt from reservoirs is available.

20. *Proceedings*, First Geneva Conference, Vol. 1, pp. 96–101.

21. *Ibid.*, p. 86, Table II.

Even for the areas of low per capita reserves the years of energy supply represented are great. For Asia, including mainland China, per capita reserves of energy, according to this estimate, are 10.8 x 10^9 BTU (or roughly four hundred tons of coal equivalent per person). Were population to double and per capita energy consumption to rise to six times its present level, to that of Western Europe, the estimated reserves would still represent nearly ninety years' supply, though problems of energy supply (and cost) would probably be encountered before many decades. Whether the reserves will prove so low as to curtail further industrialization several decades hence, as suggested by Harrison Brown, will depend mainly on the pace of industrialization attained and on advances in energy production, transportation and utilization.

Nuclear Resources

If reactor technology fulfills its current promise, the world's proved energy reserves will have been increased several times. But even if technical progress fails to achieve maximum use of all fissionable material, through extremely high breeding ratios, the coming of competitive nuclear energy will have added significantly to man's energy reserves. The potential energy of the world's economically recoverable nuclear fuel reserves (excluding shale, phosphate, granite and other high-cost sources) represents a wide range of values, depending on the efficiency of use assumed. As a minimum limiting case, probably having little long-term significance, one might assume that one half the U235 will be burned with no effort to recover and burn regenerated fuel—plutonium or U233—because it may prove uneconomic to do so. As a more significant illustration, one might assume a substantial degree of fuel regeneration conversion (short of true breeding), in view of the expected economy of reprocessing, recovering and recycling fissionable material. Finally, one might assume successful fulfillment of breeding technology in both the fast and thermal energy range, permitting the conversion of most— not necessarily all—of the fertile material, U238 and Th232, available in nuclear resources. Assuming a rough energy equivalence of the three fissionable materials and utilizing the Atomic Energy Commission estimates of free world reserves of economically recoverable metal at about 2 million short tons of uranium and 500,000 short tons of thorium,[22] three sets of aggregate nuclear energy estimates can be made:

22. Robert D. Nininger, "Geneva Conference Summary—Availability and Production of Source Materials," Fifth Annual Conference, Atomic Industrial Forum, Washington, November 10, 1958. More detailed estimates are given in AEC, *Energy From Uranium and Coal Reserves*, Washington, May 1960.

$BTU \times 10^{18}$

50 per cent U235 burn-up—no recycle	
(3,000 megawatt-days per short ton U)	.5
Assuming high regeneration	
(14,000 megawatt-days per short ton; regeneration ratio,	
1.0; 1.5 per cent burn-up of uranium and thorium)	2.9
Assuming breeding	
(590,000 megawatt-days per short ton; regeneration ratio,	
1.4; 65 per cent burn-up of uranium and thorium)	48.4

From these rough estimates it can be seen that in the first case the energy addition to proved reserves of fossil fuels would be small, less than 3 per cent. In the second, representing an advanced state of reactor technology, the addition of nuclear energy becomes impressive, far greater than proved reserves of petroleum or natural gas. Finally, if high-efficiency use of nuclear materials is ultimately achieved, their value of something like 48×10^{18} BTU would be several times greater than proved recoverable reserves of coal, reported by the U. S. Bureau of Mines as about 11×10^{18} BTU.

While technical progress in the use of nuclear fuel is highly desirable during the next few decades, uranium availability and output should impose no economic necessity for achieving high-efficiency breeding to ward off a shortage of uranium. The imperative for breeding is more, however, than scientific and technical elegance; in the long term the economic and resource imperative becomes dominant.[23]

World Energy Requirements

How fast may energy requirements grow in the next few decades and how may they affect estimated reserves? The theory that diminishing reserves of conventional fuels might call for urgent nuclear power programs was a premise of the agenda of the First Geneva Conference in 1955, which called forth numerous papers on future energy needs and resources, worldwide and by country. The conclusions, however, showed no immediate emergency. The problem of energy, it was seen, was not a matter of inadequate physical reserves on a world scale but rather the wide geographic differences in fuel costs and in dependence on unassured external sources of fuel.

Agreement on future world energy requirements is significantly greater than on ultimate or probable reserves. Nathaniel B. Guyol, in 1955 and again in

23. The controversy over the "conservation" reasons for achieving breeding is partly revealed in J. F. Kaufmann and E. D. Jordan, "Breeding Potential of Thermal Reactors," *Nuclear Science and Engineering*, July 1960, p. 85; and in A. M. Weinberg and E. P. Wigner, "Longer Range View on Nuclear Energy," *Bulletin of Atomic Scientists*, December 1960, p. 400.

1959, projected that energy requirements for some decades would increase at a compound rate of around 4 per cent annually. His projections were based primarily on historic rates of increasing consumption during periods of peace and prosperity, rather than on the long-term trend, for example, of only 2 per cent between 1913 and 1958.[24] E. A. G. Robinson and G. H. Daniel in 1955 projected requirements as growing only 2 to 2.5 per cent annually, relying mainly on the 100-year record of world consumption.[25] At the same time E. S. Mason and others, noting an historic correspondence between emergent industrialization and a high rate of energy consumption, projected that energy requirements would increase 3 per cent annually over the next few decades, by combining the different growth rates of energy consumption in the highly industrialized countries (2 to 2.5 per cent), the industrializing (5 per cent) and the undeveloped (roughly 4 per cent).[26] In general, estimated rates of increase in total world energy consumption presented at the First Geneva Conference were much lower than the "maximum plausible" per capita rates of 3 to 5 per cent (or more than 4 to 6 per cent total) projected by Palmer C. Putnam in 1953 for the period to 2000 and to 2050. According to his projections, all the world's economically recoverable energy reserves (he estimated 27×10^{18} BTU at up to double current costs) would be used up in the first quarter of the twenty-first century.[27] The 1955 Geneva conference papers on energy resources and requirements failed, however, to demonstrate the urgent need for a new energy source on the grounds of rapidly depleting world supplies of conventional fuel recoverable at approximately current costs. The topic was not included in the agenda of the Second Geneva Conference.

The Future Energy Balance

Combining disparate estimates of energy reserves for comparison with a range of hypothetical future requirements might seem to be a fatuous exercise. But not taken too literally, the results provide insight and, indeed, help demonstrate an issue of development policy: that world reserves of conventional fuels are probably an insufficient and untrustworthy guide for judging

24. *Proceedings*, First Geneva Conference, Vol. 1, p. 3; and Nathaniel B. Guyol, "World Energy and World Oil," *Petroleum Refiner*, January 1959, p. 192. Under present circumstances, it seems more realistic to project, as Guyol did, on the basis of a peacetime rate of energy increase than on a historical rate influenced by both world war and world depression.

25. "The World's Need for a New Source of Energy," *Proceedings*, First Geneva Conference, Vol. 1, p. 38.

26. "Energy Requirements and Economic Growth," *Ibid.*, p. 50.

27. Palmer C. Putnam, *Energy in the Future*, Van Nostrand, Princeton, 1953, pp. 216–55.

the urgency or character of nuclear energy development programs in this country or other countries.

Robinson's and Daniel's projections of energy requirements and estimates of reserves (80.4 x 10^{18} BTU recoverable fuel) suggest that by the year 2025 world reserves of fuel would be reduced to 300 years' supply, assuming 2 per cent increase in consumption, and to 120 years' at 3 per cent increase. Putnam's "maximum plausible" growth in per capita requirements, coupled with a "prudent" reserve estimate (27 x 10^{18} BTU of economically recoverable fuel), resulted in a projection of reserve exhaustion between the year 2000 and 2030. This combination of estimates of exceedingly high growth in requirements and very low reserves produces a projection that is grossly misleading for nuclear development policy or program planning. Richard A. Tybout has made a synthesis of the requirements and reserve estimates prompted by Putnam's work, the First Geneva Conference and the McKinney Panel that seems to put the need for a new energy source in better perspective.[28] Tybout's estimates indicate that, even assuming a high rate of growth in needs—3.5 per cent—more than one half the world's economically recoverable reserves (39.8 x 10^{18} BTU) will be available in the year 2000. Corresponding conclusions may be drawn from a comparison of world energy requirements and the 1960 reserve estimates of the U. S. Bureau of Mines, cited above.

On a global basis energy depletion does not seem to be a problem for the twentieth century. But this, as pointed out above, ignores the great regional and national differences in costs and reserves and the dependence of future oil supplies on present highly concentrated sources.

Future Fluid Fuel Consumption

How fast the shift to fluid fuel may be is conjectural, but the adequacy of petroleum and natural gas reserves may be roughly indicated by two hypothetical projections of consumption. In the United States consumption of fluid fuels has risen to two thirds of total primary energy consumption. If it is assumed that the fluid fuel share of world energy consumption will rise to two thirds by the year 2000—it was 49 per cent in 1958 and Guyol has projected that it will be 56 per cent by 1984 (Table 6-1)—this means that world fluid fuel requirements will rise at a rate of 3.8 per cent annually and by the year 2000 will have used up 5.5 x 10^{18} BTU. This is four fifths of the Bureau of Mines' economically recoverable reserve figure for liquid hydrocarbons (6.0 x

28. Richard A. Tybout, *Atomic Power and Energy Resource Planning*, Research Monograph 94, Bureau of Business Research, Ohio State University, 1958, pp. 736–53.

10^{18} BTU) and natural gas (0.7 x 10^{18} BTU); but it is much less than one half the combined "official" estimates for recoverable reserves of petroleum, oil shale, tar sands and natural gas, given earlier in this chapter. Seemingly, the shift to fluid fuels can continue, but whether it will be cramped by sharply higher real prices remains a question.

On the other hand, if one assumes continued sharply rising fluid fuel requirements, doubling in twelve years (or increasing at a rate of 6 per cent per year), as in recent experience, then the prospect for fluid fuel reserves becomes more serious. At this rate of increase, fluid fuel will represent an incredible nine tenths of total energy consumption by 1975, and all economically recoverable fluid fuel reserves will be under some pressure. Cumulative requirements by 2000, 9.9 x 10^{18} BTU, will have surpassed the Bureau of Mines fluid fuel reserve estimates. Evidently consumption of fluid fuels cannot continue to increase at the high rates of the last couple of decades without recourse to recovery from oil shale, tar sands or coal—or, alternatively, without being favored by exceedingly large new discoveries of petroleum, as in the past.

Future Electric Power Consumption

Electric power consumption characteristically grows at about twice the rate of primary energy consumption. In 1953, according to the United Nations, electric power took 5.4 per cent of total world primary energy output, nearly two and a half times the share in 1930.[29] Moreover, the real price of electricity has dropped sharply in the last two to three decades, whereas for the primary energy source, coal, the real price at the pithead has risen in all major coal-producing countries. The real prices of crude oil and fuel oil, while fluctuating, have not changed appreciably in the major consuming countries.

Nuclear power is a substitute for conventional energy sources for generating electricity and hence impinges on only a minor fraction of total energy supply and consumption, even in the more power-intensive industrial economies. (In the United States 19 per cent of total primary energy goes into electricity.) Guyol quite rightly emphasized at the First Geneva Conference that nuclear energy in the form of electric power could not widely influence the pattern of total energy consumption and supply. He pointed out that it would be necessary in time for nuclear energy to become competitive in a variety of high- and low-temperature applications in order to have a pervading impact on energy, such as petroleum has had over the last few decades.[30] Furthermore, nuclear

29. *Proceedings*, First Geneva Conference, Vol. 1, p. 92.
30. *Ibid.*, Vol. 1, p. 15.

fuel and power can materially influence power supply only by meeting a portion of the growth in demand, for conventional plants will remain in production through the balance of their useful lives, since conversion of boiler fuel to nuclear fuel is not technically feasible. The immediate importance of nuclear energy seems to rest mainly on the fact that transport of uranium is less precarious and less costly than that of coal or oil. Nevertheless, despite the adequacy of fossil fuels in short-term perspective, nuclear energy in the form of natural uranium and thorium does represent an extraordinarily great long-term addition to the world's finite energy resources.

Industrially Developed Economies

Energy Growth and Supply Inflexibility: Western Europe

The industrialized countries of Western Europe reveal, perhaps better than any other countries, the moderately urgent need for nuclear power as a new source of energy.

The most comprehensive reviews of Western Europe's energy position and prospects have been provided by a series of analyses published by the OEEC since 1955 examining the whole energy field and particularly the future effect of nuclear power.[31] In judging the usefulness of these findings, one must have in mind the key facts of Western Europe's energy trends and the sudden shift from fuel shortage to surpluses after 1957. From 1950–1957 coal production increased by only 10 per cent, despite the spur of rising energy needs. Coal consumption continued to grow and the deficit was made up by a 400 per cent increase in coal imports, which were sharply curtailed in 1959. Before 1959 imports of crude oil had trebled to help meet the energy deficit. However, little of the resulting fuel oil output went into steam electric generation. The fuel demands for the growing electric power production were met predominantly by coal; in 1957 only 6 per cent of total generation was from oil. Substitution of oil for coal has proceeded more rapidly in other sectors of industry,[32] but can be expected to occur in time in steam electric generation as well.

These developments resulted from a complex of circumstances, chief among which were the following: Indigenous energy production (primarily coal) has

31. OEEC, Paris: Louis Armand, *Some Aspects of the European Energy Problem*, 1955; *Europe's Growing Needs of Energy: How Can They Be Met?* (prepared by the Commission for Energy, known as the Hartley Commission, under the chairmanship of Sir Harold Hartley), 1956; and *Towards a New Energy Pattern in Europe* (prepared by the Energy Advisory Commission under the chairmanship of Professor Austin Robinson), 1960.

32. See OEEC, *Basic Statistics of Energy for OEEC Countries, 1950–57*, Paris, 1958.

been inflexible, leading on the one hand to great shortages of coal, as in the period 1945–1957, and on the other to excessive stocks, as in 1958–1961. The attractiveness of nuclear power has varied accordingly. In addition, rising coal production costs have threatened chronically unstable cost-price relations. Production costs of many mines owned by governments have been higher than regulated prices of coal. The spread between domestic and United States coal prices has increased greatly since the war, hence increasing the competitive pressure between imported and domestic fuels. Equally important, the shift from solid to fluid fuels has been accelerated by the rising prices of coal relative to oil. Finally, progressively greater dependence on imported oil has led to wide variations in import volume, accompanied by modest yearly changes in total energy consumption. Instability in the Middle East has posed the question of finding more reliable energy supplies and terms, despite coal surpluses after 1957.

In this complex setting scope for nuclear power is neither obvious nor certain. It will apparently depend on the manner of meeting the energy deficit through essentially unpredictable ratios of imported oil, coal and nuclear fuels.

Energy policies in Western Europe have recently been in a state of flux, resulting chiefly from coal surpluses and mounting oil production in North Africa. Whatever the outcome, a strictly economic solution seems the least probable. One may expect the social and institutional demands of domestic coal producers for a time to continue to carry heavy weight but development of petroleum imports as an alternative may be expected to occur. The example set by the United States in 1959 in fixing mandatory quotas on petroleum imports, so as to protect domestic producers, has apparently served to strengthen corresponding European policies with respect to coal.

The Robinson Commission revision in 1960 of the 1956 Hartley Commission energy projections reveals that, despite the energy shift after 1957, the long-standing energy deficit seems certain to continue during the next two decades, and that any further increase in it will be met largely by imported oil, not by coal or nuclear energy. (See Table 6-3.) The report suggests that by 1975 fuel imports will supply nearly two fifths of total energy consumption. The projections give tongue-in-cheek scope for nuclear power (6 to 7 per cent of total energy consumption in 1975), and a more striking feature is the expected doubling of domestic production of petroleum and natural gas. The implication is clear: nuclear power might reduce somewhat the imports of oil in 1975, but imported and domestic fluid fuel will be relied on to meet most of the increase in energy consumption between 1955 and 1975.

TABLE **6-3**

Consumption, Production and Imports of Primary Energy, 1950–1955 and Projections for 1960, 1965 and 1975, OEEC Countries

	1950	1955	1960	1965	1975
			Millions of tons of coal equivalent		
Consumption	583	777	870–910	960–1,060	1,160–1,360
Production	513	603	665	710	780
Coal	442	477	500	520	520
Lignite	26	30	35	35	35
Hydro	40	56	75	90	130
Crude oil, natural gas and other	6	40	55	65	95
Net import requirements	70	174	205–245	250–350	380–580
Coal	} 70	28	40	40	50
Oil		146	165–205	200–300	250–450
Nuclear energy	—	—	—	10	80
			Per cent		
Imports as per cent of consumption	12.0	22.4	23.6–26.9	26.0–33.0	32.8–42.6

Sources: OEEC, Paris: Europe's Growing Needs of Energy: How Can They Be Met?, 1956; and Towards a New Energy Pattern in Europe, 1960, p. 114. The projections made in the 1956 report by the Hartley Commission have been revised in the 1960 report of the Energy Advisory Commission (chairman, Austin Robinson). The figures shown here for 1955–1975 are the adjusted figures shown in the latter report.

    The extent to which Western Europe chooses to meet part of the energy gap by imported coal, as a supplement to petroleum, may well be influenced by the marked price advantage oil seems likely to have for some time. A probability exists that coal purchases from the United States may be progressively reduced because of the shift to oil (in part through dieselization), increased production of petroleum outside the Middle East (notably in North Africa) and the political sentiment favoring protection of home coal production—paralleling United States protection of domestic oil producers.

Petroleum and Western Europe's Energy Gap

    Western Europe's energy prospects depend largely on imported oil and the terms on which it is available. In recent years about one sixth of crude oil consumption has been met by home production, and the Hartley and Robinson Commissions have projected that by 1975 this share will rise to no more than one fifth.[33] Since Middle East supplies are precarious, speed is important in establishing alternative sources of oil at home and abroad. Domestic exploration, of course, is costly and evidently not particularly promising, although by-product benefits may appear, as in Italy, where no large oil reserves were found but large gas fields were discovered in the Po Valley.

Securing new sources of crude outside Western Europe and the Middle East raises problems and possibilities that go beyond the scope of this volume. It may be sufficient here to note that exploration and development of new overseas sources has already provided good prospect of substantial supplies. The French, British and American exploration of North Africa has resulted in exceedingly important discoveries, though the political risks are evident. Also, because the fields are at some distance from the Mediterranean, a program of pipeline construction has been necessary, which, together with development of the oilfields, has required substantial capital and several years' effort. Other Western European nations (Italy, notably) have entered into independent agreements with producer countries in the Middle East, in the expectation that crude supplies from these sources may prove less vulnerable to interference politically than present sources available through the major international oil companies.

How does prospective nuclear power rank with indigenous and imported fuels as a means of improving Western Europe's energy balance? As shown in the next section, nuclear power would clearly require more capital than either oil or coal. Over the long term nuclear power holds promise of saving more foreign exchange than does imported coal or oil (both at current prices), but not more than domestic coal or oil. In terms of time, competitive nuclear power is still some years away and provides no more immediate solution to

---

33. Among the members of the European Economic Community, West Germany is by far the largest domestic oil producer. Total output of crude oil in these countries in 1957 and its relative importance in meeting domestic demand were as follows:

	Crude output (million tons)	Per cent of consumption
Total	8.2	12.2
Belgium-Luxembourg	—	—
France	1.4	6.7
Western Germany	4.0	23.1
Italy	1.3	9.0
Netherlands	1.5	18.3

(Paul H. Frankel, "Oil in the Common Market," paper presented to the first International Congress of Studies on the Common Market, Palermo, October 6, 1958.)

the problem of Middle East oil supplies than do the alternative measures mentioned above.[34] Two advantages, however, are imputed to nuclear power: its production costs could prove competitive in only a few years; and the technology provides promise of Western Europe's becoming substantially self-sufficient in enriched nuclear fuel. However, the foreign exchange and capital requirements of nuclear power prompt further consideration.

The Prospects for Capital and Foreign Exchange Savings

Fuel and power expansion are heavy claimants for capital and foreign exchange in the energy-deficient industrial countries. Moreover, the rate of growth in capital requirements is high. For the fuel industries of Western Europe and Japan it is about as high as the increase in GNP, and for electric power generation almost twice as high. The heavy capital and foreign exchange commitments for fuel and power are well revealed in the OEEC countries by the Hartley and Robinson Commission reports. Over the next fifteen to twenty years the investment requirements for the production of fuel and of power will be about the same as the projected cost of imported fuels. Both already bulk large in the total economy: capital requirements in recent years have approached one fifth of national investment, excluding housing; and fuel import costs have represented more than one sixth of all imports of merchandise (c.i.f.) from outside the OEEC, and the share is rising. Nuclear power carries the potentiality of both capital and foreign exchange savings in the long run, though not at the outset.

The capital investment in secondary energy production (e.g., steam electric generation) in time is expected to approach two and a half times that in primary energy production. How good is the prospect that nuclear power might reduce the gross investment needed for these purposes in Western Europe? The Hartley report indicates that a major reduction in direct nuclear power plant costs—from $350 per kilowatt to $240—will be necessary to break even with the investment required for oil- or coal-fired generating plants, including their indirect requirements such as mines, refineries, transmission and distribution equipment, etc. The report estimates that nuclear power plants (including fuel facilities) require a gross investment of $380 per kilowatt, assuming no gaseous diffusion plants for enrichment of fuel; oil-fired plants,

34. In defending the proposed joint agreement between the United States and Euratom, representatives of the Department of State were compelled, upon questioning by the Joint Committee, to grant that acceleration of nuclear power in Western Europe could not be justified by the current vulnerability of the Middle East. (*Proposed Euratom Agreements*, Hearings, Joint Committee on Atomic Energy, 85th Cong., 2nd Sess., 1958.)

roughly $270 per kilowatt; and coal-fired plants, about $255 per kilowatt.[35] The winning bid by International General Electric Co. on the SENN project carried a direct nuclear power plant cost of about $330 per kilowatt. It is reasonable to expect that the costs of nuclear plants will be cut by one fourth, to reach the break-even point on direct capital requirements.

The prospect for foreign exchange savings by nuclear power substitution in Western Europe or Japan is likewise difficult to evaluate, yet the early possibilities are seemingly more favorable than for capital savings. The comparative direct import costs of fuel are suggested by the Hartley projections, as shown in Table 6–4.

Those responsible in the energy-deficient countries for guiding long-term financial and trade policies are continually sensitive to the foreign exchange effects of conventional and nuclear energy programs, even though the postwar problems of making hard currency payments have diminished. Circumstances could alter this new era, however, as was intimated in 1956 and 1957 by the impact on the balance of payments of the closing of the Suez Canal. Indeed, the major effect of that crisis was on the foreign exchange position of the Western European countries immediately affected.[36] Owing in part to the mild winter of 1956–57, when the Suez Canal was closed, ocean shipments of fuel and reserves in Europe were sufficient to sustain increasing industrial production without drastically restrictive allocation measures. The financial burden was the result of higher prices and high freight rates. While the volume of oil imports declined, their cost in foreign currencies increased for several reasons: the longer haul around Africa from the Persian Gulf; the 50 per cent increase in time-charter rates; a doubling of spot rates from the Netherlands West

---

35. Gross capital requirements (in millions) for 1 million kilowatts of capacity, at 6,500 hours and 10,000 BTU per KWH:

Type of plant	Power plant	Fuel facilities	Total
Nuclear	$350	$ 30	$380
Oil	160	110*	270
Coal	160	95**	255

* 1.8 million tons a year, at $60 per ton.
** 2.7 million tons a year, at $35 per ton.

"Future Capital Investments in Energy, OEEC Area, 1955–75," *Europe's Growing Needs of Energy: How Can They Be Met?*, Appendix VII, pp. 115–20.

These comparisons are greatly simplified. In fact, the indirect investments required for alternative power sources are difficult to establish. The Hartley estimates may have overstated the indirect investments for conventional power and understated those for nuclear power. Moreover, the indirect capital requirements for nuclear power vary widely, being smaller for natural uranium reactors than for enriched uranium reactors.

36. OEEC, *Europe's Need For Oil: Implications and Lessons of the Suez Crisis*, Paris, January 1958, pp. 39–42.

TABLE **6-4**

Costs of Imported Energy in OEEC Countries, 1955, and Projections for 1960 and 1975

Form of energy	1955	1960	1975
	Millions at 1955 prices		
Total (c.i.f.)	$2,600	$3,500	$7,000
Nuclear fuels[a]	—	—	100
Coal[b]	550	750	1,000
Petroleum products[c]	220	500	1,900
Crude oil[d]	1,830	2,250	4,000
Less insurance and freight paid to Western Europeans	−750	−1,000	−1,800
Total net disbursements	1,850	2,500	5,200
	Per cent		
Total as per cent of all imports	12.4	13.8	18.1

a. Based on 75 million tons coal equivalent. (It is assumed that 5 million tons coal equivalent will be supplied domestically.)

b. Same price assumed in 1960 and 1975 as in 1955—$10 per ton f.o.b., United States east coast; and same freight level, $9 per ton.

c. Prices are assumed to be the same as in 1955, but the composition is expected to shift toward lower priced products.

d. Import price assumed to remain at $14 per ton f.o.b.

Source: OEEC, *Europe's Growing Needs of Energy: How Can They Be Met?*, Paris, 1956, Table 13, p. 43, and accompanying text. (Based on the mean level of inland energy consumption.)

Indies to northwest Europe; and the 10 to 15 per cent increase in base prices in the Western Hemisphere. Taken together, these resulted in European-delivered crude oil prices of about $4.50 a barrel, or 40 to 50 per cent above those prevailing in July 1956. After the crisis posted prices declined, but held 6 to 8 per cent above the pre-Suez level until the recession of 1958, when they fell slightly below. (It is commonly known that, during periods of oversupply, prices actually paid are significantly lower than posted prices.)

The possibility of diminishing the burden of fuel imports on balance of payments raises the question whether, and, if so, under what circumstances, nuclear power plants might save foreign exchange. Highly tentative answers have been set down by various policy and study groups in the last few years. In the absence of data on nuclear power reactor performance and the foreign exchange component of both capital and fuel costs, these studies have had to rely on broad assumptions.

Existing studies have generally agreed that nuclear power reactors constructed in Western Europe or Japan during the next several years would probably show a greater foreign exchange requirement than would the conventional alternatives, assuming current oil and coal prices. In the long run, however, each of these studies expresses the conviction that the foreign exchange component of nuclear plant costs and fuel charges should fall sufficiently to save a significant part of the foreign-exchange costs for the fuel-importing countries.[37]

The available information on the estimated foreign exchange component of both nuclear and conventional power plants emphasizes the necessity of considering the specific circumstances—the country's capacity to produce equipment at home, the foreign component of domestic equipment production, the particular reactor design and fuel cycle, and so forth.

One of the leading economic justifications for the Euratom program rests on the prospects for foreign exchange savings resulting from the substitution of nuclear fuel for imported conventional fuels. The common notion that deliberate substitution of high-cost domestic for cheaper foreign resources is necessarily unsound economic policy and contrary to the theory of comparative advantage should be disposed of at once. In general, if the market has reasonable prospect of expanding sufficiently to carry production on an optimum scale, then justification may exist, as Tinbergen suggests, for considering domestic capital investment that exceeds the simple dictates of absolute cost-accounting comparisons. The "process of import substitution should, however, not diverge too much from what a reasonable international division of labor suggests."[38] Clearly, the industrial development of Japan, Italy, France and other advanced economies is adequate for the production of nuclear equipment and nuclear fuel elements.

Foreign Exchange Savings: Japan

The Japanese nuclear power program has been strongly motivated by the prospect for foreign exchange savings through substitution of nuclear for oil-

37. For statements on foreign exchange effects see Louis Armand and others, *A Target for Euratom*, Paris, May 1957, p. 88; also, UN, *Economic Applications of Atomic Energy: Power Generation and Industrial and Agricultural Uses*, Report of the Secretary-General, New York, 1957, pp. 12–13; and NPA, *Productive Uses of Nuclear Energy: Summary of Findings—Policy Suggestions for the Future*, Washington, September 1957, pp. 41–42. Also see Appendix A.

38. Jan Tinbergen, *The Design of Development*, The Economic Development Institute, International Bank for Reconstruction and Development, Johns Hopkins Press, Baltimore, 1958, p. 18.

TABLE 6-5

Japanese Estimates of Foreign Exchange Requirements for 150-Megawatt Nuclear and Oil-Fired Plants, 1970

Billion yen—cumulative to end of period

	Natural uranium graphite power plant			Oil-fired plant (imported fuel)		
	First 4 years[a]	5th year of operation	24 years	First 3 years[a]	5th year of operation	25 years
Total	3.8	5.7	14.2[b]	1.2	6.5	33.2
Construction	1.2[c]	1.2	1.2	0.5[d]	0.5	0.5
Initial fuel	2.2	2.2	2.2[b]	—	—	—
Fuel consumption	0.2	1.3	7.2	0.7	5.9	32.3
Interest	0.2	1.0	3.6	0.03	0.1	0.4

a. Includes 3-year construction period for nuclear plant, 2-year construction period for oil-fired and 1 year of initial operation for both types of plant. Plant to be commissioned in 1970.

b. If the nondepreciable portion of the initial charge is deducted (1.94 billion yen, or 90 per cent), the net foreign exchange requirement becomes 12.2 billion yen.

c. 7 per cent of total plant cost.

d. 5 per cent of total plant cost.

Source: Atomic Energy Commission of Japan, "The Long-Term Plan for Development of Atomic Power Reactors in Japan," Proceedings, Second Geneva Conference, Vol. 1, p. 125.

fired plants. In 1956 about 23 per cent of the country's primary energy supply was imported and this share is expected to rise to 48 per cent by 1975.[39] A combination of energy circumstances accounts for this expected extraordinary growth in fuel imports: almost all the economically feasible hydroelectric sites may be in use by 1970; the prospects for a very large increase in home coal production are poor and current output is costly, leading to steam electric generation at costs of 11 to 13 mills per kilowatt-hour; to meet the projected growth in electric generation about four and a half times as much fuel will be required in 1975 as in 1956. The multiplication of fuel import demand not only burdens the economy with continuing foreign payments problems but also raises such sensitive political questions as reinstating the prewar import trade in low-cost Manchurian coal. Japan now makes most of its own equipment for conventional generating stations and can well expect to do the same after nuclear power has been demonstrated in reactors developed elsewhere.

Official Japanese computations of the foreign exchange savings of nuclear power are based on an oil-fired steam plant, using imported fuel, compared with an advanced type natural uranium, gas-cooled, graphite-moderated reactor, following British design, to be commissioned in 1970. A remarkable and perhaps questionable assumption is made that the foreign exchange component of the nuclear plant cost will be only 7 per cent of the total, compared with 5 per cent for the oil-fired plant. The major other foreign currency costs of the nuclear plant are for the natural uranium contained in the fuel inventory and the cost of fuel consumed annually.

The yearly schedule of foreign exchange requirements for the two plants (Table 6–5) shows that during the first three years the nuclear station requires larger foreign currency payments than the oil-fired plant. The plant construction cost is much higher and the cost of the initial charge of nuclear fuel is a unique expense at the outset not required of a conventional plant. However, the foreign exchange cost of the annual consumption of nuclear fuel is only a small fraction of that for imported oil, hence the total foreign payments for the oil-fired plant become higher after the fourth year. For the whole period of the nuclear power plant's expected useful life (twenty-four years after start of construction), the Japan Atomic Energy Commission estimates the foreign currency requirement will have totaled 12.2 billion yen, compared to 33.2 billion yen in twenty-five years for the oil-fired plant. This apparent 60 per cent

39. Discussion in this section is based on the paper by the Atomic Energy Commission of Japan, "The Long-Term Plan for Development of Atomic Power Reactors in Japan," *Proceedings*, Second Geneva Conference, Vol. 1, pp. 119–34; also, Sapir and Van Hyning, *op. cit.*

foreign exchange saving is based on direct foreign currency requirements only and makes no allowance for discounting future savings to their present worth. (See Appendix A.) Also, it does not show the economic burden of the substantial additional domestic capital requirements of the nuclear plant (17,250 million yen against 9,450 million yen). In both cases the assumed domestic costs contain a significant but inestimable fraction of foreign exchange contained in components.

Despite the inadequacies of the data, the prospect for foreign exchange savings over the long term seems excellent—provided the plant can be built in Japan with only nominal foreign currency expenses. This cannot be true of the first demonstration reactors. Declining costs of nuclear fuel and plant are future economic probabilities reinforcing the projected foreign exchange benefits.

Foreign Exchange Savings: Italy [40]

A new perspective, different from that of the preliminary Japanese approximations, is provided by the foreign exchange prospects of the SENN Project and revealed in the accepted bid of the International General Electric Company. In this case the foreign component of the nuclear power plant cost is estimated at 30 to 50 per cent, compared with the 7 per cent assumed in the Japanese example. The prospect for foreign exchange saving is thus less clear and a more rigorous method of analysis is required.

An estimate of the savings may be undertaken by starting with the hypothetical case shown in Table 6-6, which is intended to conform generally with Western European conditions during the next few years (150-megawatt plant, 80 per cent lifetime plant factor).

On these assumptions, the excess foreign exchange requirements (and capital costs) for nuclear plant are far more than offset by the foreign currency savings on nuclear fuel, leaving a net saving of $10.6 million on a nuclear plant compared with an oil-fired plant. The assumptions used are close to those on which projected costs of the SENN project are based, yet projecting for the full life of either a nuclear or oil-fired plant implies serious contingency factors. Favoring the oil-fired plant is the possibility that useful life may be more than twenty-five years and that fuel oil prices may decline, but the major drawback is the substantial uncertainty of fuel oil prices and supply over such

40. The discussion in this section is drawn in large part from Appendix A, "Prospects for Foreign Exchange Savings: Western Europe and Japan"; also, Little and Rosenstein-Rodan, *op. cit.*

a long period. For the nuclear plant the uncertainties are also present, among them the possibility that useful life will be less than twenty-five years and that fuel performance may not prove as good as projected (guaranteed for the SENN project at 13,000 megawatt-days per metric ton of enriched uranium).

TABLE **6 - 6**

Hypothetical Foreign Exchange Savings in 150-Megawatt Nuclear Plant (Compared with Oil-Fired Plant) in Western Europe, Early 1960s

	Nuclear plant	Oil-fired plant	Difference between nuclear and oil-fired
Investment cost			
Per kw. (less initial fuel)	$330	$150	
Total (thousands)	$49,500	$22,500	$27,000
Foreign exchange component (thousands)[a]	24,750	3,380	21,370
Lifetime (25 years) fuel and operating expenses			
Per kilowatt-hour (mills)	4.8	5.5	
Total (thousands)	$126,000	$144,000	18,000
Fuel (thousands)	100,000	118,000	
Foreign exchange component (thousands)[b]	60,000	92,000	32,000
Operating and maintenance (thousands)	26,000	26,000	
Net foreign exchange saving in nuclear plant (thousands)			10,630

a. 50 per cent for nuclear; 15 per cent for oil-fired.

b. Foreign exchange component 60 per cent for nuclear fuel, 80 per cent for oil; 80 per cent plant factor assumed. For other examples of potential foreign exchange savings, see Appendix A.

Source: IBRD, Summary Report of the International Panel, Project ENSI, Washington, March 1959, p. 18.

Evidently the question of evaluating foreign exchange savings as a justification for nuclear power plants calls for careful treatment. (See Appendix A.) Assuming equal generating cost for the two types of plants, there are two analytical problems involved: to relate the real economic cost of the large additional nuclear plant investment to the foreign exchange benefits that may be derived;[41] and to relate the indicated annual "cash flow" of net foreign exchange savings over a long period to an appropriately adjusted (discounted) present value of these benefits. The detailed analysis of these and other problems in Appendix A suggests that, in the range of most probable near-term capital costs for nuclear power plant, significant economic benefit is likely to accrue to the investment of domestic capital for the purpose of reducing imports of conventional fuel. (This is not to say that the additional investment in nuclear power would be more productive in generating foreign exchange for Italy than the same sums applied to alternative opportunities outside the power sector.)

In Italy and other Western European countries where refineries operate on imported crude, the substitution of nuclear fuel for fuel oil in thermal power generation would ameliorate, in a limited way, the recurrent imbalance between refinery output and domestic consumption of the major fluid fuels—gasoline, middle distillates and residual fuel oil. In brief, refinery capacity is technically designed to produce more of the relatively profitable gasoline, but less of the heavier products, than required by home markets.[42] In this situation the substitution of nuclear energy for fuel oil or coal would slightly reduce the demand for imported crude, if a higher proportion of gasoline were produced; or, if the current product mix were retained, would permit greater export of fuel oil.

Nuclear power's influence on the balance of payments may also work through the restraint it imposes on the future price of fuel oil. In Italy the alternative for fuel oil is imported coal and this has been so expensive (up to $21 per ton) that the limit it can impose on delivered fuel oil is far above the recent and current price. Since coal has been an ineffective competitor for fuel oil, the imminence of competitive nuclear power—at 9 mills per kilowatt-hour, presaged by the SENN project—appears to hold some price importance for primary energy and refinery products.

Transport and Investment Benefits: The Soviet Union

Customarily, in the economic literature on nuclear power the United States and the USSR have been cited as nations that have no urgent need for central

41. There is no convenient measure for the marginal productivity of domestic capital and of foreign exchange, hence resort must be had to the convenient device of an assumed rate of return on capital for judging the real capital cost burden warranted by placing a premium on foreign exchange savings. In a world without trade and financial barriers the distinction between domestic capital and foreign exchange would be eliminated.

42. The problem of the refinery balance and its influence on Italy's balance of payments is discussed in Little and Rosenstein-Rodan, *op. cit.*, pp. 44–51.

station nuclear power, primarily because indigenous fossil fuels, notably coal, are low in cost and reserves are adequate for centuries of rising consumption. This view of the energy situation in the Soviet Union was expressed in qualified form even by USSR scientists at the First and again at the Second Geneva Conference.[43] Yet, closer examination of the future industrialization of the Soviet Union in relation to the location of fuel reserves and the remaining hydro potential suggests that the western part of the country—the central, industrial region including Moscow; the Urals region; and the northwest region including Leningrad—represents a large fuel-deficient area, partially dependent on expanding shipments from considerable distances.

Almost all of the Soviet Union's nuclear power capacity is expected to be located in the western sector. Here, too, the marginal cost of fuel is reported to be sufficiently high that nuclear power soon will be, if it is not already, competitive with conventional steam generating stations. Also, the Soviet data suggest that, measured by labor, transport and capital requirements for coal-fired stations, nuclear power plants are more economical and hence will be used to meet a substantial part of the power growth in these regions over the next decade. As a policy inference, then, one may conclude that the Soviet program, discussed further in the next chapter, is motivated by an economic need that may be as persuasive as that in Western Europe. Moreover, the existence of a demonstrable domestic need in the Soviet Union provides an economic pressure for an expanding nuclear power program which the United States has not had. The supposition that there is little urgency in the Soviet program proves false when the inescapably competitive relation of the nuclear power programs of the free nations to the program of the Soviet Union is considered. The Soviet need for nuclear power therefore requires appraisal for both economic and foreign policy reasons.

The Soviet Union seems to justify plans for nuclear power in the three western regions on the basis of comparative costs, labor savings and transport economies. As to nuclear costs, the data are not altogether convincing, in part because estimated investment costs per kilowatt fall so much closer to those of the coal-fired alternative than is suggested by similar estimates of the various free nations. Soviet estimates for the reactor types that are farthest advanced—pressurized-water and graphite-moderated—show plant costs only 25 to 50 per cent higher. The operating savings on nuclear fuel, as against coal, would recoup the additional nuclear plant investment in four to fourteen years, according to these estimates (see Tables B–2 and –3, Appendix B). Because

43. V. S. Emelyanov, "The Future of Atomic Energy in the USSR," *Proceedings*, Second Geneva Conference, Vol. 1, p. 68.

Soviet prices are generally unreliable measures of real economic relationships, we need to judge, as do Soviet planners, whether physical data—labor and transport criteria—substantiate indicated comparative costs.

Only an indirect view of the labor and transport savings is revealed by the available Soviet data. For the three fuel-deficient regions mentioned, John Hardt has estimated (see Appendix B) that meeting the planned expansion of 67 million kilowatts for 1959–1972 by coal-fired stations would require 400,000 more workers (120 per cent more) and 40 billion ton-kilometers of additional fuel transport (65 per cent more) than if the expansion were accomplished by a balanced program of coal, gas, nuclear and hydro. For the reasons given in Appendix B, however, the Soviet's planned expansion in the fuel-deficient regions indicates far greater reliance on natural gas and oil than on nuclear power to meet the growth in energy requirements.

Other Economies

The prospects for economic introduction of nuclear power in the unindustrialized and the semi-industrialized countries are less clear than in the energy-deficient industrial countries, though more public attention has been devoted to the question of the application of nuclear power to the less developed economies. The reason for ambiguity arises from the fact that industrialization and urbanization in these countries is not usually hindered by lack of energy resources. Almost invariably, disinterested studies of the question have pointed to the deeper problems that are constraining economic progress. Nevertheless, one needs to understand not merely the lack of short-term urgency in the development of nuclear power, but also the long-term contribution that nuclear power may make to economic development of these countries. Such understanding is a social and political necessity, for a lack of consensus on the role of nuclear power has already caused misunderstanding and resentment among nations.

Nuclear Power—Symbol of Economic Salvation?

For many reasons the economic gap between the advanced and some less developed economies is likely to widen during the next decade or two, and serious tension may arise through the inability of the less developed countries to take advantage of the early development of nuclear power. This tension may take the form of resentment, rooted in the notion—first evident during the negotiations on the statute of the International Atomic Energy Agency—that the less developed nations were not being fairly considered by the atomic powers in establishing the terms for the development of nuclear energy. Such resentment has been perpetuated by recurring instances in which spokesmen from the industrialized nations have gratuitously advised the less developed nations what energy policy was appropriate for them and that nuclear power was not yet suitable for their use. The resentment is fortified by the realization that control of nuclear energy development rests with a few countries—France, the United Kingdom, the United States and the USSR.

The World Health Organization reports:[44]

> Where exaggerated hopes have been aroused, there may be disappointment and disillusionment when nuclear installations do not prove feasible or do not at once produce a miracle in the form of a higher standard of living. In this aspect there is perhaps the greatest danger in the social and economic spheres which can be anticipated from atomic energy *per se*. When populations are under stress and have a tendency to nurse unrealistic hopes, nuclear energy may, indeed, be elected as a symbol of salvation. The repercussions from eventual disappointment may then be severe and take the form of hostility against the populations which draw major benefits from atomic energy.

Atomic Guidance for Industrializing Countries

Some resentment also has derived from the fact that much of the economic literature on the role of nuclear power in the industrializing economies has been designed to persuade them not to go too fast. The presumption seems to have existed among many Western observers that unindustrialized and some semi-industrialized countries have been entranced by the notion that nuclear power might start, or accelerate, an automatic process of industrialization and economic development; that they have been impatient to risk inordinately large investments on nuclear power, and have been unmindful of the serious technical obstructions to its commercially useful development.[45]

Each of these presumptions has proved to be badly founded, in the light of the new economic realism which began with the Second Geneva Conference. Each was seemingly a reaction to the sentimental optimism expressed so widely at the First Geneva Conference and inherent in President Eisenhower's

44. WHO, *Mental Health Aspects of the Peaceful Uses of Atomic Energy: Report of a Study Group*, Technical Report Series No. 151, Geneva, 1958, pp. 11–12.

45. Unfortunately, even the Advisory Committee on U. S. Policy Toward the International Atomic Energy Agency, as recently as May 1962, felt compelled to applaud the staff of the agency for critically examining "the assumption that nuclear power was a panacea of immediate value to all countries." (See *Report*, p. 11, Department of State, Washington, May 19, 1962.)

United Nations address in 1953. There is ample evidence today of a more realistic view among both the underdeveloped and industrializing countries. For example, a 1956 study prepared by an electric power committee of the United Nations Economic Commission for Asia and the Far East concluded that it might be a great many years before small power reactors (5 to 20 electric megawatts) would be available to provide power at costs comparable with hydro or thermal power stations, that the countries of the region should merely continue to study current developments in atomic energy and that careful surveys should be made of existing conventional energy sources in each country in the light of projected energy requirements.[46]

Further, not a single underdeveloped country by the end of 1960 had made a formal request to the International Atomic Energy Agency, the International Bank for Reconstruction and Development or the U. S. Export-Import Bank to secure assistance in establishing a nuclear power project. Finally, only India thus far has committed itself to a nuclear power program and the economic reasons given are of a long-term, specialized character, having little relevance to the country's vastly difficult economic development over the next decade or two. The papers submitted to the Second Geneva Conference did not indicate that any underdeveloped country was prepared at that time to appeal for assistance to proceed with nuclear power. Indeed, Burma and Pakistan, the only underdeveloped countries that addressed themselves to the question, concluded that no effort beyond nuclear research and study of energy prospects was yet justified.[47] There may be a danger that the underdeveloped and industrializing countries will dismiss nuclear power and, in doing so, may overlook its limited and specialized, but nonetheless significant, potential contribution to their economies.

In India it is felt that a multiplicity of long-term ends will be served by a nuclear program: to broaden the nation's energy resource base, which it is believed may be quite insufficient to support an industrialized economy of more than 500 to 600 million persons; to save ultimately on the amount of capital invested in the production and shipment of conventional fuel; and to exploit the abundant domestic reserves of thorium, in the absence of much uranium. More important immediately, however, is the driving motivation, repeatedly expressed since 1958 by the director of the Indian Atomic Energy Commission, Dr. H. J. Bhabha, that India and other industrializing countries

46. UN, "The Use of Atomic Power for Generating Electricity: Present Status and Possibilities," Report by the Secretariat to the Subcommittee on Electric Power, Committee on Industry and Trade, ECAFE, January 10, 1956, mimeo.

47. A. A. M. Ahmad, "The Future of Nuclear Power in Pakistan," and Hla Nyunt, "Burma's Atomic Energy Program," *Proceedings*, Second Geneva Conference, Vol. 1.

must take the opportunity to participate in the intellectual, scientific and technological advances being made in the Western world.[48] Only thus will such countries obtain the experience and judgment required to establish sound nuclear energy programs when the occasion arises.

Population Growth and Resource Limitations

SOUTH ASIA AND THE FAR EAST. A prime case for nuclear power for the underdeveloped economies rests on the belief that indigenous energy resources will prove too limited to meet future high levels of industrialization and large population growth.[49] The regional statistics of energy reserves, population and population growth to 1980 and 2000 disclose, as mentioned earlier, striking imbalances—that is, large, populous areas where energy endowment is far less than in the rest of the world, and where population growth rates are high. The apparent growing pressure of population on land, energy, water and other resources has focused attention on the so-called population explosion that is occurring in these underdeveloped areas. The result of a sharply declining death rate and a lagging, slowly declining birth rate, this rapid increase in population could extend over several decades[50] and may lead, as many observers fear, to a dangerously widening gap between the levels of living in the underdeveloped and industrialized nations. The question is whether and how soon nuclear energy might help to alter the apparent imbalance between population and domestic resources.

Regional per capita energy reserves and consumption, shown in Table 6-7, are based on United Nations data used by Bhabha. On these estimates it is apparent that the countries of South Asia and the Far East (SAFE) have comparatively small per capita fuel reserves and water-power potential. In order to evaluate the problem of future energy requirements against supply, Bhabha selected an industrialization target for the underdeveloped countries of 25,000 thermal kilowatt-hours per capita yearly—fifteen times the current

48. Press conference, September 1, 1958, following Session 2 of the Second Geneva Conference.

49. For the leading exposition of the case see the evening lecture, September 5, 1958, by Dr. H. J. Bhabha (India) on "The Need for Atomic Energy in the Underdeveloped Countries," *Proceedings*, Second Geneva Conference, Vol. 1, p. 395.

50. On the basis of "medium assumptions," the United Nations in 1958 reported that the population of underdeveloped countries (Africa, Central America, Tropical South America, Asia outside Japan and the Soviet Union, and the Pacific Islands other than Australia and New Zealand) will increase from 1.64 billion in 1950 to 2.67 billion in 1975 (or by 2.0 per cent annually) and to 4.8 billion in 2000 (or by 2.4 per cent during the last quarter of the century). "If a general decline of fertility in the underdeveloped countries begins in the near future," the Secretary-General states, "their rates of natural increase will not slacken appreciably for a long time to come." Memorandum submitted by the Secretary-General, *World Population Situation and Prospects*, Population Commission, UN Economic and Social Council, New York, December 22, 1958.

SAFE rate. This level is also somewhat higher than that of Western Europe currently, but far below that of North America. Such a rate of consumption is far higher than the per capita hydropower potential would permit and is high relative to the fossil fuel reserves of several underdeveloped areas. For example, at that rate the fossil fuel reserves of SAFE would be exhausted in thirty-five years and of Latin America in about forty-three years, without any

TABLE 6-7

World Per Capita Annual Consumption of Commercial Energy and Per Capita Reserves of Fuel, by Area, 1953–1954

Area	Population, mid-1953 (millions)	Per capita energy consumption, 1954 (tKWH)	Per capita reserves of fuel (tKWH X 10³)	Per capita water power[a] (tKWH per year)
World	2,616.8	9,600	12,410	1,815
Africa	189.3	1,920	3,246	8,061
North America	174.6	60,720	71,715	2,531
Latin America	173.2	4,320	1,085	2,673
Middle East	91.0	2,000	1,720	1,110
South Asia—Far East	775.8	1,600	888	557
China (inc. Taiwan)	590.9	1,520	4,195[b]	1,184
Western Europe	309.4	19,120	12,207	1,700
Eastern Europe & USSR	298.9	15,200	39,510	1,713
Oceania	13.7	22,560	17,530	3,431

a. Converted to thermal equivalent at 1,000 KWH = 0.6 metric tons of coal.

b. On the basis of later coal reserve estimates, an adjusted total would be more than three times as large.

Source: H J. Bhabha, "The Need for Atomic Energy in the Underdeveloped Countries," *Proceedings, Second Geneva Conference*, Vol. 1, Tables 2 and 3, pp. 395 ff.

further increase in population. The conclusion, assuming the reserve estimates are reasonable, is that "the industrialization of these regions will not be possible on the basis of indigenous supplies of coal (and oil), and recourse will have to be had eventually to the import of vast amounts of conventional fuels, or to nuclear energy." The implication is clear: the strong preference will be to use domestic source materials—nuclear and fossil—and minimize energy imports of any kind.

The major weaknesses of Bhabha's evaluation are the time perspective assumed, the period required to achieve the implied levels of industrialization and the adequacy of immediately available reserves of fossil fuels and hydro-power to support rapid industrial development during the next few crucial decades. Such levels of energy consumption may not be reasonably expected before the year 2000. Consider merely the economic implications of increasing the per capita level of energy consumption in SAFE from 1,600 to 25,000 thermal kilowatt-hours yearly. During the rest of this century the SAFE population is expected to rise 2.0 per cent yearly.[51] To sustain a 2000 A.D. population of nearly 2 billion at the target level of 25,000 thermal kilowatt-hours per capita implies total energy consumption in the year 2000 forty times that of 1954 and about as great an increase in GNP. These figures merely underline the crucial difficulties involved in raising per capita energy (and GNP) in this underdeveloped area to a reasonable level, short of half a century or even more.

Nevertheless, unless energy reserves in this area are drastically expanded by additional discoveries, further development and improved technology of re-covery, the currently indicated energy reserves may require, during the first half of the twenty-first century, great supplementation by imports and by nuclear energy. Since the underdeveloped areas, such as SAFE, have been very poorly prospected, substantial increases in reserve estimates might rea-sonably be expected. The necessity of introducing nuclear energy rapidly to make up for a long-term potential deficit of domestic energy supplies is not demonstrated by the reserve data now available. Indeed, examination of indi-vidual countries reveals that energy costs and their regional differences are much stronger motivations for an alternative energy source in particular areas. Furthermore, other natural resources, particularly water for irrigation, appear in more immediate danger of being inadequate at reasonable cost than does energy supply.

ISRAEL: WATER.[52] Because of the Arab embargo, Israel has had to secure its oil primarily from the Western Hemisphere and to a lesser extent from the Soviet Union and the Persian Gulf. Israel produces only about 5 per cent of its domestic consumption of petroleum and has a limited output of natural

51. UN, *The Future Growth of World Population*, New York, 1958, Appendix C, Tables I A and I B, show a medium projection for this area of 1,964 million by 2000, based on a growth rate of 1.7 per cent to 1975 and 2.2 per cent for 1975–2000.

52. The material in this section is dependent on data furnished by Victor Salkind, hydrologist and former scientific adviser to the Israeli legation, Washington, and on Landsberg and Perazich, *op. cit.*

gas. It has no other substantial domestic source of energy. Thus Israel's rapidly growing economy, its expanding power requirements and the opening of the Negev (southern desert area) to settlement and agriculture are largely dependent upon a source of energy that is more than 5,000 miles distant. Fuel oil costs about 50 cents per million BTU—not substantially more, however, than the cost in Western Europe generally in recent years. About one third of all petroleum consumption goes into electric-power production and nearly one third of electric energy consumption is for irrigation and water supply. Finally, about one third of the cost of irrigation is power. Thus, oil, water and power supply are inseparable and bulk large in the Israeli economy as a whole.

Israel's primary resource problem is insufficient water for irrigation. At present the natural water supply is barely adequate and the Landsberg-Perazich study, based on both official and independent appraisal, indicates that all available natural irrigation water will be in use by about 1965–1967. International arrangements on disposition of Jordan River water may alleviate this situation for a time, as would the conversion of brackish water. But, in any case, growth of the Israeli economy and irrigation agriculture in time will compel conversion of sea water. Israel, as a matter of national policy, has therefore been establishing long-term plans that assume an adequate water supply through sea-water conversion.

Whether nuclear power might materially influence the economics and technology of the conversion of sea water in Israel, or in other arid lands, is a subject that has attracted the attention of technicians in the United States and in Israel. As a result of these investigations, Israel is now considering an "intermediate" solution to the conversion of saline water that defers the application of nuclear power for a decade or more, until reactor technology has been further advanced by other countries. The plan being developed is to use a conventional oil-fired generating station in which the exhaust steam from the turbines, instead of being condensed, would be used as the source of heat for distillation units or evaporators. However, generating power and heat in this relatively inefficient fashion means that fuel requirements (and fuel costs) would be increased by roughly 50 per cent. The cost of fresh water would be approximately 26 cents per cubic meter. This is prohibitive for irrigation but not for urban or household use.

Within the next two decades might nuclear energy prove an economic alternative to high-cost imported oil in connection with more promising conversion methods? The principal avenue appears now to be the use of reactors that produce very low-temperature heat (under 300⁰ F.) in combination with sea-water evaporators. Higher temperature heat (steam) required for turbogenerator units would have to be supplied by superheating with oil. Since a low-temperature reactor is more suitable as a source of heat than of electric power, it is being considered by the Israelis particularly for use with small multieffect or multistage evaporators, rather than with power-intensive distillation equipment. Schematic costs for a combination of a reactor of 500 thermal megawatts and an evaporator of 42 million cubic meters, to be located near the sea, are estimated at 23 cents per cubic meter (or 87 cents per 1,000 U. S. gallons, or $284 per acre-foot). This is several times as costly as water used for irrigation now in the northern Negev, hence the economics could not justify such use under foreseeable circumstances. However, an interesting fact is that the nuclear heat from the 500–thermal megawatt reactor is estimated to cost 52 cents per million BTU, roughly competitive with imported oil. The technical gap in sea-water conversion methods is evidently far greater than the gap in nuclear energy technology. Since all methods of saline-water conversion—except solar—require a substantial input of commercial heat or power, low-cost or even marginal-cost nuclear power would be a long term economic benefit to the many arid areas of the world that lack a low-cost indigenous energy supply.

India: Capital Availability and Potential Capital Savings [53]

The early stages of economic development are now generally considered to be closely bound to an increasing supply of capital and new capital formation. Hence, it is pertinent to examine the question whether (as has been held by Bhabha, the leading exponent of nuclear power for the underdeveloped economies) this new source of energy might require significantly less capital, directly and indirectly, than would conventional electric power. Though, as indicated earlier in this chapter, nuclear energy offers scant prospect of capital savings for the industrial nations of Western Europe, the same need not be true for a less developed country, such as India, where energy supply lines are far longer. The Atomic Energy Commission of India has tried to establish direct and indirect capital requirements for nuclear as compared with coal-fired thermal plants located several hundred miles from the coal fields of central India.

53. See the following sources: Gold, *op. cit.*, pp. 78–80, and 121–25; H. J. Bhabha, "The Role of Atomic Power in India and Its Immediate Possibilities," *Proceedings*, First Geneva Conference, Vol. 1, p. 103; H. J. Bhabha, "On the Economics of Atomic Power Development in India and the Indian Atomic Energy Programme," *The Advancement of Science*, British Association for the Advancement of Science, London, December 1957; and H. J. Bhabha and N. B. Prasad, "A Study of the Contribution of Atomic Energy to a Power Programme in India," *Proceedings*, Second Geneva Conference, Vol. 1, p. 89.

India plans to develop its nuclear power program, and achieve the thorium breeder, by successive stages. First, natural uranium power reactors are intended to produce plutonium; the plutonium will then be used as fuel in second stage reactors designed to produce U233 from thorium; this will lead to the third stage, breeders, fueled with U233 and producing additional fuel from fertile material, thorium. The capital-cost data, given by Bhabha, show that capital savings are unlikely in the first two stages. However, if present unsubstantiated estimates of the costs for the breeding stage prove valid, then in a matter of a decade, but probably more, nuclear power may yield significant capital savings.

The AEC of India summarizes the comparative capital costs of nuclear and coal-fired plants as follows: In the first generation of natural uranium graphite power reactors, totaling 1 million kilowatts, the cumulative capital costs—in mines, fuel fabrication, fuel reprocessing and reactors—are roughly estimated at about 2,500 million rupees (about $500 million) compared with the corresponding total costs for equivalent coal power (including rail transport of 700 miles) of 1,600 million rupees ($320 million). The estimated capital costs of the second stage plutonium reactors, comprising 250,000 kilowatts, are 500 million rupees ($100 million) against 400 million rupees ($80 million) for equivalent coal power. In the third stage of thorium-U233 breeder reactors the AEC of India projects substantial capital savings, based on order-of-magnitude cost estimates for such breeders in U. S. literature. On a per-kilowatt basis the comparative capital costs are given as 1,350 to 1,390 rupees (or $270 to $280) for a thorium-U233 breeder against 1,600 rupees ($320) for a power plant based on coal.[54]

These estimates, for both coal and nuclear power, suffer from such grave weaknesses that the prospect seems very doubtful for capital savings in the present program even beyond the next decade. Among these weaknesses, for example, are the use of a 4.5 per cent interest rate in computing the comparative cost of nuclear and coal-fired power, while real rates of interest in India are much higher; the assumption that coal would be moved as far as 700 miles, though the central India coal fields in Madhya Pradesh, for example, are less than 500 miles from Bombay and Madras; and the assumption that the benchmark capital cost of a coal-fired power plant should be set as high as 1,600 rupees (or $320) per kilowatt, which is far more than the most costly plants in Western Europe and even in the United States, where construction costs are higher than in Europe. Despite these and other misgivings about the

54. Bhabha and Prasad, *op. cit.*, pp. 95 ff. Critical examination of the cost estimates for India strongly suggests that capital requirements of nuclear power would be less if the program were to take advantage of enriched fuel available from other countries and thus save time and capital by eliminating the intermediate stage.

validity of the capital cost comparisons, there is little doubt that nuclear power could produce important capital savings in India, provided that the capital cost of nuclear power plants could in time be reduced (from the third-stage estimate) by more than one quarter to 1,000 rupees (or $200) per kilowatt. This may be achieved, as indicated in Chapter 2, but it is not foreseeable within the next decade.

Development of Energy-Remote Areas

The so-called "remote areas" long have been considered theoretically promising sites for application of nuclear power. Small reactors, 2,000 to 10,000 kilowatts, are usually thought of as appropriate for these areas, though not as direct substitutes for diesel units, customarily of 1,000 kilowatts or smaller. The case for the small reactor in the remote area is usually based on a situation in which unexploited natural resources, particularly minerals, are distant from tidewater or from other access to fossil fuels and can therefore be exploited only with extremely high energy costs. Closer examination, however, generally reveals that serious economic and technical constraints are placed on early application of nuclear power in such an area. Canada and Australia are illustrations.

The available studies of Canada suggest the possibility of some use of small nuclear power plants in mining and milling districts that are relatively inaccessible, though their national contribution would be modest in comparison with the principal role of plants with a large base load.[55] The primary competitive threshold for small nuclear power plants, 2,000 to 3,000 kilowatts, is established in the remote areas of Canada by diesel electric units. Eliminating the regions where the plant factor would be low and the diesel fuel no more than about 20 cents per gallon, the demand for small power plants is restricted mainly to the large mining communities developing in the far north, where power at 20 to 30 mills per kilowatt-hour would be competitively useful. A few far northern mining sites, in the Yukon, for example, have exceedingly high diesel fuel and generating costs—25 to 50 mills per kilowatt-hour. Moreover, since transport is open only a couple of months each year storage capacity must be very large. At the Eldorado uranium mill at Beaverlodge on Lake Athabaska diesel storage capacity is 4.3 million gallons.[56]

55. J. U. Mowll, "Power Requirements in Remote Regions," Atomic Industrial Forum—National Industrial Conference Board, New York, March 17, 1958; John Davis, *Canadian Energy Prospects*, Royal Commission on Canada's Economic Prospects, Ottawa, March 1957, Chap. 10.

56. J. U. Mowll, "Prospects for Nuclear Power in Canada," *Martin Nuclear Marketing Research Bulletin*, Baltimore, August 22, 1957.

Somewhat more promising might seem to be the application of medium-sized plants of 10,000- to 30,000-kilowatt capacity, providing electricity at 10 to 12 mills per kilowatt-hour and process heat for use in manufacturing pulp and paper in the maritime provinces and in the northern part of interior provinces. But more than 95 per cent of Canada's power output is very low-cost hydro and only in a few areas is the hydro potential small, so there appear to be few openings for nuclear power.

In many respects Australia may appear to present a more promising region for small or medium-sized nuclear power plants in mining operations than Canada, in part because major mineralized areas are several hundred miles from tidewater or from coal mines, or the hydro potential is small. Two sites serve to illustrate the prospects and economic constraints. In the northeast sector, at Mount Isa, Queensland, substantial deposits of copper and other minerals are several hundred miles from the nearest coal mines and from the east coast ports. Delivered fuel costs to this remote area, which is connected by rail, are high but not prohibitive and would require nuclear power to meet a cost threshold of 10 to 12 mills in a medium-sized unit, if smelting and refining were to be undertaken near the mining operations. However, it is possible that the copper ore could be reduced to blister, at small power requirement, then shipped to a lower cost energy site for refining near the coal mines.[57] On economic grounds, then, there is no obvious advantage in nuclear power at present foreseeable costs. But to make a useful judgment of the question would require detailed analysis of alternative energy sources, of various sites for electrolytic refining and of joint power requirements within transmission distance of the copper mines which might justify larger, more economical power plants. Another remote site, involving no mining operations, is the midcontinent town of Alice Springs (population 2,785) situated at railhead more than 800 miles from ports on the southern coast of Australia. A small power reactor at this site could serve the town's requirements, but the economic benefits would appear to be marginal. Notwithstanding the lack of any striking opportunities for small, remote nuclear reactors even in Australia, it would be presumptuous to dismiss the possibilities of such plants without detailed studies.

The economic implications of these and other surveys of "energy-remote" sites seem rather clear and in general contradict the commonly accepted view

57. In the United States copper mining and milling requires only 8 to 23 KWH per metric ton of product, whereas electrolytic refining requires 2,645 KWH per ton. (UN, *Economic Applications of Atomic Energy: Power Generation and Industrial and Agricultural Use*, Report of the Secretary-General, New York, 1957, p. 97.)

of nuclear power's prospects in such areas. Distance from tidewater does not usually result in what might be termed prohibitive fuel costs that would make very high-cost nuclear power in small reactors competitive. The seeming pattern of diesel generating costs of 20-30 mills per kilowatt-hour at low plant factor in remote areas suggests that small nuclear power plants might in time prove competitive in cost with larger diesel units at some remote locations. But the nuclear plant would still suffer from comparison with the relatively safe and simple diesel. In addition, the probability of finding many areas of unexploited natural resources that require power-intensive processing at the site and at the same time lack an economically available energy supply is very small, a conclusion based on several investigations made since the 1955 Geneva conference. This is not to say that none will be found. Finally, if small nuclear power reactors are to serve remote mining, agricultural or urban areas in less developed countries, it will be of the utmost importance that the units meet two requirements—reliable, continuous operation and virtually no nuclear maintenance.

These constraints on the applicability of nuclear power also suggest that the "eligible" remote area has been poorly defined. The remote area which offers a more promising chance for economic nuclear power in the foreseeable future is of a different character and best described as "an industrial enclave." For such a remote area or enclave to be suitable for nuclear power, it should have not merely an energy import requirement but also a demand sufficiently large to justify a large reactor, a diversity of load permitting rather high plant factor and the possibility of interconnection with alternative power sources so as to reduce the impact of reactor shutdown. Since the economies of scale for nuclear power plants especially favor large loads, populous or industrialized enclaves located at some distance from indigenous conventional energy sources are more promising "remote areas" for nuclear power's special transport benefits than the isolated small-load area considered above. There are a great many large-load industrial enclaves: Bombay and Madras, India, each 400 to 500 miles from central coal fields, are illustrative. Such remote areas would call for large units and these would represent a much greater addition to national power capacity than a large number of small reactors.

For policy purposes, therefore, the United States atoms-for-peace program should avoid encouraging the pursuit of a will-o'-the-wisp in the form of the small power reactor for use in isolated areas. At the same time, however, there are good economic reasons for encouraging nuclear power in industrial enclaves handicapped by high energy costs.

CHAPTER 7

Foreign Programs and Resources

Outside the atomic nations a few industrialized countries and only one semi-industrialized country, India, have embarked on programs of nuclear power construction.[1] Each program, as shown later in this chapter, exhibits special national characteristics, just as the economic need and urgency for nuclear power in each country are unique, as shown in the preceding chapter. The early origins of the Canadian power program in heavy water and natural uranium, of the United States program in water-cooled and enriched-fuel submarine reactors, of the United Kingdom program in gas-cooled, natural uranium reactors and of the Soviet Union program in plutonium-production reactors all attest to diverse historical antecedents. Yet each of these is now encountering new economic and technical conditions, common to nuclear power development everywhere, that may compel a break with the past.[2] For the other countries national considerations—economic policies and objectives, size of GNP, domestic nuclear resources and technical capability—will bear

1. Aside from the United States, the United Kingdom and the Soviet Union, the only countries engaged, strictly speaking, in nuclear power programs are: Belgium, Canada, France, Germany, India, Italy, Japan, the Netherlands and Sweden. See *Proceedings*, Second Geneva Conference, Vol. 1; and the AEC summaries for sixty-three countries, current to March 1960, in the McKinney Review, *Background Material*, Vol. 3, pp. 495 ff.

2. Walter H. Zinn, "Similarities in the Technical Features of Nuclear Power Development in the United States and Other Countries," *Proceedings*, American Power Conference, Nineteenth Annual Meeting, Chicago, 1957, p. 19.

TABLE **7 - 1**

Uranium: Economically Recoverable World Reserves Compared to Production, by Area, 1960

Short tons, U_3O_8		
Area	Economically recoverable reserves[a]	Production rate, 1960
Total	1,100,000	44,000[b]
United States	240,000	18,000
Canada	400,000	16.000
Western Europe	40,000	2,000
Latin America	3,000	...
Australasia	10,000	1,000
Africa	400,000	7,000

a. Recoverable at $10 or less per pound.

b. Production capacity was probably 15 per cent greater.

Source: Division of Raw Materials, AEC, in McKinney Review, Vol. 4, pp. 1605 and 1608.

heavily on the choices made. The scale and direction of national programs will also depend in part on capital resources and on access to outside technical assistance and materials.

Major Economic Considerations

Nuclear Materials Available in the Free World

Stimulated by military requirements, the free world output of uranium has expanded in the last decade from only a few thousand tons to about 44,000 tons in 1960. Economically recoverable reserves, widely dispersed among nations, are such as to permit great expansion in output at no great increase in cost. The AEC has reported the free world reserves recoverable at $10 per pound or less to be 1 million tons, and roughly 10 million tons at up to $40 per pound.[3] Uranium reserves are so great that they can impose no limitation on even the most rapidly expanding programs of civilian nuclear power foreseeable. Indeed, for many years the reasonably anticipated growth of uranium

3. AEC, "Uranium Resources of the United States and Allied and Neutral Countries," McKinney Review, *Background Material*, Vol. 4, pp. 1598–1612; also, AEC, *Energy from Uranium and Coal Reserves*, Washington, May 1960 (TID 8207).

consumption for civilian purposes will account for only a fraction of current production.

The 1960 production rate is small compared with indicated reserves and those likely to be found by further exploration. Reserves recoverable at up to $10 per pound in known areas, totaling more than 1 million tons (Table 7–1), may well be doubled by new discoveries.

In addition to the major producers a large number of other countries produce or are preparing to produce uranium. Among these are Argentina, Denmark, Egypt, India, Italy, Japan, Spain and West Germany, which have developed or partially developed uranium reserves estimated at between 500 and 5,000 tons each and exploitable at no more than twice the average cost of major producing countries.[4]

Thorium reserves and production are smaller, in part because attention has not been stimulated by military requirements. Only India and Brazil are actively interested in thorium. Known free world reserves recoverable at $10 per pound or less are, however, rather widespread (short tons, ThO_2):[5]

Total	500,000
United States	20,000
Canada	200,000*
Western Europe	—
Brazil	10,000
India	250,000
Other	20,000

* Dependent on uranium production.

Some economic implications are clear. Supplies of low-cost uranium, even if military requirements continue for several years, are so large that nuclear power development by any nation can be undertaken with assurance that real prices for uranium will remain favorable to reactor operators, and probably even decline. Also, the large number of countries possessing low-cost uranium reserves suggests that some may be strongly stimulated to develop and use them in preference to importing nuclear fuel. They have an economic bargaining position and may be encouraged to undertake nuclear power programs that will be independent of enriched uranium suppliers. Moreover,

4. Robert D. Nininger, "Geneva Conference Summary—Availability and Production of Source Materials," Fifth Annual Conference, Atomic Industrial Forum, Washington, November 10, 1958.

5. AEC, *An Analysis of the Current and Long-term Availability of Uranium and Thorium Raw Materials for Atomic Energy Development*, Washington, July 1959.

as already noted, large surpluses of uranium are likely after 1966, when AEC procurement contracts abroad are scheduled to terminate. Nuclear power programs therefore need not be constrained in the foreseeable future by the price or availability of natural uranium.

Capital Resources: Capacity for Debt Servicing

Nuclear power plants, as has been pointed out, are likely to remain for some years more costly per kilowatt than conventional alternatives, even when indirect capital savings are considered. (See Chapter 6.) On the other hand, nuclear power may provide significant foreign-exchange savings to energy-importing industrialized nations. However, many underdeveloped countries have insufficient capital resources to permit rapid economic development. Most of them have borrowed substantial funds from the International Bank for Reconstruction and Development for the construction of conventional thermal and hydroelectric power stations and may well turn to the IBRD again for financing nuclear power stations. Except for the SENN project in Italy, the IBRD has thus far provided no encouragement for nuclear projects, nor has the Export-Import Bank, beyond its routine participation in the financing of joint projects of Euratom and the United States.

The crucial question for the particular country and the IBRD will not be whether the nuclear power plant will produce power as cheaply as a conventional plant would, but whether the debt-servicing capacity of the particular economy is sufficient to carry the additional capital burden involved in nuclear power. A long-standing issue in IBRD financing of different types of power stations—not new with nuclear power—is whether the return will support high-capital-cost projects. (The IBRD staff, for example, has urged some applicant countries proposing hydro projects at a high cost per kilowatt to undertake steam plants demanding less capital but much higher operating costs.) It is desirable, then, to review how serious and how prevalent a constraint an inadequate debt-servicing capacity may be. However urgent the need for nuclear power—and whatever the possibilities of its becoming competitive—in a particular country may appear, the limited debt-servicing capacity may prove controlling.

The relevant statistical criteria of debt-servicing capacity have been developed by the staff of the IBRD. The first guidelines are the ratios of debt-service payments to national income, savings, government revenue and foreign exchange receipts, of which the ratio of debt service to foreign exchange receipts is believed analytically most useful. The second criterion is the trend and rate of change of the balance (after debt-service payments) of income, savings, government revenue and foreign exchange earnings.[6]

By these standards the energy-deficient countries of Western Europe had a substantial debt-servicing capacity in 1958. For the industrializing countries the picture has been less uniform. Although most of them have had unused debt-carrying potentialities in recent years, a few have shown such high ratios of debt-service payments to export earnings that doubt has been raised as to further borrowing. For example, by 1958 the ratios had risen to rather high levels (above 7 per cent) for Brazil, Chile, Colombia, Israel and Mexico. However, for most of the semi-industrialized countries the public debt service has been less than 7 per cent of net export earnings, and for several the low ratios have been historically stable. On the basis of the statistical record through 1958, one may assume that the increments in national income, savings, public revenue and foreign exchange earnings of most of the under-developed economies have been sufficient to cover higher levels of debt-service payments.

Among the debtor countries that appear, according to the statistical criteria, to possess a high potential capacity for financing construction of capital-intensive power projects and also are identifiable as energy-deficient countries are Argentina and Uruguay in Latin America; Ceylon, India and Japan in Asia; and Australia—not to mention most of the countries of Europe. Thus, debt-carrying capacity of a great many countries appears adequate to permit nuclear power programs. This judgment is, to be sure, only a point of departure and it may well be that closer, current examination of a country's position would disclose an unfavorable prospect for international financing of nuclear power plants, competitive though they may soon be.

Enriched Uranium: Capital Investment in Gaseous Diffusion Capacity

The capital cost of plants for enriching uranium is so heavy that only a few countries can contemplate adding the cost of producing enriched uranium to the high capital cost of nuclear power plants themselves.[7] During the early

6. D. Avramovic, *Debt Servicing Capacity and Postwar Growth in International Indebtedness*, Johns Hopkins Press, Baltimore, 1958, p. 60; and D. Avramovic and R. Gulhati, *Debt Servicing Problems of Low-Income Countries, 1956–1958*, Johns Hopkins Press, Baltimore, 1960, p. 53.

7. However, estimates by Starr suggest that ultimately the comparative capital burden of plants for enriching uranium may not be large. Assuming capital investment of $45 billion in nuclear power plants (roughly equivalent to 135 million ekw.), the corresponding investment in three gaseous diffusion plants (each producing about 5,000 tons annually of 1.5 per cent enriched uranium) would be about $2.4 billion, or only 5.3 per cent of the nuclear plant. (See Chauncey Starr, "Fuel Enrichment and Reactor Performance," *Proceedings*, Second Geneva Conference, Vol. 13, p. 282.)

phase of program expansion, when the cost of building up fuel inventory is large, access to enriched uranium may prove critically important for all countries electing enriched systems.

There would be obvious strategic value in owning gaseous diffusion capacity if, for example, recycled plutonium should prove much less attrac- tive as fuel than enriched uranium. In that case some countries might judge the capital cost of gaseous diffusion plant worth while for the sake of inde- pendence from external sources. On the other hand, if by-product plutonium can be made economically attractive as a fuel, the heavy investment in plant to supply enriched uranium may prove unnecessary. Considering the growing emphasis on plutonium in present fuel technology, it is to be expected that plutonium fuel will become a suitable complement of enriched uranium fuel.[8] For a very few countries, however, slightly enriched uranium could become the incidental by-product of weapon-grade production in gaseous diffusion facilities built primarily for military purposes.

An important technical distinction between uranium and plutonium, based on their fuel and weapon utility, must be remembered. While Pu239 and U235 can be used both in weapons and as fuels, slightly enriched uranium is useful only as fuel. Plutonium, however, even when containing high proportions of Pu240 and Pu242 resulting from long irradiation and superficially considered useful only as fuel, may possess significant weapon value.[9] Therefore, where capital is limited, as it is in most industrializing nations, the use of plutonium offers a "poor-man's" route to weapon material as well as to reactor fuel and hence raises the problem of safeguards. Furthermore, the terms on which enriched uranium is available help to determine the early direction of a na- tion's reactor program.

Whether the United States pricing policy for enriched uranium and heavy water is "fair" cannot be lightly dismissed. A common feeling in the United Kingdom is indicated by the following:[10]

> There is no doubt that many smaller countries are dazzled, as well they might be, by the size and immense scope of the American atomic effort and the lure is all the stronger for the suspicion that the U. S. A. might be prepared to supply atomic wares at less than cost. Certainly, materials like uranium 235 and heavy water appear to be supplied at a fee that just covers the running costs of the plants

8. AEC, *Major Activities in the Atomic Energy Programs, January-December, 1960* (Annual Report), Washington, January 1961, p. 53.

9. AEC Commissioner Vance in 1958 stated that it was no longer true that $12 (per gram) plutonium could be used only as fuel. Section 202 Hearings, 1958, p. 65.

10. Mary Goldring, *Economics of Atomic Energy*, Butterworths Scientific Publications, Lon- don, 1957, p. 139.

making them. Their capital costs must be written off against military research. If the economic argument is right, and enriched reactors are more expensive to operate than natural uranium reactors, then Britain has nothing to fear. But it is always possible that American selling prices will be revised downwards simply in order to dispose of the mounting surplus of fissile materials and that the Atomic Energy Commission will dump its uranium 235 abroad in the belief that this will stimulate . . . civil atomic developments in foreign countries.

However, as discussed in Chapter 5, it appears quite doubtful that the AEC price schedules for U235 are "low," in the sense of having eliminated properly assignable costs. On the contrary, the "full-cost" principles followed by the AEC, and subject to review by the General Accounting Office, may have resulted in somewhat "high" prices, from the point of view of reactor operators. The U. S. cost of power for operating the gaseous diffusion plants is so low and the economies of scale are so pronounced that production costs are obviously far less here than in the United Kingdom and appear to be a sufficient explanation of "low" prices. The allegation of dumping is unjustified, though not demonstrably so, in the absence of published data.

So long as U. S. enriched uranium prices are not unreasonable, capacity is ample and capital costs of gaseous diffusion plant are great, one may assume that uranium enrichment capacity will not be justified in other countries and that their reactor programs need not be burdened by this claim on capital. At the same time the United States has made large quantities of enriched uranium available to other countries. The commitment to supply enriched uranium was increased by President Kennedy to 65,000 kg. of contained U235 in September 1961. At the time it was indicated that further commitments would probably become necessary and that U. S. capacity was sufficient to meet all foreseeable civilian use in addition to U. S. weapon requirements.

Role of Private and Publicly Owned Utilities in Western Europe

As is true in the United States, the conflicting interests of private and public power groups have provided strong motivation for early development of nuclear power, and in some cases have also led to controversy and delay in legislation. The proportions of public and private power in Western European countries are shown in Table 7-2. Before examining the figures, however, it should be understood that "joint undertakings"—private utilities in which public authorities have a financial interest—are much more common

TABLE **7 - 2**

Production of Electricity by Public and Private Utilities, Selected OEEC Countries, 1960[a]

Country	Total (10⁹ KWH)	Percentage distribution[b]		
		Public	Private	Joint
Total	501.1	62	21	17
Germany	108.4	40	6	54
Austria	16.0	90	10	—
Belgium	14.1	7	93	—
France	69.5	81	9	10
Greece	2.3	16	84	—
Ireland	2.1	100	—	—
Italy[c]	55.9	10	60	30
Netherlands	15.6	100	—	—
Portugal	3.1	—	49	51
Norway	31.0	50.5	49.5	—
Sweden	34.8	46	54	—
Switzerland	20.7	53	38	9
United Kingdom	127.6	100	—	—

a. Total production figures are for 1960; percentage distribution is as of 1953.

b. 1953; excludes plants that do not supply current to a system.

c. Estimated.

Sources:

    Total—FPC, *World Power Data, 1960: Capacity of Electric Generating Plants and Production of Electric Energy*, Washington, August 1961 (multilith).

    Percentage distribution—OEEC, *Electricity Rates*, Paris, 1957, Table 1, p. 14.

than in the United States. They are especially important in Germany and Italy.

The figures in Table 7-2 indicate that in Western Europe as a whole public power is the predominant institutional form, accounting for about two thirds of total generation in 1953. (The ratio is about the same for the distribution of electricity.) Only two countries—Belgium and Greece—have as high a proportion of privately owned generating capacity as the United States.

How significant is the institutional factor as an explanation of the speed with which particular countries have established nuclear power programs? Certainly in the United Kingdom and France, for example, where public power predominates, the approach to nuclear power has been direct and unambiguous; whereas in Germany and Italy there has been a rather obvious legislative conflict, stemming in part from institutional considerations, similar to those apparent in the United States power program.[11]

National and Regional Programs

United Kingdom

The British, being cut off from American reactor technology after the war, found it best to build natural uranium, gas-cooled, graphite-moderated reactors, because all the materials could be secured at home or in the Commonwealth and because the large safety distances of the water-cooled reactors (like those at Hanford, Washington) were unnecessary.[12] Since the rather inflexible indigenous supplies of coal could meet no more than about one fifth of the annual increment in foreseeable energy requirements, the British early concluded that, for balance-of-payments and security reasons, the dependence on imports of coal and oil could well be moderated by immediately available nuclear power plants of the type described. From this conception, born of economic and technical expediency, the British program has progressed along three main lines.

The so-called "Calder Hall program," consisting of four reactors at Calder Hall and four at Chapelcross, is essentially a military plutonium production effort with by-product, low-temperature heat being used for generating electricity—thereby making the cost of the power dependent on the accounting method used. The program is operated by the U. K. Atomic Energy Authority. Plant operation and fuel handling are optimized for plutonium production rather than for power.

The second main line of effort, based on the general success of the Calder Hall reactors, has consisted of the construction of several civil stations by the Electricity Boards of Great Britain. This program called for twelve nuclear stations of two reactors each, with a total capacity of 1,500 to 2,000 megawatts by 1965; but in March 1957, partly as a result of the Suez incident, the program was trebled—to between 5,000 and 6,000 megawatts by 1965. Since

11. In 1962 the government of Italy sought legislation to nationalize private utilities.

12. Sir John Cockroft, "Nuclear Power and Radio-biology," Lecture to the Royal Society of Medicine, March 25, 1959, printed in *Atom*, United Kingdom Atomic Energy Authority, London, May 1959. Also, Sir Christopher Hinton, "The Evaluation of Nuclear Plant Design," lecture at the Royal Society's Tercentenary Celebrations, July 20, 1960; and Sir Christopher Hinton and others, "The Economics of Nuclear Power in Great Britain," Sixth World Power Conference, Madrid, 1960, IVB/8.

then the program has been stretched out twice, so that in 1961 the reduced pace implied that 5,000 megawatts would be achieved in 1968, with nearly 4,000 megawatts by 1966. The basic objectives and policies have not been altered.[13]

The third line of effort has consisted of a power reactor research program, anticipating the circumstances of the late 1960s and 1970s. Part of the research program is aimed at improving the gas-cooled reactor by securing higher operating temperature, greater fuel burn-up and lower capital costs, using slightly enriched uranium fuel. An important economic objective is lower capital cost to offset the declining plant factor that will probably occur as nuclear power supplies an increasing share of total generation.[14] In addition, the reactor research program is aimed at developing, for use in the 1970s, high-temperature, gas-cooled reactors (700° C.), possibly suitable for operation with the thorium-U233 fuel cycle. Further long-term research on the plutonium fast breeder is evidently contingent on the success of the experimental Dounreay fast breeder, brought into operation in 1961. Additionally, the Authority has studied the outlook for merchant-ship propulsion, but the prospects do not appear very promising. The available types of reactor design are unsuitable for propulsion because of their size, and the advanced gas-cooled designs remain to be developed. Also, Britain's hopes for further developing export trade encounter problems of reactor scale. The belief has been held that medium-sized reactors—30,000 kilowatts or less—may be best suited to the foreign market, yet this size range is not promising for the Calder Hall type, nor, in fact, are there substantial markets for reactors in this size range.

The problems of reducing the capital investment in nuclear power and the 1958 decision to move toward enriched fuel are necessarily connected. The total annual capital investment by Britain's electric generating authorities, including 6,000 megawatts of nuclear capacity, will average £400 million ($1.1 billion) in the five fiscal years ending 1966. If the program were all conventional plants, the annual investment rate would be £130 million ($360 million) less.[15] To moderate these excess capital costs, the British have put their hopes on the economies of larger plants and the future use of enriched fuel. The estimated reduction in unit costs is shown in Table 7–3.

13. Sir Roger Makins, "Nuclear Power Policy in the United Kingdom," United Kingdom Atomic Energy Authority, London, March 1961.

14. United Kingdom Atomic Energy Authority, London: *Fourth Annual Report, 1957–58*, p. 62, and *Seventh Annual Report, 1960–61*, pp. 10–11.

15. OEEC, *The Trend of the Selling Price of Electricity and Its Relation to the Financing of New Plant*, Paris, November 1958, p. 34.

TABLE **7 - 3**

Projected Investment per Unit in Nuclear Power Plants, Great Britain, Mid-1961 to Mid-1966

Midyear on load	Net station capacity—two reactors (mw.)	Projected cost	
		Plant, per kw.	First fuel charge, per kw.
1961	300	$426	$98
1962	500	350	77
1963	500	328	63
1964	500	302	53
1965	500	280	48
1966	1,000	232	39

Source: R. D. Vaughan, "The Technical and Economic Development of the Gas-Cooled Reactor," Sixth World Power Conference, Madrid, 1960, Paper IVB/11, p. 11, Figure 5.

Securing the economies of enriched fuel may raise more difficult issues for Britain than securing the economies of larger plant size.[16] The capacity of the British gaseous diffusion plants to produce enriched uranium is believed to be rather limited, although for security reasons the data have not been publicly released. The United Kingdom faces difficult choices in establishing a supply of enriched fuel, but a number of paths do exist. Diversion of gaseous diffusion capacity from weapon material to slightly enriched material is possible, but may be an unacceptable national policy. Expansion of existing diffusion capacity would seem too costly in capital and power requirements. The remaining possibilities would be to utilize by-product plutonium, to secure enriched uranium from the United States or to produce enriched uranium in

16. The scale of base-load power consumption available for nuclear power plant may become a problem. Compared with optimum size nuclear plant (400–800 mw.), the base load demand for power (75 per cent plant factor or higher) is not large in the British Central Electricity Generating Board. Duckworth and Jones estimate that while it should be possible to operate 7,000 mw. of nuclear capacity at 75 per cent plant factor as early as 1965, the system's rate of increase in base load in the period 1965–1970 will be only about 400 mw. annually, or roughly one additional plant each year. (With the 1958 revision of the program schedule, this is no longer a serious obstacle.) The seeming constraint of limited base load has led to consideration of imaginative ways to take advantage of comparatively low fuel costs for nuclear power plant. Principal among these is pumped-water storage at off-peak periods, with the stored water being released to generate hydroelectricity at peak-load periods. The capital cost of pumped storage plants varies widely between sites, available sites are not numerous and capital cost is not small, ranging between $120 and $155 per kw. in three cases. In August 1961 a pumped-storage plant was under construction in North Wales near the 500-mw. Trawsfyndd nuclear power station. (J. C. Duckworth and E. Hywel Jones, "Economic Aspects of the United Kingdom Nuclear Power Programme," *Proceedings,* Second Geneva Conference, Vol. 13, p. 576.)

TABLE **7 - 4**

Estimates of Conventional and Nuclear Power Costs in the United Kingdom,[a] 1958

	Nuclear plant		Coal-fired plant	
	Completion date, 1960–61	Completion date, 1962	Low-cost fuel site, 1959	High-cost fuel site, 1959
Plant capacity, net (emw.)	275–300[b]	500[b]	1,000	1,000
Capital cost, ex. initial loading (per kw.)	$406	$336	$154	$126
Fixed charges[c] (per cent)	8	8	6.7	6.7
Power cost (mills per KWH)	8.2–9.0	7.0–7.8	6.55	7.49
Capital charge (inc. that on initial fuel)	6.0–6.1	4.8–4.9	1.64	1.29
Fuel replacement	1.5–2.2	1.5–2.2	4.33	5.62
Operating & maintenance	0.7–0.7	0.7–0.7	0.58	0.58

a. Nuclear plant life, 20 years; conventional, 25 years.

b. Two reactors.

c. At 5 per cent interest and 75 per cent plant factor.

Source: J. C. Duckworth and E. Hywel Jones, "Economic Aspects of the United Kingdom Nuclear Power Programme," Proceedings, Second Geneva Conference, Vol. 13, p. 576. The 1958 estimates were modified in 1960, notably for reduced cost of conventional power; see Sir Christopher Hinton and others, "Economics of Nuclear Power in Great Britain," Sixth World Power Conference, Madrid, 1960, Paper IVB/8.

new facilities, perhaps using the centrifuge method. The quantities of pluton-ium available for fuel enrichment during the 1960s, and perhaps even the 1970s, may or may not prove sufficient. The United Kingdom might, for example, extend its enriched uranium capacity by purchasing weapon-level material from the United States for military purposes,[17] releasing domestic gaseous diffusion capacity for civilian purposes. In any event, enriched uranium from the United States would probably cost far less than the same grade of material produced at home or in joint facilities that might be built in Western Europe. To be sure, such dependence on the United States might be short-lived, because of rapid development of the use of plutonium.

17. Public Law 85-479, July 2, 1958, amending section 91 of the Atomic Energy Act of 1954, permits the United States to furnish weapon-grade fissionable material to a foreign nation that "has made substantial progress in the development of atomic weapons."

The resources—in capital, fissionable materials and manpower—which the United Kingdom may be prepared to invest in nuclear power expansion after 1966 will depend chiefly on comparative generating costs in conventional plants. The British estimates, presented at the Second Geneva Conference and again at the Sixth World Power Conference in 1960, are shown in Table 7-4. They reveal the generally high expectation of achieving competitive nuclear power in the United Kingdom by the early 1960s. As there are no privately owned utilities, the British estimates are particularly aimed at providing a guide to the scale of public investment. Relative magnitudes rather than precise data are deemed sufficient for this purpose. Actual costs will vary with particular institutional and financial arrangements, geographic locations, load conditions and alternative energy supplies.[18] An important qualification of the British estimates is that they have been derived from experience with plants that are optimized mainly for production of plutonium rather than for power, and only limited experience exists on which to project the performance of reactors designed primarily for power.

The comparative costs shown in Table 7-4 do not reveal certain major uncertainties, for example, the 5 per cent interest rate, already raised from the 4 per cent quoted by Jukes at the First Geneva Conference in 1955. Since the Second Geneva Conference the cost of conventional power has fallen and the credit for by-product plutonium has been drastically reduced. As a result, nuclear power plants being ordered in 1960 and 1961 were expected to provide power at a cost 25 per cent higher than best conventional plants. Comparable generating costs at high plant factor are expected some time between 1965 and 1970.[19]

The Soviet Union[20]

The USSR program of nuclear power development and plant construction resembles in many respects a composite of the United States and United Kingdom approaches. Like the British Calder Hall power program, it involves large, dual-purpose plant construction and, like the American program, it is diversified by research and prototype construction covering a variety of long-term reactors.

18. J. A. Jukes, "Economics of Nuclear Power," *Proceedings,* Second Geneva Conference, Vol. 13, p. 499.

19. Sir Christopher Hinton, *op. cit.*

20. For a detailed analysis of the nuclear power program of the Soviet Union see Appendix B; also, "The Atomic Energy Programs of Communist Countries," McKinney Review, *Background Material,* Vol. 4, p. 1276; Arnold Kramish, *Atomic Energy in the Soviet Union,* Stanford University Press, 1959; and AEC, *Costs of Nuclear Power,* Washington, January 1961.

In 1958 the plan appeared to include the following: under construction—three large stations, 420 megawatts at Voronezh, 400 megawatts at Beloyarsk in the Urals and 600 megawatts in Siberia; two additional stations of 400 to 600 megawatts were still to be built, probably one at Leningrad and the other at Moscow; and in operation—100 megawatts of the 600-megawatt station in Siberia, and the 5-megawatt experimental plant near Moscow which was reported at the First Geneva Conference.[21] But by 1961 the program had been cut back and the status appeared to be as shown in Table 7–5.

TABLE **7 - 5**

Soviet Power Reactor Program, 1961

Plant	Status	Initial operation	Net capacity (emw.)	Type
APS-1	Operable	1954	5	PWR
Voronezh	Being built	1961	196	PWR
Ulyanovsk	Being built	...	50	BWR
Beloyarsk	Being built	1962	94	BWR superheat
Ulyanovsk	Planned	...	50	Sodium graphite
BN-50	Planned	...	50	Fast breeder

Source: AEC, *Costs of Nuclear Power*, Washington, January 1961, pp. 8–9 (TID-8531 rev.). For a more detailed description, differing in certain respects, see Table B-6.

The Soviet reactor research program appears to be technically aggressive, as evidenced by the origination of nuclear superheating within the reactor core, by the emphasis on fast reactor technology[22] and by some research on small mobile power units (2,000 kilowatts). Research and development on ship- and submarine-propulsion reactors using the pressurized water concept is much like that of the United States program. Western scientists have therefore suggested that Soviet technical progress may be rapid.[23] The supply of enriched uranium appears not to be a seriously limiting factor. Also, power station construction may proceed more rapidly, once its economy is clearly

21. V. S. Emelyanov, "The Future of Atomic Energy in the USSR," *Proceedings*, Second Geneva Conference, Vol. 1, p. 68.

22. See "Fast Reactors: A Soviet Outlook," in *Nuclear Engineering*, April 1962, pp. 137 ff. Temple Press, Ltd., London, based on "The Future of Fast Neutron Reactors," *Atomic Energy*, October 1961 (USSR).

23. Walter H. Zinn, letter to the Joint Committee on Atomic Energy, October 21, 1958, printed in Section 202 Hearings, 1959, pp. 48–51.

demonstrated, than in the United Kingdom, for example, since power consumption has been expanding about 15 per cent annually, more than twice the rate in the United Kingdom, and the average plant factor is appreciably higher.

Significantly, too, the Soviet program appears to be relatively large, compared with its apparent nuclear materials production capability. Little unclassified literature on the USSR's nuclear resources exists, but information available indicates that inputs of uranium and of electric power into the atomic energy establishment may be no more than one fifth those of the United States. Biörklund's scrutiny of the available literature suggested that the Soviet Union in 1955 had available to it in the communist bloc an annual production of roughly 3,300 metric tons of U_3O_8. Later, in 1960, the annual production in communist-controlled countries was estimated to be 12,000 to 23,000 tons.[24] In contrast, United States procurement of U_3O_8 by the AEC was 32,000 tons in 1960. Turning to electric power consumption, the atomic energy installations of the Soviet Union probably consumed roughly 10,000 million KWH in 1955, according to the approximations of two U. S. specialists on Soviet industry.[25] In the same year the AEC is reported by the Federal Power Commission to have consumed about 50,000 million kilowatt-hours. Assuming the general validity of such crude estimates, what tentative economic inferences might be drawn concerning the Soviet capacity to undertake a manifestly large civilian nuclear power program?

Scarcity of natural uranium is not a serious constraint on the civilian or military program. Also, a strong incentive probably exists to use dual-purpose reactors for power and plutonium production. Enriched uranium supply is probably sufficiently tight to encourage use of plutonium and of fast breeder reactors. Furthermore, the military supply of fissionable material apparently is not so large as to permit substantial contributions of materials to the IAEA or to other foreign applicants. The United States evidently has had a striking advantage in its capacity to supply fissionable material to other countries for peaceful purposes. The Soviet Union would probably find it difficult, for example, to match the United States offers of 65,000 kilograms of U235 to other countries, without curtailing its military requirements. Finally, the original Soviet target of installing 2 to 2.5 million kilowatts by 1960 had to be "extended" in the new Seven-Year Plan. The shift to a slower schedule

24. Elis Biörklund, *International Atomic Policy During a Decade, 1945–1955*, Van Nostrand, Princeton, 1956, pp. 142–148; McKinney Review, *Background Material*, Vol. 4, p. 1613.

25. Demitri B. Shimkin and Frederick A. Leedy, "Soviet Industrial Growth," *Automotive Industries*, January 1, 1958, pp. 51–52.

was probably based on excessive costs of the program and on technical problems.[26]

The Euratom Program

In evaluating the nuclear power program of the European Atomic Energy Community (established in 1958 when the European Economic Community, or Common Market, was founded), two underlying principles need to be recognized. Euratom, an agency of the Six—France, West Germany, Italy, Belgium, the Netherlands and Luxembourg—is designed to further both the economic and political integration of Western Europe, primarily by economic means. Also, American foreign policy since the Marshall Plan has lent support and encouragement to the unification of Western Europe as a means not merely of strengthening resistance to the communist bloc but also of improving the political and economic welfare of this region, friendly in its relation with the United States.[27]

The immediate purposes of Euratom were the speedy establishment of nuclear industries[28] and the maintenance of a system of safeguards and controls over fissionable materials allocated for peaceful purposes. It acts as broker of all nuclear ores and fissionable materials produced or received in the Six. It promotes research and development on atomic energy in common and ensures dissemination of the resulting knowledge. It also enters into international agreements with other countries—among them the United States and the United Kingdom—in order to promote progress in atomic energy.

The bold plans of Euratom were revealed in *A Target for Euratom*[29] in May 1957. This first view of the energy problem of the Six was deeply influenced by the Suez crisis and proved to be misleading. *A Target* was not intended to be a program but rather a provisional statement of desirable objectives and the major conditions necessary to their achievement. The report indicated the scale of the fuel import problem, outlined in the preceding chapter, by estimating that 15,000 megawatts of nuclear capacity would be needed by 1967, if it was assumed that the imports of coal and oil by the Six

26. *Public Works Appropriations for 1961*, testimony of AEC Chairman J. A. McCone before the Committee on Appropriations, House, 86th Cong., 2nd Sess., 1960.

27. Ben T. Moore, *Euratom: The American Interest in the European Economic Community*, Twentieth Century Fund, New York, February 1958, pp. 31–34.

28. Article 1, *Treaty Establishing the European Atomic Energy Community* (Euratom) and connected documents (undated).

29. Louis Armand and others, Paris, 1957.

were to be stabilized at the level they are expected to reach in about 1963. Yet only a year after the publication of *A Target*, Euratom expected that no more than about 4000 megawatts would be in existence by 1965. Later, in 1960, the projection was reduced to 2,000 megawatts.[30] The easing of the supplies of conventional fuel was the main reason for the shift.

The Euratom reactor program consists in the main of projects undertaken in cooperation with the United States and the United Kingdom. France, to be sure, has had decades of research experience in atomic energy, has several dual-purpose, power-plutonium reactors under construction and may be proceeding with a gaseous diffusion plant. But Euratom has found that its main need is for the advanced reactor technology and enriched uranium the United States has been prepared to offer. Capital assistance has been a desirable, but not a necessary, condition of Euratom plans.

The joint twenty-five–year U. S.–Euratom agreement, approved by the U. S. Congress in 1957 (signed in 1958), covered a $350-million investment in nuclear power plants totaling about 1 million kilowatts. Of the total capital requirement, $215 million was to be provided by European power companies; the United States, through the Export-Import Bank, was to provide $135 million in long-term credit. Furthermore, the U. S. Government established a contingent fuel guarantee of up to $90 million. Finally, Euratom and the United States each pledged $50 million for research and development over the first ten years. In 1959 it was expected that five European public utilities would come forward with proposals for undertaking joint reactor projects to be completed between 1963 and 1965. By mid-1962, however, only one was underway. This lack of response was considered a serious blow for Euratom, since critics had earlier expressed serious doubts that European utilities would make proposals.

In March of 1959 Euratom, together with six other European governments, joined in a project (Dragon) to build by 1962 an advanced type of high temperature, gas-cooled reactor employing British technology. The arrangement provides for the United Kingdom to supply and reprocess the nuclear fuel, but it does not include the financial features of the treaty with the United States. In effect, the agreements mean that the European market is open to both American and British reactor technology until Europe itself has absorbed that technology, as it should be able to do within a few years. Even then, however, the region will continue for a time to be dependent on United

30. Euratom, *Berichte über die Lage der Kerrindustrien in der Gemeinschaft*, Brussels, June 30, 1958 (report due at end of first six months, under Article 213 of the treaty establishing Euratom); and Euratom, "Outlook for the Development of Nuclear Energy," statement in McKinney Review, *Background Material*, Vol. 4, p. 1217.

States enriched uranium supplies, unless other measures are taken, presumably in common. The French gaseous diffusion facilities may prove too small and too costly to be a practical alternative source.

If Euratom capacity grows as rapidly in the late 1960s and 1970s as its revised (1960) plans imply, there may be a substantial inventory requirement for enriched fuel then. To meet it, other than by continued imports from the United States, may require careful advance planning for adequate gaseous diffusion capacity at low-cost power sites.[31] Fortunately it seems unnecessary to make a decision on this question before the mid-1960s, when the comparative economics of natural uranium and recycled plutonium should be known. Aside from enriched uranium supply, there is no doubt about the future capability of the Six in indigenous nuclear power technology and production. On the other hand, improved prospects for conventional fuel supplies have not proved conducive to rapid reactor development.

In the business recession of 1958 and 1959 energy demand dropped sharply and stocks of coal, already built up owing to the 1956–57 fuel crisis following the Suez Canal incident, reached 25 million tons at the mines—10 per cent of 1958 output in the Six. As coal markets became the "number one" problem of the European Coal and Steel Community, as unemployment in the coal mines rose and as Germany canceled contracts for United States coal and imposed taxes on coal imports, the economic wisdom of accelerating nuclear power development was seriously questioned by industrial interests in early 1959. Growing energy consumption was expected to relieve the pressure of coal stocks and hence counteract the economic objections to the Euratom program.[32] By mid-1961, however, continued surplus stocks of coal and oil made an accelerated reactor program still seem unwarranted.

The question was posed in 1959 whether Euratom effort and United States assistance should not better be diverted from power reactors to other, perhaps broader, lines of technical endeavor. The most explicit statement of this view was by Robert McKinney, former U. S. Representative to the International

31. With this possibility in prospect, and noting that in time a portion of the AEC gaseous diffusion capacity would probably become surplus to long-term military requirements, the National Planning Association in 1957 suggested that such capacity might well be leased to Euratom or other groups of friendly countries. (NPA, *Productive Uses of Nuclear Energy: Summary of Findings—Policy Suggestions for the Future*, Washington, September 1957, p. 56.)

32. In its 7th Annual Report, the High Authority of the ECSC indicated that energy policy may have reached a crossroad. The High Authority asked whether the coal market system, going back to pre-Community days and different circumstances, was still valid and, since the days of rigidly protected national markets were ended, whether the quasi-monopoly of coal in the field of energy might not also be ended. (*Bulletin*, European Community Information Service, Washington, May 1959, p. 4.)

Atomic Energy Agency.[33] Asserting that U. S. policy toward Euratom required complete reexamination, he argued that joint power reactor development with Euratom was not itself enough to provide the expected by-product benefits to American technology and, at the same time, that the Suez incident had led to excessive targets (15 million kilowatts by 1967). He noted that the foreign exchange problems of Western Europe ended with renewed currency convertibility in January 1959, and that coal and oil surpluses showed the economic need for nuclear power had receded. A key point was that the 1956 Suez crisis had not shown Western Europe vulnerable to Middle East oil, but rather had demonstrated its growing independence and the relatively weak bargaining positions of political regimes in the Middle East. McKinney suggested that since competitive nuclear power was more dubious than it had at first seemed, the emphasis ought to be shifted toward the widest type of atomic research and development.

McKinney's criticism was symptomatic of misgivings about Euratom long held in sectors of European industry, particularly in German coal mining. Some implications of the McKinney criticism and proposal should be noted.[34] If the power program should be severely cut, then American reactor manufacturers and the United States program would probably be unable to benefit by the relatively high-cost demonstration "platform" provided by the conditions of Western Europe.[35] Even at recession fuel prices and amidst surplus coal stocks, fuel costs there were still higher than those in major consuming markets in the United States up to mid-1962. Moreover, with the 1946–1956 fuel shortages and balance-of-payments problem seemingly past in 1959, the relative generating costs became of primary economic importance. This posed a serious question for both the U. S. domestic program and U. S. cooperation with Euratom. On the other hand, if nuclear power was in fact close to becoming competitive in the United States, as suggested by the estimates for the Bodega Bay plant, then the proposed redirection of Euratom research away from near-term power reactor stations was poorly timed and uncalled for. If nuclear power could not achieve competitive feasibility in Western Europe soon after 1965, then, the prospects for its becoming competitive soon in the United States would be even poorer.

33. "A New Look at Euratom," statement to the Joint Committee on Atomic Energy, May 20, 1959, reproduced in McKinney Review, *Background Material*, Vol. 4, p. 1250.

34. See the study by Arnold Kramish soon to be published by the Council on Foreign Relations, "International Aspects of the Peaceful Uses of Nuclear Energy" (working title).

35. McKinney Review, *Background Material*, Vol. 4, pp. 1241–42. Data presented by Euratom in May 1960 suggest conventional fuel costs of 45 to 55 cents per million BTU, or roughly 40 to 70 per cent higher than in the high-cost fuel areas of the United States.

Other Western European Countries [36]

The nuclear power plans of the Scandinavian and northern European countries are noticeably different from those of the United Kingdom, Euratom and the Soviet Union. Denmark, Finland, Norway and Sweden lack fossil fuels; and while the hydro potential is large in the northern countries, it will be taken up in the foreseeable future in Sweden and Finland. These countries meet their fuel needs largely by imports and, since they are maritime nations, the fuel requirement for shipping is large. Several of these countries are therefore planning to use nuclear energy for process steam and space heat, and a few are exploring the potentialities of merchant-ship propulsion. The energy position of the Scandinavian and Baltic countries may be radically altered by an oil pipeline—being constructed by the Soviet Union—the terminus of which is on the Baltic coast in Latvia or Lithuania.

Finland has a large pulp and paper industry using process steam at high plant factor and much of the heat for this and other purposes is obtained by burning wood. The country has some uranium ore and a pilot plant for concentrating uranium, built by a consortium of five Finnish pulp and paper companies. However, the need for nuclear power has been judged as not urgent.[37]

Denmark has had an obvious long-term need for nuclear power, since it has virtually no natural energy resources. Imported fuel costs are high (50 cents per million BTU in 1960) and the country imports electric power from Sweden. Despite its apparent promise, nuclear power is not being pressed by the Danish Atomic Energy Commission. Instead, a research program with three operating research type reactors has been undertaken. Design studies of several power reactor types have been made, including a deuterium-moderated and organic-cooled reactor as well as a large boiling water reactor. As to resources, Greenland has low-grade uranium and thorium and Denmark itself possesses the scientific heritage of Professor Niels Bohr and his institute at Copenhagen. Denmark is moving cautiously in its plans for nuclear power.

Norway is in the position of enjoying the highest per capita electric power consumption and about the lowest cost hydroelectric power in the world. Yet Norway lacks fossil fuel and has sought greater flexibility of energy supply for process heat and, in particular, ship propulsion. Heavy water production has long been a Norwegian specialty, hence the country's power program centers on the 10- to 20-megawatt experimental heavy water-moderated,

36. See *Nuclear Power*, London, January 1959, pp. 102–07, and January 1961, pp. 56–64; *Nuclear Engineering*, London, October 1958, pp. 419–22, and December 1960, pp. 542–46.

37. IAEA, *Prospects of Nuclear Power in Finland*, Technical Report Series No. 2, Vienna, 1960 (Joint Study by IAEA and Finnish Atomic Energy Commission).

boiling water reactor operating at Halden, primarily for process heat, using British natural uranium fuel. In addition, Norway has collaborated with the Netherlands in establishing a joint research center at Kjeller, Oslo.

Sweden, confronting a problem of inadequate fossil fuel and diminishing hydro potential sufficient for only fifteen to twenty years of further expansion, has been concentrating on heat reactors. The large imports of oil are mainly used for industrial process heat and space heating. The Second Geneva Conference revealed that the economics favored multiple-purpose over single-purpose reactors, hence the Swedish program has dropped the earlier plan to build a number of small, heat-producing plants. Sweden's program includes a combined heat and power unit to be operating in 1963, two power-producing units—of 50 megawatts and 100 megawatts, respectively—by 1967 and perhaps one or more large power plants by the end of the decade. Sweden produces uranium from shale, a low-grade source containing an estimated total of some 770,000 metric tons of uranium, recoverable at $16 to $20 per pound.[38]

Japan

Japan's program is designed to reduce dependence on imported fossil fuel and also to develop its own reactor technology.[39] Since energy requirements for the near future can be met by present means, Japan's Atomic Energy Commission is approaching nuclear power in a deliberate fashion dictated primarily by economic considerations. In the first stage the program includes purchase of a 150-megawatt natural uranium, gas-cooled reactor from the United Kingdom and a small 10- to 15-megawatt enriched uranium, boiling water reactor from the United States, both to be completed in 1962 or 1963.

The immediate preference for the British type of reactor has arisen because natural uranium is easily procured, the British have demonstrated the reactor's reliability, the fuel terms are simple[40] and the plant, though large, holds

38. AEC, *Energy from Uranium and Coal Reserves*, May 1960, p. 3 (TID 8207).

39. Atomic Energy Commission of Japan, "The Long-Term Plan for Development of Atomic Power Reactors in Japan," *Proceedings*, Second Geneva Conference, Vol. 1, p. 119.

40. An official British statement: "The United Kingdom Atomic Energy Authority have not given separate figures for the prices at which they would sell and repurchase nuclear materials and for the cost of reprocessing, as have the United States. Atomic Energy Authority representatives have however stated, subject to the same provisos as apply to the United States figures (i.e. depending on the type of fuel element), that the selling price for fabricated natural uranium fuel elements for the early gas-cooled graphite-moderated nuclear power stations is unlikely to exceed £20,000 per ton and may well be less. They have also suggested that the United Kingdom would repurchase irradiated fuel elements at a price of not less than £5,000 per ton. Assuming an average irradiation level of 3,000 MWD/T, net fuel costs for this type of station would then be about 2 mills per kWh, excluding inventory charges on the core." (Corbin Allardice, ed., *Atomic Power: An Appraisal*, Pergamon Press, New York, 1957, Appendix C, p. 143.)

out the promise of being easily duplicated by Japanese manufacturers. Japan will need to import natural or enriched uranium, and the first stage of the program assumes natural uranium fuel. Later stages leave scope for enriched fuel, since research is being directed toward both fast and thermal breeder reactors, and indicate that Japan has no intention of building gaseous diffusion capacity. It may be assumed that recycled plutonium will ultimately be the primary domestic route to enriched fuel.

The program projects several hundred megawatts in existence at the end of 1965, rising to 3,000 megawatts by 1970 and to 7,000 or 8,000 megawatts by 1975. Such a rate of growth is contingent on nuclear power's becoming competitive in Japan by 1965, on adequate domestic capital and, during the interval 1960–1968, on the foreign exchange to cover excess foreign currency requirements. From 1970 to 1975 the capital cost of domestic reactor equipment is projected at twice that of conventional steam plants and the foreign currency requirement for the imported equipment is more than eight times that for the corresponding steam plant.[41] Thus, capital and foreign exchange availability may well determine the scale of economic benefits Japan may hopefully expect.

Approaches to Nuclear Power by
Less Developed Countries

India's Program

India thus far (mid-1962) has been the only less developed country to embark on a nuclear power program, and its plans have held special interest for underdeveloped countries, as well as for the atomic leaders who are in a position to provide nuclear assistance. As mentioned in the preceding chapter, India intends to make full use of indigenous nuclear materials (chiefly thorium), and to lessen the fuel transport problem for areas remote from the coal fields. In the long run the hope is to save capital investment and to avoid the restraints of limited fossil fuel reserves on a high level of industrialization.[42] The Atomic Energy Commission has assumed that nuclear power will soon be competitive in the energy-remote areas and, indeed, may already be

41. Atomic Energy Commission of Japan, *op. cit.*, p. 132; and *Nuclear Power*, London, January 1962, p. 64.

42. In particular see H. J. Bhabha and N. B. Prasad, "A Study of the Contribution of Atomic Energy to a Power Programme in India," *Proceedings*, Second Geneva Conference, Vol. 1, p. 89; and, more recently, H. J. Bhabha, "Atomic Energy in the Indian Economy," address before the American Nuclear Society, Chicago, November 7, 1961.

competitive there, according to Bhabha. In this framework India has recently set the following target: 300 megawatts by March 1966, the end of the Third Five-Year Plan, and hopes of 10,000 megawatts by 1986.

In undertaking such early nuclear power development—some observers believe it premature[43]—India is relying heavily on foreign nuclear assistance, although her long-term objectives have been to emphasize use of indigenous resources. Estimates of nuclear reserves, initially reported at the First Geneva Conference (1955), have been increased substantially to between 250,000 and 300,000 tons of thorium in monazite, located in Kerala and Madras, and to 30,000 tons of uranium, located in Bihar and Rajasthan. While the total natural uranium requirements of even a 1,000-megawatt program would be only 6,700 to 8,000 tons, spread over twenty years, the Indian authorities believe it prudent not to plan a long-term program based on uranium. The first generation of natural uranium reactors is expected to produce sufficient plutonium to be used as fuel in a second generation of power plants in the more distant future. To circumvent the technical problems of the plutonium fast reactor, India plans to burn the plutonium in a thermal system yielding U233 from thorium.[44] If the second generation plants succeed, then the Indian planners project a start on thermal breeders, in the thorium-U233 cycle, which should be sufficient to meet the power growth rates of India, doubling every five years.

One need not be hypercritical to observe that India has embarked on an exceedingly difficult technical and economic program, one that has been made no easier by apparent insistence on producing domestically all nuclear fuel required—even though this implies high technical skill in handling plutonium and U233, both of which are already known to be "difficult" materials.[45] Some economists and reactor technicians have suggested that India might well reduce its handicaps by securing U235 from abroad.[46]

Aside from nuclear fuels, however, India has been willing to seek technical and industrial assistance abroad. For its first full-scale, 300-megawatt station (two reactors) India in 1961 received bids from manufacturers in Canada,

43. "National Power Programmes—A World Survey," *Nuclear Power*, Rowse Muir, London, January 1959, pp. 108–09.

44. Though the assumed conversion ratio, 0.45, is much lower than in a fast reactor, the time required to produce the fuel (U233) necessary for the inventory of the third generation plant is expected to be much shorter, 1.9 years against 6.7 years.

45. The desirability of stressing thorium is not questioned, since technical considerations reveal its potential promise. See, for example, R. A. Charpie and A. M. Weinberg, "The Outlook for Thorium as a Long-Term Fuel," presented at Trombay, India, January 1961.

46. For example, see Norman Gold, *Regional Economic Development and Nuclear Power in India*, NPA, Washington, 1957, pp. 119–20.

France, the United Kingdom and the United States (two companies). It has already received much assistance, under the Colombo Plan, from Canada in the joint construction of a heavy water research reactor. Germany is supplying India with a heavy water plant to yield 14 tons per year, and the United States has sold India 15 tons of heavy water for research. India has not, however, turned to the International Atomic Energy Agency for multilateral assistance—for reasons explored in Chapter 8.

While it is the intention of India's Atomic Energy Commission "to produce all the materials required for a full atomic program," it will welcome external assistance, preferably in long-term credits rather than in the form of gifts.[47] The plants will therefore have to meet strict competitive criteria, after the second generation demonstration units, in making a claim on India's scarce capital and foreign exchange resources.[48] Since first and second generation plants are likely to require substantially more capital than do conventional alternatives, their estimated capital requirements may well prompt the closest scrutiny. In a contest over the allocation of limited supplies of capital and foreign exchange, economic considerations suggest that self-sufficiency may be of less immediate importance than forms of international cooperation that will draw less heavily on these scarce resources. By buying enriched nuclear fuel abroad, India could move more rapidly, at less investment cost, toward full utilization of its special resources in thorium and uranium.

Unindustrialized Countries

Because of the early stage of reactor technology, the heavy capital requirements and the rather specialized contribution of nuclear power, underdeveloped countries have been showing discretion and restraint in undertaking nuclear power projects.

47. H. J. Bhabha, "On the Economics of Atomic Power Development in India and the Indian Atomic Energy Programme," *The Advancement of Science*, December 1957 (Evening Discourse, Dublin Meeting of the British Association for the Advancement of Science, September 6, 1957).

48. It should be noted that India has no plans for costly small power reactors. Also, strictly competitive nuclear power in large units is not projected until third generation plants appear, presumably coming on the line no earlier than 1970. And the estimates for these thermal breeders have been taken from the United States liquid-metal-fuel concept, which has still to be demonstrated as technically feasible. The order of assumed cost reduction, according to Bhabha and Prasad in 1958 (*op. cit.*), is as follows:

	Capital cost per kw.	Net cost of power per KWH
Coal-fired station	1,050 rupees ($250)	.0405 rupees (8.5 mills)
Nuclear station		
1st generation	2,367 rupees ($490)	.0451 rupees (9.5 mills)
2nd generation	1,900 rupees ($400)	.0508 rupees (10.7 mills)
3rd generation	1,350 rupees ($285)	.02662 rupees (5.6 mills)

Burma, for example, has adequate conventional energy resources at reasonable cost, and intends during the next several years to confine its efforts largely to personnel training, radioisotope research and uranium prospecting until the competitive feasibility of nuclear power can be demonstrated.[49]

Pakistan, similarly, while foreseeing a future place for competitive nuclear power in certain remote areas, as suggested by the National Planning Association study, has no specific plans for proceeding with the small power reactor (12.5 megawatts) being studied for a section of East Pakistan that is remote from hydro and natural gas sources.[50] In 1961 two U. S. engineering firms made a study[51] of the economic feasibility of nuclear power that suggested a larger role for nuclear power than did the NPA study.

Uruguay foresees, some decades ahead, a possible place for competitive nuclear power, to supplement hydro as it becomes fully exploited, but has no immediate reactor program.[52]

Israel, in contrast, seems well situated to employ nuclear energy productively in economic development at the proper time. The country has a number of scientific institutions through which it can secure the trained personnel for an imaginative program. Among these are the Hebrew University in Jerusalem and the Weizmann Institute in Rehovoth, where a pool-type research reactor was constructed by the Israeli Atomic Energy Commission with a contribution of $350,000 from the United States. Israel aims to have about 400 persons engaged in nuclear research and development within a few years—almost as many as in India.

In 1958 a leading United States electric utility executive urged the Israeli government to work toward construction of a 50-megawatt reactor in about 1965, but not before. It was recognized that such a project could place a burden on the Israeli power economy of $1 million to $2 million a year. On the other hand, atomic power costs were expected to decrease with time, there would be a gain in national security and there would be the advantage of making a start and gaining experience.[53] Yet, Israel at mid-1961 was

49. San Shin, "Burma's Electric Power Needs and Resources," *Proceedings*, Second Geneva Conference, Vol. 1, p. 209; and Hla Nyunt, "Burma's Atomic Energy Program," *Ibid.*, p. 201.

50. A. A. M. Ahmad, "The Future of Nuclear Power in Pakistan," *Ibid.*, p. 172.

51. Pakistan Atomic Energy Commission, *Study of the Economic Feasibility of Nuclear Power in Pakistan*, Karachi, November 1961.

52. Uruguayan National Atomic Energy Commission, "The Production of Electrical Energy from Nuclear Sources in Uruguay in the Course of the Next 25 Years," *Proceedings*, Second Geneva Conference, Vol. 1, p. 176.

53. Philip Sporn, President, American Electric Power Company, "Israel and the Atom: A Rational Program for the Development of Nuclear-Fueled Electric Power," an address delivered before the First World Assembly of Engineers and Architects at the Haifa Technion, May 30, 1958.

TABLE **7 - 6**

Free World Conventional Power Capacity, 1960, and Projected

Region and country	Conventional power, 1960 (emw.)	Nuclear power			
		1965		1970	
		Low	High	Low	High
Free world total	433,923	6,300	10,800	15,300	34,400
Western Europe	153,578	4,200	5,500	10,100	20,600
Euratom	74,637	1,500	2,000	4,500	9,600
United Kingdom	38,920	2,400	3,000	5,000	10,000
Other	40,021	300	500	600	1,000
Asia and Middle East	35,180	500	1,300	1,100	4,400
Japan	22,660	300	600	600	3,000
India	5,000	200	600	400	1,000
Other	7,520	—	100	100	400
North America (inc. Central America)	212,953	1,600	3,500	3,200	7,800
U. S.	186,193	1,500	2,500	2,500	5,800
Canada	23,199	100	800	500	1,600
Other	3,561	—	200	200	400
South America (and West Indies)	13,742	—	300	500	800
Argentina	3,010	—	100	200	300
Brazil	4,555	—	100	200	300
Other	6,177	—	100	100	200
Oceania	8,193	—	100	200	400
Africa	10,277	—	100	200	400

a. Generating capacity at the end of the year.

Sources:

Euratom—Based on "Outlook for the Development of Nuclear Energy," printed in McKinney Review, *Background Material*, Vol. 4, pp. 1196 ff.

United Kingdom—Based on the Hartley Commission Report (1956), p. 118; The Robinson Commission Report (1960), p. 114; and report of the Atomic Energy Authority to the Joint Committee on Atomic Energy (1960) in McKinney Review, *Background Material*, Vol. 4, pp. 1262 ff.

Japan—Based on Atomic Energy Commission of Japan, "The Long-Term Plan for Development of Atomic Power Reactors in Japan," *Proceedings*, Second Geneva Conference, Vol. 1, pp. 119 ff.

India—In part based on H. J. Bhabha and N. B. Prasad, "A Study of the Contribution of Atomic Energy to a Power Programme in India," *Proceedings*, Second Geneva Conference, Vol. 1, pp. 89 ff.

Nuclear Power Capacity, 1965–1980, by Region and Country[a]

(emw.)				Estimated total, 1980	Per cent nuclear, 1980		Region and country
1975		1980					
Low	High	Low	High	(emw.)	Low	High	
37,200	73,400	89,900	178,300	1,143,000	8	16	Free world total
21,500	32,000	43,000	84,000	444,000	10	19	Western Europe
10,000	15,000	20,000	40,000	240,000	8	17	Euratom
10,000	15,000	20,000	40,000	100,000	20	40	United Kingdom
1,500	2,000	3,000	4,000	104,000	3	4	Other
4,000	9,400	8,900	18,200	106,000	8	17	Asia and Middle East
3,000	7,000	7,000	12,000	72,000	10	17	Japan
800	1,600	1,500	5,000	19,000	8	26	India
200	800	400	1,200	15,000	3	8	Other
							North America (inc.
10,100	28,800	34,200	67,900	521,000	7	13	Central America)
8,000	25,000	30,000	60,000	460,000	7	13	U. S.
1,700	3,000	3,600	6,300	54,000	7	12	Canada
400	800	600	1,600	7,000	9	23	Other
							South America (and
800	1,600	2,400	5,000	32,000	8	16	West Indies)
300	600	1,000	2,000	8,000	13	25	Argentina
300	600	1,000	2,000	12,000	8	17	Brazil
200	400	400	1,000	12,000	3	8	Other
400	800	800	1,600	20,000	4	8	Oceania
400	800	600	1,600	20,000	3	8	Africa

United States—Chauncey Starr, statement before Joint Committee on Atomic Energy, Section 202 Hearings, 86th Cong., 2nd Sess., 1960, pp. 295 ff.; Philip Sporn, *Energy Resources and Technology*, statement before Joint Economic Committee, 86th Cong., 1st Sess., 1959, pp. 49 ff.; "AEC Estimates of Nuclear Power Capacity," in *AEC Authorizing Legislation, Fiscal Year 1960*, Hearings, Subcommittee on Legislation, Joint Committee on Atomic Energy, 86th Cong., 1st Sess., 1959, p. 680; and Keith L. Harms, "Economic Considerations Bearing on Civilian Nuclear Power Development," Supplement II to the *Report of the Ad Hoc Committee on Atomic Policy of the Atomic Industrial Forum*, New York, 1962.

Canada—Interpolated from W. B. Lewis, "Canada's Steps Toward Nuclear Power," *Proceedings*, Second Geneva Conference, Vol. 1, p. 58.

Other areas—Estimated by author.

Conventional power, 1960—FPC, "World Power Data, 1960," Washington, 1961 (multilith).

planning to meet its emergent water problem in the Negev through an "intermediate," conventional power scheme that would by-pass nuclear power for at least several years. In 1961 Israel revealed that a 24-megawatt reactor had been constructed in the Negev south of Beersheba, but details have not been released.

Projections of Free World Nuclear Power Capacity, Fuel Requirements and Plant Investment

At this stage of technical development projections of nuclear plant capacity and fuel requirements beyond the next five years must be viewed as conjectural, since they are not supportable with economic data on which different investigators should be expected to agree. If viewed not as forecasts but rather as experimental tools for analyzing possible interrelationships, projections to 1975 or 1980 may provide useful perspective, both on the broad range of uncertainty and on certain issues of economic policy.

Such projections are shown in Table 7–6, in which the maximum ("high") nuclear power capacity was derived, in the main, from official or semiofficial estimates presented at the Second Geneva Conference, 1958, and modified thereafter. The minimum ("low") projection, it need hardly be said, is the more likely outcome, although the analytical purpose is not to impose a specific forecast. In any case, a few points are evident. All but a small part of the nuclear capacity will be in the industrial countries, throughout the twenty-year period. Furthermore, the high-cost, energy-importing countries—Japan and Western Europe—will account for roughly three fifths of nuclear capacity, and the United States for a large part of the balance. In addition, the rate of nuclear power expansion after 1970 could be very rapid, even on the minimum projection and on the assumption that nuclear power will become competitive by 1965 to 1970 only in the high-cost-energy regions. Finally, despite the maximum presumed rapid growth in nuclear power, even in 1980 conventional plants will still be producing many times more energy than nuclear plants.

The projected large Western European nuclear power capacity offers a convenient point for judging roughly the scale of foreign requirements for natural and enriched uranium fuel, as well as the extra capital investment implied. The staff of the European Nuclear Energy Agency, associated with the OEEC, estimated in 1959 that the seventeen Western European nations might be expected by 1965 to have a maximum of 8,500 megawatts of nuclear

capacity, representing 4 per cent of total generating capacity in those countries (200,000 megawatts). Moreover, it was estimated that by 1965 the annual
nuclear power increment would be 2,500 megawatts. Reflecting the predominant place of the British reactors, almost three fourths of the capacity was
expected to be operating on natural uranium fuel. On these projections, the
relevant requirements for fuel and capital, as estimated by the ENEA, are
shown in Table 7–7.

Western Europe and the United States

From the United States point of view, the figures in Table 7-7 contain
some surprises. Assuming the predominance of natural uranium reactors in
1965, as the European Nuclear Energy Agency did, the enriched uranium fuel
expenditures in dollars would be roughly $80 million in that year. Although
ENEA also included a dollar requirement for natural uranium, it seems
likely that it could be obtained from nondollar sources. There is also a $40
million dollar requirement for plant.

The dollar requirements for enriched uranium may be compared with imported coal (or oil). If we take the 2,500 electric megawatts of plant capacity
originally planned for 1965 as the basis of comparison, we find that dollar
payments for United States coal, which might otherwise be required, would
be on the order of $113 million (on an annual coal requirement of 7.5 million
metric tons, and at a delivered cost of $15 per metric ton). Thus, the enriched
uranium fuel requirement in dollars would be roughly three fourths that for
the equivalent in coal supplied by the United States. In view of the dollar
requirements for plant, the absence of any major dollar saving on imported
fuel means that Western Europe would not be improving appreciably its
financial commitment on current account with the United States.[54]

From the Western European point of view the figures reveal that, in relation
to the total balance of payments of the area, the dollar requirements for both
plant and fuel would be small by 1965. For 8,500 electric megawatts of nuclear
capacity (originally planned for addition by the end of 1965) the investment
cost would be $2,900 million against $1,300 million for conventional plants,
at $160 per electric kilowatt. This large excess capital requirement exerts a
strong compulsion, as in the United Kingdom, for research to reduce capital
costs. The most economically promising approach seems to be the recycling

54. In effect, the extra plant cost of nuclear power is a price Western Europe is prepared to
pay in order to get started; technically, in time the recycling of plutonium might well diminish
the dollar requirement for enriched fuel. Moreover, deferral of fuel payments for ten years, as
under the Euratom agreement, avoids the immediate burden of purchase.

TABLE 7-7

Projections of Fuel and Capital Requirements for Nuclear Power Plants in OEEC Member Countries, 1965

	Total	Natural uranium reactors	Enriched (2 per cent) uranium reactors
Capacity (emw.)			
Installed capacity, end of 1965	8,500	6,000[a]	2,500
Capacity added in 1965	2,500	1,625	875
Fuel requirements (metric tons)		5,000	500
Initial inventory (plants added in 1965)		2,500	150
Annual make-up (all plants)		1,700	200
Pipeline additions, etc. (all plants)		800	150
Expenditures for fuel (millions EMA[b])			
Gross	$380–$445	$210–$275	$170
Net[c]	335–400	190–255	145
Requiring dollars	110–120	30–40	80
Capital investment (millions EMA[b])			
Cumulative to end of 1965	2,900	2,100	800
Annual rate in 1965	750	500	250
Dollar requirements to end of 1965[d]	160	—	160
Dollar requirements increment in 1965[d]	40	—	40
Investment per kw.		350	320

a. 4,500 emw. in United Kingdom.

b. European Monetary Agreement unit of account (equivalent to $1).

c. After allowing for credits of unburned and by-product fuel.

d. The European Nuclear Energy Agency assumes no dollar requirement for natural uranium plants, and 20 per cent of plant cost in case of enriched uranium.

Note: Basic assumptions are: 75 per cent plant factor; 3,000 megawatt-days per metric ton burn-up in natural uranium and 10,000 megawatt-days per metric ton in enriched material; 27 per cent thermal efficiency; fuel-element manufacture to be in Europe; 1961 prices for U and U235; fuel is purchased, not leased; no plutonium recycling is assumed.

Source: OEEC, European Nuclear Energy Agency, Estimates of Nuclear Energy Production in Europe, 1958–1965, Paris, 1959.

of plutonium, for this calls for less capital than would gaseous diffusion facilities and less dollar exchange than would the purchase of United States enriched uranium.

Fuel Requirements

Now, if the coefficients of fuel requirements, fuel expenditures and capital investment implied by Table 7-7 are applied to the short-term projections (to 1965 and 1970) contained in Table 7-6, it may be possible to estimate roughly the minimum and maximum requirements for nuclear fuel and capital in the various countries, assuming different possible ratios between natural and enriched uranium reactors. For example, if the projected minimum nuclear capacity in the United Kingdom, Canada and India in 1970 (5,900 megawatts) is all in natural uranium reactors and the projected minimum capacity of the rest of the free world (9,400 megawatts) is in enriched (2 per cent) uranium reactors, the minimum free world projection of capacity in 1970 (15,300 megawatts) would imply a fuel requirement (inventory plus make-up) in that year of roughly 3,500 metric tons of natural uranium fuel and 1,400 metric tons of enriched (2 per cent) uranium fuel.[55]

On these assumptions, the total natural uranium requirement for both enriched and unenriched fuel in 1970 would be roughly 8,300 tons. This is only one fifth of the annual supply (40,000 metric tons U_3O_8) projected by the AEC at no increase in production cost. The 1,400-metric ton requirement for enriched uranium in 1970 would be the equivalent of one tenth the output of United States gaseous diffusion capacity, as roughly estimated by Karl Cohen.[56] Hence, the minimum projection of nuclear power capacity to 1970 appears quite insufficient to sustain the U. S. gaseous diffusion plants in the absence of continuing, large military requirements.

For policy purposes, then, a fast or slow introduction of nuclear power during the next ten years will, in the absence of continuing, large military requirements, determine whether fuel production capacity, here and abroad, can be shifted soon from predominantly military to civilian purposes. Since the rate of progress seems likely to be slow rather than fast, prospects for the nuclear fuel supply industry seem poor, certainly until the end of the decade, and are contingent mainly on decisions in the government, rather than in the private sector.

55. For this purpose the following coefficients were used: for natural uranium initial inventory, 1.5 metric tons per mw., on 1,000 mw.; for natural uranium replacement, 0.4 metric tons per mw., on 4,900 mw.; and for enriched uranium initial inventory, 0.17 metric tons per mw., on 1,500 mw.; and for enriched uranium replacement, 0.14 metric tons per mw., on 7,900 mw.

56. "Charting a Course for Nuclear Power Development," *Nucleonics*, January 1958.

In view of the uncertainty of hoped-for progress, it is difficult to attempt a quantitative analysis of such requirements beyond 1970.[57]

Requirements Placed on the United States

To the nations where nuclear power capacity will be built in greatest volume, the United States represents primarily a source of enriched uranium, advanced reactor technology and financial assistance. Among these elements only the capacity to supply enriched uranium may have a critical, practical limitation in the terms being discussed here.

Surpassing all other influences in importance will be the U. S. military requirements for highly enriched uranium. Since this is necessarily conjectural, one can only explore the extreme range of possibilities. If weapon requirements were to take up substantially all the available enrichment capacity, accommodation of civilian needs would, of course, necessitate an expansion of capacity, but this expansion would not have to be great to meet the demand in prospect by 1970. At the other extreme, if strategic military requirements for nuclear materials are substantially met by 1965, then civilian requirements would for some years fail to utilize all the available capacity. Also, were disarmament proposals to carry through by that time, or sooner, the effect might be similar. Moreover, if technology should solve the problem of recycling plutonium economically the civilian requirement for enriched uranium would be reduced, though only after a considerable period of development.

Self-Sufficiency Versus External Nuclear Assistance

Nuclear energy is technically capable of diminishing dependence on outside sources for conventional fuel supplies and hence may be attractive to nations that seek economic autarky. But nuclear energy also requires many countries to enter into close cooperative relationships with one or more of the atomic leaders, and these may lead to fears of dangerous dependence.

The need for external assistance in nuclear power is apparently more urgent in Western Europe and Japan than in the less developed countries. The industrialized nations possess greater freedom of action than do the less developed countries, since the former can, if necessary, produce their own equipment and even enriched fuel. The lack of numerous sources for enriched uranium and the uncertainty of plutonium and U233 technology tend to make

57. A useful assessment of the long-term possibilities has been made by R. A. Laubenstein and Chauncey Starr, "The Availability of Uranium for a Nuclear Power Industry," Section 202 Hearings, 1960, pp. 660–76.

the underdeveloped countries watch and wait before embarking on either a costly self-contained program or one implying indefinite strategic dependence on external sources. India may be the only exception to the general rule that underdeveloped countries cannot hope to overcome the obstacles to nuclear development by undertaking "made-at-home" programs and projects.

Bilateral and multilateral arrangements have both been shown to hold a particular place in meeting the objectives of American foreign policy. Yet, the bilateral arrangement clearly is more vulnerable to the charges of atomic domination and intervention.[58] The country that wishes to avoid any threat of encroachment on its sovereignty, implied by bilateral arrangements, still may secure cooperative assistance through the International Atomic Energy Agency or through regional organizations.

In the free world bilateral agreements have been the governmental complement of private export activities: governments have authorized the release of nuclear fuel and frequently have provided the financing, while industry has contributed management, equipment and technical skills. It may then be asked whether reduced reliance on bilateral arrangements might also curtail the market potentialities of export nations. This seems doubtful, for multilateral arrangements normally will also lead to opportunities for private business.[59]

Fortunately, the IAEA, Euratom and other regional groupings offer a long-term escape from dependence on bilateral arrangements. The nuclear power programs and resources of other countries reveal that there is considerable scope for international economic cooperation as the desirable alternative to both nuclear nationalism and nuclear domination. The economic footings for such cooperation are already evident: nuclear materials are widely distributed and are not conducive to monopolization; capital requirements for nuclear power, while large, are not prohibitive; electric utility systems are mixed and permit both privately and publicly owned enterprise; reactor technology is varied and no system is controlling; and, finally, enriched fuel supply is not an economic or technical constraint on well-conceived programs.

58. Consider the terms of U. S. bilateral agreements calling for U. S. inspection of facilities and for the processing of irradiated fuel in the United States or in other mutually agreed facilities. In both cases security against the diversion of materials to weapon use is the prudent and immediate purpose, but the effects are far wider, involving the sovereignty of the foreign country.

59. In 1958, for instance, the IAEA requested bids to supply three tons of natural uranium for Japan. The three tenders illustrated the contrast between commercial and noncommercial considerations, in the short run: a United States company bid $54.34 per kilogram, a Belgian company bid the equivalent of $34.00 and the Canadian government offered the fuel free of charge (f.o.b. Canadian seaport). The material was destined for a 10-tmw. research reactor designed and built entirely by Japanese technicians. (Press Release 58-40, International Atomic Energy Agency, Vienna, December 12, 1958.)

CHAPTER **8**

Nuclear Power and Foreign Policy

Atoms for Peace and for Power

The policy of atomic isolation established immediately after World War II was promptly undermined by a combination of foreseeable domestic and foreign events. At home industrial firms, acting as AEC contractors, had come to believe in the economic potentialities of nuclear energy and soon pressed the government to allow increased participation of private industry. Abroad the Soviet Union soon broke the monopoly of nuclear weapons and was moving swiftly toward the hydrogen bomb. The United Nations attempts to bring about sensible international control of atomic energy were foredoomed to failure, partly because of Soviet intransigence with respect to inspection.

The event formally marking the end of the isolation policy was President Eisenhower's December 1953 address before the General Assembly of the United Nations, dramatically calling for international cooperation and launching the atoms-for-peace program. To implement this program, it was necessary for Congress to grant to the President a certain degree of authority to enter into bilateral or multilateral international cooperative agreements. However, the loosening of congressional controls, both domestically and internationally, was not a matter of granting unrestricted freedom but rather one of establishing carefully circumscribed fields of executive action, with a variety of checks retained by the Congress. Just as new government-industry relations were being worked out by the AEC, so the executive branch was called on to create new international relations under which the Congress would act as joint guardian and promoter of the nation's foreign interest, despite the fact that foreign relations have been considered the responsibility primarily of the executive branch.[1] These constraints have proved far less significant, however, than the foreign policy objectives.

Objectives—Real and Fanciful

Considering the central importance of the atoms-for-peace program, it is striking that President Eisenhower's 1953 address was—and still is—the only comprehensive administration statement of foreign policy for peaceful uses of atomic energy.[2] The program's objectives were numerous, overlapping and, in several respects, illusory. In particular, the premises on nuclear power proved to be unrealistic and misleading. Even highly sympathetic observers described this "farsighted" program as "only moderately successful," whereas critics condemned it as a "failure." The reasons for such limited success may be found in the objectives of the program. These were as follows:[3]

To strengthen a peaceful "foreign image of the United States" abroad by stressing the civilian applications of nuclear energy, by providing leadership and resources to promote peaceful uses, and by maintaining technical world leadership.

To strengthen the "national security and safety" by securing international agreement on health and safety standards, by reducing the amounts of fissionable material available for military use, by delaying the emergence of a

1. The requirement that the Joint Committee on Atomic Energy "authorize" appropriations for reactor and other projects (Sec. 261) is an example of congressional encroachment on domestic matters, while required Joint Committee approval of certain international atomic arrangements (Secs. 123 and 124) is an illustration in the area of foreign relations. For innumerable other illustrations of such encroachment see H. P. Green and Alan Rosenthal, *The Joint Committee on Atomic Energy: A Study in Fusion of Governmental Power*, George Washington University, Washington, 1961.

2. In contrast with the comparative silence of the State Department, AEC Commissioners frequently commented on the program. For example, Commissioner W. F. Libby in an address at the University of Oregon, Eugene, Oregon, January 15, 1958; and Commissioner Robert E. Wilson, "U. S. AEC Policies Relative to Foreign Reactors," remarks prepared for delivery at the Second Joint Conference on Nuclear Power, U.S.–Japan Atomic Industrial Forums, Tokyo, December 5, 1961.

3. Klaus E. Knorr, "American Foreign Policy and the Peaceful Uses of Atomic Energy," in *Atoms for Power: United States Policy in Atomic Energy Development*, The American Assembly, Columbia University, New York, December 1957, pp. 100–29.

"fourth country" with weapon capability, by providing experience helpful in ultimately achieving a workable disarmament plan and by reducing international tension between the United States and the Soviet Union through cooperative action in preventing the spread of military capability in nuclear energy.

To help in "waging the cold war" against communist bloc expansion by using atomic energy to raise the general standards of living in underdeveloped areas, by strengthening the energy-deficient economies of Western Europe and by jointly participating with Euratom in support of the eventual unification of Western Europe.

Finally, to "promote American business enterprise abroad" by establishing intergovernment arrangements to encourage U. S. exports of nuclear equipment and supplies.

Critical appraisal of this loose conglomeration of policy objectives reveals that a large number were quite unrealistic. For example, as long as the United States continued to pursue a highly diversified program of military nuclear propulsion and weapons research, testing and production—though the USSR was doing the same—its "image" was not likely to be fundamentally changed for the better.

It became clear that the "national security and safety" objectives were equally tenuous, that the quantities of fissionable material required for civilian power reactors could not soon affect the stockpiles of weapon-grade materials or the priority of military over civilian nuclear programs. In fact, the growth in civilian reactors will result in an expansion rather than a contraction of fissionable material production capacity that is available for military purposes. "The fourth country problem" could not be met by a mere process of "diffusion" of the control of civilian reactors.[4] France, the first of possibly several "fourth countries," had produced plutonium in weapon quantities and in early 1960 tested a nuclear device (and thus raised the "Nth country" problem). Indeed, the worldwide availability of natural uranium and the propagation of nuclear reactor technology seemed certain to result in signifi-

---

4. No one could demonstrate how control of peaceful uses was to be transformed into control of weapon uses. Congressman Sterling Cole suggested progress would occur "by example." In a statement recommending Senate ratification of the statute of the IAEA, he said, on the subject of inspection and control: "The Agency's operations can produce that technology and that confidence in international control which will lead to complete international control of atomic energy at an appropriate time later on. Since the Soviet Union has been the country principally opposed to international inspection of atomic areas, perhaps it will learn that international inspection will not be as unpalatable as anticipated." (*Statute of the International Atomic Energy Agency*, Hearings, Committee on Foreign Relations and Senate members of the Joint Committee on Atomic Energy, 85th Cong., 1st Sess., 1957, p. 171.)

cant plutonium production in areas outside controls exercised by the three atomic powers, by Euratom or by the IAEA.[5]

The hope that nuclear energy might help greatly in resisting expansion of the communist bloc among underdeveloped countries was based on an inflated theory of the primary role of electric power in economic growth and development.[6] Nuclear energy for a decade or more seems unlikely to influence appreciably the standard of living in the developing economies exposed to possible influence by the communist bloc.

Finally, the commercial objective of promoting U. S. exports of nuclear equipment has remained subject to harsh economic limitations. Industrial nations seeking nuclear power will soon be able to produce most of their own equipment and supplies. U. S. manufacturers seeking markets in these countries will find that special arrangements, such as cross-licensing and joint-equity participation, will be required.[7] It is likely to be many years before there is a substantial market in the underdeveloped countries. Moreover, numerous economic obstacles still stand in the way of a substantial export trade by United States suppliers. Nuclear power is not yet marginally competitive in the high-cost areas, and the drastic easing of conventional fuel supplies after 1958 has made the prospect more remote than in 1956, the year of the Suez crisis. In some countries foreign exchange available for purchases in the United States has remained a difficulty, and indemnification of liability for reactor accidents that might occur in foreign countries is a complex problem internationally.[8]

Nevertheless, the fact that many supposed objectives of the atoms-for-peace program were mistaken should not obscure the wisdom of the program's valid purposes and the broadening means for accomplishing them—through the IAEA, Euratom and bilateral agreements. These objectives that were valid and timely in the program need to be recognized. They are best revealed

5. It is a common public misconception that source and fissionable material supplies have been "brought under control" by formation of the IAEA. Such material control as the IAEA has is confined to the materials that are made available to recipients through its auspices. Countries, such as India or Brazil, which produce source materials and others which procure these materials may be potentially capable in terms of economic and technical resources to undertake programs of fissionable material production for weapon purposes. The limited scope of IAEA safeguards is revealed by the agency's initial statement, *Agency Safeguards*, Vienna, April 14, 1960.

6. See Stefan H. Robock, *Nuclear Power and Economic Development in Brazil*, NPA, Washington, April 1957, pp. 67–68.

7. See testimony of Michael Michaelis, Arthur D. Little, Inc., Section 202 Hearings, 1957, Vol. 2, pp. 581–98.

8. See "*Financial Protection Against Atomic Hazards: The International Aspects*" (preliminary report of a study under the auspices of Harvard Law School), Atomic Industrial Forum, New York, May 1958.

against the background of general foreign policy objectives of the United States which are, briefly: first, to promote the defense of the country by "winning the cold war"; second, to contribute to economic prosperity at home by assisting worldwide economic development; third, to maintain domestic opportunities for social and economic improvement in a manner consistent with U. S. leadership in international relations; fourth, to encourage an environment conducive to free institutions everywhere; fifth, to achieve world prestige and influence, based on respect; and sixth, to satisfy a moral sense of justice in foreign relations.[9] Each of these broad objectives was strengthened in some measure by the atoms-for-peace program.

The program contributed to the achievement of the first of these objectives by providing constructive international experience in the handling of fissionable materials and nuclear facilities, through Euratom and the IAEA, that may prove important in ultimate agreement with the Soviet Union on nuclear weapons control. (One must not presume, however, that this experience in international cooperation in promoting peaceful uses of atomic energy will, of itself, win the cold war or that nuclear weapons control will automatically follow.)

The atoms-for-peace program should in time contribute to the second objective by strengthening the industrial economies of Western Europe, as nuclear energy begins to provide a partial alternative to insecure fuel imports. Also, some of the industrializing economies have highly specialized, though limited, needs for nuclear energy. Meeting these needs will be significant, pending the more distant time when these countries will need nuclear energy in quantity.

Nuclear energy can be expected to contribute marginally to the third objective, though it will not begin to make a significant contribution to continued economic growth in the United States as soon as it will in Western Europe or Japan.

The declassification of civilian reactor technology furthered the fourth objective, since it opened the door to a vast store of knowledge for all countries wishing to undertake nuclear research and development. Moreover, unfettered access to knowledge, the cornerstone of free institutions generally, was promoted by the U. S. grants of research funds, the allocation of fissionable materials and the provision of technical assistance to individual countries and international agencies.

9. For a more detailed statement see Philip C. Jessup, "Ends and Means of American Foreign Policy," *International Stability and Progress: United States Interests and Instruments*, The American Assembly, Columbia University, New York, June 1957, pp. 18–21.

U. S. initiative in the atoms-for-peace program clearly contributed to the fifth objective. It won the respect of most countries and resulted in a considerable measure of international prestige and influence for the United States in shaping the safe introduction of nuclear energy. Sixth, and finally, the program went far to satisfy the foreign policy objective of a "moral sense of justice," since foreign peoples could see that an elemental force, first used by the United States in World War II, was being turned toward productive use for man's welfare. Had nuclear energy continued for long to be used only for military applications, the growing moral repugnance of peoples here and abroad might have destroyed foreign relations benefits accruing from a strong weapons position.

There is little reason to doubt that the United States still leads in the peaceful development of nuclear energy, even though progress in the 1950s was not on a scale sufficiently large to meet the requirements of foreign policy objectives. The manner in which this leadership has been exercised is a matter for serious consideration. For example, the donor-donee relation in economic assistance programs has long been recognized as dangerous and undesirable. On the other hand, all-out competition for world markets by government-subsidized United States firms could also lead to great resentment by less fortunately situated countries hopefully developing nuclear equipment for export. Either a pure giveaway program or cutthroat competition could lead to domination of other countries by the United States or a lively fear of it.

Illustrative of a U. S. attitude that has troubled many foreign statesmen is the following statement by a U. S. official:[10]

> The United States occupies an absolutely commanding position in the atomic power development of the future. We supply the cheapest heavy water and we are one of the world's principal producers of uranium. It is not too much to say that whatever the future development and in whatever direction atomic power moves, our position will be an absolutely commanding one from the point of view of raw materials alone.

Fear of United States domination will lead almost all countries that accept bilateral agreements with the United States to avoid long-standing dependence on imported technology, equipment or materials. The so-called "absolutely commanding" position of the United States is neither commanding nor absolute in any sense and the pretense that it is can serve only to arouse hostility in friendly countries. As has been pointed out, uranium and thorium are widely available throughout the world at moderate costs; reactor technol-

10. Libby, *loc. cit.*

ogy, now almost entirely unclassified, is available to all nations; industrialized economies are in fact independent of the atomic leaders and seek their help mainly to get a faster start. Even the underdeveloped countries, if they do not feel safe in accepting aid from the United States or the Soviet Union, can turn to Canada, France and the United Kingdom as sources of help.

Having briefly identified some interrelations of United States general foreign policy and the atoms-for-peace program, one should also judge how effectively the national policies for nuclear energy were executed until 1961. Nuclear energy has fitted into none of the customary categories of foreign economic policy. The atoms-for-peace program, as carried out, has not been precisely mutual assistance, technical assistance or economic assistance. It has been separate and apart from the main body of foreign policy.

Foreign Policy Leadership

During the Eisenhower administration the AEC took the initiative in expounding foreign policy and programs for nuclear energy. The State Department remained virtually silent—except where official support of Euratom and the charter of the IAEA were at issue. The two agencies revealed differing degrees of enthusiasm for the potential role of peaceful nuclear energy as an instrument of American foreign policy. State was deeply skeptical of the atoms-for-peace program and quietly made clear the view that the AEC and the White House were misguided in emphasizing nuclear power prospects abroad. Believing that the initial policy statement in 1953 went to dangerous extremes in committing the nation to foreign nuclear assistance that could not be fulfilled without major governmental measures, State used the bilateral research agreements as a stopgap device for avoiding the issues raised by nuclear power, particularly among the industrializing nations. Consequently, State never overtly supported the fundamental view, commonly accepted in Congress and elsewhere, that peaceful nuclear power should be "accelerated" primarily to accomplish important foreign policy objectives. On the other hand, State did with foresight secure administration and congressional support of U. S. cooperation with Euratom. In brief, State demonstrated little enthusiasm for nuclear energy as such, had misgivings about the dangers it entailed and, in the main, considered it not as an end in itself but more as a special "device" for advancing particular aims of American foreign policy.

The foreign policies and programs of the AEC up to 1961 were differently oriented and motivated. At the outset, in 1954, the Commission and its staff had the atoms-for-peace program thrust upon it with virtually no prior preparation and with little experience in foreign affairs. Indeed, President Eisenhower's UN address was prepared hastily, without the assistance or knowledge of the Commission or its staff. In "starting from scratch" to rationalize a policy statement based on faulty technical and economic assumptions, the AEC soon found itself fashioning a program that was aimed at achieving a "dominant" position in world trade. With the AEC assuring supplies of nuclear fuels and industry supplying "know-how" and equipment, high hopes were raised for a grand partnership in developing large foreign markets. Thus, the AEC was motivated strongly by commercial objectives in the cold-war setting: to demonstrate industry's capacity to compete with the Soviet Union in foreign countries, and to advance the competitive position of American equipment manufacturers and exporters vis-à-vis those of the United Kingdom.

Progress of reactor technology and the economic circumstances surrounding it proved unpropitious, however. Like the atoms-for-peace address, the objectives of the AEC were remote from and inconsistent with the realities of the domestic reactor development program.

There were other disparities in the AEC and the State Department approaches to the peaceful atom in foreign policy up to 1961. State "downgraded" the role of atomic power so greatly that it ignored the tremendous resources being brought to bear on development. Today the depth and variety of the U. S. development program, plus the scale of nuclear resources and plant capacity, provide unequaled opportunity for the United States to maintain responsible initiative in the wise promotion of nuclear energy. In contrast, the AEC failed to realize that an aggressive foreign program had to be compatible with the realities of the domestic program. Thus, for example, in evaluating particular reactor concepts and fuel cycles or in establishing pricing policies for materials and services, the AEC failed to give sufficient weight to foreign policy considerations.[11]

Programs and Instruments

When President Eisenhower committed the nation in 1953 to a policy of promoting the peaceful uses of nuclear energy, he was also committing the AEC and the State Department to a task for which these agencies were scarcely prepared. Both agencies recognized that the atoms-for-peace address

11. Today, for example, the AEC cannot judge the merit of laboratory support for thorium-U233 systems without considering their importance to India and Brazil, both properly concerned with future use of their large thorium reserves as an alternative source of energy. Similarly, the AEC's 1959 decision to maintain obsolescent price schedules for enriched uranium should not have been made solely on domestic considerations.

raised premature expectations at home and abroad. The instruments chosen to meet this problem were varied and ingenious and capitalized on the nation's nuclear resources. One of the first was the proposal to hold the first international conference on the peaceful uses of atomic energy, which led in 1955 to the public release of much of the reactor technology known at the time. Bilateral research agreements were promptly negotiated with many friendly countries to provide technical assistance and funds (up to $350,000 each) to help purchase U. S. research reactors. Somewhat later a few bilateral agreements for nuclear power were negotiated, the IAEA was formed and the United States agreed to encourage and assist Euratom. Furthermore, large quantities of enriched uranium were offered for sale in support of the bilateral agreements, Euratom and the IAEA. But, despite all these ramified efforts, by the end of 1961 the tangible benefits were difficult to see and Joint Committee critics of the Eisenhower administration suggested that the atoms-for-peace program had proved a fiasco.[12]

Bilateral Research Agreements

Recognizing that the immediate success of the atoms-for-peace program would be in serious jeopardy if all it could offer was the distant hope of low-cost power, the Department of State in 1955 concentrated instead on the negotiation of as many bilateral research agreements as could be managed by the time Congress adjourned in the summer of 1955 (being mindful of the thirty-day waiting period while Congress is in session). This tactic might plausibly have been interpreted as a belated response to the fact that too much effort was being devoted to negotiations on the so-called "international pool."[13]

The real problem lay deeper. Ambassador Morehead Patterson, the U. S. Representative for International Atomic Energy Negotiations, who held primary State Department responsibility for the atoms-for-peace program, recognized that the President's statement in December 1953 embraced spurious objectives and assumptions, that it was much too early in the technology to expect economic benefits from nuclear electric power and that it was dangerous to raise such expectations.[14] The State Department therefore

---

12. Senator Clinton P. Anderson, "The Peaceful Atom: Fact or Fable?" remarks before the Congressional Club, Washington, January 15, 1960.

13. Cf. John Lear, "Ike and the Peaceful Atom," *The Reporter*, January 12, 1956, pp. 11–21.

14. See, among his other statements, Ambassador Morehead Patterson's address at the opening of the School of Nuclear Science and Engineering, Argonne National Laboratory, Lemont, Illinois, March 13, 1955 (in *Atoms for Peace Manual*, Joint Committee on Atomic Energy, 84th Cong., 1st Sess., 1955, pp. 353–56.)

avoided explicit policy positions on nuclear power and emphasized the non-power contributions of nuclear energy. The Department took the position that while nuclear energy had become an essential aspect of foreign policy nuclear electric power had not, partly because it involved some difficult problems of international relations (explored in the next section).

By the end of 1961 some thirty-eight bilateral research agreements were in force, hence the main question is what progress has been achieved under the agreements to fulfill foreign policy objectives. Such an evaluation can be only inferred from the activity reported, including the construction of research reactors.[15] At first, action by almost all cooperating countries to secure the benefits of the research agreements was slow, but more recently signs of increased activity under many agreements suggest that they are more than mere pieces of paper negotiated in haste. By the end of 1961 grants had been authorized for twenty-three foreign research reactors. Research reactors are not necessarily effective tools of education and in some instances have proved rather costly and difficult pieces of equipment. However, comparatively few policy issues have been raised by the research agreements and the program is aptly described as having been "mainly political in character."[16] By 1958 the emphasis of negotiation had shifted to bilateral power agreements, where more important commercial and policy issues were encountered.

Bilateral Power Agreements

In the fall of 1961 the Atomic Industrial Forum reported that seven power reactors had been sold for export by U. S. manufacturers. Of these, three were under construction, two were operating and two were planned. Other exporting nations were no more successful. Five years earlier the McKinney Panel had expressed the "hope" that, by 1960, "our bilateral partners" would have

15. Research agreements, to be in force from five to twenty years, provide primarily for the exchange of information, but most of them also authorize the transfer of specific amounts of special nuclear material for reactor fuel and for research purposes. The exchange of information (unclassified) covers general research, research reactors and health and safety problems, but in each case language is included anticipating later comprehensive agreements including power reactors. The reactor fuel is generally leased for approved reactor projects in amounts of no more than 6 kilograms of U235, not including "pipeline" requirements, in enrichments up to 20 per cent. Exceptions have been made to these standards. The United States also has the right to secure records to assure accountability of special nuclear material. Lease agreements state that the cooperating government will hold the U. S. government harmless against all liability (including public liability) arising from use of special nuclear material made available by the AEC. Provision is also made for the United States to grant up to $350,000 toward the construction cost of a research reactor. The foreign reactor aid program expired June 30, 1960, and since then applications have fallen under the general U. S. foreign aid program.

16. Clark Vogel, "International Bilateral Agreements for Cooperation in Atomic Energy," *The George Washington Law Review*, April 1957, p. 507.

installed a million kilowatts of nuclear generating capacity, based on a program of U. S.–supplied technical assistance and nuclear fuels.[17] This is almost double the capacity of the seven American reactors which had been contracted for construction abroad by the fall of 1961. These projects are shown in Table 8–1.

Thus by the fall of 1961, under the thirteen bilateral power agreements which had been signed, U. S. manufacturers had been able to sell seven power reactors, three of them full scale. Since nuclear power was still far from being economically competitive, these reactors were in effect "demonstration" projects and faced the same problems as their counterparts in the United States. Indeed, under the U. S.–Euratom joint agreement (1958) it became plain that "export sales" were in fact noncommercial extensions abroad of the AEC reactor demonstration program, and likewise required a variety of forms of U. S. (and foreign) government assistance. The disappointing U. S.–Euratom development program revealed the fallacy of expecting to demonstrate nuclear power abroad as an alternative to doing so at home first and of expecting to develop soon a conventional type of export business in power reactors.

Since most foreign countries, including the semi-industrialized, soon became aware of the technical and economic obstacles to nuclear power, only those few industrialized nations that felt compelled to secure early participation in the nascent technology were prepared to assume the risks and costs. Hence, until nuclear power can be demonstrably competitive, the export of U. S. power reactors will remain dependent on noneconomic motives and on special assistance from the United States. Technology and nuclear fuels have been far more important forms of assistance than direct financial help—which has been small.[18]

Bilateral power agreements establish the safeguards over the use and production of nuclear fuel to prevent diversion to weapons purposes. As in the research agreements, the cooperating country must guarantee, in accordance with Section 123 of the 1954 act, that the material to be transferred under the agreement "will not be used for atomic weapons, or for research on or development of atomic weapons, or for any military purpose" and "will not be

17. McKinney Panel, Vol. 1, p. 8.

18. By June 30, 1960, the cost to the United States of international activities, excluding Euratom, consisted of the following: for reactor and equipment grants, mainly provided by the Mutual Security Program, $9.2 million approved; value of heavy water and fissionable material leased, $6.2 million on which $141,000 in use charges was earned in fiscal year 1960. During fiscal year 1960 the costs totaled $6.0 million, consisting of: grants, $1.2 million; training and education, $1.3 million; and "other," $3.6 million. (AEC, *Major Activities in the Atomic Energy Programs, January-December 1960* [Annual Report], Washington, January 1961, p. 533.)

transferred to unauthorized persons or beyond the jurisdiction of the cooperating party, except as specified in the agreement for cooperation." But, in addition to this statutory control requirement, the agreements carry a 20 per cent limitation on enrichment and clauses stating that spent fuel elements will be reprocessed in AEC or AEC-designated facilities and that the AEC has first option to purchase by-product fissionable material for its own use in peaceful applications.

Except in its agreements with Canada and the United Kingdom, the United States also reserves the right to review reactor designs, to require materials accountability reports, to require deposit of by-product materials in designated storage facilities and to have free access to all places and data in verifying compliance with the agreement. It is significant that these control provisions are intended to be consistent with those of the IAEA and with those contained in agreements negotiated by Canada and by the United Kingdom with other countries. (Control provisions of agreements negotiated by the USSR are not known.) In the most recent bilateral agreements entered into by the United States (e.g., with Japan) provision is made for the possible transfer of the safeguard functions from the United States to the IAEA. The safeguard provisions of the early agreements were an obvious source of concern.[19] For neutral countries, such as India, the safeguard provisions of the bilateral agreements, as well as the dependence on U. S. supplies of enriched fuel, have remained an obstacle. Nevertheless, India early in 1962 indicated an interest in having U. S. suppliers bid on a two-reactor, 300,000-kilowatt station burning either enriched or natural uranium. In light of India's long-standing objection to inspection, her inquiry raised a sensitive policy issue for the United States that might endanger the prospects of concluding an agreement. The United States had to decide whether to insist on international inspection by the IAEA (which India has long opposed) or to apply the customary inspection by the United States under bilateral agreements (bypassing and thus weakening the IAEA).

In economic terms the more critical features of the power agreements are the charges for nuclear fuel, the plutonium "buy-back" prices and the charges for reprocessing. The charges for nuclear fuel exported abroad are the same

19. During 1961 the AEC made safeguard inspections of forty-one facilities in eighteen foreign countries. On November 30, 1961, there were fifty-seven reactors and critical assemblies, subject to U. S. safeguards, in twenty-four foreign countries. (AEC, *Major Activities in the Atomic Energy Programs, January-December 1961* [Annual Report], Washington, January 1962, Appendix 12, p. 491.) Under the Euratom agreement it would be possible for the Euratom Commission to "inspect" the chemical processing facilities of the United States, if it were necessary for spent fuel elements of the reactors covered by the joint agreement to be returned to the United States for recovery and reprocessing.

as those in the published price schedules.[20] Whereas nuclear material under the research agreements is customarily leased, under the power agreements it is generally to be sold.[21] The 1954 statute prohibited the sale of special nuclear material within the United States but not abroad. The chosen policy of foreign sale, rather than lease, was heavily influenced by the staggering value—several billion dollars—of the materials that in time would be out on lease.[22] In selling nuclear fuel abroad, the United States has moderated the cost burden of the initial reactor inventory by offering long-term, low-interest credit through the Export-Import Bank (as in the arrangement with Euratom). Unless the purchase payments are deferred, as under Euratom, the foreign reactor operator buying U. S. fuel may be under a slight economic disadvantage compared with the domestic operator, who leases at a 4.75 per cent use charge.

In case the cooperating country does not need its by-product plutonium or U233 in its own program, then the United States has an option to purchase at prevailing prices or to approve the transfer to another nation or international organization. The AEC pays the domestic "fuel-value" price schedule for these materials and has agreed that foreign-produced plutonium would be used only for civilian purposes. However, in explaining why nuclear power can now provide only limited help in achieving foreign policy objectives, set out at the beginning of this chapter, the policy aspects of the bilateral power agreements are less important than the obvious economic and technical obstacles. On the one hand, the thirteen bilateral power agreements have failed to meet the special needs of the industrializing economies; on the other, the joint U. S.–Euratom agreement, which held such great hope of combining the objectives of foreign policy and accelerated reactor demonstration, has faltered under the new energy conditions in Western Europe.

Regional Approaches: Euratom

The encouragement of regional approaches has been an important, but not altogether successful, feature of nuclear energy foreign policy. In Latin America the United States assisted in establishing the Puerto Rico Training Center, in conjunction with the University of Puerto Rico, to help provide

20. Before the AEC price schedule for enriched uranium was publicly announced (in 1956) a range of prices—$15 to $30 per gram of U235—had been used, in unclassified documents, with the approval of the Office of Classification, AEC. At one time during this period it appeared that the AEC was considering a two-price system, a lower price for domestic users and a higher for foreign users. Such price discrimination, fortunately, was rejected.

21. Wilson, *loc. cit.*

22. Vogel, *op. cit.*, footnote 28, p. 499.

training for students of all the Spanish-speaking American republics. The United States also cooperated with the Inter-American Nuclear Energy Commission, formed in 1957. In Asia the U. S. proposal in 1956 to establish an Asian nuclear center at Manila came to nothing, in large part because India was unable to see the need for such a center. In Western Europe the United States encouraged the seventeen-nation Organisation for European Economic Cooperation to form the European Nuclear Energy Agency. But most important for U. S. foreign policy was the strong support given the six-nation, supranational European Atomic Energy Community (Euratom), established in 1957. Among the regional groups only Euratom and the European Nuclear Energy Agency have given primary attention to nuclear power rather than to the more general fields of isotopes, atomic research and training.

The material and financial assistance the United States has provided Euratom in the joint power reactor and research program has eclipsed that offered to all other regional organizations, primarily because U. S. interest and regional need have been complementary. Euratom has fitted into both the U.S. policy of encouraging political and economic integration in Western Europe and the U. S. need for early demonstration of planned reactor types. The six nations composing this group lacked the indispensable reactor technology and fissionable materials that the United States could provide. Moreover, the Euratom nations, motivated by an economic urgency and a high political objective, were prepared in 1958—though not in 1960—to invest substantial sums toward rapid nuclear development, the benefits of which were expected to redound to the U. S. demonstration program as well. By the fall of 1959, however, it had become clear that the new improved fuel supplies of Western Europe had ended the urgent need for nuclear power, though not its long-term role.[23]

The joint U. S.–Euratom program in 1958 contemplated the construction of five or six reactors between 1963 and 1965, totaling 1 million kilowatts capacity, and an investment of $350 million in plant and $100 million in research and development. Yet by mid-1962 only one of the reactor projects (SENN) was underway and one new project (SENA) had been proposed. (See Table 8–1.) The proposals of electric utilities for the remainder had been deferred or withdrawn. Euratom representatives, throughout the negotiations with the State Department and the AEC in 1958 and 1959, had expressed assurance that a number of electric utilities would bring forward acceptable proposals in response to the Euratom invitations. When they were not forth-

23. OEEC, *Towards a New Energy Pattern in Europe* (prepared by the Energy Advisory Commission under the chairmanship of Professor Austin Robinson), Paris, January 1960.

TABLE 8-1

Overseas Power Reactors Completed or under
Contract by U. S. Contractors, Fall 1961

Country	Name and location	U. S. contractor	Capacity (kw.)	Completion date
Total			651,500	
Italy	SENN, Punta Fiume	General Electric	150,000	1963
Belgium	CEN, Mol	Westinghouse	11,500	1962
West Germany	RWE, Kahl-am-Main	General Electric	15,000	1960
Italy	SELNI, Trina	Westinghouse	165,000	1964
Japan	JAERI, Tokai-Mura	General Electric	12,000	1963
France-Belgium	SENA, Chooz	Westinghouse	242,000	1965
Sweden	Simpevarp	Allis-Chalmers	56,000	...

Sources: Atomic Industrial Forum, "Progress Chart: U. S. Nuclear Power Projects," New York, September 1, 1961; and AEC, Major Activities in the Atomic Energy Programs, January–December, 1961 (Annual Report), Washington, January 1962, p. 479.

coming, the United States and Euratom agreed to shift the emphasis of the joint program from 1963 to 1965 for new projects following SENN.[24]

With this faltering of the joint U. S.–Euratom arrangement, grave doubts were raised about the prospects for the atoms-for-peace program as a whole and the consistency of policy in pursuing bilateral agreements while also supporting the IAEA. Robert McKinney's evaluation of the atoms-for-peace program in 1960 suggested that the former emphasis by Euratom on near-term, marginal nuclear power should be modified, in favor of long-term investigations aimed at low-cost power.[25] Also, he saw a need for greater laboratory collaboration, possibly through the coordination of the OEEC. Yet the vitality of Euratom in 1961 seemed to depend as much on the prospects for nuclear power as on closer coordination of laboratories. Furthermore, U. S. policy toward Euratom appeared to be inseparable from the issue of wise support for the IAEA.

U. S. Role in the IAEA

The International Atomic Energy Agency, established in 1957 and having seventy-seven member nations in 1962, has generally been considered the key instrument for accomplishing the manifold objectives of the atoms-for-peace program. After more than four years of work, however, the international agency in 1961 was still in the process of determining what functions would be most suitable for it to perform and the United States had not yet established a policy toward the agency.

In general the Department of State, until 1961, looked on the international agency as having a lower priority than bilateral agreements or the U. S.–Euratom program. To be sure, when ratification of the statute for the international agency was being considered by the Committee on Foreign Relations of the U. S. Senate, Secretary of State Dulles supported it, partly on the ground that it would permit neutral and uncommitted nations to secure nuclear assistance without having to negotiate bilaterally with any of the atomic powers.[26] Thereafter, however, the State Department remained almost silent on the international agency and the optimum degree of U. S. support. The AEC, on the contrary, sought to improve the status of the international

---

24. See exchange of correspondence between W. W. Butterworth, U. S. Ambassador to the European Community, and Etienne Hirsch, President of the Commission, European Atomic Energy Community. (*Nucleonics*, April 1960, pp. 24–25.)

25. McKinney Review, Vol. 1, pp. 73 ff.

26. *Statute of the International Atomic Energy Agency*, p. 8.

agency by increasing U. S. support and by diminishing the role of bilateral arrangements.

It was doubtless a foregone conclusion that the international agency would have trouble in meeting the excessive and partly illusory expectations raised by the original proposal. At the end of 1961 few of the original purposes of the IAEA seemed likely to be accomplished soon. Universal health and safety standards, as well as indemnification for reactor accidents, were still to be established, whereas in the European Nuclear Energy Agency they were moving toward conclusion. Safeguards against diversion to military purposes were incomplete, though a start had been made by adoption of limited proce-dures and principles in April 1960. The concept of the agency's becoming a bank or clearing house for making nuclear fuels available from the nuclear "haves" to the nuclear "have not" countries was early dropped in favor of more practical arrangements. By mid-1962 no nuclear power project had been sponsored by the agency in any of the misnamed "power-starved" countries.

For these and other reasons scientists and statesmen of the industrializing countries—India notably—have tended to question the sincerity of the atomic leaders in having established the international agency. Despite its shortcom-ings, however, the agency has contributed to communication between East and West and between the atomic powers and the developing countries on a variety of technical matters: waste disposal, applications of radioisotopes, training and education, technical assistance missions, scientific conferences and radiation protection. The IAEA has also made significant contributions to the evaluation of the role of nuclear power in the energy economies of member countries. Studies have also been made that provide economic guid-ance, among them reports on Finland and the Philippines, and on nuclear power costs. The agency has done this work on an exceedingly small budget— in 1962 totaling $8.3 million, composed of $6.3 million for "regular" expenses, $1.6 million for technical assistance and fellowship programs, $168,000 for research contracts and $40,000 for operating two mobile laboratory facilities.[27]

The U. S. policy toward the international agency through 1961 evidently was one of limited encouragement and support, meeting necessary minimum demands and avoiding engagement in visionary projects—particularly those involving power reactors. This policy of "hardheaded realism" was founded on the State Department's skepticism of the prospects for nuclear power and on the historical political problems that had attended United Nations activi-ties in nuclear energy, beginning with the UN Atomic Energy Commission. Among these long-standing issues are safeguards and controls and the Nth

27. IAEA, *Bulletin*, September 1961, p. 22.

country problem, to be discussed later. Under the circumstances—lukewarm support by the United States, opportunistic participation by the Soviet Union and disenchantment among the developing countries—the international agency seemed in 1962 to stand little chance of becoming a viable institution, at least until progress could be demonstrated on the broader stage of nuclear weapons control or competitive nuclear power. Yet, up to 1961 the United States continued to express in the UN General Assembly complete satisfaction with the progress of the international agency and its ability to become the main channel through which the more advanced countries could provide nuclear fuels and assistance to other countries.[28] Evidently the Eisenhower administration was not prepared to make of the international agency more than a "holding action." The Kennedy administration was faced with the issue of whether to abandon the agency, maintain lukewarm support or provide vigorous aid. Abandonment seemed least likely.

In 1962 the Advisory Committee on U. S. Policy Toward the International Atomic Energy Agency recommended "active U. S. support of the IAEA."[29] In brief, the committee found the agency had filled a useful function in promoting the peaceful uses of atomic energy; expressed the judgment that development of nuclear power is the key issue determining the fate of the agency; and especially emphasized the importance of establishing a uniform world system of safeguards to discourage the diversion of nuclear materials to military uses. The committee failed, however, to treat specifically the following questions: the relative degree of U. S. cooperation with Euratom and with the IAEA; how to meet the "double standard" argument of India and other countries that have been unwilling to accept the proposed safeguards system; and how to reconcile the failure to secure weapon-test control by the atomic leaders, with their insistence on safeguards for materials secured through the IAEA. Nevertheless, the Smyth Committee Report represented the first comprehensive statement of policy to guide the AEC and the Department of State since President Eisenhower's address eight and a half years earlier.

Nuclear Fuels

The United States has used many other instruments to support the atoms-for-peace program: offering nuclear materials in quantity at reasonable prices, providing technical assistance, offering educational and training opportunities

28. IAEA, *Bulletin*, January 1960, p. 24.

29. U. S. Department of State, *Report*, Washington, May 19, 1962; referred to hereafter as the Smyth Committee Report. Former AEC Commissioner Henry DeWolf Smyth was U. S. representative to the IAEA at the time of the report.

for foreign students and specialists, exchanging technical information, co-operating in scientific conferences and symposiums and making available for export sale a wide range of stable and radioactive isotopes. While each of these has held foreign policy significance, the offering of nuclear fuels obviously has carried the greatest economic value, as enriched uranium and certain other nuclear materials have not yet become abundantly available in other countries.

In 1956 the United States offered to supply to the international agency the equivalent of 5,000 kilograms of U235 and to match offers of fissionable material to the agency made by other countries through July 1, 1960. Other countries had offered only 70 kilograms of U235 up to December 31, 1959. Further, the United States offered to make available enriched nuclear fuel for 500,000 kilowatts of generating capacity, on a deferred payment plan similar to that for the Joint U. S.–Euratom program, and by the fall of 1961 65,000 kilograms of U235 had been allocated by the President for distribution to friendly foreign countries (under Section 54 of the Atomic Energy Act).

Despite such inducements, the actual amount of nuclear fuel assistance has proved to be small—by the end of 1961 shipments transferred abroad, almost exclusively for research reactors, totaled only 1,050 kilograms of U235.[30] The explanation for such a record is not found in the price or availability of U. S. nuclear fuels and materials but rather in the technical and economic problems that have impeded nuclear power plants at home as well as abroad. To these have been added a variety of special obstacles that have arisen in the atoms-for-peace program itself.

Problems of Policy

Safeguards Against Diversion

The Baruch plan for international control of atomic energy had the merit of treating atomic activities—military and civilian—as a "package," inseparable and requiring common control. The atoms-for-peace program, however, was conceived on the contrary and still dubious thesis that materials for civilian nuclear power could be controlled separately. Such control of civilian nuclear fuels as now exists is partial and is effected mainly under bilateral arrangements of the atomic leaders. This has not yet seemed a pressing problem because, so far as is known, plutonium in weapon quantities is produced only in the United States, the United Kingdom, the Soviet Union and France.

30. AEC, Annual Report for 1961, p. 226.

However, the possible spread to other countries has raised the Nth country problem and the possibility that in time more and more countries will have atomic weapons.[31]

Early in 1960 France tested its first nuclear "device" in the Sahara and became the fourth country to have nuclear weapon capacity. The development of civilian nuclear power plants in France had nothing directly to do with this event. Yet, the fear that wide knowledge of nuclear power technology will lead to the proliferation of ability to produce plutonium and U233 has shackled the atomic leaders. Without international controls any country producing nuclear power will be tempted to make weapons from the by-product plutonium. Canada has not done so, for obvious reasons. France, the prime illustration, had been producing significant quantities of plutonium from domestic natural uranium long before its 1960 tests. The political decision to produce atomic weapons was almost inescapable.[32]

In traveling the route to an operational power reactor, we are told by scientists, a country is "well over half-way toward an operational plutonium bomb." This suggests, too, that within perhaps five and certainly ten years the manufacture of atomic weapons will be within the reach of several more countries, aside from the present four. Communist China may be one of the first. Since it is to the mutual interest of the present atomic powers to avoid the diffusion of nuclear weapons, there has been some reluctance in these countries to see peaceful nuclear power possibly expedite this diffusion. Although the terms of bilateral agreements, Euratom and the IAEA all provide some control of nuclear fuels, the greatest hope for civilian control seems to rest on the effectiveness of the IAEA in establishing safeguards. However, success in establishing safeguards could not greatly delay the proliferation of weapon capability, because many countries—with or without the help of the

31. There has been a tendency to assume that a fifth country, following France, might promptly join the ranks. However, if one examines the list of other countries potentially capable of producing weapon quantities of plutonium, the conclusion appears that none, aside from communist China, will in fact be in a position to do so for several years. Ultimately almost all will.

32. It easily overcame the cautious misgivings of a small group (other than the Communists, who were obviously opposed) who felt that France's production of atomic weapons would subject it to the tensions already prevailing between the big three. The question came to a head with the Euratom treaty. France rejected the first draft of the treaty, which prevented weapon production by participants. Later, France's insistent reservation to the Euratom treaty, permitting her to make atomic weapons, was based on recognition of several nuclear realities: that atomic bombs might be the "low-priced weapon of the weak," that production of smaller "tactical" nuclear weapons was technically feasible and that such weapons would help to protect metropolitan France while her military forces were committed in Algeria. For an interesting account of France's shift toward "nuclear mindedness" and her relation to Euratom, see Christian de la Malène and Constantin Melnik, "Attitudes of the French Parliament and Government Toward Atomic Weapons," Research Memorandum, the Rand Corporation, Santa Monica, Calif., May 14, 1958.

atomic powers—could proceed independently if the motivation were sufficiently great.[33] Indeed, a country bent on rapid atomic weapon capability could achieve it faster by concentrating on making plutonium in single-purpose reactors. If weapon capability in the long term were the end sought, then dual-purpose reactors, subordinating efficient power generation to production of weapon-grade plutonium, would also be effective, though more demanding of national resources and technology. This method was followed by the United Kingdom.

Today the most thorny issue existing between the United States and the Soviet Union in the IAEA is the question of safeguards. Believing that a direct approach to weapons control was not yet feasible, the Eisenhower administration early concluded that establishing separate safeguards for civilian applications was feasible in advance of weapons control. The State Department recognized that safeguards under the IAEA would be discriminatory, but this fact, it was hoped, would be ameliorated by the atomic powers' voluntarily accepting IAEA safeguards, and by the expectation that discrimination would prove only temporary—pending general weapons control. This conception of the safeguards problem failed because the atomic powers did not volunteer to come under safeguards, the less developed countries (led by India) refused to accept the discrimination and the United States decided at the outset not to press the safeguards issue in the IAEA.

The construction of effective international controls has met countless problems, arising partly from the long-standing disagreement between East and West on the need for inspection. But in addition there have been the conflicts between bilateral and multilateral methods of promoting civilian nuclear energy, while assuring accountability of source and fissionable material. For example, the control the United States requires under its bilateral agreements appears to conflict with national sovereignty. In the U. S.–Euratom agreement, for reasons of sovereignty, Euratom negotiators insisted on what critics have referred to as "self-inspection" and avoided either United States or IAEA safeguards. This was interpreted as weakening the prospects for universal safeguards to be established by the international agency—since other regional groups, perhaps in the communist bloc, could refuse to come under the system. The system being established by the IAEA seems to impose a "double standard" of safeguards—one for the "have not" countries, which secure materials through the agency, but none for the nuclear "haves."

33. NPA, *The Nth Country Problem and Arms Control, A Statement by the NPA Special Project Committee on Security through Arms Control*, Washington, January 1960. (See particularly pp. xiii–xiv.)

Furthermore, bilateral agreements may tend toward progressive deterioration of standards, as rival nuclear powers compete for position.[34] Despite the need for universal safeguards, the negotiations in the IAEA on control and inspection have moved slowly, owing to common recognition by the members that the issue goes to the heart of the agency's operations and raises the most sensitive political problems.[35] Finally, huge surpluses of natural uranium are in prospect within the next few years and, unless these are brought under control, any nation may be able readily to buy the uranium needed to make weapon material.

Numerous proposals have been made for overcoming the obstacles to adequate international control.[36] For example, the United States has already taken steps in the language of its current bilateral agreements to have IAEA safeguards, when they are established, supersede U. S. control. Also, an international register of all peaceful atomic installations would provide a useful step toward more intensive control. In addition, all international traffic in source and fissionable material might well be "certified" and reported via the international agency, just as international traffic in certain narcotic drugs is subject to international control. Finally, the atomic powers could take steps looking toward application, to them, of agency safeguards, as contemplated under Article XII of the statute, and thus end the "double standard." The United States did so unilaterally at the fourth general conference, 1960, with respect to four civilian reactors, thus encouraging conference support of initial steps toward safeguards procedures.

These are essentially political problems requiring careful political solutions. The economic considerations in international control are secondary, though not insignificant in terms of manpower requirements. For example, it has been

34. The USSR has made much of the claim that it has put no "strings" on recipient countries under its bilateral agreements. Whether the USSR is prepared to permit equal freedom in power agreements involving weapon quantities of materials is not known. But the presumption is that the USSR, in its own interest, will avoid the spreading of nuclear weapon capabilities among its satellites. (Note that the USSR has supported the desirability of "safeguards"—as distinct from strict inspection—both in the short-lived UNAEC and, to date, in the IAEA.)

35. The statute provides (Art. XII) that inspectors ". . . designated by the Agency after consultation with the State or States concerned, shall have access at all times and places to data and to any person who by reason of his occupation deals with materials, equipment, or facilities which are required by this Statute to be safeguarded, as necessary to account for source and special fissionable materials supplied and fissionable products and to determine whether there is compliance with the undertaking against use in furtherance of any military purpose. . . ." Under the statute a country not a recipient of material may request the agency to apply its safeguard system to the atomic energy activities of that state (Art. XII).

36. In particular see the study by Arnold Kramish soon to be published by the Council on Foreign Relations, "International Aspects of the Peaceful Uses of Nuclear Energy" (working title).

estimated that carrying out inspection of nuclear reactors in the United States would require between six hundred and fifteen hundred persons and for fissionable material production plants, between three hundred and twenty-four hundred.[37] However, the view of the United States, expressed in previous discussions on its participation in the IAEA and in Euratom, has emphasized the fact that the degree of safeguards imposed should be commensurate with the monetary value of the material and the inherent biological and safety hazards involved.[38] Adequate safeguards against diversion should prove no economic block to nuclear power here or abroad.

Meanwhile, the bilateral power agreements of the United States, the United Kingdom and Canada will provide controls that are consistent with the statute of the IAEA. The agency is hopefully expected in time to take over these responsibilities. However, the "folding in" of bilateral agreements will still leave the possibility that countries outside either form of international control might undertake nuclear power projects and turn them to military purposes. Until this gap is closed there can be no assurance that the worldwide growth of nuclear power for peaceful purposes may not also spread nuclear weapons.

Nuclear Affluence

The United States, the only country evidently possessing "surplus" supplies of enriched uranium, has had the advantage of using enriched fuel as an instrument of foreign policy—making generous offers, unmatched by the Soviet Union, to sell or lease U235 to the IAEA, to Euratom and to many friendly foreign countries. This instrument has, however, led to a fear among some countries of becoming dependent—strategically and economically—on the United States as a source of supply. The lessons of dependence on Middle East petroleum cannot be ignored. At the same time, this reaction has encouraged a kind of "nuclear nationalism" elsewhere. It is expressed in a variety of ways, depending mainly on the availability of indigenous resources. In India it took the form of apparent insistence on achieving the thorium-U233 cycle without timesaving recourse to enriched uranium from the United States, or elsewhere. Canada has considered the possibility that gaseous

37. Seymour Melman, ed., *Inspection for Disarmament*, Columbia University Press, New York, 1958, p. 49.

38. See, especially, statement of Richard L. Kirk, Assistant Director for International Organizations, AEC, at the Hearings before the Senate Foreign Relations Committee, on the *Statute of the International Atomic Energy Agency*, 85th Cong., 1st Sess., May 14, 1957, p. 93.

diffusion plants, located at low-cost hydroelectric sites, might materially ease the Canadian problem of surplus natural uranium. In Western Europe there is the latent desire to demonstrate the technical capacity to produce enriched uranium, a capacity formerly confined to the big three.

For the time being the low prices at which the United States has offered enriched uranium have gone far to remove the economic rationale for such proposals. The motivation, however, remains and raises a problem for U. S. foreign policy.

The national compulsion to seek independence from exclusive external sources of fuel and, perhaps, cognate weapon ambitions, have led France and Germany to consider seriously the prospects for domestic plants to enrich uranium. The Smyth report on the Manhattan Project indicated that the United States had used a number of methods before the MED settled on gaseous diffusion. Up to the Second Geneva Conference, 1958, sufficient investigation had been carried out in Western Europe to indicate beyond reasonable doubt that the knowledge required to build practical plants for enriching uranium was no longer confined to the big three. The numerous conference papers on this subject, notably by the French, revealed that "in Western Europe the knowledge and experience needed to produce U235 on a commercial basis now exists," in the expert opinion of Professor Manson Benedict, Massachusetts Institute of Technology.[39]

Both the Department of State and the AEC have followed a policy of lending no encouragement to the aspirations of Western European continental countries looking toward the construction of capacity for enriching uranium. The economic justification for such capacity in any Western European country is nil; while the proposition is not simply an economic problem, the cost burden would have to be counterbalanced by extraordinary national goals and interests. Whether any country or group of countries in Western Europe or elsewhere will soon be prepared to assume the large costs involved appears doubtful, but the issue of independence will remain.

The United States has had powerful instruments, in the form of the Euratom arrangement and the low price of enriched uranium, to discourage the Western European desire for independent enrichment facilities. The fuel terms of the Euratom arrangement are so favorable to Euratom countries that the immediate incentive for independence has been greatly weakened. Beyond the developmental stage, the demonstrable need for such capacity will rest largely on the outcome of plutonium recycle technology, on the

39. Second Geneva Conference, Press Release ACG/34, September 8, 1958.

relative disadvantages of natural uranium fuel and on the cost of chemically processing irradiated fuel.[40]

Considering the uncertainties surrounding each of these, it is in the interest of the United States and Western Europe to continue with joint fuel arrangements that help avoid the expense of enrichment capacity in Western Europe. U. S. capacity to provide enriched uranium is sufficient to meet continuing military requirements as well as domestic and foreign civilian programs for many years. Since the growth of civilian nuclear power is unlikely to be very fast, the United States is assuming a justifiable responsibility in committing itself to supply enriched fuel to friendly foreign countries, while maintaining for a time a high rate of production for military purposes.[41] Fuel supplies therefore impose no restriction on a broad and imaginative foreign policy for nuclear power development. The restraints lie in a different direction.

Bilateralism

The IAEA has posed for the United States a dilemma of nuclear power foreign policy—whether it should continue the predominantly bilateral form of assistance and also whether it could hope, as promised in the 1953 atoms-for-peace statement, to bring nuclear power soon to the industrializing countries, primarily through the IAEA.

After the IAEA's first year of operation Sterling Cole, the Director General, made plain the fact that U. S. policy (as well as the policies of the United Kingdom and the USSR) had thus far been to continue the bilateral agreements indefinitely, with no apparent intention of bringing them into a complementary relation with the IAEA. If the IAEA were to be more than another UN specialized agency, he indicated, it would be necessary to provide it with additional responsibilities and support.[42] A similar point of view was expressed by him in 1962, following his four-year term as Director General. Among the tasks originally suggested were international control over reactors established through bilateral agreements and provision of fissionable material through the IAEA at more attractive prices than those obtainable bilaterally. Little progress toward either of these has been achieved and the broader issue remains to plague the atoms-for-peace program.

40. As noted in Chapter 2, if commercial chemical processing costs remain high, then the incentive for using enriched uranium fuel, which requires reprocessing, will be dampened and may lead reactor operators to use natural or only very slightly enriched fuel, without expectation of its being immediately reprocessed.

41. Wilson, *loc. cit.*

42. Address before the Atomic Industrial Forum, Washington, November 1958.

AEC officials and American staff members of the IAEA have indeed expressed the view that bilateral arrangements—particularly with Euratom— would undermine the functions of the IAEA. The issues are most sharply drawn by U. S. policies toward the two organizations, and by proposals to revamp the arrangements with Euratom. Indeed, criticism of Euratom and support of the IAEA have often had a common origin.[43]

The apparent incongruity of U. S. policy toward Euratom and the IAEA has arisen from differing approaches to safeguards and controls, from sharply divergent degrees of assistance and from different expectations of by-product benefits for the reactor development program at home:

First of all, the United States has supported IAEA safeguards and controls, except in its agreement with Euratom, in which it consented to safeguards procedures that would be consistent with IAEA safeguards. At the same time, United States assistance to the IAEA has been trivial compared with that offered to Euratom. Clearly, the assistance to Euratom reflected the fact that the joint program was, in effect, intended to be an extension of the domestic power reactor program. Finally, the United States may have slighted the needs of the developing countries. Considering the slow progress of Euratom, it might appear that greater attention should be given to strengthening the market position of the United States—via the IAEA—in the industrializing countries. In fact, however, the slow progress of foreign development (and U. S. exports) comes back to the slow progress the United States has made at home.

The IAEA and the Industrializing Nations

Some industrializing countries in the IAEA have apparently felt that the dominant nations in the organization do not intend to use the agency effec- tively in bringing nuclear power to these areas of the world. Their evidence for this view is, in addition to the pointed comments of spokesmen for the industrial nations at the Second Geneva Conference, the carefully drawn Report of the Preparatory Commission of the IAEA. After mentioning the potential long-run benefits of nuclear power, the Preparatory Commission said:[44]

There are, however, important limitations to the initial scope of the Agency's reactor programme. On the basis of strict current economics, and considering the existing types of power reactors, nuclear power will first be competitive on a large

43. See statement of Robert McKinney, "A New Look at Euratom," submitted to the Joint Committee on Atomic Energy, May 20, 1959. (Printed in McKinney Review, *Background Mate- rial*, Vol. 4, pp. 1250 ff.)

44. *Report: The Programme, Staff, Budget and Financing of the Agency During Its First Year*, New York, 1957, p. 13.

scale with conventional sources of electric power in a relatively small number of Member States which are highly industrialized and densely populated, have high conventional fuel costs and in which electricity supply is fed into distribution grids permitting continuous full load operation of power reactors. On a similar basis it is probable that medium-sized power reactors will provide electricity at competitive rates for the needs of industrially less-developed countries only at a somewhat later date except in certain limited locations. Furthermore the Agency cannot itself finance reactor projects, and the outside sources of finance at the disposal of its Members are limited. The Agency's reactor programme must reflect a balance between these technical and economic factors and the interest which Member States have displayed in developing atomic power at an early date.

Representatives of the developing economies, notably India, understandably resented this harsh view of nuclear power prospects in their countries. On economic grounds it is inaccurate to state that nuclear power "will first be competitive" in the highly industrialized, densely populated, high-load countries. As noted in Chapter 6, these are regional or area characteristics, found in enclaves of several countries broadly defined as "industrially less developed." Furthermore, the philosophy of the Preparatory Commission, fully accepted by the United States and other atomic powers, became an excuse, in the eyes of the developing countries, for the IAEA to discourage nuclear power projects in their areas. To be sure, with its strictly limited resources, the IAEA has been neither able nor willing to promote nuclear power projects anywhere. Thus, bilateral agreements have been the only effective alternative and the route India has finally been prompted to pursue.

For several years the atomic leaders of the West have apparently approached the problem of nuclear power in the developing countries with an invalid assumption and an awkward mental attitude. In brief, the emerging nations were expected to plunge into uneconomic nuclear power projects for reasons of "prestige," it was said, and it thus became the responsibility of the Western atomic powers with superior technical knowledge to discourage them from doing so. Indeed, the early emphasis on research reactors and training assistance was designed in large part to draw attention from nuclear power, so exaggerated in President Eisenhower's UN address. Numerous papers at the Second Geneva Conference in 1958, and at the annual conferences of the IAEA later, were designed to reinforce the argument that the developing countries should exercise patience and restraint in undertaking nuclear power projects.

That United States officials early adopted an attitude of "restraining" the less developed countries was unfortunate. First, the attitude implied that the leaders of the less developed countries were generally incapable of making their own decisions on such a technical matter. Not a single underdeveloped country throughout this period has committed itself to inordinate nuclear power plans. Even among the industrializing countries, only three nations (Brazil, India and Israel, each a special case) have demonstrated sufficient interest to undertake sizable investments and long-term plans. All the rest, recognizing the technical and economic obstacles to nuclear power, have limited their participation to research reactors, training programs and investigations with radioactive isotopes. Among these countries there has indeed been little overt, practical interest in nuclear power. The hard "reality" of nuclear power development has long been recognized by both less developed and industrialized nations.

Second, the State Department's practice of minimizing nuclear power had proved untenable because it ran at cross-purposes with both the stated plans and reputed progress of the domestic development program and reasonable long-term expectations for the practical contribution of nuclear power to the economies of several industrializing nations. For example, at home the AEC and U. S. industry could not publicize the expectation that the proposed nuclear power plant of the Pacific Gas and Electric Co. would be competitive within the next few years, while the government allied itself with the expressed views of French and British officials that the less developed countries should not become involved yet. Furthermore, the AEC ten-year development program has contained an explicit short-term goal of achieving competitive nuclear power in high-cost fuel areas of the country before the end of the decade. If that reasonable goal is achieved, there will be great need for having completed preparatory work in several less developed countries where similar plants should be competitive at that time.

Fortunately, the Smyth Committee helped to correct the early distorted views toward nuclear power. While noting that in a majority of the newly developing countries "nuclear power is not of immediate urgency," the committee stated that there were a number of industrializing countries which would be "well-advised to start planning and building their first nuclear power plants," on the reasonable assumption that nuclear power in large-sized units will be competitive in plants completed by 1966–67 in areas of high fuel cost (40 cents per million BTU). This view of nuclear power, coupled with the need for establishing uniform safeguards, provided the footing for the committee's recommendation that the United States support the IAEA "with increasing vigor."[45]

45. See Smyth Committee Report, p. 10.

Commercial Policy

Enjoying all the advantages of fissionable material production capacity and diversified reactor technology, American industry and American policy makers early came to the conclusion that the pressing foreign need for energy would result in a substantial and growing export demand for American nuclear reactors and equipment. In 1956 the McKinney Panel recommended that the United States provide fuel and technical assistance and encourage contracts for at least 1 million kilowatts of generating capacity outside the United States by 1960, if possible.[46] Many equipment producers voiced equally optimistic expectations during this period, but they soon acquired a hollow sound, as foreign orders for U. S. or other power reactors failed to materialize. Michael Michaelis, appearing before the Joint Committee in 1957 after a survey of foreign markets, stressed the need for foreign demand in the absence of a large immediate market at home.[47] He also mentioned the serious problems of liability, foreign exchange and capital shortage which would need to be overcome before the potentialities of the apparent export market could be realized. Yet, by the end of 1958 the consensus of industry was that, while the export market might develop in time, probably first in the advanced industrial nations and later in the industrializing, it could not sustain a large industry during the interval before substantial domestic demand could appear.

As on the domestic scene, first hopes proved false. The return to a realistic view of the limited export demand in 1958 was confirmed by the collapse of Euratom plans covering 1 million kilowatts of capacity.

Size of the Export Market

Most of the free world's nuclear capacity that is expected to be built during the next ten years is in continental Europe, the United Kingdom, Japan and the United States. (See Table 7-6.) In 1957 Michaelis estimated that from 1958 to 1968 about 6 million kilowatts of capacity might be built abroad, using components from the United States that would bring in between $500 million and $1 billion of business, or roughly one half the total cost.[48] The Atomic Industrial Forum in 1958 projected about 6.5 million kilowatts of U. S.-supplied capacity in the period 1960–1970, representing no more than

46. McKinney Panel, Vol. 1, p. 8.
47. Section 202 Hearings, 1957, Part 2, pp. 581 ff.
48. *Ibid.*, p. 598.

$650 million of business.[49] Working from the Forum's projection, Aley Allen estimated that the foreign market for U. S. equipment and services during the next decade, based on 6.5 million kilowatts, would be between $500 million and $1 billion, not including enriched uranium and other materials and services supplied by the U. S. Government, estimated at up to $385 million.[50] While these appear to be attractively large numbers, they are small in relation to industry's former expectations and present capacity.

Thus, although the projections differ moderately, agreement seems to prevail on the essential elements of the export problem. None of the considerable growth in U. K. nuclear generating capacity is expected to be U. S.-supplied. Continental Europe and Japan generally offer "one-time" opportunities, pending the development of their own manufacturing capacity. The market in the industrializing countries is likely to be small for at least a decade. Finally, the United States advantage in producing enriched uranium is subject to erosion, especially as other countries develop systems for recycling plutonium as fuel and using natural uranium.

The real prospect, therefore, of a large nuclear export market for the United States in the next decade or two is severely limited by economic circumstances.

AEC Commercial Policy to 1961

During the Eisenhower administration, U. S. commercial policy in nuclear power was primarily made in the AEC, it will be recalled, rather than in either the International Cooperation Administration or the Department of State. Before the Euratom proposal the AEC had rather unsuccessfully attempted to encourage export sales primarily by offering enriched fuel on favorable terms. This device failed, because the reactors to use it profitably were not yet developed and the proffering of such large amounts of enriched uranium was judged pretentious rather than helpful. Not until the content of the U. S.–Euratom agreement was examined in 1958, and again in 1959, did coherence and consistency begin to appear in the AEC's varied policies for promoting future U. S. exports.

According to the AEC staff, the guiding policies of export promotion since 1958 have been:[51] to make fissionable materials available only under appro-

49. *A Growth Survey of the Atomic Industry, 1958–68*, prepared by Pickard-Warren-Lowe Associates, for the Atomic Industrial Forum, New York, 1958.

50. "Atomic Energy and World Trade," A Symposium on Nuclear Energy and the Law, *Vanderbilt Law Review*, December 1958, pp. 56–60.

51. See in particular Myron B. Kratzer, "U. S. Export Policies," *Nucleonics*, August 1958, p. 82; and Wilson, *loc. cit.*

priate safeguards against diversion, insofar as possible to offer the same prices and conditions abroad as in the United States and to make the use of enriched material attractive by deferred payment (as well as by lease under the joint program with Euratom).

By the end of 1961 the United States had allotted 65,000 kilograms of U235 for peaceful purposes abroad. All but a small part of this amount was committed under the bilateral and Euratom power agreements and the 5,000-kilogram commitment to the IAEA. Since an assured supply of enriched uranium over the long term has been considered necessary by all foreign countries, the AEC plans to extend the ten-year period of the early bilateral agreements to twenty years (as for Italy, Japan and Euratom). Equally important as an export inducement has been the AEC's assurance that receiving U. S. fuel does not bind the country to using reactors manufactured in the United States.

An important nondiscriminatory aspect of commercial policy has been evident in the prices established for U235 and other materials or services available only from the AEC. For example, when reactor fuel is sold to a foreign operator on the deferred payment plan, no payments on principal are required in the first ten years and the interest rate on the unpaid balance is close to the current use charge in the United States. In effect this combination tends, during an interim period, to equalize the terms on which U235 is made available to foreign and domestic operators.[52] Euratom has the privilege of purchasing fuel under the deferred payment plan or leasing the fuel at domestic rates, including the 4.75 per cent use charge.

Foreign reactor operators may stand to benefit from the AEC's attractive terms for processing irradiated fuel. These terms, however, meet keen competition from British suppliers of nuclear reactors and equipment. The United Kingdom, as has been mentioned, appears to warrant the fuel cost of its export reactors, including reprocessing costs.[53]

The AEC, under the Eisenhower administration, approached its export policy mainly in terms of competition with the British, particularly in Western

52. Under the deferred payment plan payments are extended over a twenty-year period, with the recipient paying only 4 per cent interest during the first ten years. Payment on the principal would be made in ten equal increments during the following ten years, with an interest rate of 4 per cent on the unpaid balance. (AEC, Annual Report for 1961, p. 227.)

53. The UK Atomic Energy Authority indicated in 1957 that the selling price for fabricated natural uranium fuel elements in early gas-cooled, graphite-moderated power stations should not exceed £20,000 per ton and that the United Kingdom would repurchase irradiated fuel elements at not less than £5,000 per ton. At 3,000 megawatt-days per ton, net fuel costs would be about 2 mills per KWH, excluding inventory charges. This is a substantially lower net fuel cost than promised by any U. S. reactor supplier—for enriched uranium designs.

Europe and Japan. The UK's competitive position, however, was inherently weak, and this has become more evident as the technology of enriched fuel has advanced and the price of U235 has been progressively reduced. Apparently the United Kingdom's major export advantage has been a natural uranium reactor that promises low fuel cost, but that advantage has been offset by high capital cost. If, however, the United Kingdom is able to develop a high-temperature, gas-cooled reactor ahead of the United States, it might be able to reestablish a part of the export potential that once appeared so promising. Even so, U. S. commercial policy for nuclear power would seem to call for more important objectives than successful competition with British exporters. If the Soviet Union were to expand its nuclear assistance to neutral countries, it might well resolve the question whether the United Kingdom is more a partner of the United States than a competitor in international nuclear power equipment trade.[54]

In continental Western Europe the framework of U. S. commercial policy was established by the U. S.–Euratom agreement. U. S. manufacturers of reactor equipment and supplies at the outset viewed the prospects for business with the six Euratom countries with mixed feelings. On the one hand, Euratom was considered on the political level as a desirable step toward unification of Western Europe; also, it was expected to encourage the introduction of American technology, in the absence of participation by the United Kingdom.[55] On the other hand, until the functioning of both Euratom and the Common Market had become clearer and their foreign trade better known, little enthusiastic support of Euratom was likely to come from U. S. exporters of nuclear supplies and equipment. Prospects for foreign patent rights were improved in 1960, however, when the AEC adopted a policy of authorizing its contractors to file for patents and to retain private rights under certain conditions.

Competition with the USSR

Direct worldwide competition between the United States and the Soviet Union in the peaceful applications of nuclear power has not yet appeared, but it is a potential element in the economic strategy of both free nations and the communist bloc. Since early 1960 India has been considering bilateral power

54. Cf. Oliver Townsend, "Report to the Panel on the Impact of the Peaceful Uses of Atomic Energy," McKinney Panel, Vol. 2, p. 332.

55. It should not be forgotten that the United Kingdom has been cooperating with the European Nuclear Energy Agency (OECD) in the construction of a high-temperature, gas-cooled power reactor, the Dragon Project, in England. Euratom is also participating.

agreements with the United States, the Soviet Union and other countries. In the long run nuclear power programs of the United States and the Soviet Union are inescapably competitive as other nations watch the technical and economic progress of the two.

The Soviet Union launched its general offensive in "the peaceful field of trade" in 1953, the same year in which President Eisenhower announced the atoms-for-peace program. The Eisenhower program was new and spectacular; the Soviet trade program was launched quietly. It appeared to be a belated reaction to the successful series of U. S. programs—Marshall Plan, Point IV, mutual assistance and foreign aid. The communist bloc is well able to sustain a large foreign program, for example, by exchanging exports of capital equipment for imports of agricultural products and raw materials.[56]

In considering nuclear trade competition with the Soviet bloc, certain technical and economic circumstances are common to both sides. First, the Soviet bloc has found the promotion of nuclear power as a means of economic growth no more promising in the developing countries than have the United States and the United Kingdom. Moreover, the IAEA, whose activities are still being directed mainly toward nonpower applications, has in effect preempted the most immediately fertile fields in these countries. However, looking toward the future, there is still substantial room for the bilateral programs of the United States and the Soviet Union.

Second, less than one fifth of the foreign assistance grants and loans made by the United States have gone to the developing economies. Similarly, by far the greater part of nuclear energy assistance has gone to the industrial nations and only a fraction to the less developed. Hence, neither foreign aid in general nor nuclear assistance has yet been strongly directed toward the major "problem" areas. At an appropriate stage, therefore, U. S. nuclear assistance ought to shift its emphasis to the developing areas. Too heavy reliance, however, may have been placed on the limited capabilities of the IAEA, and seeming neglect of the developing areas may already have opened opportunities for "ruble diplomacy."

The total aid extended by the communist bloc to the developing countries is relatively small, but the programs are opportunistically administered, more for political than for economic purposes. In certain key countries in the Far East and Middle East the communist aid is comparable in scale to aid from the United States. Customarily, the aid of the Soviet bloc is in loans, usually at 2 per cent interest for twelve to fifteen years, repayable in local currencies.

56. Cf. Michael Sapir, *The New Role of the Soviets in the World Economy*, Committee for Economic Development, Washington, April 1958, pp. 28–30.

The loans are thus more favorable on interest burden but less favorable on time period than loans offered to governments by the Development Loan Fund.[57] The USSR-supplied equipment to build a large steel mill in India will increase India's steel capacity by 60 per cent and provide foreign exchange savings of about $80 million annually. The Soviet equipment was financed by a twelve-year loan ($132 million) at 2.5 per cent, repayable in convertible currency or goods.[58]

The implications of the Soviet foreign economic offensive for U. S. nuclear energy foreign policy are unclear. Thus far the USSR has shown no disposition to compete in projects or to offer assistance in atomic energy, but this policy is subject to change. The USSR may confine its assistance for the time being to research programs, because of problems in its domestic power development and its apparently limited supplies of enriched nuclear materials available for civilian purposes.

As long as power reactor technology remains problematical, the Soviet Union will also probably avoid encouraging exports to other members of the communist bloc. If and when the Soviet advanced power reactor technology is demonstrated, apart from the production of weapon-grade plutonium, then the USSR may be in a position to use bilateral nuclear power agreements as an instrument of foreign policy with other bloc nations and, also, with free world countries. Such nuclear energy agreements as the USSR has thus far negotiated have probably been motivated more by political considerations than free world bilateral agreements customarily have been. The Soviet motivations are to expand trade, to be sure, but only as a means of improving its bargaining position in the economic and political destinies of these nations. Whether nuclear power agreements can soon play much of a role as a part of the aggressive communist trade policies toward the uncommitted nations seems dubious at the moment.

57. The Development Loan Fund (now administered by the Agency for International Development) can, however, be operated in a flexible manner in meeting special situations to overcome critical economic problems and counteract the aid programs of the communist bloc. Loans made to India in 1958 provide a possible clue to the manner of financing highly capital-intensive nuclear power plants in the industrializing countries. One loan to India under the Development Loan Fund was to finance imports into India of motor vehicle components (truck and bus parts to be assembled there), for steel and steel products required by India to build railway rolling stock, for equipment to expand the cement industry and to modernize the jute industry. Important features of loans from the fund are these: They are repayable in local currency; for the railway project, in the public sector, the interest rate is only 3.5 per cent, with repayments over twenty years, whereas the loans for the other three projects, in the private sector, are for fifteen years and at 5.25 per cent interest. (Department of State, Bulletin, March 24, 1958, p. 464.)

58. Statement of Douglas Dillon, Deputy Under Secretary for Economic Affairs, before the Senate Committee on Foreign Relations, March 3, 1958 (State Department Press Release 96).

In Brief

This review of nuclear power as a part of U. S. foreign policy up to 1962 has emphasized the birth pains, rather than the promise, of an emerging technology. The objectives of the atoms-for-peace program have been viewed as pretentious and premature. The bilateral research agreements have been, indeed, essentially stopgap devices thrown into the hiatus until power reactor technology can become competitive. Unfortunately, the imaginative joint program between the United States and Euratom was retarded by sudden fuel surpluses in Western Europe. Also, the IAEA was carefully restricted by the atomic powers to a minimum program covering isotopes and training in the developing countries and made little progress toward the basic problem of the times—safeguards and control of nuclear fuels and power reactors. In brief, the atoms-for-peace program lacked the force it required because the faltering pace of the domestic development program had fallen behind the demands of U. S. nuclear power foreign policies. The issue remains one of reconciling foreign and domestic policies, programs and objectives.

Yet, for all its weaknesses, the atoms-for-peace program has contributed to the aims of foreign policy—to foster a world system of law and order, to assist the developing countries through science and technology and to help strengthen the Atlantic Community. In particular, it gives countries outside the atomic powers an opportunity, with generous U. S. help, to participate and become involved in the new science of the mid-twentieth century. Indeed some less developed countries have "seized upon atomic energy as the base upon which to build the technical development of their countries" and thus have provided "an unparalleled opportunity for the advanced nations to aid the newly developing countries to promote their scientific and engineering programs."[59]

59. Smyth Committee Report, p. 14.

CHAPTER 9

Partial Reconciliation

The timeworn principle that foreign policy begins at home was ignored in the atoms-for-peace program, although discerning scientists and reactor experts pointedly remarked, soon after passage of the 1954 act, on the incompatibility of the grandiose expectations encouraged abroad with the real state of reactor development at home. This situation resulted from the divergent policy objectives—expansion of nuclear power abroad through U. S. help and, on the other hand, excessive reliance on the initiative of the private utilities at home—which hobbled effective U. S. cooperation abroad. The persistent effort to treat these conflicting policies as separate was futile. They necessarily affected each other.

For example, despite domestic policies which stood in the way, the equipment industry, the electric utilities and the Eisenhower administration all agreed that "accelerated" development of competitive nuclear power was desirable, primarily because atoms-for-peace objectives seemed to demand it. Furthermore, at the administrative level most members of the Joint Committee welcomed Euratom in 1958 because it seemed to offer an escape from problems delaying development at home. Finally, at the technical level, the AEC's early preoccupation with enriched uranium reactor systems had permitted only modest work on plutonium recycling and other problems of special interest to foreign countries.

From 1955 on, as recognition of the lagging progress grew, successive statements by such groups as the McKinney Panel in 1955, advisory committees of the Joint Committee in 1958 and of the AEC in 1959 all called for domestic development programs that would strengthen foreign policies. These policies, the Edison Electric Institute in 1959 stated, "may require efforts that exceed those indicated by domestic considerations" and "are a collective responsibility of all segments of the economy."[1]

In retrospect one might reason that the policy conflict could have been relieved either by promptly eliminating the extravagant aims and pretensions of the atoms-for-peace program or by adopting a domestic development program capable of acceleration or, more sensibly, by doing both—which is about what has been happening in the evolution of national policy since 1959. Thus, on the one hand, the Department of State proceeded, inconspicuously, to be sure, to deflate atoms-for-peace objectives by largely ignoring nuclear power, except as a necessary element of Euratom, and by providing minimum support to the IAEA. But the Department did not propose abandoning the atoms-for-peace program. On the other hand, the AEC, under strong Joint Committee pressure, persuaded the reluctant electric utility industry to accept a variety of presumably "disquieting" expedients—such as the construction of a very few prototypes of less than full-scale by the AEC itself—in order to accelerate the program. Furthermore, the joint U. S.–Euratom program represented an imaginative device for combining foreign and domestic policies.

United States policy makers also perceived that, at the current pace of development, the maximum foreseeable claims of civilian power plants at home and abroad could account for only a small fraction of the available nuclear supplies and capacity for many years. In the meantime, it appears certain that weapon requirements will decrease—and may already have decreased. Question arises, then, why is civilian nuclear power continuing for so long to lag behind the obvious military accomplishments of reactor technology—in ship propulsion, generating stations at remote military sites and reported progress toward use of nuclear power in rockets and space satellites?

The failure to achieve competitive nuclear power in the United States, even in high-cost fuel areas, as soon as had been expected partly explains the refusal of electric utility systems in Euratom to offer project proposals in 1959 under the joint program. The slow rate of progress became so obvious that in 1960 the AEC was compelled to establish a long-term development program, aimed at achieving competitive nuclear power in some areas within ten years.[2] Moreover, the style of the U. S. program, which had been characterized by

1. Section 202 Hearings, 1959, p. 383.

2. See "Civilian Power Reactor Program—Plans for Development," *AEC Authorizing Legislation, Fiscal Year 1961*, Hearings, Subcommittee on Legislation, Joint Committee on Atomic Energy, 86th Cong., 2nd Sess., 1960, pp. 474 ff.

exploration of a wide variety of reactor concepts, was changed in 1959 and 1960 to greater concentration on the reactor types most closely approaching competitive feasibility. But well before these reasonable modifications could be adopted it was seemingly necessary to explore and reject a number of devices—some almost quixotic—for accelerating development in the interest of atoms-for-peace objectives.

Grand Designs for Reconciliation

Since 1954 a variety of schemes has been put forward that served, unintentionally in some cases, to reconcile the domestic and foreign programs for nuclear power. One proposal was for a worldwide "Marshall plan" in atomic energy, supported by massive public subsidy. Others urged reduced emphasis on nuclear power at home and abroad, thus permitting development to take a course dictated more by commercial considerations. Between these extremes were clustered numerous variations showing differing degrees of reliance on private or public resources. A few contributed in some measure to the emerging reconciliation of foreign and domestic policies and programs.

A "Marshall Plan" for Nuclear Energy

In November 1956, during the period immediately following the Suez crisis, an ambitious proposal was made by a leading industrialist in the nuclear energy field, John Jay Hopkins.[3] He urged the free nations to take immediate steps toward becoming independent of Middle Eastern oil through "a massive Free World program of nuclear energy development not only for power but for all those additional applications which are technically feasible and which will be necessary before nuclear power may ease significantly the Free World's current dependence on dwindling oil and coal resources."[4] The proposal for this "new economic alliance" was motivated by the view that "for the West, energy self-sufficiency is a prime condition of economic survival." Through a "massive cooperative effort" of free world governments and industrialists, he believed nuclear power developments necessarily should be accelerated far beyond current or projected programs. Hopkins conceded that nuclear power would require long and costly development before it

3. John Jay Hopkins, "Unatom: A Plan for the Development of a United Atomic Treaty Organization of Free World Nations," an address to the Third International Conference of Manufacturers, National Association of Manufacturers, New York, November 29, 1956.

4. *Ibid.*, p. 19.

could become an economic benefit, and that it was problematical whether this end could be achieved within the five-year period he optimistically believed might be left before the "inevitable" debacle he foresaw in the Middle East. Though Hopkins may have been unduly pessimistic about dwindling free-world reserves of fuel, he recognized the danger of political strain in the Middle East and the need for nuclear power to relieve the threat of unpredictable events in that area. For rather obvious reasons, chiefly the good progress toward Euratom and the IAEA, nothing tangible came of his proposal.

Military Reactors First, Then Civilian

Before 1953 the priority of military reactors dictated an AEC policy of undertaking civilian reactor research only if it involved no "interference" in AEC laboratories. At the same time the obvious success of the naval program lent prestige to the military reactors as pointing the way to the best civilian designs. Later, when a substantial civilian market failed to develop, it was proposed that commercial acceptance of civilian reactors be sought through emphasis on those designs that were meeting the needs of remote military installations. One view was that acceptance of this devious approach would be merely a reflection of the force of economic circumstances. Others felt that it would show a realistic appreciation of the fact that military technology could break the way that civilian technology should follow.[5] A combination of these views was revealed in Joint Committee testimony (1958) by the representative of a "newcomer" in equipment manufacturing, who had found the sale of "package-power" reactors unrewarding and suggested that "a major military program for the development of nuclear energy is the most plausible solution" to the problem of achieving early nuclear capacity in industry.[6] Members of the Joint Committee were unreceptive to the suggestion, chiefly because they believed the incentives for cost saving would be small and the peaceful uses of nuclear energy would be caught in the "mesh of military secrecy." Apparently, too, the failure of the Department of Defense to follow up the Fort Belvoir package-power reactor (APPR) raised understandable misgivings about the wisdom of the civilian reactor program's becoming "a natural by-product of a successful military program."

5. Military development of diesel engines for use in submarines and their subsequent use in locomotives provided a simplified historical precedent.

6. See statement by Tibor F. Nagey, General Manager, Nuclear Division, The Martin Co., Baltimore, Md., before the Joint Committee on Atomic Energy, February 21, 1958. (Section 202 Hearings, 1958, pp. 218–24.)

Despite the proposal's evident drawbacks, the scheme to transfer the major government effort to the military reactor program held tacit relevance for reconciling foreign and domestic policies. The type and size of reactors were pertinent considerations. Ship-propulsion reactors for civilian purposes are similar to those for naval vessels and their development was closely associated. Similarly, after some delay and Joint Committee prodding, the package-power reactor is being developed by the military in a variety of forms.[7] There is, however, no military requirement for large central station units.

The greatest drawback to this proposal, therefore, is that it failed, on the one hand, to provide for accelerated development of the larger reactors needed by most electric utilities in the United States and abroad. On the other hand, the development of ship-propulsion and package-reactor units for civilian purposes was already meshed with military development of these types. Nor could the proposal assure more rapid technical development, since the technology already had a common origin in the AEC laboratories and contractors. Finally, shifting major civilian development to the military reactor program was repugnant to both sectors of the electric utility industry and perhaps to most equipment manufacturers, who had accepted both the necessity of a long developmental period and the objectives of the Atomic Energy Act of 1954. Evaluation of this scheme, however, does reveal that domestic programs and policies up to mid-1958 were deemed insufficient to bring about "a capable nuclear industry at the earliest possible time" and that forceful public measures were needed.

An "International Atomic Power Demonstration Program"

In 1955 the Joint Committee Panel on the Impact of the Peaceful Uses of Atomic Energy cautioned the public that during the next decade more nuclear power capacity would probably be constructed in foreign countries than in the United States. Furthermore, it recommended that the U. S. provide assistance toward construction of 1 million kilowatts of nuclear power capacity outside the U. S. "as soon as possible—we hope by 1960."[8] Soon after the panel's

---

7. In 1960 the AEC submitted to the Joint Committee a report on the use of small nuclear power reactors at continental and remote military sites. At four of the ten sites the estimated costs indicated advantages for nuclear over conventional plants at McMurdo Sound, Antarctica; Thule, Greenland; Okinawa; and Guam. (Joint Committee on Atomic Energy, Release No. 266, April 4, 1960.) At the end of 1961 two small, military electric power reactors were operable at remote installations, two others were being built and a fifth was planned. (AEC, *Major Activities in the Atomic Energy Programs, January-December 1961* [Annual Report], Washington, January 1962, Appendix 10.)

8. McKinney Panel, Vol. 1, p. 8.

report was issued, the chairman, Robert McKinney, made explicit the connection between the domestic development program and support of the atoms-for-peace program by urging "an international atomic power demonstration program" of this scale.[9] This proposal now appears more realistic and convincing than the "Marshall plan" and "military by-product" approaches set forth above. Its primary strength was accepting the fact that, in the absence of an immediate domestic market for high-cost power, a complementary relation existed between large U. S. nuclear resources and foreign needs for power. Promising though it appeared, the proposal failed to win action by either the Joint Committee or the executive branch and the concept withered— though it was, to be sure, to find partial revival in later joint U. S.–Euratom arrangements.

The economic reasons for rejecting McKinney's proposal are not easily discerned. Important, no doubt, was the persistent, misguided assumption that competitive nuclear power might soon be achieved without the necessity of transferring primary initiative back to the AEC from the electric utility industry.[10] In retrospect it can be seen, too, that any power reactor project proposed for construction in a foreign country was necessarily a "demonstration," since none beyond the experimental stage had been operated in the United States by 1955. Also, fear naturally existed in the United States and abroad that the technical reliability of power reactors was insufficiently established to risk their being operated under sensitive international conditions.[11] Further, it became evident that the reactors U. S. manufacturers might confidently construct abroad were generally the same—though perhaps not the latest models—as the reactor designs already being constructed for demonstration in the United States. Finally, McKinney's assumption that demonstration plants should be built "where they can be economically competitive [and] therefore they should yield a return on the investment" proved fanciful. Despite higher fuel costs abroad, even by mid-1962 no manufacturer had

9. Robert McKinney, "American Industry's Stake in an International Atomic Power Program," an address before the Atomic Industrial Forum and the Denver Research Institute, Denver, Colo., June 25, 1956.

10. The McKinney Panel report, for example, in undisguised language, recommended "in the event that industry does not take on the full risks and burdens, the Commission should support a program to bring atomic power to a point where it can be used effectively and widely on a competitive basis, even to the construction with public funds of one full-scale 'demonstration' plant of each major reactor size and type." (McKinney Panel, Vol. 1, p. 2.)

11. Excessive emphasis on the domestic benefits of reactors built abroad during the demonstration period at one time lent support to the sordid inference that foreign areas might be used as "guinea pigs." Reactor experts insisted that no reactor should be considered for American construction abroad that had not first been carried to the prototype stage in the United States, to establish its safety and reliability of operation.

proposed a demonstration reactor that was guaranteed to provide competitive performance under normal methods of financing.

Deemphasizing Nuclear Power

Representatives of the State Department held that the nuclear power segment of the atoms-for-peace program was unwise, the objectives appeared propagandistic and practical means of accomplishment were lacking. In their view the reconciliation of foreign and domestic policies should be achieved by ignoring nuclear power in the atoms-for-peace program and by leaving reactor development to be carried on by industry and utilities at a rate justified by private economic criteria.[12]

Vestiges of this "hands off" view have appeared in policy discussions from time to time, in part because certain technical assumptions of the program were indeed badly founded, as explained in the preceding chapter. Also, in partial defense of this position, it should be recognized, for example, that the need for the United States to maintain a strong competitive position "against" the United Kingdom or the need to counteract economic penetration of Asia by the USSR or to build an important export trade could not be used, convincingly, as justification for the scale and pace of special atoms-for-peace programs. Yet foreign programs were undertaken with U. S. encouragement and there is no need now for the United States to withdraw.

Lacking both technical and economic reality, these various and extreme approaches proved abortive. Aside from the merits of the Euratom program, the effective compulsion for reconciliation of the atoms-for-peace program and domestic reactor development arose primarily from the force of reactor technology itself and from external events. For example, the twin legislative policies in 1953 and 1954 of increasing publicly available information and encouraging wider industry participation grew out of the Soviet Union's unexpected progress in both nuclear and thermonuclear weapons.[13] Similarly, the Suez Canal crisis in 1956 was a spur to action. On the other hand, the fuel surplus in Europe in 1958 and 1959 led to a contraction in 1960 of the Euratom program.

12. See, for example, Ambassador Morehead Patterson, in *Atoms for Peace Manual*, Joint Committee on Atomic Energy, Senate Document 55, 84th Cong., 1st Sess., 1955, p. 353 ff.

13. Arnold Kramish (*Atomic Energy in the Soviet Union*, Stanford University Press, Stanford, Calif., 1959, p. 127) reports that AEC Chairman Strauss stated there was good reason to believe, in 1954, that the Soviet Union had "begun work on this [thermonuclear] weapon substantially before we did."

In the main, however, the pressure has been toward more aggressive domestic action, as it has become increasingly obvious that progress in the atoms-for-peace program depends on reactor development at home. The various reactor development programs set down by the AEC through the years best reveal each administration's attitude toward bringing the domestic program into effective support of the established foreign policy.

Reconciliation of Plans and Goals

The Atomic Energy Act of 1954 sharply separated the foreign and domestic phases of nuclear energy—as it did the civilian and military aspects. Not surprisingly, then, the AEC's Five-Year Reactor Development Program (1954) failed to take cognizance of its relevance for the foreign program. The main point of emphasis was private industrial participation. Progressively, in succeeding program statements greater attention was given to "positive steps of assistance to other countries," mentioned in the 1955 program,[14] until, finally, in 1958 the AEC explicitly stated that the "urgency" of the development program was "dictated primarily by international considerations."[15] The Commission also made explicit the hope of achieving competitive nuclear power "within five years" in high-cost areas abroad and "within ten years" at home. Finally, the long period that would be required for development began to be recognized.

One of the great barriers to effective program planning up to 1959 was the sheer inability of the Joint Committee and the AEC to agree on primary objectives and means.[16] Successive program statements, ostensibly the primary responsibility of the AEC, were often prompted by outside initiative, usually by the Joint Committee. The result was a continuous process of "successive approximation" to a coherent statement of ends and means. Not until the comprehensive AEC program of 1960 did it appear that the six-year process

14. *Current Statement of the Atomic Energy Commission on the Five-Year Reactor Development Program to the Subcommittee on Research and Development*, Joint Committee on Atomic Energy, 84th Cong., 1st Sess., May 4, 1955.

15. Statement on the Atomic Energy Commission's Civilian Power Reactor Program before the Joint Committee on Atomic Energy, June 4, 1958. *AEC Authorizing Legislation, Fiscal Year 1959*, Hearings, Subcommittee on Legislation, Joint Committee on Atomic Energy, 85th Cong., 2nd Sess., 1958, pp. 214 ff. (particularly p. 234).

16. In closed seminars with the Joint Committee, reactor experts and equipment manufacturers complained that the primary need was for "clear-cut national objectives, both with respect to domestic and international development." (See Section 202 Hearings, 1958, pp. 583–84.)

of policy accommodation might be approaching a moderately satisfactory conclusion.[17]

As might be expected of a predominantly technical organization, basic economic considerations were given insufficient attention by the AEC. This fact helped to explain why the problem of achieving competitive nuclear power in the United States was so gravely underestimated by the Commission and its staff. Correcting this distorted timetable also provided the basis for correcting the more egregious errors in the atoms-for-peace program.

The AEC's 1960 program, described as long range, contemplated a ten-year development effort, involving successive stages of experimental, prototype and full-scale plants. Earlier the AEC programs had looked forward not more than five years and presumed rather speedy success.

The AEC's avoidance of government-owned demonstration plants was zealously adhered to, with only minor deviations imposed by the Joint Committee. Thus, the AEC insisted in 1960 that "reactor experiments should be built and operated by the Commission," whereas "prototypes should be built and operated by publicly or privately owned utilities independently or in cooperation with the Commission. Alternatively, prototypes could be built and operated by the Commission." Moreover, "industry should assume the primary responsibility for large commercial-size nuclear power stations," although the AEC "will consider possible assistance on initial plants in various concepts useful for demonstration purposes."[18] This formulation of policy on a sensitive issue meant that, in order to maintain the pace of the program, the AEC itself would be obliged, as administration critics on the Joint Committee had insisted, to construct prototypes if satisfactory proposals from utilities were not forthcoming.[19]

17. The origination of these program statements is revealing. The first AEC program (1954) and its revision (1955) were prepared on request of the Joint Committee. In 1958 the Edison Electric Institute, sensing a program vacuum, established a Technical Appraisal Task Force which assayed the status and prospects of nuclear power. Many of the findings of this task force were included in the mid-1958 report of the Joint Committee staff (and scientific consultants) on the "Proposed Expanded Nuclear Power Program." In early 1959 the AEC's Ad Hoc Advisory Committee submitted its statement, which was incorporated soon thereafter in the AEC's reactor program presented to the Joint Committee. Finally, in the spring of 1960 the AEC provided its "ten-year program" of development, which conformed closely with the ad hoc committee's findings a year earlier. Significantly, a few scientists (Henry DeWolf Smyth and Walter H. Zinn, notably) provided the "connective tissue" running between successive statements and attempted to bridge the split between the Joint Committee and the AEC.

18. *AEC Authorizing Legislation, Fiscal Year 1961*, pp. 474 ff.

19. The first test of this policy came early in the spring of 1960 when two proposals came from public power systems to undertake boiling water projects, under the AEC's "second-round" demonstration program, whereas none was received under the "third-round" invitation for an organic-cooled and -moderated reactor. Yet, by the end of 1961 the AEC had not taken steps to build the latter plant itself.

Furthermore, the belabored issue of whether or not full-scale plants should be built at an early stage received some clarification. In 1955 the AEC had stated that the most rapid progress would come from actual construction and operation of large-scale reactors on a commercial basis. By 1959 this concept had been rejected. Chairman J. A. McCone stated that existing technology "must be built into plants of a prototype nature as rapidly as possible if we are to make maximum progress," and explained "if we attempt to build that technology into large plants, . . . a delay will result."[20] This revised policy, curiously, received little criticism from the customary administration opposition on the Joint Committee and the question of full-scale plant construction was seemingly put to rest—on AEC terms. However, with the setback of Euratom in 1959, it seemed that both prototype and full-scale construction would have to be deferred until the utility systems were prepared to assume, in a period of high interest rates, the heavy additional capital costs involved in nuclear power plants. In the three years 1959 through 1961 only two full-scale private projects were proposed—the 355,000-kilowatt plant of the Southern California Edison Co. and the 313,000-kilowatt plant of the Pacific Gas and Electric Co.

Explicit Goals

A year before the AEC's 1960 announcement of its ten-year program the interrelation of the objectives of foreign and domestic policies had been clearly stated by the Commission's Ad Hoc Advisory Committee, headed by former Commissioner Henry DeWolf Smyth:[21]

> Since the development of nuclear power is in fact proving to be difficult and expensive, the Government has been faced with a hard choice. Either this country continues its leadership at the cost of heavy expenditure or it accepts the probability that there will be no significant nuclear power industry in this country until the technology has been developed elsewhere and can be reintroduced here. This Committee knows of little support for the latter alternative. . . .

> Were there no hope of bringing the cost of nuclear power into the general range of present costs for power from fossil fuel, it would be a waste of money to push the development of nuclear power for domestic reasons. Since there is good reason to hope that the cost of nuclear power may decrease over the next ten or twenty years to the point where it is comparable to the cost of power from stations burning coal, a development program for domestic reasons alone is sensible, though

20. Section 202 Hearings, 1959, p. 45.

21. AEC, *Civilian Nuclear Power*, Report of Ad Hoc Advisory Committee on Reactor Policies and Programs, Washington, January 2, 1959 (printed in Section 202 Hearings, 1959, pp. 513 ff.).

not urgent. Whatever urgency there is in this development rises from our concern for national prestige and our desire to assist the development of nuclear power in other countries. There is, however, not a very great discrepancy between the program which might be laid out for domestic reasons alone and the program we are recommending.

This report was favorably received by electrical equipment and nuclear reactor manufacturers, but an important sector of the electric utility industry had serious reservations.[22] Thus, the long controversy over program objectives was not fully resolved, but sufficiently so that the most obvious inconsistencies were reduced and the connection between foreign and domestic objectives was generally accepted.

The Ad Hoc Advisory Committee covered the objectives in these five points: fortify the U. S. position of leadership in the technology of civilian nuclear power; within ten years achieve competitive nuclear power in some areas of the United States;[23] in less than ten years achieve competitive nuclear power in friendly foreign nations having high-cost energy, through a comprehensive program of assistance, clearly defined and vigorously pursued; reduce nuclear power costs substantially over the next twenty or thirty years by continuing studies which are unlikely to be fruitful in the next ten years; and make fullest possible use of nuclear energy latent in both uranium and thorium, especially by breeding.[24]

When the AEC restated its program objectives it made the same five points, substantially without change, but inexplicably reduced to fourth rank the desirability of maintaining U. S. leadership in reactor technology.[25] Significantly, too, neither the Ad Hoc Advisory Committee nor the AEC explicitly included wide "private participation" as a major objective, as had been true of early program statements. The AEC program principles were readily accepted and unchallenged by the Joint Committee, in part because the committee staff had previously drafted similar objectives and had secured a large measure of acceptance from reactor experts, equipment companies and electric utilities.[26] As an incident, then, of reestablishing harmony between the

22. Section 202 Hearings, 1959, p. 240.

23. The AEC defined competitive nuclear power as having been achieved "when utility executives can decide to build nuclear power stations based on economic considerations." This decision might well occur four to five years before nuclear power would be generated. Also, by high fuel cost, the AEC meant fossil fuel at 35 cents per million BTU or higher. (See Table 3–5, p. 89.)

24. Ad Hoc Advisory Committee, *op. cit.*

25. See Section 202 Hearings, February 1959, testimony of AEC Chairman McCone, pp. 38 ff.

26. Joint Committee on Atomic Energy, 85th Cong., 2nd Sess.: *Proposed Expanded Civilian Nuclear Power Program*, August 1958, p. 4; and *Comments of Reactor Designers and Industrial Representatives on the Proposed Expanded Civilian Nuclear Power Program*, December 1958, pp. 182–218.

Joint Committee and a reconstituted AEC on the scale and direction of the program, a partial reconciliation of foreign and domestic objectives was accomplished in 1959. Whether it penetrated to the economic and technical details of the development program itself remained a question.

However nicely domestic and foreign program objectives were finally stated, critical members of the Joint Committee remained skeptical of the constrained means the AEC used to achieve them. Experience fortified such skepticism. Congressman Holifield in 1958 declared "we want to get on with the building of reactors and the second and third generation reactors because of the international situation" and criticized the AEC for having wasted time with the utilities on projects that the government later would have to rescue. Holifield pointedly cited the Pennsylvania Power and Light project with Westinghouse Electric Corporation for construction of a homogeneous power reactor, based on long, difficult research at AEC's Oak Ridge National Laboratory, operated by Union Carbide Corporation. In this case, the utility system originally declared its intention to undertake the developmental project without direct government aid, then in 1957 found it necessary to request such aid, and, finally, in 1958 abandoned the project primarily because of the technical obstacles encountered in this advanced system. As similar delays had occurred on several private and public nuclear power projects, Congressman Holifield decried AEC policy and the lag that "comes about as a result of the failure of industry to do the job."[27] The AEC long considered such delays a valid cost of encouraging outside participation in the absence of an urgent domestic need for nuclear power. Whether a more realistic approach might be found still remains to be seen.

The Technical Level

Despite the inconsistencies of program administration, by the end of 1961 the AEC had made some progress in establishing consistent ground rules for assisting domestic and foreign reactor operators in matters of pricing nuclear fuels, charges for services, etc. Reactor systems have proved to offer particular foreign or domestic advantages, hence the technical goals themselves have been influenced by economic circumstances abroad as well as at home. For example, development of small- and medium-sized reactors is not especially needed for foreign programs, whereas large reactors are needed in the large-load centers of industrialized and industrializing nations.

27. *AEC Authorizing Legislation, Fiscal Year 1959*, pp. 247–49.

The U. S. development program, covering at least eight reactor types, is well designed to accomplish these diverse objectives. The pressurized water, boiling water and organic-moderated reactor types, which were expected to be the heart of the U. S.–Euratom program, seem nearest to competitive costs in Western Europe. Concentration of development effort on these, as well as on the gas-cooled type, was emphasized by the Ad Hoc Advisory Committee in 1959. In another category fall the sodium graphite reactor, the heavy water–moderated reactor and the fluid or molten fuel reactor, representing more advanced types. These are economically less promising immediately, but they have long-term potentialities, which might permit power at lower cost than the first group. Moreover, heavy water technology may prove important to countries wishing to exploit natural uranium and to avoid importing enriched uranium. Finally, there are the breeder types, which promise less in terms of low-cost power than in terms of conserving available nuclear resources.

Greater emphasis on reactor systems most nearly approaching competitive feasibility, through strong encouragement of prototype plants, represented a material redirection of program administration by the AEC in 1959 and 1960. This was expected to add force to the reactor program and to support of atoms-for-peace projects. For one thing the shift meant that representatives of foreign countries would ordinarily have only a few systems to evaluate. At the same time this would not prevent investment by foreign countries in advanced systems that had not yet reached the "near-proven" class. The freedom of industrial nations to experiment with more exotic systems was revealed in the U. S.–Euratom negotiations.[28] Countries, such as India and Brazil, wishing to pursue natural uranium systems or possibly the more difficult thorium-U233 breeders, were expected to welcome continued U. S. investigations in these directions. Similarly, more intensive work on gas-cooled systems was expected to keep the United States abreast of the advanced gas-cooled reactor being pressed by the British. Furthermore, by the nature of the competition with the Soviet Union, one would expect that success would rest more on highly advanced systems, particularly breeders, than on "proven" types.

Finally, the AEC's research on fuel technology had by the end of 1960 given larger, though belated, attention to the recycling of plutonium. Except for some work on heavy water reactors, the natural uranium systems had been given comparatively little attention.

28. See line of questioning by Congressman Holifield and the exchange of correspondence between Max Kohnstamm (Euratom) and Richard W. Cook (AEC), in *Proposed Euratom Agreements* (with associated documents and materials), Hearings, Joint Committee on Atomic Energy, 85th Cong., 2nd Sess., July 1958.

Clearly, as stated by AEC Commissioner Harold S. Vance in 1958, "assistance to other countries may require projects even in the domestic program which might not be required otherwise; also . . . the results from assistance to other countries will contribute greatly toward meeting the domestic objective. The urgency is dictated primarily by international considerations, but the over-all program should be an integrated one."[29] By the end of 1960 one could foresee the time when this might be true—though the halting progress of Euratom and the IAEA was discouraging. The new ten-year program of the AEC, it was hoped, might provide an "answer" to the domestic need for greater progress, and, as a by-product, the atoms-for-peace program as well.

Economic Assistance

Despite the innumerable forms of economic assistance available up to 1961, the AEC succeeded in maintaining consistency and avoiding discrimination in the terms on which assistance was granted to foreign and domestic nuclear power projects. Among the various types of aid available to each were: access, under private contract or government agreement, to the technology of industry and AEC laboratories on a wide range of power reactors and fuel cycles; guaranteed enriched fuel supply for the life of the reactor; fair charges for the reprocessing of irradiated fuel elements; contracts to assure the purchase of by-product plutonium; sale to foreign operators of enriched fuel inventory on a deferred or installment basis (fuel inventory leased to Euratom projects).

Differences in the type of assistance at home and abroad were justified, the AEC held, by differences in objectives. For example, the AEC guarantees of fuel performance under the Euratom agreement were not extended to domestic projects.[30] It appeared that the AEC was providing more intensive aid for foreign industry than for domestic. However, assistance to foreign and domestic utilities has been closer to conformity than suggested by the line of questioning of critical Joint Committee members.

Nuclear fuel prices for domestic and foreign reactor operators have been identical, a major advance over the two-price system that appeared to be emerging in 1952 to 1954. In 1955 the AEC was quoting a classified U235 price schedule to prospective domestic operators, while publicly, for papers presented at the First Geneva Conference and for other purposes, it used a

29. *AEC Authorizing Legislation, Fiscal Year 1959*, p. 254.

30. For a detailed qualitative comparison of assistance offered to domestic and Euratom utilities, see statement submitted by the AEC in *Proposed Euratom Agreements*, p. 211.

range of $15 to $30 per gram of U235. The subsequent publication of the AEC price schedule[31] was an important policy step, not only because it provided essential public information but also as a declaration that all qualified buyers, domestic and foreign, would pay the same prices. This action helped to give assurance of more compatible foreign and domestic reactor policies.

The terms for "buy-back" of foreign and domestic by-product plutonium differ because, for the time being, the AEC is still prepared to buy some domestic plutonium at "weapon-grade" prices. This situation will presumably change with the expiration of the first seven-year guarantee in mid-1963, when fuel-value prices should prevail for foreign and domestic by-product plutonium.

The charge for chemical processing of irradiated fuel is the same for both domestic and foreign operators. Transportation costs in both instances are paid by the operator.

Government guarantees of performance of fuel elements are nonuniform. At home the AEC has guaranteed nuclear fuel in AEC-owned reactors operated by publicly owned utilities. The AEC has given limited guarantees to Euratom but thus far none to other foreign reactor operators. To be sure, in the United States and overseas American manufacturers have themselves offered certain guarantees of minimum fuel-element performance.[32]

What economic justification is there for the AEC to give fuel guarantees to Euratom but not to private utilities at home? If the foreign and domestic conditions of reactor operation and manufacturers' incentives are substantially similar, there would seem to be no economic justification for withholding governmental fuel guarantees from private operators in the United States. The primary difference is that conventional fuel costs in the United States, even in high-cost areas, are somewhat lower than in the Euratom countries, therefore the hope of nuclear power's competing may be better in Europe. But this difference is not controlling, for even the U. S. guarantee of fuel performance does not make nuclear power competitive in Euratom countries; indeed, the figures used in the working papers attached to the proposal presented to the Congress in 1958 show that unless fuel performance is better than the guarantee the total nuclear power costs will still be 1 to 3 mills per KWH higher than for coal-fired plants in Western Europe.[33] Hence, in Europe or here, all the guarantee does for the reactor operator is to set a limit

31. Ranging from $5.62 per gram of U235 at 0.72 per cent concentration to $17.07 at 90 per cent concentration.

32. In the international competition on the SENN project the General Electric Company included in its winning bid a fuel-life guarantee of 12,500 megawatt-days per ton of fuel, compared with AEC's guarantee of 10,000 megawatt-days per ton in the Euratom agreement.

33. *Proposed Euratom Agreements*, pp. 39 ff.

on possible excess fuel costs, but does not eliminate the excess. The guarantee policy would seem then to be equally applicable at home and abroad.

The terms on which capital is made available domestically and under the Euratom arrangement differ, but this is to be expected for institutional reasons. Domestically, private utilities secure financing at various rates, customarily ranging from 4 to 6 per cent on bonds, whereas the rural cooperatives secure funds at 2 per cent, though somewhat higher rates are usual for municipal systems and public utility districts. Under the Euratom agreement up to $135 million credit from the Export-Import Bank is to be available to utilities at 4.5 per cent; but the balance, to be secured in Europe, will probably carry a somewhat higher interest rate.

Until the Euratom agreement the amount of private or governmental assistance for the atoms-for-peace program was exceedingly small. A major explanation would seem to be that whereas a host of special interest groups, private and public, were outspoken on the domestic necessities of reactor development in the United States, only a few saw a need for speaking with as much conviction about the desirability of U. S. readiness to meet its implied foreign commitments.[34]

Wider economic support of reactor development by the government has tended to reduce the disparity between foreign policy objectives and the means of achieving them. The elusive "export market," for example, was originally viewed primarily as a matter of customary commercial development, since the government could assure the nuclear fuel supply. This oversimplification broke down under the weight of foreign liability problems, the necessity of financing the purchase of fuel inventories and the dubious prospect of doing business abroad without conventional private patent protection. In each case the government has "intervened." The arrangements for governmental liability insurance and for inventory financing are examples. The AEC also has attempted to protect American industry in foreign markets by promptly filing AEC patents there and in 1961 made it possible for AEC contractors to secure substantive rights abroad under certain conditions.

The Political Level

Political motivation has doubtless been one of the prime sources of continuing controversy between the Joint Committee and the AEC on nuclear

34. One of the earliest was Henry DeWolf Smyth in *Foreign Affairs*, October 1956. The most consistent organized support of a strong foreign program in nuclear energy has come from a rather unexpected quarter, organized labor as represented by the AFL-CIO. (See discussion in Chapter 1.)

power development. Political considerations seemingly fall outside the realm of economic analysis, but selected aspects of them may throw light on how the reconciliation of domestic and foreign policies has begun to emerge.

The greatest pacifying agent in the political conflict over nuclear policies has been the almost universal fear among both conservatives and liberals that insufficient measures might jeopardize U. S. leadership in the race with the USSR. This fear underlies the seeming consensus among Joint Committee members that the administration should employ measures that do more than merely encourage private participation.

The political atmosphere in the Joint Committee partly explains the apparent ease with which successive steps were taken to fortify the lagging atoms-for-peace program and to bring the domestic program more in line with the needs of foreign policy. Far-reaching international cooperation in bilateral agreements, in Euratom and in the IAEA was accepted by the Joint Committee with little objection.[35] On the other hand, the Joint Committee majority opposed government subsidies for export reactors.[36]

As time passed it had also become politically unacceptable for the United States either to discard the atoms-for-peace program or to ignore the necessity of taking practical measures to achieve its essential purposes. In the end it appeared that the federal government would have to assume greater initiative in both the domestic and foreign programs. The crucial problem was to assure all concerned that in doing so it would not upset the existing sensitive balance between private and public power.

The major obstacle to harmonization of the somewhat divergent foreign and domestic programs was the theory of the Eisenhower administration that its atoms-for-business policy could be kept separate from its atoms-for-peace program and that it could bring nuclear power to competitive reality promptly enough to satisfy foreign objectives. Underlying this theory were the unfortunate assumptions that the technical problems of nuclear power could be surmounted without long and costly development effort and that

35. Note the comparatively mild objections expressed by Senator Dworshak to Euratom and to the International Atomic Energy Agency. More serious were Senator Hickenlooper's numerous misgivings concerning U. S. ratification of the IAEA charter. (See his list of forty-eight questions in the *Statute of the IAEA*, Hearings, Committee on Foreign Relations and Senate Members of the Joint Committee on Atomic Energy, 85th Cong., 1st Sess., 1957, pp. 55 ff.)

36. See, for example, Joint Committee Chairman Sterling Cole's proposal in 1957 that the U. S. provide construction subsidies for American demonstration reactors built abroad. Cole proposed that for developmental reactors built abroad the United States provide half the difference between the capital cost of a conventional plant and the nuclear power station. (See Atomic Industrial Forum, *Forum Memo*, April 1, 1957, p. 14.) Cole renewed his proposal in 1962 following his four-year term as Director General of the IAEA.

industry's ability to undertake reactor demonstration was not so limited that it would block the road to the nation's foreign policy objectives.

Six years after passage of the 1954 act most sectors of the industry, as well as government policy makers, had come to see that to accomplish competitive nuclear power at home or abroad and to achieve unpretentious foreign and domestic economic objectives required strong AEC initiative, large public investment and—as had long been urged by nuclear scientists—a long-term plan that covered both foreign and domestic reactor programs. The long-term plan was already at hand in 1961, but the strong AEC initiative and the public and private investment necessary to implement it were in doubt.

Although some coalescence of domestic and foreign policies had been achieved by the end of 1960, no consensus had been reached on the key issue— where should responsible initiative for power reactor demonstration properly rest: with the private utilities and equipment manufacturers or with the AEC? In 1961, to be sure, less reliance than formerly was being placed on private initiative to achieve reactor development commensurate with both domestic and foreign policy objectives. Nevertheless, as late as mid-1962 the AEC was still pursuing the economically vulnerable policy, established years earlier, that the scale and pace of power plant demonstration should be determined primarily by the investment decisions of the private utilities.

The always contentious question—how best to secure the prompt construction of full-scale demonstration plants—remains to be resolved by the Kennedy administration and the Joint Committee. It has become clear that for reasons of technology and economics full-scale plants must be built and operated in utility systems—both private and public—so that the managements of domestic and foreign utilities will have a sound basis for making future investment commitments.

Finally, the fundamental economic objective remains to be dealt with— the achievement of competitive nuclear power abroad as well as at home. Until current foreign cost thresholds can be crossed, nuclear power is likely to remain a dubious instrument of American foreign policy generally. However, since there are common long-term interests in reactor research and development between Euratom and the United States, a foundation already exists for achieving important foreign policy objectives.

CHAPTER **10**

Future Public Policy

The Kennedy administration in 1961 inherited a body of policies for nuclear power development whose original rationale in many respects lacked economic footings. Outstanding examples are the persistently false views on the imminence of competitive nuclear power in the United States, the exaggerated role of nuclear power in underdeveloped and "power-starved" areas of the world and the excessive weight given to assumed increasing costs of domestic energy resources. Development also was hindered by the AEC's price system, by doctrinaire misinterpretation of the ability of private utilities to undertake full-scale plant construction and by the early disposition to embroider the prospects for early appearance of a substantial, profitable export market. Political considerations—in both the private and public sector—exerted great force.

In a subordinate role thus far, political economy may well be expected to contribute more to future atomic policy formation here and abroad than it has done, although the "best" economic solutions may not be attainable. Even so, it need not follow that "democratic planning must inevitably be an economically irrational compromise of divergent political interests." But it does mean, as added by E. S. Mason, that "the economic calculus operates within a fairly severe set of limitations."[1] The Kennedy administration has the opportunity to apply the lessons of economics to several aspects of future nuclear energy policy such as assuring the growth of technology, enforcing

1. *Economic Planning in Underdeveloped Areas: Government and Business*, Millar Lectures, No. 12, Fordham University, New York, 1958, p. 66.

317

dynamic government price setting, unifying national energy policies and evaluating alternative investment opportunities.

Bearing in mind the limits of economic criteria, policy makers will also recognize that American nuclear policy formation is taking place in a world scene:[2]

> People everywhere see the abundance of a minority of mankind before their eyes, but for them affluency is a rather elusive mirage. . . . Advances in technology must be seen not only in our own domestic perspective but also in the perspective of the rapidly growing populations in many of the less developed countries.

The administration will need to find both political and economic solutions in keeping with the promise nuclear technology holds out for the long-term improvement of human welfare abroad as well as at home.

Expanding Technical Knowledge

During the industrial revolution in the seventeenth and eighteenth centuries, technology found its nurture in the emerging science of the period. Since then the proximity of technology to science has grown ever closer. In some instances the significance of the separation is often, mistakenly, ignored.[3] Atomic energy development has been perhaps the most extreme example of the permeation of technology by science, at least until the appearance of research on controlled thermonuclear reactions and space vehicles. Nevertheless, real distinctions remain between science and technology, and it has now become a fact of highly advanced industrial life that the stock of technical knowledge cannot be extended significantly without first extending the range and depth of fundamental scientific understanding. Technology, formerly the casual offspring of natural science, is seen now in nuclear energy and related fields as the insatiable and demanding taskmaster of science.

Against this background the economics of nuclear power policy not only illustrates universal principles but also reveals unique features, the most conspicuous of which are the growing need for "public risk capital," the

2. Gerhard Colm, "Economic Factors of Scientific Development," *The Scientific Revolution— Challenge and Promise*, Gerald W. Albers and Paul Duncan, editors, Public Affairs Press, Washington, 1959, p. 85.

3. One of the great economic advantages of science is that it, unlike technology, is not "tied to the inertia of existing industry." Henry DeWolf Smyth, "Basic Research and Atomic Energy," paper prepared for delivery before the Atomic Industrial Forums of the United States and Japan, Tokyo, May 13, 1957.

future role of the national atomic energy laboratories and the dilemmas confronting publicly sponsored research aimed specifically at achieving "economically competitive" results. A theory of the economics of publicly sponsored research and development, based in part on nuclear power experience, is overdue.

Publicly Sponsored Research and Development: Nuclear Energy

For good or ill, publicly financed reactor research has distinguishing economic characteristics:

Technical problems are large and complex and involve sustained effort by many disciplines and stable institutions, hence economies of scale have compelled a concentration of effort, at the AEC's national laboratories and to a lesser extent at the laboratories of the largest industrial corporations. Nuclear scientists like to describe this minimum scale as "critical mass."

The long period between initial investment and economic return may be decades (for example, breeder reactors), hence an exceedingly low rate of discount is implied by the relation of future benefits to present private and public expenditures.[4]

A variety of reactor concepts is being supported to avoid senseless gambling on early selection of the ultimate "best," hence wide duplication of research effort seems indispensable when the uncertainties of technical and economic feasibility are so great.

Almost profligate application of nonpecuniary incentives and public assistance seem necessary to sustain private research when tangible economic returns are as remote as in reactor research.

Perhaps the most revolutionary concept, and one that has never been critically examined, is that in nuclear power the federal government has tacitly assumed the necessity of—though not full administrative responsibility for—shepherding a new technology through to competitive commercial feasibility. This is apparently without precedent in U. S. industrial experience, though not unlike federal participation in agricultural experiment stations and in aircraft development, for example. It raises the possibility that future developments, such as achieving controlled thermonuclear power, shall be treated in the same way. It should also reopen the question of the deliberate

4. General Electric Co., for example, in reputedly sinking many millions into the Dresden project, in effect was applying a far lower rate of discount to future return from present outlays than is characteristic of its other commercial operations. In this sense, G. E. was acting more like a public agency, for which the discount rate might well approach 3 per cent or less annually, than a profit-seeking corporation with a high time preference.

abandonment of the shale-oil problem and the liquefaction and gasification of coal by the federal government.

In large areas of research and technology the federal government has become an entrepreneur and must judge the wisest investment course to pursue, moreover, on principles that may appear rather remote from neoclassical theories of alternative-opportunity cost and marginal productivity in the allocation of private resources. Allocation of public resources among large national research programs, such as nuclear energy and space exploration, places a heavy burden on the Bureau of the Budget, the executive branch and the Congress to judge the wisdom of public investment based on social costs and social gains and on the productivity of private investment. At this point the economist should not, against his instinct, withdraw and "turn the matter over to the political scientist and statesman," unless he is prepared to assume that resources have become as unlimited as space.

Finally, protection of the public interest in patentable inventions made through publicly financed research appears to be in conflict with customary industrial practice and expectations. A new institutional device in place of full private patent rights may be needed. Nuclear power experience, possibly to be repeated under the space exploration and thermonuclear energy programs, has raised the unavoidable issue, whether to protect the skills developed under government research contracts by providing a temporary advantage to particular companies in an industry already marked by a very high concentration of companies. Although the nuclear power case is inconclusive, may J. A. Schumpeter's notion of providing temporary restraints on competition as a way of fostering new technology have something to commend it?[5]

Research As Capital Formation

Investment in research and development, whether privately or publicly sponsored, may best be evaluated as capital formation. As such, research and development is not closely related to the short-run rate of profit nor to consumption; instead, it is closely related to secular growth of the market and to necessary technical advances in the methods of production. Furthermore, research and development, considered as capital, is peculiarly subject to the characteristic features of overhead costs, principally in that pertinent costs are not easily identified with units of product, that significant waste occurs

5. Cf. Richard Cosway, "Antitrust Provisions of the Atomic Energy Act," *Vanderbilt Law Review*, December 1958, pp. 181–82; and J. A. Schumpeter, *Capitalism, Socialism and Democracy*, 3d ed., Harper, New York, 1950, pp. 81–106.

when resources are not used to full capacity and that relatively constant costs are inherent.[6] In all these respects private and publicly financed research and development appear to be similar. Such differences as exist are in the main complementary. Perhaps the simplest example of a difference between private and public reactor research and development is that private research necessarily consists predominantly of applied, market-oriented development, whereas public research, in complementary fashion, stresses more basic inquiry.

Owing primarily to the uncertainty of results and the number of reactor concepts, the AEC assumes that the most effective way to find competitive nuclear power is to follow multiple routes. Yet, because each reactor route is exceedingly costly, careful culling out of the least promising soon becomes necessary. This is difficult, aside from the narrow question of entrenched company positions, because concepts that hold long-term promise, as do the fast breeder and homogeneous-fueled reactors, may prove unprofitable in the short run. These are the types of effort that direct AEC research should sustain, in contrast to the proved reactor concepts which private industry and the Euratom nations already appear prepared to develop, with some governmental assistance, to be sure. Thus, one can see that, like other forms of research and development, the economics of nuclear reactor research implies some of the vices of undisciplined freedom and competition—heavy duplication, rampant eclecticism and abhorrence of centralized direction or planning.[7]

The National Laboratories

The major repositories of scientific and technical knowledge of reactors are the national atomic energy laboratories, an imaginative contribution of the Manhattan Engineer District and one which should influence strongly the future stock of technical knowledge in nuclear power. Despite their great

6. The theory of overhead costs is central, of course, in the analysis of dynamic cost-price relationships, since unused capacity may well justify prices at less than average cost, but more than variable (or out-of-pocket) expenses. Competition between reactor equipment manufacturers has been similarly motivated: with their established technical and scientific staffs and existing plant investments both being used at less than capacity, companies are prone, in the initial stage, to bid less on the few available jobs than estimated total costs would dictate. Any return above direct costs is advantageous, permitting the company to hold its staff and to hope for later recoupment.

7. For a perceptive analysis of the application of private competitive principles to military research and development, see Charles J. Hitch, "Character of Research and Development in a Competitive Economy," *Proceedings of a Conference on Research and Development and Its Impact on the Economy*, National Science Foundation, Washington, 1958, pp. 129–139.

contribution, within the next few years these laboratories may be in danger of ceasing to exist as creative institutions generating new knowledge.

One view is that the laboratories should be considered merely a transitory phase of public atomic development, ultimately to become "surplus" and be sold, presumably to the company or institution now the operating contractor. In general, according to this view, there is no important long-term function for the laboratories as public institutions and, indeed, this view reveals some fear that the laboratories may possibly usurp the proper functions of industry. It tends to look upon contraction or liquidation of the laboratories as a desirable step away from government domination and the wartime heritage of state monopoly.

Another, more conservative, view is that long-term research objectives should be established soon, recognizing the laboratories as unique and valuable national resources deserving imaginative future employment as a matter of public policy. Until such objectives are fashioned, however, the laboratories may suffer accelerating attrition by losing their best personnel to industry and perhaps to education. The Kennedy administration faces this issue now, recognizing that nuclear reactor technology may not remain indefinitely the major function of any of the laboratories and, further, that the basic research going on in the laboratories may become less directly related to atomic energy.

The economic ground rules for guiding such publicly financed efforts are easy to state in generalized terms. In order to complement the development work of industry, the laboratories should emphasize scientific research, though not to the exclusion of engineering development. In order to complement the basic research of educational and nonprofit institutions, the laboratories should emphasize the scientific research that is contiguous to or required by the practical applications being explored. Depending as they do on federal support, the laboratories should especially emphasize the long-term goals of research and development, because neither industry nor educational institutions have sufficient resources to pursue such ends.

The growing demands technology is placing on basic research thus call for a wiser public policy than contraction or liquidation of the AEC laboratories. Broad as the possibilities are, reasonable limits on their future use and disposition do exist. These installations are exceedingly large, as noted in Chapter 4, and possibly beyond the capacity of even the largest corporations or universities to own and operate without heavy public subsidy. Each of the laboratories is unique, having a different emphasis and being staffed with men of differing technical talents and motivation. Further, the scientists and technicians are the main values of the laboratories, rather than the buildings and equipment, and many of the personnel may not wish to be transferred with the plant.

Putting aside the obvious, but probably undesirable, possibility of giving (or selling) the installation to the present operating contractor, one is free to explore other avenues. One or more of the national atomic laboratories (perhaps Argonne) might well be operated by the AEC with emphasis on long-term civilian nuclear and thermonuclear power purposes, in much the same fashion as National Aeronautics and Space Administration installations are operated in the field of aeronautics. For certain others the National Science Foundation might be considered in time a more logical point than the AEC for long-term laboratory administration. This might provide better coordination of public assistance to complementary research programs and provide leverage in bringing about a better balance between basic and applied research in all fields. At this stage, however, the NSF lacks sufficient operating experience for such large-scale research. It has been suggested that certain AEC laboratories could be transferred to the Department of Defense to engage in the widest application of reactor technology to defense problems. Now that atomic energy and nuclear weapons have permeated all parts of the armed forces, it may be time to reexamine some of the old clichés. One is the current appropriateness of the alleged reluctance of atomic scientists to work for the Department of Defense.[8] Finally, the director of the Oak Ridge National Laboratory has suggested that the mission of the national laboratories might be widened to include research on such national problems as water desalinization.

None of the above ideas represents a solution of the laboratory problem and the national laboratories may continue to be considered a threat to research and development by private industry. When the MED established the laboratories, it was expected that they would become, among other things, an additional incentive for the operating contractors—corporate and educational—to maintain strong participation in atomic energy development after the weapon aspects had decreased in importance. More recently the "competitive" role of the AEC laboratories has been called into question, not by the major operating contractors themselves but by others not so fortunately associated. The fears of "government competition with business" have been heightened, in part, by the failure of commercial business to grow as had been expected in 1954 and by the fact that the "stock of knowledge" in the labora-

8. Transfer of the Bettis Laboratory, where naval vessel propulsion has been pursued so successfully, might be considered. Transfer of this facility to the Navy could provide an effective center for all types of nuclear ship development, not to mention strategic and tactical study, as the U. S. Navy becomes almost exclusively nuclear-propelled.

tories is being accumulated through large, continuing government appropriations.[9]

The United States Chamber of Commerce, the National Association of Manufacturers and the Manufacturing Chemists Association in 1960 protested that the AEC was giving to its laboratories research and development work that could and should be done by private industry. The AEC, however, reiterated its general policy that the government laboratories would continue to do preliminary research and pursue development projects until technical feasibility had been demonstrated and then they would rely on private laboratories to undertake development that might lead to economic feasibility.[10]

Again, as in many other instances, the sharp distinction made between the private and public sector is unrealistic, for with one minor exception the AEC laboratories are operated by private contractors from industry or education, not the government. Furthermore, in certain instances both industry and government have found the AEC an instrument of private and public necessity. For example, in technically evaluating the competitive bids of American reactor manufacturers submitted to the International Bank for Reconstruction and Development and the Italian government for the SENN project, the AEC quite properly arranged with the principal reactor research center, the Argonne National Laboratory (for which the University of Chicago is the contractor), rather than with a private group or company, to perform the sensitive task of technical review. Similarly, as might be expected, the AEC has long operated its own facility for assaying uranium ore samples. These illustrate, of course, only the minimum necessary functions of AEC facilities and leave a vast area of work where either private or government-owned facilities might be used.

Thus, the "laboratory problem" is symptomatic of government-industry relations generally in atomic energy development. Moreover, on the accom-

---

9. For thoughtful discussion of the laboratory problem see, among others, the following: Dr. Chauncey Starr, Vice President, North American Aviation, Inc., "Business Survival in the Atomic Power Business," address before the Atomic Industrial Forum, Washington, November 2, 1959; Dr. Warren C. Johnson, Chairman, AEC General Advisory Committee, address before the American Nuclear Society, Washington, November 6, 1959; AEC, *The Future Role of the Atomic Energy Commission Laboratories* (a report to the Joint Committee on Atomic Energy), Washington, January 1960; *Report to the President on Government Contracting for Research and Development*, prepared by an interdepartmental committee under the auspices of the Bureau of the Budget, Washington, April 30, 1962; and, much earlier, the report of the McKinney Panel, Vol. 2, Chap. 12.

10. "Commission Communication on Commercial-Industrial Activities of the Government Providing Products or Services for Governmental Use," AEC, *Major Activities in the Atomic Energy Programs, January-December 1960* (Annual Report), Washington, January 1961, Appendix 18, pp. 472 ff.

modation of the two sectors may depend the success or failure of technology sponsored by public means. The danger that this rate of progress may prove less than that required to keep pace with the Soviet Union has been recognized as a challenge for the AEC and industry.[11] Considering, too, the comparatively limited resources of private industrial laboratories, the AEC and the Joint Committee may be slow to accept the notion that the development

Figure 10-1   AEC Laboratory Costs for Reactor Development, Fiscal Year 1961

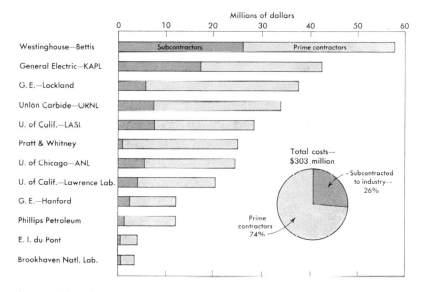

Source: AEC Authorizing Legislation, Fiscal Year 1963, Hearings, Subcommittee on Legislation, Joint Committee on Atomic Energy, 87th Cong., 2nd Sess., 1962, p. 511.

programs of the laboratories should be curtailed to strengthen industry. "To preserve a balance between freedom and authority," the United States, through the AEC in this case, has been "moving in the direction of operating patterns which may accomplish central policy without destroying corporate or academic independence."[12]

11. See the remarks of AEC Chairman McCone, on his return from an inspection of USSR facilities for nuclear and thermonuclear power development, before the Atomic Industrial Forum, Washington, November 1959.

12. Don K. Price, "Organization of Science Here and Abroad," *Science*, March 20, 1959, p. 764.

Public "Venture" Capital

One of the main economic obstacles to reactor development today is the excessive capital cost of prototype and full-scale units. By comparison, the direct costs of research and development for a specific plant are not large and, except for the most futuristic reactor types, the sources of technology are at hand in both AEC and industrial laboratories.

The shortage of large risk capital for reactor development perhaps raises a question whether the public may now have to supply venture capital for large projects having a far higher degree of uncertainty and foreseeable operating losses than private interests can normally bear. The market puts a premium on short-term, rapid pay-off advances. Would the growth of the industrial system be strengthened by a mixed private-federal finance corporation, for example, to provide industry a source of venture capital at low public rates of interest for advanced technical development?

Low-interest capital from such a source might not be a sufficient inducement for a large-scale nuclear demonstration plant, but together with other existing incentives it should prove useful. Also, valuable time between development and full-scale commercial application might be saved. Joint private and public development of nuclear power probably is only the first of an expanding number of governmentally sponsored technical advances requiring large capital investments well before their competitive or economic applications are feasible.

If nuclear power development provides proof that a new source of energy can be introduced into the economy without leading to the weakening of either public or private power, then one would have reason to hope that the same might be true of controlled thermonuclear energy. Much may depend on modification of present doctrinaire views held by both private and public power. An economic solution is not at hand, but a source of public-private venture capital, as well as greater public impatience with the obstacles to necessary demonstration projects introduced by the controversy, might prove salutary.

Toward A Dynamic Price Policy

As suggested earlier, particularly in Chapter 5, the AEC's pricing practices during the Eisenhower administration were at cross purposes. The AEC, pulled by conflicting demands, had to play multiple economic roles, hence the agency's pricing practices reveal internal tension and inconsistency. By objective economic standards the low use charge on U235—at first 4 per cent, then 4.75 per cent—is akin to providing capital at little more than government interest rates. It cannot be considered either a reasonable rental charge or a price commensurate with the cost of working capital of private utilities. The low use charge provides a subsidy. Its historical rationale has probably been lost to public evaluation.[13]

On the other hand, the prices of enriched uranium established in 1954 were made unrealistic by declining costs of natural uranium and of plant operation. The price schedule apparently yielded a "profit" to the government. The overdue reductions of prices in mid-1961 and in mid-1962 partially rectified this, but a policy issue remains. Similarly, in its plutonium "buy-back" prices, the AEC struggled to harmonize conflicting economic and political objectives: the avoidance of subsidy, while giving appropriate weight to the weapon value of plutonium. The lesson seems clear. The Congress was unable at the outset of development to legislate an economically sensible price policy for government-furnished materials and services, and the AEC on its part administered the pricing provisions of the act in a manner that rigidly adhered to the principle of recovering "full costs," which led to inflated prices of U235.

Enriched Uranium for Civilian Purposes

The keystone of the present AEC price system is the schedule of prices for depleted and enriched uranium. Today this schedule is, as shown in Chapter 5, more closely related to real costs than it was before 1961. The schedule, as revised in 1961, reestablished continuity and comparability between the prices of natural and very slightly enriched uranium, and it removed the distortion which the original price schedule exerted on the comparative position of both natural and enriched uranium reactors. The second reduction in price, 1962, was justified because the costs of gaseous diffusion separation had evidently declined appreciably. But the definition of pertinent costs still remains an issue.

13. One possible, undocumented explanation, rendered plausible only by discussions with former AEC staff, is as follows: if a use charge of 6 per cent or more had been established, this would have penalized power systems which can secure capital at lower rates. On the other hand, establishing as low a charge as 2 per cent, the REA statutory rate, would have meant a heavy subsidy to private operators of nuclear reactors. The original 4 per cent figure, which was about the current rate on U. S. Government borrowing, was selected as a convenient middle ground. Later the low rate was rationalized by the belief that both U235 and Pu have some intrinsic value, akin to the gold or silver in Treasury vaults. Though interesting, this notion was economic nonsense.

First of all, the administration needs to determine the national security significance of the cost experience. If in the judgment of the AEC and its advisers the security classification of the data needs to be retained, this would be no bar to careful reevaluation by cleared experts, the Comptroller General and the Joint Committee. This would, however, prevent public review of prices and would continue a curious anomaly: power reactor technology would be "open," but the economics of nuclear power would continue to be publicly "unknowable." In any case, the public interest would have inherent safeguards against injudicious pricing, in the surveillance of the Comptroller General and the Joint Committee.[14]

Since it is feasible, though a bit awkward, to meet the security problem by classified review of the pricing basis, the central issues of pricing then become those of economic policy—what criteria should be used in setting "fair" prices? The pertinent considerations would seem to be the response of prices to changes in underlying costs, the economies of scale and progressive plant improvements, treatment of so-called "external economies," depreciation of plant, marginal versus average cost definitions and AEC overhead. Highly important are the price implications of a large reduction in the fraction of plant capacity devoted to producing weapon-grade material.[15]

It should be expected that prices would change in time to maintain general consonance with current costs. The price schedules up to July 1, 1961, had been frozen for more than six years; apparently price stability was considered up to that time more important than consonance with changing costs. Future price adjustments, to be sure, should not be a monthly occurrence, but they should occur often enough to indicate a valid cost-price relation. If the cost-price relation departs greatly from fact, then needless economic pressures may arise and will tend to distort the choice of reactor types and fuel systems.

The economies of scale, together with steady improvements in plant operation and extremely low power costs, are perhaps the major reasons for expecting that U. S. costs for enriched uranium will remain lower than corresponding costs in the United Kingdom or elsewhere in Western Europe. Yet, it

14. The Comptroller General, of course, would be on guard against prices being below cost and the Joint Committee would be sensitive to prices so low as to amount to a subsidy. But both of these leave open the question, explored in Chapter 5, whether prices may be higher than properly defined and assignable costs warrant.

15. If the plants have not yet been fully depreciated, question arises whether the investment in war-built plant should be "written off," then, as a "cost of the war." In this sense the war is not "over," for all but a fraction of present gaseous diffusion capacity was built after World War II; moreover, its useful life for peace or war is far from coming to an end.

might be argued that economies of scale should not be reflected in lower prices, since they are now dependent on volume production for military, not civilian, purposes. Actually, the gaseous diffusion plants may be expected to continue for some years to produce both military- and civilian-grade material in complementary fashion, though presumably an increasing proportion will consist of civilian fuel. Even if the civilian output should remain comparatively small for several years, the economies of scale should redound as much to the benefit of civilian material as to military.[16]

Perhaps the most intriguing question of price theory in this case is whether the civilian price schedule should be based on average or marginal (incremental) costs of product (not marginal costs in the sense of less-than-capacity operation of a single plant, but rather as based on a supply curve, the shape of which is defined by the points representing differing costs for each of several gaseous diffusion plants). Marginal costs are significant with respect to the different sources and prices of natural uranium fed into the cascades and with respect to the lesser plant cost, but presumably lower efficiency, of the older plants (and the reverse for the newer). Thus, one might well hold that the civilian product should be required neither to bear the high marginal costs of uranium, which are a consequence of military requirements, nor on the other hand the higher costs of certain gaseous diffusion plants built to meet augmented military needs. One consequence of this theory is that progressive relative increases in civilian prices might have to be made through the years as the fraction of total plant capacity devoted to military requirements decreases.[17]

Aside from the historic divergence of cost trends and product prices, the fixed costs of depreciation and of AEC overhead need to be examined critically. Both charges are matters of administrative discretion and may be only partly derived from strict economic considerations. Depreciation rates should be based on estimated useful plant life, which may, as indicated above, be very long. Whether computed on a straight-line or sinking-fund basis, the resulting rate should be rather low, clearly no more than the standard 4 per cent implied by the AEC's financial reports and far less than the 10 per cent

---

16. There is, of course, good prospect that civilian requirements will rise to a predominant fraction of total enrichment capacity during the next twenty years. One way of assuring wide use of enriched uranium in civilian reactors is to price it on a basis that presupposes full utilization of plant when establishing overhead costs.

17. The question of marginal-cost pricing involves a subordinate issue: whether the plants are assumed to be operated at their optimum relation to the cost of natural uranium feed and of power. There is no obvious answer to this problem, since the basic data are classified. Speculation is hardly fruitful, beyond merely flagging an issue of cost-price determination.

imputed by informed specialists on gaseous diffusion plants.[18] Similarly, the allowance for AEC overhead should be small, considering the fully recorded relation between AEC administrative costs and program costs; no economic justification would be evident were AEC to apply to cascade costs the extraordinarily high 15 per cent rate used in establishing its service charge for chemical processing of irradiated fuel elements.[19]

Price Implications of Private Ownership of Nuclear Fuel

The AEC has long recognized that requiring private ownership of nuclear fuel would end two administrative problems—the responsibility for purchasing by-product plutonium and for setting the fuel-use charge. The private ownership issue, examined critically in 1962, has presented a dilemma for the private utilities, namely, whether to seek the institutionally desirable goal of private ownership, with its attendant costs, or to retain the economic benefits of the low use charge and the resultant lower generating costs. Temporizing, the industry has suggested that private ownership of nuclear fuel is desirable ultimately, but that it is premature at the present stage of nuclear development and will require a transition phase of possibly several years.[20]

Because nuclear fuel may in time become privately owned, the AEC will need to ask whether the pricing of enriched uranium should be influenced by this possibility. Various degrees or transitional stages of private ownership may be distinguished. Plutonium and U233, for example, might well become the first candidates for private ownership, since these are already produced in private plants, subject of course to strict public control for reasons of security and safety. Moreover, the quantities to be produced will be small for at least a few years. Additionally, private ownership of plutonium and U233, properly controlled for possible loss or diversion, can now scarcely be considered the national security problem it was when the 1954 act was debated and passed. The feared political consequences of permitting private ownership of weapons materials are now an anachronism.

If plutonium and U233 were to be privately owned, what pricing implications for enriched uranium might this have? None directly, for enriched

18. Karl Cohen, "Charting a Course for Nuclear Power Development," *Nucleonics*, January 1958, pp. 66–70.

19. AEC, "A Conceptual Design of a Chemical Processing Facility," Washington, February 1957.

20. Section 202 Hearings, 1962, pp. 95 ff., 509–12. Before the AEC reduced the price of U235 again in 1962, some observers believed that a further price reduction might well be accompanied by a material increase in the fuel-use charge, in preparation for the economic conditions of private ownership. (*Ibid.*, pp. 560–62.)

uranium would still be priced primarily on the basis of costs—natural uranium plus gaseous diffusion processing.[21] A more basic question is what influence the AEC-established prices of enriched uranium might have on the prices of plutonium and U233, since all three fissionable materials are expected to be energy substitutes for each other in the long run. The price of enriched uranium will set a ceiling on the fuel value of the others, as long as AEC can guarantee future supply. Were the AEC prepared to continue buying by-product plutonium and U233, even though privately owned, the alternative price of U235 would operate in the same fashion as a ceiling. The policy question whether AEC should provide a market for by-product plutonium and U233 need not be examined here beyond suggesting again that compared to U235 both fuels should have only marginal weapon value in a short time, and that such government procurement should be considered on the economic merits, which appear dubious.

Possible private ownership of enriched uranium raises somewhat more difficult questions of AEC pricing. To be sure, once plutonium and U233 have passed over, there would seem to be little justification for not treating enriched uranium in the same fashion. Accountability and controls would provide the same protection of the national security. If enriched uranium produced by the government were available for sale, then the central question would still be the economic validity of established prices. If these were to be set by the AEC on the basis of its assigned production costs, private ownership of the three fuels should make no difference in pricing. As long as the gaseous diffusion plants are owned by the federal government, the cost basis is a reasonable point of departure for pricing, provided that marginal costs of producing the civilian product are considered.

The next step, then, is to consider whether possible transfer of the present gaseous diffusion capacity to private or other hands,[22] possibly within a decade, might alter the present or foreseeable price structure. At the outset it is to be emphasized that as long as the civilian product remains only a small fraction of the total output of enriched uranium, little, if any, justification is evident for private ownership of such a military facility. Thus, private ownership of gaseous diffusion capacity presupposes a well-established nuclear

21. Indirectly, however, the ownership of plutonium and U233 might result in changing their prices, that is, if particular reactor designs or exposure levels were favored by relative prices of the three fuels.

22. The gaseous diffusion plants represent a huge capital investment, but they are to a degree divisible, thus encouraging the prospect that at least three operators (the present number of installations and contractors) could be accommodated. All three need not be private enterprises; conceivably, one of the installations might well be operated for the government by the AEC or the TVA. Moreover, multifirm leases might be considered.

power market, with expanding demands on enrichment capacity. The transition to this state of nuclear affairs, possibly in the 1970s, would probably require that the AEC maintain price control differing little from that it will be exercising directly for some years. Again, one may reason that the cost basis of pricing should remain the most reasonable economic criterion under both "government ownership in transition" and possible private ownership later. In fact, government regulation of prices would probably have to be retained indefinitely—as long as only a few producers of enriched uranium were involved. "Toll enrichment" of private uranium might be desirable.

Reasonableness of U235 Prices in the World View

For the present the United States is the only possible large-scale exporter of enriched uranium in the free world, hence the price of enriched uranium compared with natural uranium is important to foreign reactor operators. If the relative price of natural uranium declines further, the operator who has avoided dependence on the United States for enriched fuel will feel justified. Contrariwise, if enriched uranium is reduced again in relative price, the technical disadvantages of natural uranium may become more acute—as occurred when the AEC reduced enriched uranium prices twice within a year. The combined reduction of enriched uranium prices may well have had a potent effect upon the choice of enriched or natural uranium reactors, upon the future export market for U. S. reactors and perhaps, too, upon whether France or other countries build enrichment plants.

Friendly foreign countries show a wide variety of belief and disbelief in the reasonableness of U. S. prices and hence of confidence in their future stability. The British, for example, have generally held the view that AEC prices fail to cover costs and hence represent a subsidy, one presumably aimed at offsetting the apparent advantages of low-cost natural uranium fuel. Time has provided no encouragement for this view and, as indicated earlier, the prospects are for still lower rather than higher prices. In continental Europe and in Japan the main concern has been that prices be established on a firm economic basis that can assure stability over a long period of years. Reactor operators in these countries need to be assured that prices do not contain a hidden, and perhaps transient, subsidy and that they conform closely to production costs that would obtain were the plants to be operated predominantly for civilian purposes.

The views of neutral countries, many of which are pursuing the natural uranium route, suggest that the price of enriched uranium that might be secured from the United States is only an incidental consideration in their politically motivated decisions. But the strong desire for self-sufficiency and the use of indigenous nuclear fuel is effective only within limits, and such a policy will be strained if technical superiority and smaller capital requirements are demonstrated by enriched uranium reactors. Furthermore, because uranium can be enriched by the gas centrifuge process, which probably requires less capital than the gaseous diffusion process, foreign countries may now have less to fear from dependence on the United States as a supplier of enriched uranium.

Because the U. S. capacity in enriched uranium is perhaps several times that of the Soviet Union, the U. S. revised prices for enriched uranium may have been no surprise to Soviet atomic energy officials. But to comment on the attitude of the Soviet Union toward the world price of enriched uranium, set by the United States, would be sheer speculation. The AEC doubtless recognizes that a rigorously calculated U. S. price should strengthen the free world in its long-term competition with the communist bloc.

Toward an "Open" Economics of Nuclear Power

The public has been led to believe that nuclear power development and the economics of civilian nuclear power are "open" to public evaluation. They are not—yet. The validity of enriched uranium prices cannot be demonstrated because pertinent production cost data are classified. Moreover, since virtually two thirds of the fuel costs of a nuclear power plant depend on prices or charges administered by the AEC, the costs of generation will remain indeterminate for a considerable period.

In a strict sense the "economics" of nuclear power is today unknowable. Fortunately, however, private development of atomic energy and secrecy in civilian reactor technology are inherently incompatible. How long the residual restraints may be permitted by the AEC to stand in the way of "open" economics is unanswerable without first considering the national security significance of revealing U235 production rates. This rate has already been estimated, with apparent confidence, by a U. S. authority on gaseous diffusion technology (see page 125). Sound development of a private nuclear power industry with an effective price system would appear to be blocked by national security requirements. However, considering the number and varying ages of gaseous diffusion plants, it would seem that "standard" historical costs of production could be revealed without jeopardizing the secrecy of current production rates.

Serious technical issues in openly establishing AEC price schedules might arise, even though cost data were no longer classified. For example, military requirements for highly enriched material probably cannot continue long to command virtually all the output of the gaseous diffusion plants. Thus, the AEC needs to have reasonably good projections of military and civilian requirements over the next five to ten years. With such projections and using the cost accounts and the theory of cascade operation, it should be possible for the AEC to construct imputed costs for civilian product that are more in line with improved efficiency, adjusted depreciation rates, lower natural uranium prices, and with operation of the cascades more for slightly enriched fuel than for highly enriched, weapon-grade material.

Unifying Energy Policies

The presumed imminence of depletion of U. S. energy reserves has been a common misconception affecting formation of nuclear energy policies. Well-established reserve data indicate that real costs of conventional fuels are unlikely to rise enough for a few decades to threaten the present generally low level of energy costs enjoyed by most parts of the United States. Depletion of conventional fuel resources represents a false justification of accelerated government-sponsored nuclear energy development. Although real costs of producing conventional fuels hold the prospect of only moderate future increase, the existing public policies are such as to suggest that real prices may rise significantly—unless these policies are rectified. Thus, nuclear energy development is "needed" not on grounds of energy resource depletion but, among other reasons, as an additional factor to help constrain price increases induced by faulty U. S. energy policies generally (Chapters 3 and 5).

While conventional energy reserves are an insufficient basis for evaluating the adequacy of nuclear energy development programs, these programs have a long-term bearing on the nation's general energy policies.

Pertinence of Nuclear Energy

United States policy for oil, centering on import quotas, has resulted primarily from protection of domestic producers and exaggerated national security considerations, loosely defined. The policy for natural gas centers on the question whether the government should attempt to restrain natural gas prices from rising toward parity with alternative fuels. What economic significance may the emergence of competitive nuclear energy have for these energy policies and the circumstances shaping them?

Nuclear power may be expected to compete at first with coal-fired plants some distance from coal fields, and very much later, if at all, with gas-fired thermal plants. To the extent that nuclear power succeeds in becoming competitive with natural gas, it may provide a more effective ceiling on the steady upward drift in gas prices than is likely to be provided by domestic oil. But to have this much effect, generating costs of nuclear power would have to be in the range of 5 mills per KWH or lower, which appears unlikely during the next decade, and possibly longer. Presumably, then, for some years the present national policy of price control for natural gas will need to be considered independent of the prospects of competition from nuclear power.

Nuclear energy can reasonably be expected to have wider implications for the national policy of restricting crude oil imports than for natural gas prices. Within the next several years nuclear energy is almost certain to be used in nearly all large naval vessels. This will greatly reduce the strategic importance of crude oil supplies within the borders of the United States, further undermining the dubious theory of a possible oil squeeze in any conceivable general war. Other than through its use for ship propulsion, however, nuclear energy may for a time have only marginal implications for the consumption of petroleum products. Oil, it will be recalled, is not an important source of fuel for steam electric power generation, except in the New England and Pacific states. On the other hand, if nuclear energy ultimately proves able to compete in the field of high-temperature industrial process heat, then it will come into direct competition with oil, notably in metallurgical industries. More immediately, however—during the next several years—the advent of nuclear ship propulsion suggests a reexamination of the restriction of oil imports on the rationalization of conserving domestic reserves for national security reasons. The issue should be approached directly in the classical terms of protection of high-cost domestic industry.

It must be noted that protecting domestic petroleum production, by quota or tariff, will have the effect of raising (or sustaining) prices at home and may have continuing derivative foreign effects, particularly in Western Europe. The worldwide geographic price pattern for crude oil, loose though it appears from time to time, suggests that the marginal, high-cost production of crude oil in the United States may not be wholly independent of delivered prices in Western Europe. The price-sustaining influence of marginal cost U. S. oil may be reinforced by continued efforts within Western Europe[23] to achieve greater self-sufficiency in crude oil, at higher cost, to be sure, than equivalent imports. For the next few years the terms on which Western Europe secures crude oil are likely to be influenced more by increasing North African oil production (and perhaps by U. S. quota policies) than by the prospective introduction of nuclear power.

Oil Policies, Nuclear Energy and National Security

The threat to U. S. security in connection with petroleum lies in the danger that political pressure or outright denial of access to Middle East oil might so throttle Western Europe as to lead to war. Avoiding war in the Middle East, with its incalculable implications, requires the expeditious development of other petroleum sources—in Iran, the Sahara, Indonesia, as well as in the Western Hemisphere—some of which might remain open in case of trouble in the Middle East. The national security of the United States may depend upon, among other things, maintaining markets for imported petroleum from alternative sources other than domestic.

From a realistic point of view, then, the route to national security lies in the capacity of Western nations to retain a bargaining position that is sufficiently flexible to avoid a repetition of anything like the Suez crisis of 1956. The terms on which Middle East petroleum may be secured might be improved, and the danger of war lessened, if such heavy dependence on this source continues to be reduced. Development of nuclear energy is only one of the more important long-term means that might be taken to achieve this. Other means of strengthening the Western position might include construction of excess (or stand-by) shipping capacity and stockpiling of oil in Western Europe, though the need for these measures has diminished with the opening of the North African fields.

A policy aimed at stimulating alternative sources seems likely to be disquieting to American oil companies producing either in the Middle East or in domestic fields. Yet, such a policy is necessary, both to avoid the extremes of

---

23. One energy specialist, Sam H. Schurr, has suggested a contrary interpretation: namely, that by limiting its markets to oil imports the United States has thereby intensified the oversupply elsewhere and hence has lowered the price at which Western European countries would otherwise be able to purchase petroleum. ("Foreign Trade Policies Affecting Mineral Fuels in the United States and Western Europe," American Association for the Advancement of Science, 127th Meeting, New York, December 30, 1960.) This interpretation gives insufficient weight to the much lower costs of production in the Eastern Hemisphere, to the existing surplus production capacity, further added to by the North African fields, and to the international price pattern that is sustained by the major producers in the Eastern and Western Hemispheres.

having to expand excess marginal cost production of oil at home and to protect our interests in Middle East oil "with all the power at our command."[24]

Conservation of Nuclear Resources

Early emergence of conservation theories in nuclear energy development reveals a unique facet of the maturing American attitude toward conservation of natural resources generally. The first need—and plea—for conservation of other materials arose when unmistakable evidence of great waste of natural resources appeared in the early part of the twentieth century. Consideration has been given to conservation of nuclear source materials, however, at the very outset of development of nuclear energy. It has been prompted not by any obvious waste of natural resources in a national sense but rather by the technical possibilities inherent in the breeding concept and the prospect for extending the useful life of available source materials.

How important, economically, may it be to "conserve" the future energy values of nuclear source materials by rapidly developing breeding technology that would permit better use of fertile materials? The position taken by many reactor specialists who are not engaged in breeder reactor development is that converter reactors are available now and that successively more efficient converters may in time be expected to approach closely the status of true breeders. Such high-conversion-rate reactors may well be lower cost power producers than true breeders. On the other hand, proponents of breeding fear that failure to emphasize breeding technology in the immediate future will be courting trouble, because nuclear power ultimately will compel the use of not only U235 but also plutonium and U233 produced from fertile materials. This group believes that the long-term potentialities of breeders are so great that their development must be maintained to determine whether they are possible or are impractical and should be dropped in favor of other types.[25]

This mild technical controversy appears to be little more than a by-product of the recurrent question of relative budgetary emphasis—between, for example, converters, breeders and controlled thermonuclear energy. Viewed in economic terms, the necessity of giving greater relative support to breeder technology than in the past is hardly self-evident, for the primary advantage of the breeder reactor rests on its efficient use of raw material, not on its

24. Walter Levy, "Issues in International Oil Policy," *Foreign Affairs*, April 1957, p. 469. For a later view on petroleum policies see "World Oil in Transition," *The Economist*, August 19, 1961, pp. 723 ff.

25. See, for example, A. M. Weinberg, "Some Thoughts on Reactors: Geneva, 1958," *Bulletin of Atomic Scientists*, March 1959, pp. 132–37.

presumed cost of generating power. This is obviously a long-term benefit, when viewed against the current large annual output of natural uranium and the small nuclear power requirements that are likely to appear for more than a decade. Moreover, the potential economic superiority of breeders may decrease as enriched uranium reactors move toward progressively higher degrees of burn-up, and also toward higher conversion of fertile material. Thus, neither the case for conservation of nuclear resources nor for much heavier support of breeder reactor technology can be wholeheartedly accepted on domestic economic grounds. Nevertheless, it may be important for foreign policy reasons, discussed in Chapter 8, that thermal breeders using thorium and fast breeders using plutonium be developed to economic feasibility, so that countries with limited resources can employ their nuclear materials prudently. This case for developing breeder technology appears more significant and timely than the remote conservation argument.

This is not all. Generally unknown to the public, but of great economic potentiality for the future, is the fact that the United States has been accumulating for nearly two decades large tonnages of depleted uranium tailings through operation of the AEC's production reactors and gaseous diffusion cascades. This fertile material represents the potential energy equivalent of hundreds of millions of tons of coal, provided it can be employed usefully someday for conversion into plutonium fuel. These stores of U238 are conserved, awaiting the time when they can be economically used.

Federal Power Agencies and Nuclear Power Development

If the controversy surrounding construction of federal nuclear power plants had not become aggravated, the major federal power agencies—the Tennessee Valley Authority and the Bonneville Power Administration—would probably now be participating vigorously in the demonstration of nuclear power. They are not today, although the TVA has been selected by the AEC to operate the prototype gas-cooled reactor being built near the Oak Ridge National Laboratory in the Tennessee Valley.[26] These agencies possess a combination of economic conditions that would seem to justify their contributing more to nuclear power development than in the past. Owing to the exceedingly great power loads in these integrated systems, they could readily assimilate the largest power reactor stations (over 1,000 megawatts) which yield the most

26. The Bonneville Power Administration analyzed the economic feasibility of a proposal by the Washington Public Power Supply System to build facilities for generating electricity from the steam of the New Production Reactor that would otherwise be dumped. After considerable controversy the proposal was authorized by the Congress in 1962.

significant economies of scale. The public rates of financing are attractive for capital-intensive plants. Bonneville, particularly, raises the intriguing possibility of improving the economics of a hydro system by balancing variable water supply with steam-generating plants. Finally, both agencies have long been firm power suppliers to AEC installations in their service areas. Yet, more than ten years after the first experimental generation of electricity by nuclear energy and five years after the generation of nuclear power by a private utility, no federal power agency is prepared to plan an investment in nuclear power capacity.

The issue, one that has scarcely received serious public consideration, is whether the federal power agencies should continue to pursue such a passive role in nuclear power development or whether they should explore its possibilities actively through substantial investment in demonstration reactor projects.

That none of the federal power agencies took the initiative early in the program is understandable on both economic and political grounds. Public power advocates, on the one hand, did not press the issue. Perhaps they realized that to do so might jeopardize progress toward more urgent matters, such as finding an acceptable formula, which it now has, for the TVA to secure funds for expanding its steam-generating capacity. Yet, atomic energy participation by federal power agencies has been considered desirable over the long term to assure an additional degree of competition.[27] At the same time the private utilities have manifested their fear of any step toward an "atomic TVA" or federal nuclear power program. The Eisenhower administration consistently opposed government-owned plants except as a last resort, and the cooperative projects with private utilities preempted any substantial reactor development by federal power agencies. Finally, raising the question of authorizing legislation required for construction of such facilities would undoubtedly have led to an interminable legislative battle involving the protagonists of nuclear energy as well as of federal public power. Both sides have therefore accepted, perhaps with relief, the tacit understanding that this issue is still too thorny to permit early constructive debate and resolution.

Putting aside the question of political feasibility, may there be an objective, economic case now for the Kennedy administration's encouraging early participation in reactor development by federal power agencies? The burden of the argument should rest, of course, on those who hold that the federal power

27. See line of questioning and comments by Representative Bolling, Joint Economic Committee, Hearings, Subcommittee on Fiscal Policy, *Federal Expenditure Policy for Economic Growth and Stability*, 85th Cong., 1st Sess., Nov. 18–27, 1957, pp. 451 ff.

agencies should stay strictly out of nuclear power, since there is nothing in law or public policy to prevent their taking more active part. The relevant economic considerations would seem to be the degree of urgency for an alternative energy source and the prospective cost of conventional fuels, the unique features of the federal power agency's operations that might prompt special consideration of nuclear power and the possible benefits the nation's reactor development program might secure from such participation.

Conventional energy costs at both TVA and Bonneville, for example, are among the lowest in the nation and these explain, indeed, the wartime decision to locate power-intensive AEC facilities in these areas. Moreover, in the TVA area reserves of low-cost coal are adequate for many decades of future growth without encountering appreciably higher cost. The Bonneville system has no low-cost fuel resources but the Federal Power Commission estimates that the remaining hydro potential in the Columbia River Basin is ample for a couple of decades of further growth.[28]

Special considerations prompting early addition of nuclear power plants seem to prevail at Bonneville. It is probable that at Bonneville, as suggested by FPC and BPA studies, the dual-purpose nuclear power reactor (New Production Reactor) built at Hanford will be economically justified as a means of "firming-up" the variable water supply.[29]

The TVA and Bonneville policy of waiting may have been justified by the economic prospects for nuclear power in the two systems, but today that policy calls for reexamination in light of the possibility that large reactor stations may soon be competitive, by private accounting standards, in the systems of two California power companies. There is also the general welfare function of the public agencies, to work toward the lowest cost and most efficient methods of generation and transmission in hydro, thermal and, ultimately, nuclear power systems. Since interest rates, plant scale and operating conditions will differ between private and federal nuclear power plants, only indirect cost comparisons—no "yardstick"—could be derived from federal agency experience. But these should not be minimized.

28. On January 1, 1957, the Columbia River Basin had undeveloped power sites totaling 31.6 million kilowatts, the largest of any U. S. river basin, compared to developed power of 4.3 million kilowatts. (FPC, *Hydroelectric Power Resources of the U. S.*, Washington, 1957, pp. 10 and 20.)

29. As indicated in Chapter 2 the nuclear power reactor would be on base load and hydro capacity in reservoir would be used for peak load. The possible difficulties of doing this, however, are suggested by a communication from the FPC to the AEC, February 21, 1958, which stated that the value of large base-load nuclear power in good water months might be greatly reduced by necessary spillage from reservoirs. (*AEC Authorizing Legislation, Fiscal Year 1959*, Hearings, Subcommittee on Legislation, Joint Committee on Atomic Energy, 85th Cong., 2nd Sess., 1958, pp. 422–23.)

As the TVA and Bonneville experiences have demonstrated for thermal and hydro power, these federal agencies are peculiarly fitted for development of highly efficient operations. They should be expected to continue contributing over the long term to achieving low-cost generation from all available energy sources and to fitting very large plants into the interconnected grids that will exist in most parts of the country in another generation. To foreclose this contribution would seem, in the light of federal power history, to be short-sighted public policy. It could be bad economics as well because of the loss of the cost-reducing abilities of the federal systems and because nuclear power may break through to the low costs generally prevailing in these regions—and now implied by the largest private projects.

Recognizing the Economic Imperatives

Because political considerations deeply influence nuclear power development, a danger exists that the role of economic motivation will be subordinated, if not ignored, in policy formation. In fact, however, the fundamental economic imperatives are not as weak as suggested by the heat of policy controversy.

The work of the Ad Hoc Committee on Atomic Policy of the Atomic Industrial Forum[30] not only revealed the problem but the opportunity in attempting to relate quantitative economic measurement to policy formation. Their study of economic considerations indicates, for example, that the inception of competitive nuclear power will probably occur in the period 1965–1970 and that by 1980 from 12 per cent to 24 per cent of all new electrical capacity may be nuclear. Also, the "national economic benefits" derived from projections to the year 2000 of the costs of nuclear compared with conventional power provide a basis for judging the dollar scale of "benefits" over "costs." On these data the committee concluded that a "continuation of the total expenditure level, public plus private, of the past few years in support of the development of nuclear power appears reasonable for the near term."[31] Equally important were derivative policy conclusions. Private ownership of fuel, while desirable, it was said, must involve a period of transition if nuclear power growth is not to be slowed down. The committee, however, ignored a number of basic conditions, such as external economies and economies of scale, which the administration dares not avoid when judging the proper rate and scale of future development efforts. At this stage the price system and

30. Report of the Committee, New York, March 1962, including Supplements I and II.
31. *Ibid.*, p. 17.

customary incentives cannot yet provide effective guidance to the proper allocation of resources among, for example, proven reactor systems, recycled plutonium, breeder reactors and thermonuclear power.

Range of Public Investment Opportunities

Public expenditures for nuclear power development of roughly $200 million annually will probably continue at this rate for a decade, and perhaps longer. Compared with the cost of military applications or with total AEC budget or with space vehicle development, the future $2 billion investment in nuclear power extending over a decade does not appear large. Compared, however, with other peacetime programs, such as saline water conversion, the amount is very large indeed. Not without reason, then, certain scientists question the desirability of such large expenditures compared with expenditures for other public programs, such as, for example, improvement of educational facilities.[32] Furthermore, other groups express concern that undue emphasis on nuclear power might further accentuate the national shortage of scientific personnel and divert effort from such high priority programs as missiles. However, the limitations of technology rather than the shortage of scientific personnel are the primary reasons for the difficulties being encountered in developing missiles and space vehicles. Moreover, the technical problems of saline-water conversion or of improving the nation's educational situation go much deeper than additions to federal expenditures might be expected to reach. Whether the nuclear power program should become twice, or one half, as large as at present has little bearing on the prospects for these or alternative investment opportunities.

External Economies [33]

A compelling reason for the large, sustained program of nuclear power development stems from the external economies represented by the vast

32. See early statement of Dr. George Weil to the Joint Committee on Atomic Energy in response to its request for criticism of an expanded program, *Proposed Expanded Civilian Nuclear Power Program*, Joint Committee on Atomic Energy, 85th Cong., 2nd Sess., August 1958, pp. 28–30.

33. Some economists may wish to use the term "common costs" instead. A textbook version of "external economies," a term coined by Alfred Marshall, would be the decreased cost of raw materials production and transportation made possible for one consuming plant by reason of the existence of other consuming plants. Highly significant for civilian nuclear energy applications, such external economies represent in effect the social inheritance bestowed on civilian applications by preceding military applications of productive resources. They do not need to be "paid for" again.

structure of AEC's procurement, production and research activities. Indeed, over a period of time these facilities and activities are apparently subject to such rapidly declining marginal productivity for military purposes[34] that each step toward early civilian nuclear power reduces the dead weight of sunk and current costs. The scale of desirable and permissible public expenditures for civilian nuclear power is clearly larger, considering the $7 billion investment in AEC facilities, than it would have been had the civilian program been forced to "start from scratch," as in most other countries.

Economies of Scale

The economies of scale in power reactor development are not easily distinguished from the external economies just mentioned. Certainly, an important benefit of "returns to scale" is evident in the diversity and breadth of the U. S. power development program. Indeed, the advantages of such large undertakings in the AEC laboratories have been so great that deliberate effort to keep the program "within bounds" did not appear necessary until the 1959 report of the AEC Ad Hoc Advisory Committee. The returns to scale are also seen in chemical processing, waste disposal and enrichment of uranium—for which AEC prices and charges should, and in some instances do, reflect the economies of scale. Until the private atomic industry itself can achieve substantial stature—tens of millions of kilowatts capacity—the benefits of size derived from AEC facilities represent one of the more important, perhaps indispensable, forms of assistance this infant industry has had bestowed upon it. Helpful also is the fact that the electric utility systems in the United States are well set to incorporate large nuclear power reactors (more than 350 megawatts) which, owing to high capital costs, enjoy important economies of scale if used as base-load plants.

Time Preference and the Uncertainties of Success

Some observers of the reactor development program feel that rigorous appraisal of current public outlays against the future benefits, discounted to a present value basis, is called for. If the distribution of reactor expenditures among competing concepts (Chapter 4) is examined critically, one can see that it is virtually impossible to project differential degrees of future economic

34. AEC Commissioner Robert Wilson in 1961 indicated that production improvement had been slowed and certain power contracts canceled because "we cannot now see a definite need for producing U235 at the maximum rate." (U. S.–Japan Atomic Industrial Forums, Tokyo, December 5, 1961.)

benefits for each reactor concept on any convincing time scale. However, pressurized water and boiling water reactors will probably provide marginally competitive nuclear power sooner than others. While the probability is high that these concepts will now go on to achieve success at competitive levels, nevertheless future economic benefits due to their introduction in the United States are expected to be only marginal.[35] Since public and private outlays for their development have already been generous, it seems to follow that further expenditures for these should be curtailed in favor of other concepts which show greater uncertainties but better prospects for achieving very low generating cost for the future. Indeed, to justify on this basis alone the present large public outlays for reactor development, the AEC would probably have to show that nuclear reactors are likely, within the next couple of decades, to provide not merely marginal-cost power but low-cost power (4 to 5 mills per KWH).

Reactor manufacturers and private utilities utilize a higher rate of discount (time preference) than the federal government utilizes in evaluating the economic benefits, over costs, of nuclear power.[36] It is not surprising, therefore, that all of the privately financed full-scale projects—except the Detroit Edison fast breeder—fall in the class of "proven concepts," though each provides little prospect of becoming more than marginally competitive during its useful lifetime.

Research on the frontier, as expressed in "advanced" reactor systems, is not necessarily more likely to achieve low-cost nuclear power ultimately than is reactor research on less "futuristic" technology, that is, on further advances in converters and in plutonium recycle. The implied distinction is dubious. Some reactor experts believe that steady improvement in current technology of reactors and fuel systems may well result in low-cost nuclear power—and achieve marginal, competitive usefulness sooner. Other reactor experts, intrigued by the more sophisticated technology, believe that breeders will make better use of nuclear resources and will also result in low-cost nuclear power ultimately. Yet no one can assume with any certainty that of these two broad avenues either, neither or both will lead to success.

The nation does not have to make an exclusive choice of pursuing either near-term, high-cost nuclear power or long-term, low-cost power. That is not the pertinent issue, for the United States has ample technical, material and

35. That is, it is expected that some years of development will be required to bring generating costs to 6 mills or less.

36. Keith L. Harms, "Economic Considerations Bearing on Civilian Nuclear Power Development," Supplement II to the Report of the Ad Hoc Committee on Atomic Policy of the Atomic Industrial Forum, New York, March 1962.

financial resources to pursue both short- and long-term objectives under the AEC's 10-year reactor development program. Similarly, the relevant choice is not whether converter or breeder technology is to be supported. Resources are ample to pursue both to a conclusion—for domestic and foreign policy reasons. The real issue is whether the administration is prepared to take the vigorous measures required to fulfill the objectives of the ten-year program. Thus far, it appears that it is not. As a consequence reactor technology has moved well ahead of demonstration on a plant scale. The orderly sequence of demonstration plants that is necessary has not been provided by the electric utility systems, nor by the cooperative arrangements program of the AEC and the utilities.

Perspective

In attempting to develop nuclear power wisely the nation and the conflicting groups at interest have been contending with difficult questions of political economy. Reactor manufacturers have sought elimination of trade restraints, especially those on patents. The private utilities have thought mainly of how to prevent the emergence of "federal nuclear power." Public power groups have sought to avoid being shut out of nuclear power and to maintain their hard-won preference position. The electric utility industry, however, has not been deeply concerned by the transitory anomaly of government ownership of nuclear fuel. It is not seeking immediate action because private ownership would increase generating costs and perhaps rates. Moreover, while manufacturers have generally supported the private utilities in opposition to federal nuclear power, they have urged a strong, heavily subsidized program to help shorten the long, unprofitable development period. Finally, the AEC and the Congress, particularly the Joint Committee on Atomic Energy and the Appropriations Committees, have not succeeded—after eight years of conflict—in formulating a long-range program in which the AEC is made responsible for taking the initiative in power reactor development. The issue, unresolved in the statute and the legislative history, remains unsettled, providing another case of a government-industry relationship in which the "public-private" character is in doubt. In the development of nuclear power the federal initiative and responsibility for a successful outcome have not been clearly established, as they have in satellite and space technology, but instead they have remained ambiguous, involving varying degrees of private participation and motivation.

A clearer relationship has arisen between the course of nuclear power technology and the force of AEC administrative policy. The technology is not emerging "pure" from public and private laboratories. Rather, the past and future direction of development has been shaped, and in some important respects misshaped, by the AEC's price system, by the residual influence of military requirements and by inability to comprehend the depth of the conflict between private power and public power. This policy framework should be overhauled soon if the "economics of nuclear power" and, more specifically, the real cost of generating nuclear power are to acquire practical meaning. In particular, the entire AEC price system deserves reevaluation and adjustment in light of the ten-year civilian development program, rather than of the historic and possibly irrelevant circumstances of military requirements and production. Fortunately the AEC took important initial steps, first in 1961 then in 1962, when it lowered the prices of enriched uranium.

In the face of new technical and economic circumstances a reevaluation of former U. S. foreign policy for peaceful nuclear energy may be called for by the Kennedy administration.

The 1954 atoms-for-peace program was, to be sure, one of the major innovations in foreign policy during the Eisenhower administration. Today both the successes and failures of that policy and program are plainly visible. In terms of reactor technology the program was premature—though it did provide a psychological lift to development. In raising exaggerated expectations for the economic benefits of nuclear energy, the program was pretentious. In suggesting that the Soviet and U. S. weapon stockpiles of fissionable materials could thereby be reduced substantially, the program was detached from the physical facts of "nuclear plenty." In suggesting that international cooperation in the peaceful uses would help achieve agreement on nuclear arms control, the policy was visionary.

Yet, despite these faulty assumptions, the atoms-for-peace program achieved some success as an instrument of U. S. foreign policy. It provided new hope, however tenuous, for improved international relations in the cold war. It represented the United States taking the initiative and leading from a position of technical strength. It contributed to major American foreign policy objectives: to foster a world system of law and order, to help the developing countries through science and technology, and to strengthen the unity of the Atlantic Community. Most important of all, perhaps, the atoms-for-peace program gave countries outside the "atomic powers" an opportunity, with generous U. S. help, to participate and become involved in the new science of the mid-twentieth century.

The issue, then, is not whether the program has failed and whether it should be drastically curtailed. Rather, the question is how the program and relevant policies should be altered to recover unity and consistency in national purposes, both at home and abroad.

In the United States the lack of urgent domestic need for an alternative energy source superficially suggests a program of limited effort and one based on long-term commercial considerations. At the same time, however, marginal-cost nuclear power, which will probably result from such a leisurely and restrained approach, offers little economic benefit at home or abroad. Such a scale of effort is not commensurate with the scale of nuclear productive capacity already available for civilian purposes and would probably result in further industrial concentration.

This apparent dilemma, as well as the institutional conflicts present, have contributed to the lack of unity in the nation's nuclear development policies and their administration. The AEC's belated resort to "mixed methods" in the cooperative arrangements program has proved inadequate. More successful have been the separate private and governmental projects. Yet the early vigor of private efforts could not be sustained, and progressively greater public assistance—leading to the suggestion in 1959 for a capital subsidy and in 1962 for reimbursement of engineering design costs—has become the logical alternative to government or private projects. Thus, while expeditious reactor development, possibly beyond the means of private enterprise, has been generally accepted as necessary in the national interest, such acceleration in fact has been held in check. At the same time cutbacks in both the British and Russian reactor development programs seem to exonerate a less than vigorous effort. Yet more arduous measures seem called for since actual plant demonstration has fallen behind the pace of reactor technology.

The Case for Sustained Development

Under the Atomic Energy Act of 1954 the national effort to develop the peaceful atom has progressed in eight years from excessive hopes at the outset, to disillusioned skepticism somewhat later, and now to chastened resignation. The demanding realities of an unfulfilled technology, of economic boundaries and of public acceptability are now recognized.

This "new reality" is evidenced throughout the national program for nuclear power. Industry and government have together accepted the need for a long, costly ten-year development program requiring federal expenditures of more than $200 million annually. Former administration policy imposing responsibility for taking the initiative on the private utilities and industry proved unrealistic. Measures to force private development have given way to greater use of public investment and assistance in reactor research and proto-type plant construction.

Not unexpectedly, strong proposals have been made to scale down the effort and to divert it toward long-term reactor research and development, at home and abroad. There are, nevertheless, compelling reasons for sustaining the present scale of effort aimed at both long- and short-term goals:

The costs of generating nuclear power are promising. Scientists and engineers in the nation's public and private laboratories are confident that technical advances can bring nuclear power into competitive range soon under present programs and expenditure levels.

As a new energy source, nuclear fuels can become of complementary importance, alongside coal, oil, and natural gas, only if important advances beyond present technology are achieved—in high burn-up, in methods to recycle nuclear fuel and in breeding.

The nation's capacity to produce source and fissionable material, for military and civilian needs, is so great that enormous economic waste is in prospect, if these resources cannot be employed productively for peaceful purposes.

Through its recognized advantage in resources and diversified reactor technology, the United States possesses an unequaled opportunity to provide effective world leadership in both the control and promotion of nuclear power development.

The nation, therefore, should look forward to a large, sustained "public-private" program—at substantial cost, to be sure—as a necessity in meeting U. S. responsibilities in the current world situation and in achieving the long-term economic benefits of nuclear energy.

Prospects for Foreign Exchange
Savings: Western Europe and Japan[1]

The analyses in Chapter 6 indicated the general importance of potential foreign exchange savings resulting from the substitution of nuclear power for conventional thermal plants operating on imported fuel. This appendix is intended to set down more specific conditions for such savings and also to evaluate their extent, cost and imputed value in the conditions of Western Europe and Japan.

In Western Europe and Japan, where fossil fuels are imported for steam electric generation, a nuclear plant with fuel cost at about 2.8 mills per KWH[2] will provide an annual saving in foreign exchange payments for fuel over what would be required for a thermal plant, even though the nuclear fuel must also be imported. On the other hand, because capital costs for a nuclear plant, at about $420 per kilowatt, including initial fuel inventory, are considerably higher than the $150 per kilowatt required for a thermal plant (excluding fuel inventory), the additional foreign exchange costs associated with the capital may partially or fully offset the annual savings arising from the fuel. Moreover, prices of respective fuels will undoubtedly change in relation to each other and there may also be changes in the foreign exchange component. (Fabrication and processing make up much of the nuclear fuel cost and in both Western Europe and Japan it is to be expected that these functions can be performed by domestic industries.)

Capital cost may be related to operating cost by two methods: (1) the conventional "accounting method," in which the annual unit cost of power production in both a nuclear and a conventional plant is determined by using the value of the capital allocated over the life of the project, through the use of a depreciation rate and a

1. The author is grateful for the assistance of Kenneth Bohr and Robert Sadove, on the staff of the IBRD, in preparing a background paper on which this appendix is based. However, the conclusions stated in this appendix are solely those of the author.

2. For illustrative purposes the costs assumed are based on costs of an enriched uranium reactor with fuel inventory capitalized as reported in IBRD, *Summary Report of the International Panel, Project ENSI*, Washington, March 1959, Appendix C.

Figure A-1   Boundary Conditions for Foreign Exchange Savings Related to
              Conditions of Nuclear-Thermal Cost Equality: Case 1[a]

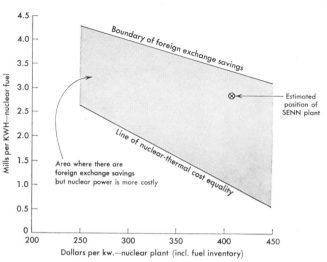

a. Assumptions are: Nuclear plants—60 per cent of the cost of nuclear
fuel and 50 per cent of the cost of nuclear plant is in foreign exchange.
Thermal plants—$150 per kw., 15 per cent foreign exchange; fuel, 40¢
per million BTU, 100 per cent foreign exchange; efficiency, 10,000 BTU
per KWH. Both plants—150,000 kw., 80 per cent plant factor.

rate of return on investment, and then combining this amount directly with annual
operating cost; or (2) the "discounted cash flow method," in which a rate of discount
is determined that will make the present value of the annual cash flow of savings in
operating costs equal to the added plant investment resulting from the choice of a
nuclear plant compared to a conventional thermal plant.

By the second method the additional foreign exchange invested as a result of
building a nuclear rather than a conventional plant can be compared with the
"present worth" of all of the annual cash foreign exchange savings resulting from
lower operating costs over the life of a project. A measure of the importance of such
savings can be indicated by the rate of discount which makes the "present worth"
of the stream of annual savings equal to the additional investment. This "return"
can then be compared with rates that may be obtained from alternative investment.

Table A-1 shows the potential net savings in foreign exchange resulting from the
use of nuclear fuel under various conditions of unit cost and under two assumptions
concerning the foreign exchange component of the nuclear fuel. All fossil fuel is
considered imported. Table A-2 shows the net additional foreign exchange required
per KWH as the result of the higher capital investment in the nuclear plant under

Figure A-2   Boundary Conditions for Foreign Exchange Savings Related to
Conditions of Nuclear-Thermal Cost Equality: Case 2[a]

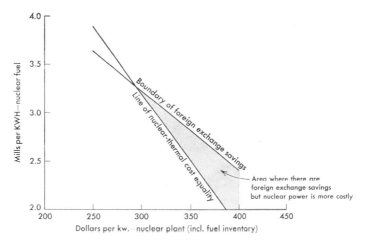

a. Assumptions are: Nuclear plants—all of the cost of nuclear fuel and 75 per
cent of the cost of nuclear plant is in foreign exchange. Thermal plants—$150
per kw., 15 per cent foreign exchange; fuel, 55¢ per million BTU, 100 per cent
foreign exchange; efficiency, 10,000 BTU per KWH. Both plants—150,000
kw., 80 per cent plant factor.

various conditions of unit cost (per kw.) and with assumed foreign exchange components that appear to be reasonable in Western Europe and Japan, at least in the
short run. It is assumed that other costs do not require foreign exchange. Obviously,
the foreign exchange savings suggested in Table A-1 would be offset, wholly or
partly, by the additional foreign exchange required for the nuclear plant shown in
Table A-2.

Figures A-1 and A-2, based on the tables, illustrate graphically the boundaries
of foreign exchange savings associated with the specified assumptions, and the
conditions under which foreign exchange savings will and will not occur. The lower
line in each figure joins the points at which the total costs, foreign and domestic, of
nuclear plants would be equal to those of thermal plants under the assumptions
given. To the left of this line nuclear power would be less expensive, to the right
more expensive. The shaded areas cover the points where nuclear power would be
more expensive but would still provide foreign exchange savings. This area is large,
even on the unfavorable assumption that 50 per cent of the cost of the nuclear plant
is in foreign exchange and 60 per cent of the cost of nuclear fuel is in foreign exchange. In other words, for countries such as Japan and those in Western Europe the
opportunities of foreign exchange savings appear quite substantial. Figure A-2

indicates that if certain assumptions less favorable to nuclear power are used, though compared with higher fuel costs for conventional thermal power (55 cents per million BTU), the opportunities for foreign exchange savings would be greatly diminished. The cross mark in Figure A-1 represents the standard assumptions for a near-term nuclear plant—the SENN Project in Italy—$420 per kw., 2.8 mills per KWH, used throughout this appendix.[3] More detailed comparisons based on this project are given in Tables A-3 and A-4. Table A-4 indicates that the large additional foreign exchange requirement for the nuclear power plant right at the outset will necessitate substantial offsetting savings in foreign exchange on annual fuel costs.

(Not reflected in the figures or the tables are the effects of variations in plant factor, in nuclear fuel charges and capital investment on the comparative generating costs, because the results are obvious and to be expected.)

Relating Foreign Exchange Savings to Excess Generating Costs

In Western Europe and Japan, where some net savings in foreign exchange seem likely even in the short run, the question is what weight should be attached to these savings in making a choice between nuclear and conventional thermal power. At one extreme such savings might coincide with lower total costs of production with nuclear plants and thus be of minor additional importance in making the determination. At the other extreme savings may be obtained at the expense of more costly power, and thus some weight would have to be attached to the value of these foreign exchange savings, if a nuclear plant is to be economically justified. These are the extreme cases. The most pertinent cases currently are those, illustrated in Figure A-1, in which there are net savings in foreign exchange but total generating costs, domestic and foreign, are somewhat higher for the nuclear plant. The problem thus is to balance foreign exchange savings against excess generating costs.

One way to relate foreign exchange savings to excess domestic costs is to determine a proper premium to be added to all foreign exchange costs so that the cost of power from all plants will be commensurate. An alternative method is to compute the net savings in foreign exchange as a return on the net investment in foreign exchange, either as an average annual quantity or as the expected accumulated amount of savings over the life of the project—that is, discounting future savings and costs so as to place them on a comparable basis of present value. An example of this type of calculation is shown in Table A-5. Table A-6 shows the effect of having a "premium" placed on foreign exchange. For Western Europe and Japan, where nuclear power

3. Figures A-1 and A-2 are based on calculations using the accounting method and assume 100 per cent debt financing at 6 per cent interest; the same results would be obtained if the discounted cash flow method were used assuming 6 per cent as the appropriate rate of return. Using the latter method, the boundary lines would pass through the points at which the additional investment in foreign exchange attributable to the choice of a nuclear over a thermal plant would be equal to the present value of the flow of savings in foreign exchange resulting from the use of nuclear fuel instead of fossil fuel, discounted at 6 per cent.

might be slightly more costly than conventional power in the near term, a 50 per cent foreign exchange premium would almost equalize the generating costs—at 8.9 mills per KWH for thermal and 9.3 mills for nuclear.

Even though such a premium were assumed on foreign currency expenditures, at present cost levels, conventional power would still cost less than that produced by nuclear plants. Whether the foreign exchange components are moderately low or high, the foreign exchange premium apparently works to the advantage of the nuclear plant, especially if nuclear fuel costs are at a high level or most of the capital cost of the nuclear plant is in foreign exchange.

Changes in technology, both in nuclear and conventional thermal plants, may be expected to alter the picture, but probably in favor of nuclear. The capital costs of nuclear plants may eventually be reduced to $200 per kw. or less and fuel costs to below 2.8 mills per KWH. (See Chapter 2.) The total cost of nuclear power would then be below the 7 mills per KWH of the conventional steam plant, if fossil fuel prices remain stable at the current European levels of around 40 to 45 cents per million BTU or the Japanese level of about 45 to 50 cents.[4]

Future variations in the cost of both fossil fuel and nuclear fuel can be expected. With no allowance for foreign exchange savings and with nuclear fuel costing 2.8 mills per KWH, a nuclear plant would be competitive with a thermal plant if fossil fuel prices were about 55 cents per million BTU—prevalent in Western Europe until 1959. If fossil fuel prices continue at the current 40 to 45 cents per million BTU in Western Europe, the competitive price of nuclear fuel will have to be somewhat below 2.8 mills per KWH; the capital cost of nuclear plants, including initial fuel inventory, around $350 per kw.; and plant utilization at 80 per cent for both types of power production. The effect of introducing a moderate foreign exchange premium (under 50 per cent), as shown in Table A-6, would not make nuclear power competitive under present conditions. However, if a higher price of fossil fuel were assumed (or a lower price of nuclear fuel), this would, of course, add to the cost advantage of nuclear power as well as to the effect of a foreign exchange premium. While the trend to convertibility in Western Europe suggests that no foreign exchange premium is justified in that area, a modest premium is probably justified in Japan. (The alternative "discounted cash flow" approach does not significantly alter the conclusions under European or Japanese conditions. See Table A-5.)

As shown in Table A-7, the estimated total net savings in operating costs over a twenty-five-year period resulting from the use of nuclear rather than conventional thermal power in a 150,000-kilowatt plant generating 1,050 million KWH annually would amount to nearly $44 million. To obtain these operating savings, however, it would be necessary to invest $30 million more capital in the nuclear facilities than would be required for a conventional steam plant. The "present worth" of the total annual savings in operating costs, when discounted at a rate of 2 per cent, would just about equal the additional investment required. In Western Europe and Japan

4. *Petroleum Press Service* (London), June 1962, pp. 203–05.

interest rates are rather high, hence this would be an extremely low return. The foreign exchange savings, however, do alter the picture.

Measuring Foreign Exchange "Return"

Under most European and Japanese conditions it is reasonable to assume that all but 15 per cent of the conventional thermal plant's facilities, compared to about half of the nuclear plant's, would be produced locally. Inasmuch as these countries have a growing requirement for imported fossil fuels, it may be assumed, initially, that all of those fuels would be imported. Some 40 per cent of nuclear fuel costs might represent foreign exchange. On these assumptions $75 million would be obtainable in foreign exchange savings over a twenty-five-year period (Table A-5). Securing this would require an additional investment of about $23 million in foreign exchange at the beginning of the twenty-five-year period (Table A-4). The "present worth" of future foreign exchange savings would more than equal this additional investment when discounted at a rate of about 10 per cent (Table A-5), indicating a far greater return on the foreign exchange investment than on the total investment.

Whether such a rate of "foreign exchange return" is justified, in view of the rather low yield on the additional investment and possibly higher total cost for nuclear power, depends on the foreign economic position of the particular country. If a large premium is placed on foreign exchange savings, then the unit costs of thermal and nuclear power might be "equalized." Any foreign exchange premium, as Table A-8 shows, would improve the return on the additional investment in nuclear compared with conventional thermal power. The foreign exchange position of most of the European countries and Japan can hardly be said to be so sound that foreign exchange savings are of no special value. A 10 per cent return on foreign exchange investment would seem to be reasonably good. This return would be even larger if a foreign exchange premium could be justified.

If the European countries or Japan could finance the foreign exchange investment ($23 million, as shown in Table A-4) by borrowing abroad at 6 per cent for twenty-five years, the contribution of the nuclear alternative to the future balance of payments would thereby be accentuated. If, for example, it is assumed that the foreign debt is amortized in twenty-five equal installments including interest (i.e., level debt service), the lifetime burden of the debt would be about $44 million compared to a twenty-five-year foreign exchange saving of $75 million (Table A-5). In other words, after all foreign debt has been serviced there is still a net foreign exchange saving for the twenty-five-year operation of $31 million. This saving would have a "present worth" of $5.7 million, discounted at a 6 per cent interest rate. Such contribution to the future balance of payments problem is worth consideration. Despite the substantial excess cost in local currency, the "present worth" of such foreign exchange saving would offset some increase in power costs, even though only a modest foreign exchange premium is considered justifiable for these countries today.

TABLE **A-1**

Foreign Exchange Savings Resulting from Lower Fuel Costs in Nuclear than in Conventional Thermal Plants

		Mills per KWH	
		If foreign exchange component of nuclear fuel is—	
Cost of fossil fuel	Cost of nuclear fuel	40 per cent	60 per cent
5.0	2.0	4.2	3.8
4.5	2.0	3.7	3.3
4.0	2.0	3.2	2.8
3.5	2.0	2.7	2.3
5.0	2.5	4.0	3.5
4.5	2.5	3.5	3.0
4.0	2.5	3.0	2.5
3.5	2.5	2.5	2.0
5.0	3.0	3.8	3.2
4.5	3.0	3.3	2.7
4.0	3.0	2.8	2.2
3 5	3.0	2.3	1.7
5.0	3.5	3.6	2.9
4.5	3.5	3.1	2.4
4.0	3.5	2.6	1.9
3.5	3.5	2.1	1.4

Note: Assumptions are—All fossil fuel is considered imported for the purpose of these calculations. Efficiency of thermal plant, 10,000 BTU = 1 KWH, so that 35¢ per million BTU is equivalent to 3.5 mills per KWH, etc.

TABLE **A-2**

Net Additional Foreign Exchange Required to Service Increased Capital Costs of Nuclear Compared to Conventional Thermal Plants[a]

Capital cost of nuclear plant per kw.[b]	Mills per KWH if foreign exchange component of nuclear plant is—	
	25 per cent	50 per cent
$250	0.48	1.18
300	0.62	1.45
350	0.75	1.73
400	0.89	2.00
450	1.03	2.28

a. Based on level debt service, 25 years at 6 per cent for nuclear and 33 years at 6 per cent for conventional thermal. Nuclear plant as shown; thermal plant $150 per kw., 15 per cent foreign exchange. Size of both plants 150,000 kw. and load factors 80 per cent.

b. Includes initial inventory of nuclear fuel.

TABLE A-3

Unit Cost Comparisons for Average Thermal and Nuclear Plants under European Cost Conditions

| | Unit cost of power generation (mills per KWH)[a] | | | | | Capital required | |
	Total	Operation and maintenance	Fuel costs	Depreciation	Other fixed charges	Per kw.	Total (thousands)
Thermal plants	6.9	1.0	4.0	0.2	1.7	$150	$22,200
Nuclear plants							
Gas-cooled reactor,[b] natural uranium–fueled	9.8	1.2	1.8	1.3	5.5	490[c]	73,500
Enriched reactor[d]	9.7	1.0	2.8	1.1	4.8	420[c]	63,000
"Optimistic" nuclear reactor	8.0	1.0	2.2	0.9	3.9	325	49,000

a. Compare basic assumptions with those used in IBRD, *Summary Report of the International Panel, Project ENSI*, Washington, March 1959, p. 4. Lower fuel cost assumed because of recent trends.

b. *Ibid.*, Appendix C, Chart IV. Lowest cost gas-cooled reactor, GC-1 with fuel inventory capitalized.

c. Includes capitalized fuel inventory.

d. *Ibid.* Lowest cost enriched reactor ER-1 with fuel inventory capitalized.

Note: Basic assumptions are—

Installed capacity, 150,000 kw.

Net generation, 1,050 million KWH.

Average plant load factor, 80 per cent.

Capital cost of thermal plant, $150 per installed kw.

Fossil fuel cost, 40 cents per million BTU.

Depreciation (sinking fund method)—for nuclear, 25-year life at 6 per cent interest rate, 1.8 per cent per annum; for thermal, 33⅓-year life at 6 per cent interest rate, 0.8 per cent per annum.

Fixed charges other than depreciation, 8 per cent (including return to capital of 6 per cent).

Efficiency of thermal plant, 10,000 BTU per KWH.

TABLE A-4

Basic Assumptions for Comparing Nuclear and Thermal Plants under Competitive Conditions with Plant Factor for Thermal Plant Based on Current Experience[a]

	Nuclear	Conventional thermal	Difference between nuclear and thermal
Installed net capacity (kw.)	150,000	150,000	
Average annual net generation (million KWH)	1,050	1,050	
Average annual plant factor (per cent)	80	80	
Investment			
Capital cost per kw.	$350	$150	
Capital investment	$52,500,000	$22,500,000	
Additional investment in nuclear			$30,000,000
Operating costs (mills per KWH)			
Fuel	2.8	4.0	
Other	1.0	1.0	
Foreign exchange components[b]			
Per cent of capital	50	15	
Initial foreign exchange requirements	$26,250,000	$3,380,000	
Additional foreign exchange in nuclear			$22,870,000
Annual cash operating costs	$3,990,000	$5,250,000	
Fuel	2,940,000	4,200,000	
Other	1,050,000	1,050,000	
Difference in annual operating costs			$1,260,000
Foreign exchange required for annual operating costs	$1,600,000	$4,200,000	
Difference in foreign exchange required for operating costs			$2,600,000

a. Assumptions same as for Table A-3, as indicated in IBRD, Summary Report of the International Panel, Project ENSI, Washington, March 1959.

b. 100 per cent of fuel costs in the case of conventional thermal and 40 per cent of nuclear assumed to be in foreign exchange. 50 per cent of the capital investment in nuclear is assumed to be in foreign currency and 15 per cent of the conventional plant's requirements. This is based on the experience in Italy, as indicated in correspondence from Professor Carlo Matteini, December 15, 1958, and modified to reflect the downward trend in the cost of nuclear plants.

TABLE **A-5**

Calculation of the Foreign Exchange Savings as a Return[a] on the Additional Investment in Foreign Exchange in a Nuclear Plant Compared with a Thermal Alternative

Years	Annual foreign exchange savings (millions)	Approximate five-year discount factor at 10 per cent	Five-year present worth of foreign exchange savings at 10 per cent (millions)
25-year total	$75.00		$25.65
1– 5	2.60	3.79	9.85
6–10	2.80	2.35	6.58
11–15	3.00	1.46	4.40
16–20	3.20	0.91	2.92
21–25	3.40	0.58	1.90

a. The additional investment in foreign exchange would be $22,870,000. The present worth of foreign exchange savings discounted at 10 per cent would be $25,650,000, indicating a "foreign exchange return" of about 10 to 11 per cent.

Note: For basic assumptions see Table A-4. It has been assumed that the foreign exchange savings would increase modestly after each five-year period.

TABLE A - 6

Effect of Variation in Foreign-Exchange Premiums on the Thermal-Nuclear Comparison

	No premium	25 per cent premium	50 per cent premium	100 per cent premium	200 per cent premium
Unit cost of power generation, thermal plant (mills per KWH)	6.9	7.9	8.9	10.9	14.9
Operation and maintenance	1.0	1.0	1.0	1.0	1.0
Fuel costs	4.0	5.0	6.0	8.0	12.0
Depreciation	0.2	0.2	0.2	0.2	0.2
Other fixed charges	1.7	1.7	1.7	1.7	1.7
Unit cost of power generation, nuclear plant (mills per KWH)	8.7	9.0	9.3	9.8	10.9
Operation and maintenance	1.0	1.0	1.0	1.0	1.0
Fuel costs	2.8	3.1	3.4	3.9	5.0
Depreciation	0.9	0.9	0.9	0.9	0.9
Other fixed charges	4.0	4.0	4.0	4.0	4.0

Note: Basic assumptions are the same as in Table A-3. Nuclear plant used in this comparison is the enriched reactor. All fossil fuel costs in foreign currency; 40 per cent of nuclear fuel costs in foreign currency.

TABLE **A-7**

Calculation of Return[a] on Additional Investment in Nuclear as Compared to Thermal Alternative by the Discounted Cash Flow Method

Years	Annual cash savings (millions)	Approximate five-year discount factor at 2 per cent (per cent)	Five-year present worth at 2 per cent of savings (millions)
25-year total	$43.85		$32.30
1– 5	1.25	4.75	5.70
6–10	1.50	4.27	6.40
11–15	1.75	3.87	6.10
16–20	2.00	3.50	7.00
21–25	2.25	3.17	7.10

a. Additional investment in nuclear of $30 million is fully paid back by annual cash savings with a present worth of $32 million, indicating a return of only about 2 per cent on the additional investment by this method. It has been assumed that the price of fossil fuel will rise modestly and the price of nuclear fuel will decline after each five-year period.

TABLE A - 8

Effect of Variation in Foreign Exchange Premiums on the Return on the Additional Investment in Nuclear Compared to a Conventional Thermal Alternative

	No premium	25 per cent premium	50 per cent premium	100 per cent premium	200 per cent premium
			Millions		
Annual operating costs					
Thermal	$5.8	$6.8	$7.8	$9.9	$14.1
Fuel	4.3	5.3	6.3	8.4	12.6
Other operating costs	1.1	1.1	1.1	1.1	1.1
Depreciation	0.2	0.2	0.2	0.2	0.2
Property taxes & insurance	0.2	0.2	0.2	0.2	0.2
Nuclear	5.7	5.9	6.3	6.8	8.0
Fuel	3.0	3.2	3.6	4.1	5.3
Other operating costs	1.1	1.1	1.1	1.1	1.1
Depreciation	1.0	1.0	1.0	1.0	1.0
Property taxes & insurance	0.6	0.6	0.6	0.6	0.6
Annual savings, nuclear over thermal	0.1	0.9	1.5	3.1	6.1
			Per cent		
Capital requirements					
Nuclear	52.5	59.5	65.5	78.7	105.0
Thermal	22.5	23.4	24.3	26.1	29.7
Additional for nuclear	30.0	36.1	41.2	52.6	75.3
Return on additional investment for nuclear	3.0	3.0	4.0	6.0	8.0

Note: Basic assumptions are the same as for Table A-3, with 100 per cent of fossil fuel cost and 40 per cent of nuclear fuel cost and 50 per cent of the capital in the nuclear plant and 15 per cent of that in the conventional thermal plant assumed to be foreign exchange costs.

APPENDIX **B**

The Soviet Nuclear Power Program[1]

The Soviet Union had one small nuclear power station in operation at the time of the First Geneva Conference in August 1955. By the Second Geneva Conference in September 1958 only one additional section of a large nuclear electric power station and a nuclear-powered icebreaker stood out as concrete accomplishments. Yet, during that three-year period an impressive program for expansion of nuclear power for domestic uses had taken shape in the Soviet Union, as well as reasonably clear outlines of a nuclear foreign aid program. The most ambitious part of these programs was the development of reactors for electric power generation.[2] Although far-reaching, the domestic program for constructing nuclear electric power capacity up to mid-1962 has been much slower than planned.[3] Nevertheless, the urgent domestic need for nuclear power capacity in certain fuel-deficient industrial areas may still make the economic necessity for a large-scale program more compelling in the Soviet Union than in many other nations. By 1965 nuclear power in the Soviet Union will still total less than 2 million kw., producing an estimated 21,000 billion kilocalories of fuel equivalent.[4]

1. This appendix summarizes a background paper originally prepared for this project in 1959 by John P. Hardt, Research Analysis Corporation, Bethesda, Md. (Unless otherwise indicated translations from the Russian in this appendix are his.) Since then there have been few references to the nuclear power program of the USSR in the Soviet literature. However, on the basis of the limited data available, we believe that this appendix gives an up-to-date analysis of the Soviet program, with projections to 1965. Other sources of information on the Soviet program may be found in the following staff papers in the McKinney Review, *Background Material*, Vol. 4: "The Atomic Energy Programs of Communist Countries," pp. 1276–1364; "USSR Uranium and Thorium Resources," pp. 1613–18; and "Production and Reserves of Primary Energy in the Sino-Soviet Area, 1959, 1975 and 2000," pp. 1644–51.

2. See Academician Kurchatov's speech at the Twenty-first Party Congress, *Pravda*, February 3, 1959.

3. V. Yemelyanov, *Izvestia*, August 27, 1961.

4. CIA, *Significant Developments in the Fuels and Power Industries of the USSR in 1961*, Langley, Va., July 1962, p. 2 (unclassified).

TABLE B-1

Increments in Soviet Electric Power Capacity
by Type, 1952–1965

	Million kilowatts	
Type	1952–1958	1959–1965
Total	31.9	61.0
Steam	24.5	35.2
Hydro	7.4	24.2
Nuclear	—	1.6

Sources:

1952–1958—*Pravda*, December 4, 1958.

1959–1965—CIA, *Significant Developments in the Fuels and Power Industries of the USSR in 1961*, July 1962, p. 20.

Three aspects of the Soviet domestic nuclear program are examined here: how soon nuclear power may be considered economically competitive with stations using conventional energy sources in the Soviet Union; what specific plans for the design and construction of new atomic electric power capacity have been formulated; and what may be some of the limiting factors on Soviet capabilities for meeting these plans.

Nuclear power capacity has been expected to represent an increasing share of the Soviet electric power plans in the period 1959–1965. Soviet plans for capacity expansion for this period, as shown in Table B-1, indicate an ambitious electrification program—a doubling of the 1952–1958 annual rate of capacity installation. This table also shows the continued importance of hydroelectric and steam capacity. The steam capacity to be added in the period 1959–1965 includes 10 million kw. of reconstructed capacity,[5] 14 million kw. of steam by-product capacity[6] and the bulk of the remaining capacity is to be in large, technically advanced steam-condensing stations using natural gas and petroleum.[7] With the resumption of the Krasnoyarsk station (4.2 million kw.), the hydro capacity to be added in 1959–1965 will be even more than in the period 1952–1958.[8] New hydro stations in Siberia and on the Volga will probably be producing by 1965.

5. The 10 million kw. to be installed in 233 individual stations. *Stroitel'naia gazeta*, August 12, 1958.

6. *Teploenergetika*, No. 11, 1958, p. 90.

7. At least 20 million kw. of the remaining 23 million kw. in twenty new steam-condensing stations of from 1 to 2 million kw. each. *Izvestia*, November 19, 1958.

8. *Pravda*, November 14, 1958, and January 28, 1959. For a discussion of the policy shift in favor of thermal over hydro, see J. Hardt, "Investment Policy in the Soviet Electric Power Industry," *Value and Plan* (G. Grossman, ed.), University of California Press, Berkeley, 1960. For policy reversal discussion see J. Hardt, "Industrial Investment in the U.S.S.R.," *Comparison of the United States and Soviet Economies*, Joint Economic Committee, 1959, Vol. I, pp. 132 ff.

TABLE B-2

Operating Cost for Solid-Fuel Steam and Nuclear Electric Power Stations, Fuel-Deficient Regions, Adjusted for Cost of Transporting Fuel, 1958

| Type of station | Source | Fuel | | | | Operating cost without fuel transportation (rubles per kw.-yr.)[e] | Operating cost with fuel transportation (rubles per kw.-yr.) |
		Average distance from consumption point (km.)[a]	Requirement (tons per kw.-yr.)[b]	Transportation requirement (ton-km. per kw.-yr.)[c]	Transportation cost (rubles per kw.-yr.)[d]		
Central industrial regions							
Solid-fuel steam	Moscow coal	100	6.6	660	19	324	343
Nuclear	Uranium	f	f	f	f	212–302	212–302
Urals							
Solid-fuel steam	Irtysh coal	1,200	3.3	3,960	119	135	254
	Karaganda coal	1,400	3.3	4,620	139	212	351
Nuclear	Uranium	f	f	f	f	212–302	212–302
Northwest							
Solid-fuel steam	Pechora coal	1,600	3.3	5,280	158	302	460
Nuclear	Uranium	f	f	f	f	212–302	212–302

a. "Accepted" or average transportation distances from *Elektricheskie stantsii*, No. 7, 1958, p. 7.

b. Calculated at rate of 485 kilocalories of conventional fuel per KWH (Ministry average 1958) and a factor of 4,500 hours of use.

c. Fuel requirements in tons per kw.-year times "accepted" transportation distances.

d. "At the present time the average cost for long-distance haulage of coal by railroad is about 3 kopecks per ton-kilometer," *Elektrichestvo*, No. 9, 1958, p. 72. Ton-kilometers times 3 kopecks or .03 rubles. The figure of 19 rubles per kw.-year for Moscow coal transport is probably low.

e. Solid fuel data from *Elektricheskie stantsii*, No. 7, 1958, p. 7. Atomic data calculated from cost indexes given in N. Nikolaev, "Razvitie atomnoi energetiki v sovetskom soiuze" (Development of Atomic Energy in the Soviet Union), *Atomnaia energiia*, No. 11, 1957, pp. 385–390.

f. Uranium consumption in weight of fuel consumed and transported is a negligible cost factor.

The figure for new nuclear capacity for 1959–1965, as noted in Table B-1, is based on an estimate by the Central Intelligence Agency (CIA). The CIA, in the same report, also compared the percentage shares of total electric power generation by energy sources in 1958 and 1965, respectively, as follows:[9]

	1958	1965
Total	100.0	100.0
Coal and lignite	56.7	39.6
Crude oil	25.3	35.5
Natural gas	5.3	15.2
Peat	3.3	2.5
Shale	0.7	0.7
Fuel wood	5.2	2.4
Hydro	3.5	3.8
Nuclear electric power	—	0.3

The change in "energy balance" is largely explained by the increasing role of crude oil and natural gas, it may be noted. It is projected that in 1965 electric power stations will consume about 21 per cent of all the natural gas consumed, or more than any other industry using gas—ferrous metallurgy, machine building, cement and others.[10] Natural gas is playing a significantly larger role in the electric power balance than anticipated, thus apparently reducing the need for nuclear stations.[11]

Comparative Cost of Coal-Burning Steam and Nuclear Capacity

The need for new power sources is felt to be acute in three "fuel-deficient" regions: the central industrial region (including Moscow), the Urals, and the northwest (including Leningrad). Development of nuclear power in other regions is not ruled out, but for the near future solid fuel sources and hydroelectric developments are considered by the Soviets to be adequate for regional electric power needs.[12] The Ukrainian electric power plan for 1959–1965 calls for no nuclear power. A nuclear station to be near Lake Sevan in Armenia, referred to in a general way by Academician Khachaturov, is apparently not for the near future.[13] However, all nuclear power projects known to be under way are in fuel-deficient regions, and Soviet writers nearly always link the development of nuclear power with the problem of providing additional electric power capacity in these regions. (See Table B-6.)

9. CIA, *op. cit.* An increase in fuel oil consumption also is indicated by other projections. See *Planovoe khoziaistvo*, No. 12, 1958, p. 34. Also see *Energo-mashinostroenie*, No. 8, 1958, p. 2. *Cf. Voprosy ekonomiki*, No. 10, 1958, p. 34. Fuel oil appears to be given a larger share of steam-generated electric power than indicated in the tabulation.

10. *Planovoe khoziaistvo*, No. 12, 1958, p. 33.

11. *Ekonomicheskaya gazeta*, March 19, 1962.

12. Hydro projects are not considered here, as they represent operational alternatives in the fuel-deficient regions only to the extent that long-range transmission is economically feasible.

13. *Elektricheskie stantsii*, No. 6, 1958, pp. 1 ff; *Voprosy ekonomiki*, No. 8, 1958, p. 35.

In order to expand electric power capacity in solid-fuel-burning plants in the fuel-deficient regions, either more use must be made of very low quality local fuel, which is expensive to mine, or fuel mined elsewhere must be brought in at considerable increase in transportation requirements. Unlike coal for the Urals, which comes from the Irtysh and Karaganda coal fields, each over 1,000 kilometers (621 miles) distant, coal for the central industrial regions from the Moscow brown coal basin does not have to be transported long distances. However, the relatively high labor costs per ton of conventional fuel make expansion of coal-burning capacity based on low-calorie Moscow coal expensive.

The operating cost figures cited in Table B-2 indicate that nuclear power may be competitive with solid-fuel steam in the fuel-deficient regions, if allowance is made for transportation costs.[14] G. Yermakov, Chief of the Administration for Atomic Energy of the Ministry of Electric Power Stations, claimed that the nuclear stations being built will generate electric power "at least as cheaply as, and possibly more cheaply than, the very largest steam-condensing stations," presumably using any type of fuel.[15]

About three quarters of the steam capacity in the Soviet Union was operated on coal in 1958 and at least that share of the steam capacity in the fuel-deficient regions used coal.[16] This would appear to make the alternative costs of nuclear to coal-burning electric power capacity important to the pattern of future expansion in those regions. Moreover, as about 300 of the additional 570-670 billion kilowatt-hours of output projected by 1972 are expected to be in the above-mentioned fuel-deficient regions (including the Volga),[17] the competitive economic position of nuclear power in these regions may be significant for meeting total future power needs.

Full confidence, however, cannot be placed in the operating cost figures as measures of the comparative efficiency of investment in either coal-burning or nuclear stations, partly because they lack proper allowance for capital charges. It would be desirable, of course, to determine whether the investment cost advantage runs counter to the operating cost advantage of nuclear over coal-burning capacity. However, even if that were so, greater investment outlays are permissible, in the Soviet view, if the operating cost advantage is sufficient to "recoup" the additional investment outlays in a time period considered short enough. In some cases hydroelectric projects have been approved with a "recoupment period" of as long as eighteen years.[18]

14. Independent verification of the fact that transportation costs are not included in the operation cost figures cited in Table B-2 has been made from data found in *Elektrichestvo*, No. 9, 1958, pp. 71 ff; *Stroitel'naia gazeta*, February 4, 1959.

15. *Stroitel'naia gazeta*, January 4, 1959.

16. *Ugol'* (Coal), No. 10, 1958, p. 37.

17. An additional 350 to 400 billion KWH are expected for European regions of the USSR—"more than one-half in Central Industrial regions (including the Northwest region and the Volga) and about one-quarter in the Urals." *Elektrichestvo*, No. 9, 1958, p. 72.

18. This may have been an *ex post facto* approval. For a fuller discussion of investment criteria, see J. Hardt, *op. cit.*

TABLE **B-3**

Investment Cost for Alternative Coal-Burning Steam
and Nuclear Capacity, 1958–1965

	Rubles per kilowatt
Large coal-burning steam station	
1958 average[a]	1,200–1,300
1959–1965 plan[b]	800–900
Additional investment in coal mines to supply new capacity[c]	
Central industrial regions	850
Urals	170
Northwest	500
Range of possible investment in station and mining, 1958–1965[d]	970–2,150
Large-scale nuclear stations, 1959–1965[e]	
Pressurized water (Moscow)	1,500
Graphite-moderated (Ural)	1,800
Heavy water (Leningrad)	2,400
Range	1,500–2,400

a. *Stroitel'naia gazeta,* August 12, 1958; *Elektricheskie stantsii,* No. 2, 1958, p. 2.

b. *Pravda,* December 4, 1958; *Stroitel'naia gazeta,* August 12, 1958.

c. *Elektricheskie stantsii,* No. 7, 1958, p. 7.

d. Minimum and maximum combination of steam station and mining investment outlays.

e. N. Nikolaev, *Atomnaia energiia,* No. 11, 1957, pp. 385–390. For further technical details, see Table B-6.

In fact, the investment cost per kilowatt of coal-burning steam capacity is less than the estimated nuclear station cost, as shown in Table B-3, if the additional outlays in new coal mines needed to supply the new stations are excluded. Even including these additional outlays, the investment cost advantage of coal-burning capacity could be recouped in a reasonably short time through savings in operating cost possible with nuclear power, as indicated in Table B-2. At the same time, as indicated in Table B-3, with the inclusion of coal mine investment the advantage of lower investment cost would shift to nuclear stations, at least in the central industrial regions and the northwest.

The accuracy of the operating and investment cost figures cited above is subject to serious reservation. There is, for example, little operating experience for large-scale nuclear power stations and little construction experience as a basis for the investment estimates. As a result, the data for nuclear power capacity may represent hopes rather than real costs.

TABLE **B-4**

Labor Requirement and Estimated Labor Cost of Coal Extraction
for Electric Power in Fuel-Deficient Regions, 1958

| | | Labor requirement for coal extraction | |
Region	Fuel requirement (tons per kw.-year)[a]	Man-years per kw.-year[b]	Estimated cost (rubles per kw.-year)[c]
Central industrial regions	6.6	.015	225
Urals	3.3	.004	85–105
Northwest	3.3	.007	174

a. From Table B-2.

b. The coal extraction rate is 460 tons per man per year for Moscow and Pechora coal and 750 tons per man per year for Karaganda coal for the Urals (production workers only). *Ugol'naia promyshlennost' SSSR, statisticheskii spravochnik* (Coal Industry USSR, Statistical Handbook), Ugletekhizdat, Moscow, 1957, pp. 232 ff.

c. Lower estimate based on figures in preceding column and average wage for coal miners, assumed to be 10,000 rubles per annum. A. Nove estimated average for all workers to be about 9,000 rubles per annum in 1958, *Soviet Survey*, October–December, 1958, p. 34. Even though it is assumed that coal workers are paid materially more than the average, the above estimate may be low. The upper range of the estimate is based on 58 per cent average of total cost to labor for Ministry of Coal production of coal in 1955, *Ugol'naia promyshlennost' SSSR*, p. 358. Pechora wages are difficult to estimate because of the use of "unfree" labor, on the one hand, and payment of "Arctic Circle supplements" to free labor, on the other hand.

At the same time, judging by past Soviet experience, some of the steam investment cost figures in Table B-3 appear low. The low investment figures for 1959–1965 are based on appreciable savings assumed to be forthcoming from the construction of very large stations with advanced technical characteristics and in much shorter construction periods than have previously been possible. Therefore, the higher 1958 figures cited are probably closer to the actual outlays than the planned costs for 1959–1965.

Labor and Transportation Requirements

Even if the Soviet cost figures were materially changed in favor of coal-burning steam, strong preference might still be shown for nuclear over coal-burning steam capacity. In addition to the index of cost reduction, reductions in manpower and transportation requirements represent important additional criteria on which decisions are made in Soviet planning. Coal mining for the fuel-deficient regions is heavily labor consuming and the transportation of coal to the fuel-deficient regions for electric power generation places a burden on the railroad transportation system.

The labor and transportation saving advantages of nuclear power could, therefore, be quite persuasive as confirming the recorded cost advantages. If the production cost figures for nuclear stations compared with coal-burning steam electric power capacity were less favorable, the physical input savings might determine the outcome.

The labor requirement rate is particularly high for Moscow coal consumed in the electric power stations of the central industrial regions, as indicated in Table B-4. Labor costs for all workers and employees represented, on the average, 58 per cent of the total cost of coal mined by the Ministry of Coal installations in 1955.[19]

The transportation requirement of coal per kilowatt-year is greater for the stations to be built in the Urals and northwest than in the central industrial regions. This contrasts with the relatively larger labor requirements for the central industrial region stations. As indicated in Table B-2, the average ton-kilometers of rail transportation per kilowatt-year of coal-burning capacity are much lower for Moscow coal in central industrial regions than for Irtysh and Karaganda coal for the Ural stations and Pechora coal for the stations of the northwest.

The labor and transportation requirements for coal to supply the additional electric power capacity planned for the fuel-deficient regions can be more clearly illustrated by referring to the total labor and transportation requirements involved. An estimated 67 million kilowatts of new capacity will be needed to supply the increased electric power production of 300 billion KWH which is planned for the fuel-deficient regions. This additional 300 billion KWH is from 50 to 60 per cent of the total expansion in the Soviet Union planned for 1959–1972 (500-600 billion KWH) and more than the total electric power generated in the Soviet Union during 1958 (233 billion KWH).[20]

Were the new capacity needed to generate this planned expansion to be entirely coal burning, as indicated in the "old fuel balance" in Table B-5, the estimated additional labor force requirement in 1972 would be 732 thousand workers or about 90 per cent larger than the comparable 1955 total of some 827 thousand production workers.[21] However, according to an estimate based on the "new fuel balance," which more closely reflects the actual Soviet plans, the additional labor force would still be 330 thousand workers.

The total labor requirement is especially high for the central industrial region, Volga and northwest as it is calculated on the basis of Moscow coal production. But modification of this assumption to allow for higher quality fuel output, e.g., Pechora coal for the northwest, would not materially change the result, because only a small share of the total electric power generation is based on this fuel. Furthermore, even more labor-consuming peat production, which would tend to increase the estimated labor requirement, is not included.

19. *Ugol'naia promyshlennost' SSSR, statisticheskii spravochnik* (Coal Industry USSR, Statistical Handbook), Ugletekhizdat, Moscow, 1957, p. 358.

20. *Elektrichestvo*, No. 9, 1958, pp. 72 ff.

21. *Ugol'naia promyshlennost' SSSR*, p. 242.

TABLE **B - 5**

Labor and Transport Requirements with Alternative Coal-Burning Steam Capacity Construction, Fuel-Deficient Regions, 1959–1972[a]

	New coal-fired steam capacity[b] (million kw.)	Fuel requirement[c] (million tons per yr.)	Transportation requirement[d] (million ton-km.)	Labor requirement[e] (thousand workers)
Old fuel balance[f]	67	366	101,106	732
Central industrial regions, Volga and northwest	44	290	29,106	660
Urals	23	76	72,000	72
New fuel balance[g]	22	122	61,075	330
Central industrial regions, Volga and northwest	15	99	33,075	225
Urals	7	23	28,000	105

a. For 1959–1972, 67 million kw. estimated from planned 300 billion KWH at 4,500 plant factor. *Elektrichestvo*, No. 9, 1958, p. 72.

b. Coal-burning steam capacity divided between regions proportionately to output.

c. Fuel requirements per kw.-year from Table B-2.

d. Transportation requirements per kw.-year from Table B-2.

e. Labor requirements per kw.-year from Table B-4.

f. Entire planned expansion of 67 million kilowatts assumed to be in coal-burning steam stations.

g. New coal-burning steam capacity minimized—22 million kw. coal-burning in fuel-deficient regions: 5 million kw. coal-burning steam in East Siberia supplied to Urals by long distance transmission; 16 million kw. nuclear; 1 million kw. hydro; and 23 million kw. noncoal steam, primarily natural gas, and gas turbine. *Elektrichestvo*, No. 9, 1958, pp. 71 ff.

The total transportation requirement for the additional capacity is some 40 billion ton-kilometers less for the "new fuel balance" than for the "old fuel balance" (Table B-5). The shift from coal to other energy sources in the 1959–1965 period for total fuel use, including iron and steel, transportation and electric power, is said to involve a saving in transportation requirements of some 400 billion ton-kilometers.[22] (This figure was probably derived by a method similar to that employed in the old and new fuel balances shown in Table B-5.) The total increase of all freight carried over the 1959–1965 period is planned to be only about 500 billion ton-kilometers.[23] So the planned reduction in transportation requirements by shifting from coal to energy sources having lower transportation requirements is significant, particularly in specific geographic areas such as the fuel-deficient regions. As only a 4 per cent increase in coal production for electric power generation is planned for the period 1959–1965, most of the coal transport would be to those areas.[24]

Whether based on cost figures, on labor and transportation minimization or on a combination of cost and physical input data, the Soviet planners have good grounds for determining that the economic advantage of nuclear as compared with coal-fired steam capacity is interesting in the fuel-deficient regions. However, the same advantages hold for natural gas- and petroleum-fired stations, and these are currently receiving priority.

Design and Construction Plans for Nuclear Reactors

A wide range of technical possibilities is being pursued in the Soviet development of nuclear power for peaceful uses. The reactor routes currently being seriously explored are indicated in the list of reactors presented in Table B-6. The large power reactors are generally of the more technically conservative, water type, whereas the more advanced models are being explored, it may be noted, only in research reactors. The 100,000-ekw. reactor in operation in the Urals (second item in Table B-6) is a dual-purpose reactor, primarily a producer of plutonium. As such it hardly represents an advance in reactor technology. Although the list in Table B-6 may not be complete, nor current, it represents all the types publicly discussed at the time of the Second Geneva Conference. Since then, information released on nuclear power has been minimal. The withholding of information may have occurred because divulging the details of downgrading the program would have tended to damage the image of the Soviet Union as a leader in the peaceful uses of nuclear energy.

22. Dieselization and electrification of railroads and increased use of gas and petroleum products in industry and the communal economy largely account for the remaining shift from coal to other energy sources in the period 1959–1965. (*Zheleznodorozhnyi transport*, No. 11, 1958, p. 10.)

23. *Pravda*, November 14, 1958.

24. *Ugol'*, No. 3, 1959, p. 3.

Soviet Domestic Reactor Types, 1958[a]

Location	Station capacity (emw.)	Moderator	Coolant	Fuel	Date of criticality
Power reactors					
Obninsk[b]	5	Graphite	H_2O	U235	1954
Troitsk	600 (6 reactors 1 operating)	Graphite	H_2O	Natural U rods (probably clad with aluminium silicon alloy)	1958
Voronezh	420 (2 reactors)	H_2O	H_2O at 1,470 psi	U235 UO_2 rods, zirconium clad	1961
Urals, Beloyarsk in Sverdlovsk Oblast	400 (4 reactors)	Graphite	H_2O	U235	1961
Northwest (Leningrad Oblast)	420	Heavy water	H_2O at 1,470 psi	UO_2 rods, zirconium clad	...
Not known	250	—	Na at 540° C. average	Plutonium	...
Obninsk	2[c]	H_2O	H_2O at 1,764 psi	...	1959
Research reactors[a]					
Volga	50	None	Na at 500° C. maximum	Pu-U alloy	...
Volga	50	Graphite	Liquid sodium	Not decided	...
Ulyanov Oblast, Volga	50	Boiling water	H_2O	UO_2	1961
Volga	35[c]	Heavy water	Fuel suspension	UO_2 suspension in D_2O	...
Other reactors[a]					
Northern sea route (Lenin icebreaker)	180[d]	H_2O	H_2O at 2,940 psi	...	1959

a. At least three additional reactors have been referred to: one as having a capacity of 50 emw., another as fueled with UF_6 gas, and a reactor in an atomic locomotive. The locomotive reactor was noted in Nucleonics, November 1958, as reported in Magyar Ifjusay, a Hungarian publication.

b. Near Moscow.   c. Mobile.   d. Thermal.

The Soviet approach of simultaneously exploring a number of reactor routes is more similar to the American program than to the British. The implication in Soviet writings is that the Soviet economic urgency for nuclear electric power is similar to that in the United States and less urgent than the British need. One Soviet writer noted that because of the "rapidly depleting coal resources and expensive imported oil . . . in England they . . . could not wait for a more economic type of reactor."[25] Therefore, the British were concentrating on the plutonium, Calder Hall–type reactor. In the Soviet Union, on the other hand, according to this Soviet writer, the immediate need for nuclear power capacity is not so pressing, and various types can therefore be explored in order to find the least costly type.[26]

The Soviets may still be able to reach a conclusion, based on the comparative costs and characteristics of reactor types now being explored, that by 1965 a stage of mass production of large standardized reactors should be undertaken. The expansion estimated by Soviet writers for 1965 and a possibly much more rapid rate of nuclear capacity expansion thereafter, is consistent with this assumption on a least-cost decision about 1965. In 1958 Zinn reported as follows:[27]

> The scientists of the USSR stated explicitly that no decision had been made as to what kind of reactor is likely to produce nuclear power at the least cost. In answer to a question as to what they would guess might be the best one at some date in the future, there seemed to be some opinion that the graphite-moderated, super-heating reactor had a good chance of being best. Naturally, it would be surprising if all the Russian technologists agreed with this point of view, and it also should be realized that that reactor is more completely Russian than any other. The next two to three years, if the USSR construction program actually follows the schedule given, should produce large-scale experience with all of the important power reactor concepts, with perhaps the exception of the organic-moderated and the homogeneous reactors.

Soviet Capabilities for Fulfilling Domestic Nuclear Program

Three scarcities may influence the pace of the Soviet domestic nuclear electric power program: skilled personnel for design, construction and operation of the reactors; the supply of uranium, especially enriched uranium; and scarce construction materials required for the new reactors, i.e., copper and other nonferrous metals.

Design engineers in the electric-machine-building industry have always been scarce. The new turbine and generator plants constructed in the south and in west Siberia, for example, have relied heavily on designers made available from the older Leningrad plants. This may well also have been true in other fields. Although the

25. *Promyshlenno-ekonomicheskaia gazeta*, November 19, 1958.

26. *Ibid.*

27. Dr. Walter H. Zinn, Section 202 Hearings, 1959, p. 48 (in letter to the Joint Committee, October 21, 1958, following the Second Geneva Conference).

design and technology may be similar to that employed in the West, Soviet reactor technology is so close to the world level of development that those engaged in it are not merely "copiers."

Information on the uranium resources and production in the Soviet Union has been for the most part withheld, but it is clear that imports of uranium from other members of the communist bloc have been important to the Soviet nuclear program.[28] One Western estimate placed the total uranium ore production in the communist bloc in 1955 at 28,000 tons, which is roughly equivalent to 3,300 tons of U_3O_8 annually.[29] By way of comparison, the procurement of U_3O_8 by the U. S. Atomic Energy Commission at the time totaled 16,268 tons.[30] The development of the capability for burning plutonium in reactors may ease somewhat the apparent pressure on uranium supplies in the Soviet Union. The Soviet interest in plutonium reactors, moreover, suggests that the Soviet development in this area may be more intense than the U. S. development.

Copper and some other nonferrous metals are known to be scarce in the Soviet economy and such shortages may be a consideration in the construction of nuclear reactors. Information on such metals, however, is closely guarded as a result of strict injunctions in the Soviet Secrets Act.[31] One may conclude, however, that none of the above-mentioned factors has retarded or will retard the program, if the Soviet leaders do not wish to permit it. Since the original deadlines for completion of the new large-scale installations by 1960 were probably not met, it would seem that the priority given the program was not sufficient to overcome all problems; or the costs may have been so much higher than anticipated that the priorities were changed. However, this program competes to some extent with the military applications of nuclear energy rather than with civilian programs; hence, examination of the past record as a basis for conclusions on priorities is of limited value.

Inferences

The Soviet program for nuclear power and foreign nuclear aid has been somewhat less than initially promised. However, planned commitments are being adhered to, albeit behind schedule. The large-scale programs of domestic development and foreign aid announced and undertaken were based on concrete domestic needs and specific foreign policy aims. In each case the program was not pushed forward

28. All joint stock companies other than those engaged in uranium mining, such as "Wismut A.G." (Soviet–East German Uranium Mining Co.), have been dissolved since the Polish uprising in 1956. See U. S. Bureau of Mines, *Mineral Trade Notes*, Washington, September 1958, Special Supplement No. 55, p. 5.

29. Elis Biörklund, *International Atomic Policy During a Decade, 1945–1955*, Van Nostrand, Princeton, N. J., 1956, pp. 142–48.

30. *Atomic Energy Appropriations for 1958*, Hearing before the Subcommittee of the House Committee on Appropriations, 85th Cong., 1st Sess., 1957, p. 39.

31. Law of April 28, 1956 in Ministerstvo Uristii RSFSR, *Ugolovnia Kodekc RSFSR* (Criminal Code of the RSFSR), Gosurizdat, Moscow, 1957,

without some sacrifice of desirable alternative projects. Once the program was undertaken, it was given maximum publicity, to gain as much prestige as possible from the technological advancement. There has been a material difference, of course, between the goals specifically set and those implied by the worldwide publicity of the program for nuclear development for peaceful uses. Plans may, of course, be revised or abandoned. Owing to centralization of Soviet decision making, a revision in over-all policy, occasioned by such events as the reorganization of industry in 1957 directed by Khrushchev, can change the order of priorities throughout Soviet society.

These generalizations can be related readily to the domestic Soviet program for nuclear electric power capacity. Firm figures for nuclear electric power capacity were set down in the sixth five-year plan in 1956. These announced goals were followed by the publication of specific plans for the construction of the large-scale stations necessary to fulfill the goals. The progress toward completion of these plans has been slower than originally planned. But it should be noted that most of the major targets set by the sixth five-year plan itself were scrapped. In this context it might seem surprising that so much progress on the nuclear program has been made. Predictions on long-term development are, of course, hazardous. For example, for accurate projections some judgment would also have to be made on the comparative cost of gas turbines and nuclear power stations. Only operating experience can provide a conclusion here. Great as the propaganda gains are in this field, it would be erroneous to assume that either the domestic or the foreign program was undertaken solely to compete in a race for world leadership in technology or to surpass the United States in some field of technical-economic endeavor.

In attempting to judge the future of Soviet nuclear aid abroad, it must be remembered that Soviet foreign economic aid programs are subordinated to Soviet domestic needs and, in the main, reflect hard bargaining on the part of the Soviet Union for whatever substantial aid it provides. At various junctures in the conduct of international relations the Soviet Union may decide it is willing to make a magnanimous offer of aid, nuclear or otherwise. However, any long-range program that would be of special benefit to countries which could also be supplied by Western nations would seem to be unlikely, based on the Soviet assistance programs thus far. This is important in its implications for the United States atoms-for-peace program.

In the future considerable progress may be made in the Soviet domestic program, based on the Soviet Union's pressing need for alternative sources to expensive coal-burning steam electric power capacity. Though the USSR is relying far more heavily on natural gas than on nuclear power, progress in peaceful uses of nuclear energy in the Soviet Union can be used to create an image of the Soviet economy as technically advanced and progressive. And the export of this image may in future years be more important to the furtherance of Soviet foreign policy aims than large-scale export of nuclear equipment.

NOTES AND ABBREVIATIONS

A number of terms, conventions and abbreviations used in this study are explained below. Specialized terms used in one chapter only are explained where used.

Reactor Types

BONUS Nuclear Superheat Power Reactor.

BORAX Boiling Reactor Experiment.

BWR Boiling Water Reactor.

EBR Experimental Breeder Reactor.

EBWR Experimental Boiling Water Reactor.

EGCR Experimental Gas-Cooled Reactor.

EOCR Experimental Organic-Cooled Reactor.

GCR Gas-Cooled Reactor.

HRE Homogeneous Reactor Experiment.

HWCTR Heavy Water Components Test Reactor.

LAMPRE Los Alamos Molten Plutonium Reactor Experiment.

MSRE Molten Salt Reactor Experiment.

NPR New Production Reactor.

OMRE Organic-Moderated Reactor Experiment.

PRTR Plutonium Recycle Test Reactor.

PWR Pressurized Water Reactor.

SRE Sodium Reactor Experiment.

Measures

BTU British thermal unit.

C. Centigrade.

e (prefix) electric.

F. Fahrenheit.

g. gram.

kg. kilogram.

km. kilometer.

kw. kilowatt.

KWH kilowatt-hour.

mw. megawatt.

psi pounds per square inch.

short ton 2,000 pounds.

t (prefix) thermal capacity.

Scientific Terms

Be beryllium.

C carbon.

D_2O heavy water.

H_2O natural water.

Na sodium.

Pu plutonium (without regard to isotopic content).

Pu239 plutonium, an isotope of.

THO_2 thorium oxide.

U uranium (without regard to isotopic content).

U233, U235, U238 uranium, isotopes of.

UF_6 uranium hexafluoride.

U_3O_8 uranium oxide (concentrate of natural uranium).

Other Technical Terms	*Symbols Used in Tabulations*
O & M operating and maintenance.	... data not available.
Plant factor power production as a per cent of generating capacity.	— nil or negligible.
R & D research and development.	< less than.
Thermonuclear power energy secured from fusion of nuclei of light elements.	> more than.

Organizations and Governmental and International Agencies

AEC   Atomic Energy Commission. Established by the Atomic Energy Act of 1946, as amended by the Atomic Energy Act of 1954, as amended. Headquarters, Washington. (See also Commission.)

AECL   Atomic Energy of Canada, Ltd.

AID   Agency for International Development. Established November 1961 as an agency of the U. S. Department of State, to succeed ICA (International Cooperation Administration).

ANL   Argonne National Laboratory, Lemont, Illinois.

APPA   American Public Power Association, Washington.

Commission, the   The five AEC Commissioners, appointed by the President.

EEI   Edison Electric Institute, New York.

ENSI   Energia Nucleare Sud Italia, a project of SENN (see below).

Euratom   European Atomic Energy Community. Member countries are Belgium, the Federal Republic of Germany, France, Italy, Luxembourg and the Netherlands. Headquarters, Brussels.

FPC   U. S. Federal Power Commission, Washington.

Geneva Conferences   International Conferences on the Peaceful Uses of Atomic Energy, held in Geneva: the first, August 8-20, 1955; the second, September 1-13, 1958.

IAEA   International Atomic Energy Agency. An agency under the aegis of the UN. Statute ratified by the President of the United States on July 29, 1957. Headquarters, Vienna, Austria.

IBRD   International Bank for Reconstruction and Development.

IGE   International General Electric Co.

Joint Committee   Unless otherwise indicated means Joint Committee on Atomic Energy of the U. S. Congress.

MED   Manhattan Engineer District. (In 1947 some of the functions of this agency, which had been established in 1942, were transferred to the AEC and some to the Armed Forces Special Weapons Project, now the Defense Atomic Support Agency of the Department of Defense.)

NASA National Aeronautics and Space Administration. Established by the National Aeronautics and Space Act of 1958.

NPA National Planning Association, Washington.

NRTS National Reactor Testing Station, Idaho Falls, Idaho.

NSF National Science Foundation, Washington.

PRDC Power Reactor Development Co.

OECD Organisation for Economic Cooperation and Development, successor (in 1961) to the Organisation for European Economic Cooperation (OEEC). Member countries are: Austria, Belgium, Canada, Denmark, France, Germany, Greece, Iceland, Ireland, Italy, Luxembourg, the Netherlands, Norway, Portugal, Spain, Sweden, Switzerland, Turkey, the United Kingdom and the United States. Headquarters, Paris, with a regional office in Washington.

OEEC See OECD.

ORNL Oak Ridge National Laboratory, Oak Ridge, Tennessee.

RFF Resources for the Future, Washington.

SENN Società Elettronucleare Nazionale.

UN United Nations. Headquarters, New York.

UNAEC United Nations Atomic Energy Commission. Established by the UN in 1946. Was replaced (along with the Commission for Conventional Armaments) by the Disarmament Commission, which was established by the General Assembly in 1952.

Bibliographic Notes

AEC Annual Reports

Major Activities in the Atomic Energy Programs. Through 1958 these reports were semiannual—January-June, published in July; July-December, published in January. Since 1958 the reports have been annual, January-December, published in the following January. Referred to in citations in this study as "Annual Report" (or "Semiannual Report"). This is the same as the *Annual Report to Congress of the Atomic Energy Commission*, except the latter includes a letter of transmittal and only a limited number of copies is issued.

Hartley Commission Report

OEEC, *Europe's Growing Needs of Energy: How Can They Be Met?* (prepared by the Commission for Energy, known as the Hartley Commission, under the chairmanship of Sir Harold Hartley), Paris, 1956.

McKinney Panel

Peaceful Uses of Atomic Energy (report of the Panel on the Peaceful Uses of Atomic Energy, Robert McKinney, Chairman), Joint Committee on Atomic Energy, 84th Cong., 2nd Sess., 1956, 2 vols.

McKinney Review

Robert McKinney, *Review of the International Atomic Policies and Programs of the United States*, Report to the Joint Committee on Atomic Energy, 86th Cong., 2nd Sess., October 1960, 5 vols.

Proceedings, First Geneva Conference, Second Geneva Conference

See Geneva Conferences under "Organizations and Governmental and International Agencies," above.

Robinson Commission Report

OEEC, *Towards a New Energy Pattern in Europe* (prepared by the Energy Advisory Commission under the chairmanship of Professor Austin Robinson), Paris, 1960.

Section 202 Hearings

Development, Growth and State of the Atomic Energy Industry, Hearings, Joint Committee on Atomic Energy. Hearings under this title have been held annually, 1955–1962, by the Joint Committee under the provisions of Sec. 202, Atomic Energy Act of 1954.

Smyth Committee Report

U. S. Department of State, *Report of the Advisory Committee on U. S. Policy toward the International Atomic Energy Agency* (Henry DeWolf Smyth, Chairman), Washington, May 19, 1962 (mimeo.).

Thomas Report

Charles A. Thomas and others, "Economics of Nuclear Power," Clinton Laboratory of the Manhattan Engineer District, Oak Ridge, Tenn., July 19, 1946 (Report CF 46-7-257, secret, declassified with deletions, February 12, 1958).

LIST OF TABLES

Chapter 4

Chapter 5

Chapter 6

Chapter 7

Chapter 8

Appendix A

Appendix B

LIST OF CHARTS

INDEX